America

AND THE CHALLENGES OF RELIGIOUS DIVERSITY

America

AND THE CHALLENGES OF
RELIGIOUS DIVERSITY

ROBERT WUTHNOW

PRINCETON UNIVERSITY PRESS

Princeton and Oxford

Fourth printing, and first paperback printing, 2007
Paperback ISBN-13: 978-0-691-13411-6

The Library of Congress has cataloged the cloth edition
of this book as follows

Wuthnow, Robert.
America and the challenges of religious diversity / Robert Wuthnow.
p. cm.
Includes bibliographical references and index.
ISBN-13: 978-0-691-11976-2 (cloth : alk. paper)
ISBN-10: 0-691-11976-7 (cloth : alk. paper)
1. Christianity and other religions. 2. Religious pluralism.
3. United States—Religion. I. Title.
BR127
201'.5'0973—dc22   2004058684

British Library Cataloging-in-Publication Data is available

This book has been composed in Adobe Garamond and
Helvetica Neue Display

press.princeton.edu

Printed in the United States of America

10   9   8   7   6   5   4

CONTENTS

TABLES

THIS BOOK is concerned with how we as individuals and as a nation are responding to the challenges of increasing religious and cultural diversity. Questions about racial and ethnic differences and questions about the impact of immigration have attracted extraordinary interest in recent years. Questions about religion and its cultural effects are just as important. They involve beliefs and convictions, assumptions about good and evil, individual and group identities, and concerns about how to live together. These questions were not resolved during the nation's formative era. And they certainly have not faded away. The growing presence of American Muslims, Hindus, Buddhists, and other new immigrant groups makes these questions more pressing than ever. The United States has a strong tradition respecting the rights of diverse religious communities. But American culture is also a product of its distinctive Christian heritage. This heritage exists in tension with the nation's religious and cultural diversity.

The tension between America's Christian heritage and its religious and cultural diversity became evident in the days following the September 11, 2001, attacks on the Pentagon and World Trade Center. In a speech to Congress, President Bush declared to Muslims, "We respect your faith." Yet Bush had also said that only Christians have a place in heaven. How did he reconcile these views? What did he mean by "respect"?

An apparent inconsistency in political rhetoric like this would hardly merit attention were it not for the fact that it points to something much deeper. American identity is an odd mixture of religious particularism and cultural pluralism. Although it is not an established religion, Christianity is the nation's majority religion, and its leaders and followers have often claimed it had special, if not unique, access to divine truth. Yet the reality of religious pluralism, including beliefs and practices different from those embraced by Christianity, has also had a profound impact on American culture. These strands of our national identity are not just contradictory or conflicting impulses. They are inextricably bound together in ways that feed our collective imagination and evoke questions about who we are.

Through a large number of in-depth interviews, data from a new national survey, and published materials about the past and present, I examine the terms in which the relationship between America's Christian heritage and its growing religious diversity is being debated. I emphasize the perceptions of ordinary Americans as well as those of community leaders and the languages in which these perceptions are framed. I argue that interpretations of religious diversity have been, and continue to be, a profound aspect of our national identity.

It has become popular among social observers to argue that American religion is so thoroughly composed of private beliefs and idiosyncratic practices that belief and practice ultimately do not matter. People pick and choose in whatever way helps them to get ahead (or, at least, to get along). Their beliefs are so shallow that inconsistencies make no difference. Some observers also argue that Americans can hold fundamentally incommensurate beliefs in their personal lives, but live amicably in public. This is a recent litany in the literature on pluralism. Let religious subgroups believe whatever they want to, the argument goes, but count on laws and norms of civic decorum to maintain social order. In this view, religion and civic life function without mutual influence. Pluralism is culturally uncomplicated.

The evidence I present here suggests that these views are wrong. I show that pluralism and religious practices are intertwined. How people think about pluralism is influenced by their religious convictions. And religious convictions are influenced by their experiences with pluralism. This means that cultural interpretations of religious questions matter. They matter, not so much as formal expressions of what theologians or religious organizations teach, but in the way that Michael Polanyi described the *tacit* knowledge in which all human behavior is inscribed. Tacit knowledge matters because we prefer to live in a world, even if it is a world of our own construction, that make sense, rather than in a world without sense. Understood this way, it makes a difference how people think about questions of God, death, salvation, heaven, good and evil, other religions, and the teachings of their own tradition. It certainly matters to the many Muslims, Hindus, Buddhists, and practitioners of other non-Western religions who now make up a growing minority of the U.S. population. It also matters to Americans who claim to be Christians or Jews, or who are self-styled spiritual shoppers. They may sometimes deny that it does. But when they confront religious diversity, and when they think about what it means to be religious or spiritual in a diverse society, they articulate tacit assumptions about what it means to be human and what it means to be an American.

Religious identities matter to the collective life of society as well as to the personal lives of individuals. Religious identities are among the ways in which cultural assumptions about what is right and good, or better and best, are organized. Americans believe they are a special people with a distinctive mission to fulfill in the world. This belief is associated historically with our understanding of religion. To say that we are a Christian nation has been a normative statement as well as a descriptive one. Christian values and practices occupied a special place in our thinking. To say that some people were Christian implied that others were not. Our moral universe included assumptions about Jews, Muslims, Hindus, Buddhists, and practitioners of Native American religions. They, too, had duties to fulfill, roles in the cultural drama to perform. Religious diversity was inscribed in the moral order.

Another popular approach to religion among social scientists is to deal with it as if it were purely an expression of something else, such as class, race, gender, and region, or to explain its trends and patterns with reference to demography, organizations, leadership styles, and theories about rational choice. These reductionistic approaches give social scientists an excuse to avoid the *content* of religion. What people believe, or say they believe, and the language in which they make sense of their beliefs and practices are somehow, in the view of these scholars, too marginal, too normative, or too difficult to measure for any self-respecting social scientist to tackle. This is the point at which narrow definitions of disciplinary boundaries get in the way of knowledge.

I choose to emphasize what people think and the cultural idioms in which they express their thoughts. This is how people make sense of their beliefs and practices. It is how they negotiate meaning when faced with multiple religious teachings and traditions. If people were guided only by demography or social position, there would be no need to know what they say or think. But there is a well-established tradition in the social sciences (counting Max Weber and George Herbert Mead among those who observe it) that says that the meaning-making activity of humans is crucial to our understanding of society. Making sense of religious diversity is one of these meaning-making activities.

Still, listening to what people say would be of little value if their views merely echoed the writings of theologians and social philosophers. If ordinary people were guided by these writings, one would want to spend the time one has for scholarly reflection understanding these tomes and writing commentaries about them. Worthy as that may be, it does not provide much of a picture of the society in which we actually live.

When rank-and-file Americans talk about religious diversity, they disclose an implicit cultural text composed of narrative fragments from personal experience, from conversations with friends and neighbors, from the media, from books and magazines, and in many instances from ruminations about questions raised in Sunday school, a high school youth group, a course in comparative religions, or a visit to another country. It is possible to identify themes and variations in this subterranean text. Some people find ways to embrace religious diversity as fully as possible. Others assert loyalty to the tradition in which they were raised (or are presently involved), but acknowledge the validity of other traditions. A substantial number of Americans adamantly reject the truth of religions other than their own. In each of these orientations, people articulate a bricolage of ideas that both reflects and subverts public images of cultural diversity. Patterns of avoidance minimizing considered engagement among religious traditions are evident. And these avoidances illuminate the behavior of religious organizations and their leaders.

I do not argue that the present encounter with religious diversity is entirely new or without precedent. My argument is rather that America and American Christianity have always existed in a world of religious differences and with some awareness of these differences. I further argue, however, that this awareness is probably greater among rank-and-file Americans now than in the past because of mass communications, immigration, and our nation's role in the global economy. In this, I am in agreement with historians such as Sydney Ahlstrom and William Hutchison who have argued that the present acceptance and welcoming of religious diversity is relatively new, dating perhaps only to the mid-twentieth century (Hutchison's book, *Religious Pluralism in America* is especially helpful in this regard).

Whereas historical treatments of religious diversity in America have typically emphasized the divisions *within* Christianity (especially those separating Protestants and Catholics, Protestant denominations, and the various sects), my emphasis here is on the encounter between American Christians and other major religious traditions, such as Islam, Buddhism, and Hinduism. I understand that the tensions between Protestants and Catholics, or even between rival branches of Presbyterianism, were sometimes as fierce as anything evident currently between Christians and non-Christians. I am nevertheless interested in the fact that Christians have always had to formulate arguments about people who were clearly outside the Christian tradition by virtue of belonging to other major religious traditions. I am interested in how these arguments played into our national identity historically and how they are being revised at present.

My aim is not to encourage readers to conclude that religions are interchangeable. Nor do I believe the best way to live in a pluralistic society is to combine bits and pieces of several religions. I do insist that the growing religious diversity of our society poses a *significant cultural challenge.* The fact that Muslims, Hindus, and Buddhists are now a significant presence in the United States raises fundamental questions about our historic identity as a Christian nation. This new reality requires is to rethink our national identity and to face difficult choices about how pluralistic we are willing to be. It requires people of all religions, as well as scholars and community leaders, to take notice. If a person's best friend in elementary school belonged to a different religion, and if this person takes religion seriously, he or she will surely think about his or her faith differently than would have been the case if everyone in school belonged to the same religion. If one's neighbors and coworkers hold beliefs vastly different from one's own, this too will evoke a response. We can try to understand and become more aware of these influences, and thus make more informed choices about how we respond, rather than letting circumstances dictate our responses.

I include the perspectives and experiences of American Muslims, Hindus, Buddhists, and Jews. These voices have too frequently been ignored in discussions of religious pluralism. They need to be heard. In addition, I focus especially on Americans who identify themselves as Christians and who are involved in churches. Christianity has been the dominant religious influence on our nation in the past and is likely to remain at the center of American religion in the foreseeable future. How Christians respond to religious diversity will be a decisive factor in shaping the future.

I write as a humanistically oriented social scientist. I view the encounter between Christianity and other religions as an instance of how we are shaped by our culture and of how we engage in cultural work. I am interested in the fact that religious diversity is embedded in cultural memory. America was not Christian when the first European explorers arrived. Settlers of Christian origin have always defined themselves through their encounters with other religions. They maintained the conviction that their own beliefs were true, perhaps uniquely so. How has this been possible? What cultural resources have made it possible? How do people frame their beliefs and make sense of them knowing that there are others who believe quite differently?

Some years ago, I became interested in the study of anti-Semitism and racial prejudice. I immersed myself in the research literature on those topics. I learned that contact between members of different religious or racial groups often reduces prejudice and hostility, that education and information generally have a positive effect on attitudes, and that tolerance has been increasing. I also learned that expressions of tolerance mask more complex attitudes and understandings, and that some of the most complex of these arise from religious teachings and traditions. For more than a decade, I have been listening to what Americans say about their faith, looking closely for clues about how they manage to choose certain beliefs and practices at a time when there are so many options from which to choose. This book is a continuation of my interest in those topics.

The research was supported through a Guggenheim fellowship and a grant from the Lilly Endowment. I am especially grateful to Craig Dykstra and Chris Coble at the Endowment for their interest in the project and for their help and encouragement along the way. Jenny Legath, Conrad Hackett, Daniel Weiss, and Jonathan McMath helped invaluably in tracking down historical and other textual materials. Natalie Searl did most of the interviewing and oversaw the transcription process. She was assisted by Libby Smith and Karen Myers. Wendy Cadge and Prema Kurien helped with Buddhist and Hindu sources, Jim Gibbon helped review the literature on American Muslims, and Sara Nephew and Cristina Mora assisted with the broader literature on religion and immigration. Interaction with the many visiting fellows and graduate students with whom I have been privileged to associate through the Center for the Study of Religion has broadened my perspectives historically and comparatively. Alan Wolfe, Wade Clark Roof, and Lynn Davidman read an earlier draft of the manuscript and provided helpful suggestions. I was also privileged to receive valuable feedback on portions of the book given as public lectures at the University of Michigan, Denison University, and Messiah College. My wife, Sara, and my children, Robyn, Brooke, and Joel, have been my faithful companions and sources of inspiration.

America

AND THE CHALLENGES OF RELIGIOUS DIVERSITY

Confronting Diversity

ON SATURDAY, September 13, 1997, millions of Americans viewed the funeral of a diminutive Catholic nun who had served India's neediest people for four decades. The internationally televised service was for Mother Teresa of Calcutta, the colorful "Saint of the Gutters" who for years ranked among America's "most admired women" and had been awarded the Nobel Peace Prize in 1979. The funeral followed by only a week that of Britain's Princess Diana, whose tragic death in a speeding automobile pursued by paparazzi in the Pont de l'Alma tunnel in Paris evoked an extraordinary international outpouring of grief.

Both of these events conveyed messages about religious diversity. The 15,000 mourners who packed Netaji stadium for Mother Teresa's funeral included representatives of the world's major faiths: Hindus, Muslims, Sikhs, Buddhists, Catholics, and other Christians. The assembled dignitaries eulogized Mother Teresa's life of compassion, calling it an ideal to which the followers of all religions could aspire. Her words, "I see God in every human being," were repeated like a mantra, as if to affirm the impression, so vividly communicated by religious leaders in a kaleidoscope of traditional robes laying garlands around her casket, that all faiths worship the same God. The religious messages accompanying Diana's death were more ambiguous. Journalists conscientiously included the quiet Islamic burial of her companion, Dodi Al-Fayed, in their coverage, but for a time rumors also circulated that an interfaith romance of such high-profile possibilities had simply been too much, causing some black conspiracy to forever halt it from maturing.

In the following weeks, neither event was remembered especially for its images of religious diversity. Public attention moved on, looking back occasionally to the sad faces of Diana's young sons, William and Harry, or to new revelations about the clouded circumstances of her hasty departure from the Ritz hotel. It moved on, remembering Mother Teresa's goodness, savoring the thought that humans can indeed aspire to noble achievements, but including questions about public welfare policy and whether charity can be successful in alleviating the suffering of the world's poor. And yet it would have been hard to watch either event without absorbing the message that the larger world, the world that encompasses so many different beliefs and faiths, is becoming smaller, crowding in on itself, forcing a new awareness of its diversity.

These are but two examples illustrating how common exposure to the leaders and followers of non-Western religions has become. News coverage from around the world includes images of religious leaders, adherents, and their places of worship. The nation's expansive economic and military activities render these images more newsworthy than they would have been in the past. Apart from media, exposure to the world's religions comes increasingly through first-hand encounters. During the last third of the twentieth century, approximately twenty-two million immigrants came to the United States.[1] Like the surge of immigration that occurred between 1890 and 1920, most of these immigrants came from countries in which Christians are the dominant religion. Yet, in contrast to that earlier period, the recent immigration included millions of people from countries in which Christians are only a small minority. Thus, in little more than a generation, the United States has witnessed an unprecedented increase in the diversity of major religious traditions represented among its population. More Americans belong to religions outside of the Christian tradition than ever before. The new immigrants include large numbers of Muslims, Hindus, Buddhists, and followers of other traditions and spiritual practices. Their presence greatly increases the likelihood of personal interaction across these religious lines.

Recent immigrants and their descendants generally do not live isolated from other Americans in homogeneous enclaves. They frequently work in middle-class occupations and live in the same neighborhoods as other Americans do. Their mosques, temples, and meditation centers are often located in close proximity to churches and synagogues. The typical American, therefore, can more readily encounter people of other religions as neighbors, friends, and coworkers.[2]

Diversity is always challenging, whether it is manifest in language differences or in modes of dress, eating, and socializing. Seeing people with different habits and lifestyles makes it harder to practice our own unreflectively. When religion is involved, these challenges are multiplied. Religious differences are instantiated in dress, food, holidays, and family rituals; they also reflect historic teachings and deeply held patterns of belief and practice. These beliefs and practices may be personal and private, but they cannot easily be divorced from questions about truth and morality. Believing that one's faith is correct and behaving in ways that reflect this belief may well be different in the presence of diversity than in its absence.

How have we responded to the religious diversity that increasingly characterizes our neighborhoods, schools, and places of work? Has it sunk into our awareness that the temple or mosque down the street is not just another church? Does it matter that our coworkers have radically different ideas of the sacred than we do? Or do we perceive these ideas as so different from our own? Are our views of America affected by having neighbors whose beliefs and lifestyles may run counter to our own? Does it bother us to read about hate crimes directed at Muslims or Hindus?

Historic interpretations of Christian teachings encourage Christians to practice the acceptance and love exhibited by Mother Teresa. Stories about Jesus' willingness to violate social boundaries separating Jews and Gentiles exemplify how Christianity may encourage openness to racial, ethnic, and cultural diversity. Yet Christianity has also taught that only by accepting Jesus as their savior can believers overcome sinfulness and gain divine redemption. According to some interpretations of this teaching, the followers of other religions must convert to Christianity if they are to know God.

Throughout America's history, our sense of who we are has been profoundly influenced by our religious beliefs and practices. Christianity's claim to be the unique representative of divine truth has been one of these influences. We have thought of ourselves as a chosen people, a city on a hill, and a new Israel. We have considered ourselves defenders of the faith, a God-fearing people, and a Christian nation. At present, we remain one of the most religiously committed of all nations, at least if religious commitment is measured in numbers professing belief in God and attending services at houses of worship. Our identity is still marked by this fact. Many Americans take for granted that we are a Christian society, even if they implicitly make a place in this notion for Jews and unbelievers. Others take pride in our national accomplishments, our democratic traditions, and our extensive voluntary associations, assuming that these reflect Christian values.

If our understanding of what it means to be American reflects our religious heritage, our collective identity is also influenced by how we think about religious diversity. Until recently, we were able to think of ourselves as a Christian civilization, divided by the historic cleavages separating Protestants from Catholics and, among Protestants, Methodists from Baptists, Presbyterians from Episcopalians, Congregationalists from Quakers, and so on. We were a diverse nation because of the national origins from which the various denominational groups had come and because of racial, ethnic, and regional divisions in which religious disunity was embedded.[3] We took pride in this diversity. It seemed like a mark of distinction.

We clearly do have a long history of religious diversity. This history has affected our laws, encouraging us to avoid governmental intrusion in religious affairs that might lead to an establishment of one tradition in favor of others. And it has taught us a kind of civic decorum that discourages blatant expressions of racist, ethnocentric, and nativist ideas. Yet it will not do, now in the face of new diversity, simply to rewrite our nation's history as a story of diversity and pluralism.

The reality of large numbers of Americans who are Muslims, Buddhists, Zoroastrians, Sikhs, Hindus, and followers of other non-Western religions poses a new challenge to American self-understandings. When Christian leaders and their followers think about it, they will have more trouble knowing what exactly to think about their neighbors who belong to these other religions than they ever did simply thinking about the differences between Methodists and Baptists or Protestants and Catholics. That is, *if* they stop to think about it.

But the truth is, we know very little at this point about how ordinary Americans are responding to religious diversity. And, for that matter, we know little more about how religious leaders are dealing with diversity. We do know, for example, that religious leaders occasionally form interfaith alliances that include representatives of the world's major religious traditions, and we know that other leaders are sometimes quoted in newspapers as saying that the followers of a particular religion other than their own are condemned to hell. Such headlines, however, seldom tell us much about how things are going in local communities or what people really believe and think.

To examine how we are responding to religious diversity and the cultural challenges that go with it, I draw on the results of a three-year research project that included more than three hundred in-depth personal interviews and a new national survey. Most of the interviews were conducted in fourteen metropolitan areas, selected to represent the several regions of the country as well as larger and smaller cities with varying experiences of immigration and diversity. The cities were New York, Philadelphia, and Washington, D.C., in the East; Charlotte, Atlanta, and Houston in the South; Columbus, Saint Louis, Kansas City, and Chicago in the Midwest; and Denver, Los Angeles, Sacramento, and Portland in the West.

In any part of the country, including cities like these, it is possible for people to go about their daily lives without thinking about religion or religious diversity. To increase the chances of finding people who had thought about these issues, I selected a Muslim mosque, a Hindu temple, a Buddhist temple or meditation center, and (for purposes of comparison) a Jewish synagogue in each city, taking care to choose ones belonging to different traditions and varying in size and location. I then identified a church in the immediate vicinity of each of these fifty-six organizations—often right next door or across the street and never more than a few blocks away.[4] Interviews were then conducted with the pastors at each of these churches and with at least one of the members.[5] Interviews were also conducted with the religious leaders at forty of the Muslim, Hindu, Buddhist, and Jewish organizations, and with forty of the Muslim, Hindu, Jewish, or Buddhist members. These interviews were supplemented with thirty-two interviews conducted among people who were either Christians married to non-Christians or non-Christians married to Christians and with forty interviews conducted among people who were eclectic in their religious beliefs and practices.[6] Forty-five interviews were also conducted with local and national leaders experienced in dealing with interreligious issues through work in law and government, public education, chaplaincies, theological education, and interfaith organizations.[7]

The survey—which I will refer to as the Religion and Diversity Survey—was conducted with a national sample of 2,910 adults, selected to be representative of the adult population of the United States. It was conducted by telephone and each set of questions lasted approximately thirty-five minutes. Each person in the survey was asked questions about his or her contacts with people of religions other than Christianity, attitudes toward these religions, personal religious beliefs and practices, and a variety of other social and demographic characteristics.[8] After the survey, we contacted two hundred of the respondents who were church members and asked them twenty to thirty minutes of open-ended questions about their beliefs and the activities of their churches. We also contacted the pastors at fifty of their churches to find out from them what their churches had been doing vis-à-vis followers of other faiths.

To put this contemporary evidence in historical perspective, I examined hundreds of primary and secondary documents from the past, ranging from books and letters to journal articles and statements issued by religious organizations. The historical material provides information with which to see how Americans at key moments in the past, beginning with the first European explorers and settlers and moving through subsequent phases of American history, made sense of the religious diversity with which they were confronted.

In sorting through the historical and contemporary material, I have focused on the following questions: How have Americans been able to maintain their conviction that Christianity is uniquely true and that theirs is a special nation with a distinctive (even divine) destiny? How has this been possible, given our frequent and now increasing encounters with other religions? And as we do face increasing diversity, how are our beliefs and identities changing to accommodate this diversity?

Behind these empirical questions is an important normative concern: How well are we managing to face the new challenges of religious and cultural diversity? Are we merely managing in the sense of making do, muddling our way by avoiding the issues whenever possible and responding superficially whenever we must? Or are we managing better than that? Are we taking advantage of the opportunities that diversity provides and moving toward a more mature pluralism than we have known in the past?

These are, in my view, among the most serious questions we currently face as a nation. In our public discourse about religion we seem to be a society of schizophrenics. On the one hand, we say casually that we are tolerant and have respect for people whose religious traditions happen to be different from our own. On the other hand, we continue to speak as if our nation is (or should be) a Christian nation, founded on Christian principles, and characterized by public references to the trappings of this tradition. That kind of schizophrenia encourages behavior that no well-meaning people would want if they stopped to think about it for very long. It allows the most open-minded among us to get by without taking religion very seriously at all. It permits religious hate crimes to occur without much public attention or outcry. The members of new minority religions experience little in the way of genuine understanding. The churchgoing majority seldom hear anything to shake up their comforting convictions. The situation is rife with misunderstanding and, as such, holds little to prevent outbreaks of religious conflict and bigotry. It is little wonder that many Americans retreat into their private worlds whenever spirituality is mentioned. It is just easier to do that than to confront the hard questions about religious truth and our national identity.

A Special People in a Diverse World

A POPULAR RESPONSE to questions about religious diversity, both from rank-and-file Americans and from community leaders, is that the topic is essentially unworthy of serious reflection: either because religious diversity has not been part of one's experience or because it is satisfactorily covered among our constitutional rights. Yet if one examines discussions of religion in the past, it becomes clear that diversity was seldom divorced from thinking about ourselves and our identity as a nation. Contributors to these discussions believed that America was a special place and that its distinctiveness was somehow related to a divine purpose. That purpose necessarily carried implications for their understanding of the various religions they encountered. Particularly when America's purpose was associated with a distinctly Christian view of God and of God's people, as it often was, the founders and promoters of America were compelled to adopt a position toward other religions. They often articulated views of these religions that corresponded with their own sense of destiny and social location.

Max Weber's influential writing about religion nearly a century ago provides a helpful framework for thinking about the relationships among religious convictions, views of other religions, and ideas about purpose and destiny.[1] Weber understood that religion, among other things, provides people with a way of transforming an existence of apparent chaos into one having ultimate meaning. Religion renders existence meaningful by reinforcing the assumption that reality makes sense intellectually and intuitively. But any religious system that provides meaning in this fashion, Weber realized, must also address the problem of evil. Answers must be given and comfort provided in the face of those events that do not make sense and are not on the surface desirable. They may be explained variously as the work of an inscrutable God or the devil, or in terms of fate or a cycle of rebirths, but they must be explained. And how they are explained, Weber argued, shapes what people value and how they believe they should live. Their behavior is, in a word, *channeled* by their understanding of good and evil.

A problem similar to the more general one Weber identified arises whenever people regard themselves individually or collectively as special, at least if they cloak this view in a larger divine, philosophical, or metaphysical framework. Regarding themselves as special necessarily implies that some other group is not special and thus raises the question of why this should be so. The question is not simply a matter of idle curiosity but is integrally connected to a people's sense of identity and purpose. The "other" serves as a point of comparison and contrast, providing a sense of how we are different from and similar to the rest of the world. If our own identity is part of a divine or transcendent plan, then those who are not us must have an identity within this understanding as well—perhaps as our antagonists or as people who for some reason cannot share in the divine plan. How we conceptualize our relationships with them and how we formulate our priorities more generally will be tacitly guided by our understandings of those we are not.[2]

Throughout our history, we have formulated understandings of who we are individually and as a nation. These understandings have characteristically assumed that American culture and identity, including its distinct purpose in the world and the moral fiber of its people, are explicitly or implicitly related to Christian values. When the first European explorers and settlers came to North America, they faced a multiplicity of religious practices that were not part of the Christian world. By the end of the eighteenth century, European Americans and their descendents imagined themselves to have created a special nation that, if not distinctively Christian was at least a high expression of Western civilization.[3] Many of them understood themselves as a Christian people who had formed a vast network of congregations, spread the gospel, and established a rule of law based on Christian principles. Yet they had done so, not simply by converting the indigenous population to Christianity or by eliminating this population, but by developing a complex set of interpretations of it. These interpretations preserved and protected their understanding of what it meant to be Christian on the American continent and of why Christianity was uniquely true. During the nineteenth and twentieth centuries, new interpretations were added to make sense of the nation's growing contact with the wider world and the wider diversity of its population.

What we see at present, as Americans make sense of themselves in relation to neighbors and coworkers with different religions, is a continuation of this history. Believing that we are special, we have always found it necessary to explain how and why this should be so. At the deepest levels of our culture, these reasons have been religious. They have associated us collectively and individually with a divine purpose conceived of largely through the Christian heritage of those who came from Europe and created institutions to carry on its traditions. By association, the Christian claim of having a unique relationship with God gave Americans a special place in the world as well. The fact that others did not have this special relationship had to be understood. These others have provided us variously with a mission to fulfill, foes to conquer, visions of evil to avoid or go to war with, intellectual puzzles to resolve, opportunities to exploit, and reassurance about our moral goodness and cultural progress.

A detailed history of America's encounters with religions other than Christianity is beyond the scope of the present chapter. However, tracing the highlights of these encounters will serve as background for considering the present period. We shall see that Americans came early to accept the idea that their society, while diverse, was fundamentally Christian and that the meaning of diversity should be understood primarily in reference to the Christian majority. We shall also see that Christians' attitudes toward other religions reflected Americans' understandings of themselves and their own religion. Over the centuries, these understandings have changed; yet the struggle between a theology of exclusivism and a civic code of pluralism has remained constant. The tension between these two profoundly important aspects of American culture has generated a set of responses to other religions that are still very much in evidence today.

First Encounters

When Europeans first came to the American continent they were of course encountering a world that could scarcely be considered Christian. They were nevertheless optimistic. In fact, Christopher Columbus and his crew thought the making of a Christian land in the

New World would happen easily. Despite badly miscalculating where his journey had taken him, Columbus was a careful observer of his new surroundings. His diary describes a stalk loaded with rose berries that gave the Pinta's crew its first indication of approaching land on October 11, 1492. He describes the naked beauty of the men and women who came out to welcome him, how tall they were, and the color and length of their hair. After spending more time with them, he discusses the shape of their foreheads, the scars some of the men had received in skirmishes with neighboring islanders, what they ate, and the spears they used for fishing. He endeavors to learn about their economy, how they governed themselves, and what they appreciated in jewelry and in art. It is notable, therefore, that his account of the people's religious practices does not reflect the same consideration of detail.[4]

Columbus's voyage was undertaken with several goals in mind, not the least of which was to discover treasure for the Spanish crown and to ensure his own fortune and place in history. But the voyage was also inspired by a religious mission, one that not only reflected his own faith and the rising influence of the Spanish monarchy in western Christendom but that also illustrated the larger reasons for Europe's eagerness to believe that America would become a Christian land. When Columbus left Granada on May 12, 1492, three recent religious developments were fresh in his mind: the war with the Moors in Granada that had just been concluded, the expulsion of Jews from Spain, and Jerusalem remaining in the hands of Muslim forces. Thus the time appeared propitious for Columbus to set sail in an effort to further the Christian cause. Believing himself to be living in the end times prophesied in the Bible, he was buoyed by the possibility of being able to find treasure that could be used to pay for armies to liberate Jerusalem from the Muslims, not to mention being able to make contact with the "Grand Khan" of India who had supposedly sent messengers to Rome asking to be instructed in the Holy Faith.[5]

Columbus's perception of the indigenous peoples he encountered in the New World occurred against the backdrop of these developments in the relationships, some real and some assumed, between Christianity, Islam, Judaism, and the leaders of India. He was optimistic that Christianity was on the ascendancy and that his own voyage was foretold in biblical prophecy. An amateur theologian himself, he was well prepared to perceive whatever he encountered in the New World through interpretations provided by Christianity. He believed, for example, that mankind had descended from a common ancestor and that the various peoples of the world had migrated to different continents and adopted different customs after the flood described in the Bible. Many of these people were living in bondage, guided by evil rulers who were playing an unwitting role in God's eventual plan of redemption.[6] The Indians Columbus encountered were remarkably free of these influences, residing as they did outside the boundaries of the ancient kingdoms that Christian scholarship had interpreted in these ways. Columbus described the Indians as being eager to hear about and to understand the Christian truth being brought to them. Indeed, Columbus appears to have believed that Christianity was the only religion present in the New World since he could find no evidence of any other religion. "I believe," he wrote, "that they [the Indians] would become Christians very easily, for it seemed to me that they had no religion."[7]

What persuaded Columbus that the American continent was devoid of other religions is not entirely clear because he does note that there were "many statues in the shape of women and many mask-like heads," which may have been worshipped as well as being produced for their beauty.[8] Still, it struck him that the Indians apparently did not pray or worship idols and that they were free from the kind of religions he had read about that were imposed on otherwise innocent people by rulers such as the Grand Khan. In any event, the Indians seemed eager to become Christians as evidenced by the fact that they "say the *Salve* and the *Ave Marie* with their hands to heaven as the Spaniards show them; and they make the sign of the cross."[9] Besides their willingness to engage in Christian practices, which reinforced Columbus's belief that his mission was destined for success, the Indians appeared to have the qualities of young children who, according to the teachings of his own church, remained innocent and in a special relationship with God. Thus, his diary describes them as "lacking in evil," "naked as their mothers bore them," "credulous," "very gentle," and "very timid."[10] Columbus concludes that "given devout religious persons knowing thoroughly the language that they use, soon all of them would become Christian" and he repeats the same argument suggesting that efforts to make Christians of the Indians "will be done easily, since they have no false religion nor are they idolaters."[11]

Columbus's arguments would be echoed again and again by later European explorers and settlers. Although the idea that American Indians had no religion of their own would gradually be recognized as erroneous, indigenous religious practices would be classified as superstitions and magic and derided as meaningless rituals performed by ignorant people rather than being regarded as evidence of full-fledged religions. Efforts would be launched by Catholic and Protestant missionaries to convert native peoples to Christianity. But these efforts would also be tempered by another idea evident in Columbus's thinking and in the European background in which this thinking was shaped. That was the idea of a Christian commonwealth. In late medieval and early modern Europe, efforts to convert people outside the boundaries of Christendom were not common.[12] Priority was given to building a strong Christian commonwealth characterized by uniformity of belief and practice among those to whom citizenship was granted. Thus, Jews were more likely to be expelled, persecuted, or marginalized than turned into objects of proselytization, and Muslims were more likely to become objects of war. In the American colonies, it thus became possible to imagine that the emerging nation was Christian simply by excluding indigenous peoples from membership.

When European settlers started arriving early in the seventeenth century, another characteristic way of understanding non-Christian religions gained prominence. This was the idea that Indian religion consisted mainly in devil worship. Accusations of devil worship had grown in the years following the Protestant Reformation, especially in areas of Europe where Protestants and Catholics were engaged in heated struggles for control.[13] Each side charged the other with being in league with the devil. As conflict with Indians in the American colonies developed, it was easy to view them as devil worshippers as well.[14] John Smith, John Rolfe, David Ingram, Henry Hawkes, George Percy, Walter Raleigh, José de Acosta, Samuel Purchas, William Strachey, Roger Williams, and Cotton Mather all expressed this view, supporting it with observations about child sacrifice, cannibalism, mysterious body rituals, and superstition.[15]

Like Columbus, the American colonists believed the Indians were capable of being converted and civilized—the two going hand in hand, just as civilized Christians in Europe had sought to do in converting the heathen (literally, "people of the heath") who continued to follow superstitious practices. To this end, the English crown ordered a general contribution in 1615 and in 1617 in all Anglican parishes to assist the Virginia Company in building a college for the Indians. The money was diverted and the college never built, but in 1649 Puritan leaders in New England solicited a collection in England and formed the Society for Propagation of the Gospell in New England, the first of many such organizations.[16]

Colonists' encounters with Indians also evoked questions about how these people fit into the biblical story of human origins. Most writers were satisfied to trace the Indians back to Adam and Eve. They also sought support for common ancestry in similarities of word usage, dress, and other cultural traits between Indians and ancient Greeks, Scythians, Tartars, and biblical Hebrews. The possibility that Indians were one of the Ten Lost Tribes described in the Bible, first proposed by José de Costa in 1590, grew in popularity, as did the idea that Indians had come to America across a land bridge from Asia.[17] But if Indians had descended from Adam and Eve, it remained to explain why their customs were so different from European Christians'. The idea of degeneracy provided an answer. After the flood, the Indians' ancestors turned their backs on God, resulting in evil, corruption, and decline. Cotton Mather, for instance, described the Indians as "the veriest ruines" of mankind, and Roger Williams wrote of them having lost the true God and substituting from their own invention "false and fained Gods."[18]

Toward a New Nation

Earlier beliefs about the satanic influences in Indian religion and its degeneracy continued in the eighteenth century. But as the American colonies moved toward nationhood the twin ideas of Christendom and civic republicanism took on greater prominence in Americans' self-understanding. With these ideas, religious diversity at home and abroad also acquired new connotations. European Americans grew more confident for a time that Indians could be Christianized and thereby brought into the commonwealth at least as peaceful neighbors if not as citizens. Deist notions of God tempered more restrictive ideas about Christian salvation, refocusing debates about non-Christian religions around their belief or lack of belief in God. Strands of Enlightenment thinking also resulted in more systematic efforts to locate American religion and civilization within a broader comparative framework.

The idea that Indians might be converted to Christianity grew less from the optimism of the Spanish explorers than the reflections of early Protestant leaders who found remnants of biblical religion in native practices. In the first decades of American settlement, writers such as William Morrell, John White, William Strachey, and Roger Williams remarked on Indians' apparent belief in a monotheistic God, divine creation, and life after death, all of which gave rise to hopes that Indians had a foundation on which to receive instruction in the Christian faith.[19] Roger Williams went further than most, writing in 1643 of Indians in New England who believed in an omnipotent creator God to whom they prayed and offered laments or of whom they expressed fear, likening their belief in lesser gods to that of "Papist" worship of saints, and finding parallels between the religious functionaries of the Narragansett and those of the Israelites.[20]

The changing relationship between Christian America and Indians or followers of other religions can be seen in comparing the views of Cotton Mather at the start of the eighteenth century and those of Jonathan Edwards a half century later. Mather regarded New England as a place in which God's purposes could be worked out, repeatedly characterizing it as the New Israel, and his writing was often directed at critics in England who saw the New World more as a feeding ground for heathenism and savagery.[21] Mather was more confident than his English interlocutors that God's hand would stay the Indians' devilish proclivities, but he pictured the world as a vivid struggle between the forces of good, represented by Puritan settlers, and those of evil, embodied in the local savages, but also in "Mahometans," "Papists," and "Socinians."[22] What the historian Conrad Cherry has termed a "sense of precarious occupancy" ran through Puritan thought from Plymouth onward but seemed to be especially evident among second- and third-generation leaders.[23] The colonists' covenant with God was always threatened, from both within and without, by the forces of evil. To the extent that Puritan leaders took Indians, savages, and heathen as a negative reference point for a vision of Christian America, they did so almost defensively as a reminder of colonists' need for vigilance and purity. Living in a world of "heathenism, idolatry, and devil worship," Mather felt it necessary to be watchful, but refrained from enthusiastically promoting proselytizing.[24] The extension of Christendom would come about more by displacing the heathen than by converting them.[25]

Edwards was a more expansive thinker than Mather, writing about Jews, Muslims, and other religions as well as Indians, and puzzling about their place in divine cosmogony.[26] He too wrote often with English clerics in mind, but was influenced by writing against Deism in a way that Mather could not have been. As the historian Gerald McDermott has argued, Edwards was intent on countering the Deists' claim that reason was sufficient to guide people at all times and places to a knowledge of God, arguing that true faith came only as a result of divine revelation.[27] Thus, God's initial revelation to the Jews and later through Christ influenced other cultures to the extent that they had contact with Jews and Christians; at the same time, these other cultures were subject to slippage or degeneracy as they ceased having this exposure.[28] Muslims, for instance, benefited from having roots in Judaism and being taught some truth about Christ, but in Edwards's view they stifled free thought and grew only by offering sensual rewards and appealing to base human desires.[29] Edwards also posited, however, that individuals have differing "affections" or dispositions to receive divine revelation, thus opening the possibility of regeneration.[30] While scholars differ in interpreting the implications of Edwards's argument for missions, it appears that he opens the door for considering the possibility that other religions may contain vestiges of Christian truth that can be awakened through positive exposure to Christian preaching.[31]

In comparison with Mather, Edwards also renewed and tightened the connections between America and the idea of God working in history. The view that America may be the means by which all the world will be redeemed took on new meaning in the context of the Great Awakening and, of course, subsequently in the American Revolution.[32] Edwards insisted that all of humankind is capable of knowing God's design through the "light of natural reason" and thus can be saved, but is also subject to divine wrath for rejecting God.[33] Proselytizing therefore takes on greater urgency—which finds expression in Edwards's own efforts in behalf of Indian conversion, especially after 1751 at Stockbridge in western Massachusetts.[34] Non-Christians are no longer just an enemy to be vigilant against but a people to be redeemed.[35] America thus becomes, in the historian Bernard Bailyn's words, "a special place . . . in the architecture of God's intent," having a mission that goes beyond merely protecting the purity of its Christians.[36] As a redeemer nation, America is special in relation to Europe but even more so in contrast with the non-Christian world.[37] In addition, Edwards brings to the foreground an eschatological emphasis or "note of expectation" that gives America its special vocation at a propitious time in history.[38]

Edwards and the religious awakening that occurred in the mid-eighteenth century through his preaching and that of his contemporary, George Whitefield, are usually credited with giving impetus to the American Revolution, especially by elevating a divine mandate above conformity to an oppressive civil jurisdiction.[39] The nation-building process that took place over the next half century, however, required coming to terms with the considerable diversity of Christian groups represented in the American colonies. Thus, it is not surprising to find a growing emphasis in the second half of the eighteenth century on religious freedom. Although religious freedom usually pertained only to the various expressions of Christianity, the major architects of the new nation also shared a vision of Christianity that gave it less exclusive authority than in Edwards or Whitefield. John Adams, Thomas Jefferson, and Benjamin Franklin, in particular, questioned the divinity of Christ and championed a kind of "theistic perspectivism" that provided wider latitude for religious freedom.[40] Adopting the view that God cannot be known fully, but approached humbly through reason and virtue as well as revelation, allowed them to avoid the hard questions of whether people outside of Christianity have a relationship with God. They could, however, maintain the conviction—one that became stronger during the next century—that a combination of reason and Christian morality gives the new nation a special place in the advancement of civilization. It is thus through reason primarily that the moral values associated with Christianity will prevail. This idea by no means ended religious violence or the use of force against Indians or followers of other religions. Yet it established a foothold from which to argue that different religious perspectives might share common ideals.

Through Jefferson in particular, a framework of religious pluralism was established that permitted diverse religious groups to coexist without having to address their specific interpretations of divine truth. The Virginia Act for Establishing Religious Freedom articulated a policy of toleration and freedom not only for diverse Christian groups but for all religions, including at least symbolically "the Jew, the Mahometan, and the Hindoo."[41] Jefferson did not feel compelled to take a position with respect to the teachings of these religions other than to assume that different religions could be regarded as expressions of conscience and thus worthy of protection. He did worry about religious dogmatism and ignorance, but appears to have been convinced that reasonable people would find the same moral principles through different faiths and, as far as salvation was concerned, would find God in their own ways.[42]

Jefferson's emphasis on religious toleration, with his sense that all reasonable people somehow worship the same God, permitted him to treat Indians largely as a political entity, rather than as representing a spiritual threat to Christianity. Throughout his writings, Jefferson's most frequent references to Indians occur in the context of discussing land purchases, treaties, and alliances, often appearing alongside British, French, Spanish, and Canadians with whom business is being conducted. Although he describes varying degrees of barbarity among the Indians, he carefully distinguishes among the Cherokees and Chickasaws, Kaskaskia Indians, Powhatans, and other groups, emphasizing their resources and political interests and often characterizing them as behaving rationally and intelligently.[43] On the occasions when he writes about their religious beliefs and practices, he sometimes portrays them as believers in a Great Man above, a high god or principle that seems to resemble the one he himself associates with reason and morality.[44]

If Jefferson's thought provided a political framework in which religious diversity could be tolerated, this framework was nevertheless governed by a more general understanding of the limits of acceptable diversity. Few contemporaries wrote as extensively about religion as did Joseph Priestley, whose writings and inclinations toward Unitarianism had a significant influence on Jefferson's own thought.[45] Priestley takes a position between that of Voltaire, whom he criticizes for crediting too much rationality and morality to heathen religions, and that of Roman Catholics and Protestant sects, whom he fears pay too much attention to saints and even Jesus rather than worshipping the one superior God.[46] Monotheistic belief, expressed in the essentials that Priestley draws from Christianity, is in his view the highest source of morality and reason. In comparison, heathenism debases the mind and corrupts morality to such an extent that Priestley is loath to describe its results (but does so to disprove Voltaire). "Indostan" tortures women and causes widows to be burned alive; the religions of Mexico result in thousands of human sacrifices each year; North American Indians are barbarous and ignorant; and "Mahometanism" is only slightly better than the others because of the principles it has derived from Judaism and Christianity. Likening present-day heathenism to that of the ancient world, Priestley remarks that it was "for the good of mankind that such nations should be extirpated from the face of the earth."[47]

Priestley stops short of invoking warfare against heathen societies, but is at pains to understand why a sovereign God permits their existence. Like other writers, he describes a downward trajectory following a common origin as these cultures lost contact with Judaism and Christianity. Lacking knowledge of God, they found it necessary to explain mysterious events through recourse to animals, planets, the sun, and other forces which they turned into objects of worship. Such worship naturally stifled their ability to reason and resulted in debauchery. God knew about their wickedness and permitted it to continue, but for reasons that remain inscrutable. All that can be known is that God allowed evil on this scale in order to produce a greater good at some proper time in the future.

In Priestley, then, many of the standard ways of understanding religions other than Christianity are evident, even though his emphasis on monotheism discourages religious discrimination on the basis of sectarian interpretations of Christian doctrine itself. Reason and divine revelation come together in support of broad freedom within the Christian world, apparently extending to Judaism as well, at the same time that an understanding of heathenism sets limits on how broadly these freedoms are likely to be extended. Coupled with the more explicit defense of religious freedom evident in Jefferson, and the emphasis in Franklin, Adams, and others on resolving religious disputes through reason, these understandings fit well with the founders' desire to create a nation that embraced diversity while functioning within a framework of values derived broadly from Christianity.[48]

From Missions to Comparative Religion

The influences of Deism and Enlightenment philosophy on the founders of the early republic achieved the possibility of religious tolerance and freedom for diverse religious expressions by moving largely away from the particularistic teachings of biblical Christianity. The very tolerance encoded in the American Constitution, however, permitted religious groups that advocated more aggressive interpretations of Christianity to flourish. During the nineteenth century, especially after the second religious awakening in the 1830s and 1840s, evangelical Christianity became the source of a vibrant missionary movement both at home and abroad. Especially through the latter, American missionaries and other religious leaders came into direct contact with people of other faiths. The gospel mandate motivated missionaries to reach beyond their own shores, overcoming what they viewed as parochialism and prejudice by treating all people, whether "Hindoo or Hottentot" as if they were brothers.[49] Thus, missionaries became the largest contingent of American travelers to remote corners of the world and, unlike in Britain, where colonialism and imperial trade put larger segments of the middle class in contact with other cultures, missionaries became the chief interpreters of remote societies and religions for people at home. These encounters and interpretations opened new questions about the meanings of Christianity and of being Americans in a world of religious diversity.

The American missionary movement began in earnest with the founding of the American Board of Commissioners for Foreign Missions in 1810. In little more than a decade, its annual budget far surpassed those of comparable organizations devoted to temperance, benevolence, peace, and the distribution of Bibles.[50] A half century later, with the heyday of U.S. missions still in the future, missionary leaders could already speak confidently of triumphs around the globe. As one leader, writing in 1861, declared, American missions had risen over the past fifty years to such a position of power and prominence in the world as to "reproach all critics and cavillers."[51] Although the missionaries' successes at making converts were small numerically, their symbolic significance was immense. Through missionaries' interpretations, Americans could readily imagine that other religions were as corrupt as their host civilizations and that their further decay could be envisioned in the foreseeable future. Hinduism in India, one report concluded, showed every sign of total demise: "Sutti and widow celibacy are abolished. Polygamy is doomed, and what Hindu, knowing all this, raises a hand? There is no heart left in the creed, and though it may exist for generations, as the corpse of Roman Paganism did, its downfall is assured."[52] Elsewhere, in the Middle East, Africa, Fiji, China, and the Hawaiian islands, the idolatry of Muslims, Confucians, pagans, and tribalists was said to be crumbling in the face of Christianity.[53]

As missionaries provided first-hand accounts of other religions, Americans' perceptions expanded beyond earlier accusations of mere idolatry and heathenism. The more telling sign of other religions' inferiority to Christianity was their lack of appreciation for the finer aspects of Western civilization. Writing in 1872 of his travels in India, one writer observed: "When you enter a Hindoo home you are at once struck with the naked look of the room—no chair or sofa to sit upon, no pictures on the walls, no piano or musical instrument, no library of books, no maps, no table with the newspaper or periodical or album upon it, and you wonder how they can bear to live such a life." He continues: "But you are a Christian, and your holy religion has made you to differ, and taught you the nature and value of a Christian home and its conveniences and joys."[54]

Besides first-hand exposure, religious leaders drew increasingly on historical discussions of other religions, sometimes providing more nuanced accounts of their achievements, but also managing to mold these impressions to fit ideas of Christian and American superiority. The Orient, a Methodist bishop conceded in 1870, had "much knowledge and a wonderful history," its astronomy and mathematics surpassing that of the West for many centuries and its philosophy rivaling that of the Greeks. Drawing on current theories about the history of religions, he likened the Vedic tradition to a wellspring of mythology as rich as Egyptian, Roman, and early Germanic civilizations—all containing ideas of a deity (perhaps even trinitarian), divine origins of the earth, the Garden of Eden, the fall, and possibility of reunion with God. He nevertheless described a downward trajectory in all these traditions. "The ancient mythologies are the solid gold of truth beaten into flimsy tinsel, and molded by a depraved imagination into forms which dazzle and bewilder, but are no longer capable of being the current coin of the moral universe." The present situation in the Orient was thus deplorable: "Beginning with the true God, they advanced to the triad, then multiplied their avatars, finally worshiped things inanimate, till now the waters, the sun, the monkey, are worshiped, and the gods of the country are more numerous than the men, while the objects most adored are those that are most disgusting."[55]

Few observers of other religions during the middle decades of the nineteenth century wrote as authoritatively as Rufus Anderson, the indefatigable missionary, writer, and traveler who served as head of the American Board of Commissioners for Foreign Missions from 1832 to 1866.[56] During and after his years with the Board, Anderson visited India, the Mediterranean, Hawaii, and the Sandwich Islands, lectured at Andover seminary, and wrote numerous books and articles. He was confident that Christian missions would prevail in all the regions he visited, especially with the aid of America's rising technological and economic prowess.[57] He was nevertheless persistent in emphasizing how hard the work of missionaries was when they had to labor in such culturally unfavorable conditions. The heathen communities, he wrote, "are thoroughly sensual, earthly, and selfish; unaccustomed to be influenced by, or to think upon, intellectual or moral subjects, unused to change, without enterprise, with no models of excellence before them, and little inclined and little able to appreciate them when presented; full of prejudice and love of sin." It was almost impossible for an American audience, he observed, to understand "how unlike [the heathen] are to an active-minded, enterprising, progressive community in such a Christian land as this."[58]

For Anderson, civilization could be a means to evangelization, since the lack of civilization was an impediment to understanding the gospel. But he also considered it important to distinguish the two and not divert energies from evangelization into reforming other societies. However they might differ in degrees of cultural progress, Jews, Catholics, Mohammedans, Buddhists, and Brahminists were, in his words, "wonderfully alike" as an "undistinguished mass of rebellious sinners" in need of salvation.[59]

A generation later, at the end of the nineteenth century, the distinction between evangelization and civilization was becoming blurred.[60] As westernizing influences spread, the missionary movement appeared more sure of success than ever. Whereas sixteen missionary societies had been present in 1860, the number now was closer to ninety.[61] Civilization and Christianity were being advanced through preaching, the founding of schools, and the distribution of medicine, all peaceful means that appealed to the interests of rational people. The followers of other religions were not as advanced or reasonable, not as free of superstition or as acquainted with the spirit of science and technology as American Christians, but they could be appealed to in terms of self-interest. American ingenuity would accomplish what missionaries from more backward nations, such as England and France, had failed to do. Evangelization would prevail as soon as heathens discovered the benefits of civilization.[62]

Often well-educated and cosmopolitan, missionary leaders were not averse to supporting their observations with evidence collected by scholars or by scholarly means, including the budding methods of social science. In his three volume *Christian Missions and Social Progress*, published between 1897 and 1906, James Dennis sent questionnaires to more than three hundred missionaries soliciting their opinions about the religions and cultures with which they were most familiar.[63] Through conscientious analysis of the results, he concluded that heathen cultures were on the whole intellectually vacuous, confused, unwholesome, and mentally crooked. Ahead of many of his peers, he advocated on this basis that missions be devoted more explicitly toward the regeneration of societies rather than focusing narrowly on saving souls.

Throughout the nineteenth century, missionary writings seldom omit emphasizing that the worst deficit among the followers of other religions is their lack of eternal salvation. Yet it is almost as if this deficiency goes without saying, or at least can be mentioned briefly, whereas pages and pages must be devoted to demonstrating how lacking these cultures are in civilization. They do not accord their women a proper place in the home where their God-given talents can flourish. They do not have a broad middle class in which norms of equality and mutuality prevail. They do not provide adequate schooling for their children, but expend money foolishly on palaces and fine costumes. They do not wear practical clothing and fail to keep appointments. All of this is because their religion has not been a wellspring of appropriate values. To be sure, the longstanding images of heathen as devil worshippers continue, at least in the sense that Satan has somehow managed to keep their societies in darkness; but it is the lack of civilization that increasingly becomes more salient. Civilization is the shining light that overcomes darkness. The uncivilized world is not the unsullied state of nature that had sometimes been romanticized in the past, but a realm of chaos and confusion. It is ruled by passion rather than intellect, by animal desires rather than scientific principles, the result being unspeakable moral irregularities, mischief, and irrational behavior; only the Christian gospel, often characterized as one of *purity* as well as sanctity, could redeem it.

Knowing that missionaries are the source of these writings, we would not be surprised to find point by point arguments about other religions' lack of belief in God or the trinity, their misunderstandings of sin and salvation, or how they misconstrue the afterlife. Although such arguments are present, they do not stand out as much as phrases describing the heathen as "content with mental inactivity," "untaught in the principles of science," "absorbed in sensual indulgences," and "weak of character." Heathenism, having "exhausted its resources" and capable only of hawking "ideas of a dead past," signifies what Americans are not—or at least what they hope they are not.[64] Civilization, with its broad emphasis on learning, science, reason, and progress, begs for an identity defined by its opposite. By the end of the nineteenth century, as public concern about the salvation of heathens became less fashionable, leaders paid even greater attention to the contrasts between American civilization and other countries' lack of civilization.[65]

A parallel development in the nineteenth century that also contributed to American understandings of religious diversity was the growing interest in comparative studies of religion. Several scattered works that included descriptions of other religions besides Christianity were published before the Civil War. One of the first was Hannah Adams's *Dictionary of All Religions and Religious Denominations, Ancient and Modern*, published in 1784 and reprinted in several editions over the next two decades—written in confidence, as a religion scholar would note a century later, "that Christianity could easily be shown to be immeasurably superior to all earlier or contemporary religions."[66] Another was an edited compendium published in 1823 with chapters on Judaism, "Mohometanism," "Hindoos," and "Ceremonies of Other Pagan Nations." Yet another was *A Pictorial and Descriptive View of All Religions*, published in 1851 by Charles A. Goodrich, a popular author and educator who wrote or edited some 170 volumes.[67] The authors of these works often had scant material with which to work and thus provided relatively brief descriptions that focused more on historical religions and religious texts than on actual practices.

Although differing in impulse, the Transcendentalists' interest in Asian religions can at least broadly be associated with the development of comparative religions as a scholarly field. Ralph Waldo Emerson's interest in Asian religions began to appear in 1841 with his first volume of *Essays* and developed during the next two years as he collaborated with Henry David Thoreau on a series of translated selections of Eastern scriptures. In the 1850s Emerson read extensively in Hindu materials, the influence of which is evident in *The Conduct of Life*, published in 1860. Besides Emerson and Thoreau, several others within the Transcendentalists' circle expressed interest in Asian religions, including Theodore Parker and his student William Rounseville Alger, the editor in 1856 of a volume of Asian poetry. Samuel Johnson, who graduated from Harvard Divinity School in 1846 and later became active in the Free Religious Association, went on to produce some of the first systematic scholarly works on the religions of China and India.

During the second half of the nineteenth century American writers increasingly referred to the adherents of other world religions in an emerging quest to identify universals in human experience. This quest was not incompatible with the idea that Christianity and American civilization were more advanced than other cultures. It was rather an effort to show that the advanced ideas of American thinkers were not simply parochial inventions but pointed to general laws of human nature. Usually the followers of other religions continued to be regarded negatively in such comparisons. For instance, James Redfield illustrated an argument about the physiological bases of human dispositions by describing a Hindu who looked like a rat and behaved like one, and Orestes Brownson wrote about Hindu villages in making a more general argument about patriarchy being the earliest form of government.[68] Other references, however, were more sympathetic or neutral. Susan B. Anthony, for example, regarded Hindu, Jewish, and Muslim women as examples of the need to overcome oppression by empowering women, and Dawson Burns wrote about Greeks, American Indians, and Hindus in arguing that abstinence from alcohol is associated with longevity.[69]

Comparative religion as a scholarly field emerged especially from growing interest in the study of similarities and differences among languages. This philological approach to religious diversity had already been of interest in the late 1700s. Thomas Jefferson, for instance, recognized its value, writing in a 1789 letter to James Madison from Paris that he wished "to collect all the vocabularies I can of the American Indians, as of those of Asia, persuaded, that if they ever had a common parentage, it will appear in their languages."[70] In the nineteenth century, students of comparative languages became increasingly interested in the interrelationships of Sanskrit, Greek, Latin, and European languages.[71] The German-born Oxford philologist, Max Muller, became one of the most prolific and influential of these scholars. Muller edited a fifty-one volume collection of sacred texts from the East and in 1880 published a series of lectures proposing a new "science" of comparative religion.[72] Skeptical of arguments about ancient Judaism having been the source of all religions, Muller asserted the value of examining the evolution of language within the various traditions. Doing so persuaded him that all religions evolved by shedding arcane elements and progressively "growing up" from "the simplest childish" patterns to the "highest metaphysical abstractions."[73] Although he believed that non-Western religions were inferior, Muller posited that all religions contain truth insofar as they represent the soul's yearning for God.[74] In a similar vein, Lewis Henry Morgan, credited with founding American anthropology, combined philological and ethnographic evidence to develop a broad theory of cultural evolution that outlined a theory of religious development starting with primitive animism, moving through phases of pantheism and polytheism, and culminating with the monotheism of Judaism and Christianity.[75] This view encouraged some scholars to view non-Christian religions more positively than in the past. For instance, the Yale linguist and Sanskrit scholar William D. Whitney distinguished early "race religions" that reflected only the collective wisdom of a community from later religions founded by individual leaders, among which he included Zoroastrianism, Mohammedanism, Buddhism, and Christianity. The latter, he argued, were significantly more effective at propagating themselves.[76]

Against the natural evolutionary view, conservative Christian theologians argued that close scrutiny of the history of other religions demonstrated that they showed a pattern of decline. Princeton Theological Seminary's Charles Hodge argued that a notable change was evident in documents that he took to have been produced about sixteen hundred years before Christ: earlier documents, Hodge claimed, showed devout acknowledgment of a monotheistic God, whereas later documents included increasing evidence of pantheism, paganism, and moral decay, thus suggesting that non-Western nations could only be redeemed through aggressive exposure to Christianity.[77] These disagreements encouraged scholars to devote greater effort to translating and interpreting the texts of non-Western religions and to pay closer attention to the histories of these religions. At the start of the twentieth century, anthropologists increasingly challenged philological assumptions about common linguistic and religious origins.[78] Yet much anthropological writing in the United States remained compatible with the idea of American superiority. Evolutionary notions of religious development, even when questioning biblical ideas of common ancestry or theological arguments about moral degeneracy, continued to be constructed in ways that placed American Christianity—and especially Protestantism—on top.

Although the comparative study of religion was profoundly important as an academic development, its impact on popular thinking about religious diversity was limited. Few Americans received college training at all and fewer still were exposed to courses in which comparative religion was taught. A half century would pass before religious studies departments were founded in which students could study religions comparatively, and not until television found a surprisingly receptive audience for his work would a comparativist such as Joseph Campbell be able to popularize the idea that many religions expressed similar truths.[79] Yet the early comparativists, convinced as they were that Christian truth was inherently supreme and therefore able to withstand all comparisons, did establish the scholarly norm of examining different religions in terms of their own teachings, encouraging the view that value could be obtained by understanding religions other than one's own, and assuming that the various religions could stand or fall on their own merits.

Toward the end of the nineteenth century an event was organized that dramatically brought together the missionary impulse and emerging interests in comparative religion. This was the World's Parliament of Religions, part of the World's Columbian Exposition in commemoration of Columbus's discovery of America, which convened in Chicago for seventeen days in September 1893. Officially part of the Exposition but held seven miles north at the Art Institute, the Parliament was one of the fair's more attractive events: despite sweltering temperatures and a rash of pickpockets, it drew an estimated 150,000 visitors. Historians and students of comparative religions have viewed it as a watershed episode in America's response to religious diversity, signaling a new acceptance and opening the door for non-Western religions to gain institutional footing, as well as for comparative religious studies to be incorporated into university curricula.[80] Recent treatments have even described it as a "new dawn," presaging the religious pluralism of the twenty-first century.[81] Yet the story is more complicated, suggesting both the continuation of an ascendant Christian America and unresolved questions about religious diversity that would still need to be addressed more than a century later.

The Columbian Exposition celebrated the triumph of American civilization, which, in the words of the exposition's director general, was the culmination of "the ceaseless, resistless march of civilization, Westward, ever Westward."[82] "White City," the central venue of the fair (which some visitors likened to heaven itself), represented America, the pinnacle of civilization, while the "Midway Plaisance" exhibited other cultures as a kind of sideshow.[83] The World's Parliament was under the supervision of John Henry Barrows, a Presbyterian minister who hoped to promote the comparative study of religion and more important, to demonstrate the superiority of Christianity through these comparisons. All other religions, he believed, would be absorbed into or replaced by the higher truth of America's faith—symbolically enacted during the opening ceremony in the Roman Catholic cardinal James Gibbons's leading the assembled Jews, Muslims, Buddhists, and Christians in a multilingual rendering of the Lord's Prayer.[84]

The event did give representatives of various religions a platform alongside Christianity, albeit on unequal footing. Buddhism, Hinduism, Shintoism, Zoroastrianism, and Confucianism were well represented, while Islam was present mainly in the person of one New England convert, and "primitive" religions from Africa, the Americas, and other parts of the world were not represented at all. For the first time, representatives of some of these religions had an opportunity to describe their own beliefs and practices, rather than having them interpreted by Christian missionaries or travelers. Hindu leaders were able to point out that they were not idolaters; Zoroastrians, that they were not fire worshippers; Buddhists, that they did not believe that Buddha created the world; Muslims, that they respected human life; and so on.[85] Yet, as significant as it was for them to be represented, these leaders collectively comprised only one-sixth of the program while Christian speakers made up the remaining five-sixths, using the occasion to speak on topics such as "the idealism of American civilization," the "strategic certainty" that only Christianity provides "deliverance from sin," "the truthfulness of Holy Scripture," the "shame and mischief" of divorce, "our civilization essentially Christian," the conquest of India by England as a "marvel of history," and "the world's religious debt to America."[86]

A few scholars (including Max Muller) saw the Parliament as a significant accomplishment, but many of the religious leaders themselves came away with misgivings.[87] Buddhists and Hindus commented that they had not been heard or understood, and Christians' responses ranged from rapidly languishing interest, to polite concern about the promotion of religious universalism, to calls for more zealous proselytizing.[88] A few big-city newspapers applauded the event's promotion of tolerance and unity, viewing these as the highest marks of civilization.[89] But in smaller cities and towns, the event received hardly any visibility at all compared to the weekly coverage of local sermons and church gatherings. One newspaper, other than those in Chicago, that did give the Parliament extensive coverage was the *New York Daily Tribune*. At the close of the event, it offered this observation: "Christianity is an integral, if not an essential, element in the only civilization in the world today that is worth propagating—the only civilization, in fact, that contains within itself any hope of progress, enlightenment and happiness." As if to underscore the point, it concluded: "Christianity holds a place of supremacy in a civilization which is itself incomparably superior to any other civilization that the world has ever seen."[90]

Christianity's superiority over other religions was a view that would remain. Following a visit to India, Mark Twain wrote in 1897 that Hinduism was a religion of idol worshippers promoted by yogis chiefly intent on making money, and of Banares he observed, "[It] is a vast museum of idols—and all of them crude, misshapen, and ugly."[91] The few Asian Indians who came to the United States at the start of the twentieth century were frequently subjected to hostility and violence, and in 1917 Congress severely restricted immigration from India. Between 1870 and 1904 a series of exclusion laws barred Chinese workers from the United States, and in 1924 the Immigration Act denied entry to virtually all Asians. Journal articles, such as "American Women Going After Heathen Gods" (1912), and books, such as *Mother India* (1927) and *The Indian Menace* (1929), warned Americans of the dangerous designs of other religions.[92] Even among more liberal religious leaders, the view of other religions remained far from positive. In 1930, one of the more widely read and authoritative treatises on world religions, written by Robert Ernest Hume, a Union Theological Seminary professor and translator of numerous Sanskrit religious texts, declared that Hindus "have worshipped any object which they prefer, or virtually none" and "have followed any standard of morality, or almost none."[93] Buddhism's weaknesses included its general pessimism, its inhibition of individual initiative and social responsibility, the "empty idea of a blissful Nirvana," and its founder's "moral handicaps," while Muhammadanism was described as a religion that relied on force, motivated its followers by fear, discouraged progress, and was constrained by "certain pathetic weaknesses in the founder's moral character."[94]

During the coming decades, the wider acceptance of religious diversity envisioned by some participants in the World's Parliament would also be greatly overshadowed by what the historian R. Laurence Moore has termed a "historiography of desire."[95] This was the desire for greater unity within American Protestantism itself, a central preoccupation of mainline leaders who sincerely believed that Christ's pleasure was best expressed through the unity of the church, rather than through diversity, but who also worried about the inroads that Catholicism could make against a divided Protestantism and who equally disliked the brash sectarianism that seemed so endemic among fundamentalists. It was this desire for unity that, perhaps ironically, contributed to a new spirit of accommodation among mainline Protestants that eventually made room for Catholics and Jews as well. This tripartite arrangement would constitute a significant development in the larger movement toward greater acceptance of religious diversity.

The Tripartite Settlement

By the middle of the twentieth century, American Christians could fairly easily convince themselves that the society in which they lived was in fact Christian or at least guided by Christian values. Churchgoing was at an all-time high. Public leaders routinely pledged to uphold the principles of God-fearing people against the threat of godless Communism from abroad. Missionaries reported that people in little-known corners of the world were eager to receive Christ, while more liberal church leaders who may have backed away from the aggressive missionary programs of the nineteenth century still believed Christian values could be spread in the name of humanitarian relief and modernization. Within the United States, churchgoers worried about fringe groups, such as Mormons and Jehovah's Witnesses, that strayed from orthodox Christian teachings, and they knew that atheists could make trouble in the public arena. Yet, with polls showing that 96 percent of Americans believed in God, these fringe groups could for the most part be ignored. The main challenge to the idea that American religion and American Christianity were synonymous was the presence of American Jews.

Will Herberg's widely read *Protestant-Catholic-Jew*, published in 1955, was emblematic of the approach to religious pluralism that came to characterize the United States during the middle decades of the twentieth century.[96] Although discussions of heathenism had usually placed Jews in a separate category because of their role in the history of Christianity, Christian leaders had stigmatized Jews as Christ-killers or as unrepentant holdouts against the truth of the Messiah.[97] The emphasis on civilization as a mark of Christian virtue that had emerged in the nineteenth century forced some observers to concede that Jews must be closer to divine truth than other religions because of their educational and cultural accomplishments. But grassroots ethnocentrism still pervaded much of the population, and even the Holocaust had been regarded with surprising indifference in many quarters. When public opinion surveys began asking questions about religious attitudes in the 1950s and early 1960s, a sizable percentage of American Protestants and Catholics expressed misgivings about interacting with Jews.[98] Increasingly, though, Americans came to regard Judaism in the manner that Herberg's title suggested: as a legitimate third option alongside Protestantism and Catholicism.

Herberg's own biography is helpful for understanding how this idea of religious pluralism came to be formulated. Ethnically Jewish but raised with more of a commitment to Marxism than Judaism, Herberg underwent a religious awakening that led him to study at Union Seminary in New York, reading appreciatively the work of Reinhold Niebuhr and Paul Tillich, and for a time considering converting to Christianity.[99] Eventually returning to Judaism through Christianity, as it were, he saw deep similarities between the two religions.[100] They were, he wrote, "two religions sharing a common faith," which included faith in God, faith in the Bible, recognition of human sinfulness, trust in divine love, and recognition of the individual's need for a religious community.[101] While acknowledging the differences between Judaism and Christianity, he minimized their importance, referring to "the church" in a way that embraced synagogues and suggesting that the differences between Protestants and Catholics were as great as those between Christians and Jews. Third-generation Americans' need for identity, he argued, encouraged them to identify with one tradition or another within the "triple melting pot," but to recognize that they were, above all, people of a common faith.

Like many popular books, Herberg's was more a description of developments having already taken place than a vision of a future reality. Christian and Jewish leaders had been working to bring about greater harmony and understanding for a number of years. Several of these efforts began during the 1920s, which were otherwise characterized by vigorous Ku Klux Klan activities and a resurgence of religious, racial, and ethnic nativism. Among the first of these efforts were the Federal Council of Churches of Christ Committee on Goodwill between Jews and Christians (1923) and the American Good Will Union of Reverend Edward Hunt (1924). Jewish leaders played a reciprocal role through the Central Conference of American Rabbis Committee on Goodwill (1924) and Rabbi Isaac Landman's Permanent Commission of Better Understanding between Christians and Jews (1927).[102] Prompted by these developments, as well as by a renewed focus in other organizations on proselytizing Jews, the National Conference of Christians and Jews (NCCJ) was founded in 1927 to promote civic cooperation among the various faiths.[103] Anticipating Herberg's thesis by almost three decades, the NCCJ was organized around a tripartite representation of Protestants, Catholics, and Jews and helped to voice the idea that American religion was basically a pluralistic meeting point among these three cultural groups. Although the NCCJ did not seek to foster cooperation among religious groups other than Christians and Jews, it did work out precedents that would later serve for such wider efforts, including frank acknowledgment of the conflicting truth claims of the groups involved and the value of working together despite disagreements.[104] Another step toward the idea of parity among religious groups came about as a result of the chaplaincy in World War II. Although Jews served as chaplains as early as the Civil War, fewer than thirty had served prior to 1940, whereas this number grew to more than three hundred during World War II. More significantly, the armed forces' administrative structure for appointing chaplains became more centralized and thus required more deliberate coordination among the various faiths, while chaplaincy training more frequently included instruction about interreligious cooperation.[105]

The most distinctive feature of the tripartite perspective that emerged in the 1950s was its treatment of Judaism as a kind of branch or denomination within the larger Judeo-Christian framework—a religion peopled by believers who just happened to attend churches called synagogues, as Elia Kazan's 1945 film *Gentleman's Agreement* had characterized it.[106] Herberg argued that Protestants, Catholics, and Jews all shared a common heritage, their differences reflecting historic divisions rooted in nationality, ethnicity, and even social class, much like the differences H. Richard Niebuhr had identified as sources of denominationalism within Protestantism.[107] Now, with pressures to "Americanize," many of these particular differences were subsiding, making it possible to downplay the distinct beliefs of Lutherans as opposed to Presbyterians or Orthodox Jews as opposed to Reform Jews. "All were becoming American," he wrote, "and therefore more and more like each other."[108] Indeed, Americans' preference for Protestantism, Catholicism, or Judaism was itself largely a reflection of their desire for roots, rather than a matter of deeply held religious convictions.[109] Ironically, Herberg criticized the shallow sameness of the three traditions, arguing that they succumbed too much to the materialism and self-interestedness of American culture; yet his own analysis rested on assuming away the deeper theological differences that might have served as an antidote for this superficiality.

Responses to Herberg's book suggest how limited and controversial the tripartite arrangement was. Social observers who emphasized ethnic diversity generally thought Herberg's analysis was not only brilliant but socially desirable.[110] Among theologians, especially Jews, the response was more guarded. If Herberg was right, they argued, American Judaism was in trouble. Its historic essence lay in more than simply attending weekend services, like Christians, and praying to a God who could comfort one's Cold War insecurities. Jews should be wary of fitting in with the normality of American life, selling their birthright in order to be accepted.[111] Others saw dangers in Herberg's own emphasis on the similarities between Christianity and Judaism.[112]

These concerns notwithstanding, the tripartite idea gained acceptance in the decade following publication of Herberg's book, especially as Protestants and Jews came to regard Catholics as a more reliable partner in this arrangement. The Second Vatican Council's statement on non-Christian religions included language that suggested more willingness on the part of Catholic leaders to accept Judaism as a legitimate alternative to Christianity. Jewish leaders pointed out that the Council's language did not adequately clarify the Church's position with respect to Jewish salvation, but they applauded the Council for its support of greater respect and under-standing.[113] Jewish leaders also increasingly saw Catholics as a potential ally because of their common history of marginalization by Protestants.[114] Without fully addressing the theological differences dividing them, Catho-lics and Jews were able to embrace religious pluralism on grounds of greater tolerance and freedom of expression.

Whatever the tripartite settlement did to promote accommodation among Christians and Jews, it nevertheless did little to anticipate the wider religious diversity that the United States would face in subsequent decades. In emphasizing the similarities between Christianity and Juda-ism, Herberg drew a circle that explicitly left out Muslims, Hindus, Bud-dhists, and other non-Western religions. When "one professes oneself a Buddhist, a Muslim, or anything but a Protestant, Catholic, or Jew," he observed, "it may imply being foreign ... or obscurely 'un-Ameri-can.' "[115] His understanding of the situation was both empirical and nor-mative: religions other than the Jewish-Christian faith *were* popularly regarded with as much suspicion as atheists and agnostics, and the good thing about interfaith cooperation was that it combined Christians and Jews who shared a similar theological tradition and did not extend to any and all who might claim to be religious. The common ground between Christianity and Judaism, he wrote, is "sufficiently real and important ... to make it possible to speak significantly of Jewish-Christian faith in a way that no one could conceivably speak of Jewish-Buddhist or Christian-Hindu faith."[116] Others addressing the question of religious diversity looked to the wider world, where the impact of Islam, Hindu-ism, and other religions required more careful scrutiny.[117] Yet few of these statements, other than calling for greater respect, encouraged Americans to think about what it might mean to live in a society where diversity meant more than being Protestant, Catholic, or Jewish.[118]

Beyond Christian America?

The common theme running through five hundred years of encounters between European American Christians and other religions is that these encounters have not simply reflected the actual presence of religious diversity, but have been decidedly shaped by Christians' own perceptions of themselves and of their place in the world. Whether they were in a small minority, as was true of the early explorers and settlers, or truly the majority religion, as they were in the nineteenth century, American Christians have thought of themselves as the reigning power and the dominant cultural influence. It was thus possible to ignore the presence of devotees of other religions or to regard them variously as proto-Christians, potential converts, degenerate heathen, or in some other way that did not fully take into account the complexity of their beliefs and practices.

In all of this, the democratic structure of American government functioned reasonably well to maintain civic harmony and constrain the worst excesses of religious intolerance within the United States itself. Through the battles that Christian denominations often fought with one another, case law developed that focused more on civil rights and less on the distinctive teachings of particular religious groups. The courts also served a pedagogic function, encouraging rank-and-file Americans to behave civilly and respectfully toward their neighbors despite religious disagreements. Americans were able to practice their faith within particular and often local communities without paying much attention to the ways others were practicing their faith. Tolerance proceeded without having to carry the burden of genuine interreligious understanding or interaction.

By the end of the twentieth century, American Christians were well prepared in one sense to accommodate the wider range of religious diversity that was rapidly becoming a reality. They were prepared to approach these new differences in a spirit of tolerance and to hammer out the practical difficulties of living together by applying the same legal standards that had served them in the past. Yet in another sense the new religious diversity posed a challenge that would not so easily be met. This was the challenge of having to rethink the presumption that America itself was basically Christian (or Judeo-Christian). For many Americans, it had been possible in the past to separate their civic selves from their religious convictions and thus to think of America as a Christian nation even though they knew this not to be true constitutionally. Although they were sincere about their religious beliefs, they believed in the truth of their own religion without thinking very much about the presence of other religions. Even when they encountered people who were not Christians, as the explorers and settlers did when they interacted with Indians or as missionaries and traders did when they lived among people in other parts of the world, they had been able to treat them as if they were almost invisible, ignoring their presence, lumping them into broad categories, and perceiving them through an interpretive lens that minimized the value of their traditions and culture. Would Americans now continue to ignore other religions, even when adherents of these religions were living in their own neighborhoods? Would they begin borrowing from the wider variety of religious options in their midst? Or would they come to a deeper understanding of their own tradition as they compared it with others?

The New Diversity

THROUGHOUT most of the nation's history, Americans of European descent viewed the adherents of religions other than Christianity from a distance. The distance was either geographic, as in the case of people living in the Middle East or Asia, or socioeconomic and cultural, as in the case of American Indians. Both kinds of distance inhibited interaction of the type that might have furthered genuine understanding. In comparison, the novel aspect of the new diversity that has come to characterize American religion in recent decades is that these older forms of distance no longer prevail. Hindus, Buddhists, and Muslims now live in significant numbers within the boundaries of the United States itself. And, despite the fact that many are immigrants and thus differ in cultural heritage from residents of longer duration, most are middle-class, college-educated professionals who live in the same kinds of neighborhoods as other Americans, send their children to the same schools, vote in the same elections, shop at the same stores, and watch the same programs on television. Religious diversity has become a fact of ordinary life. American Christians and Jews now have opportunities to work in the same offices with people of other religious persuasions, become acquainted with them at community gatherings, visit or at least drive past their places of worship, and hear about or participate directly in their services.

While Americans of European ancestry may still find reasons to isolate themselves or to let their impressions of other religions be guided by the mass media rather than firsthand knowledge, the members of these religions themselves provide ample evidence of the diversity that now exists. Their traditions are not, as Americans a century ago believed, simply antiquated precursors of a more vibrant Christianity or decadent practices nearing extinction. Contrary to some arguments that became popular in the twentieth century, these traditions are not disguised expressions of Christianity or of some universal religious system, either. They are truly distinctive in origin and in the manner in which they are currently practiced. In adapting to the American environment, their adherents are also experiencing new tensions and misunderstandings that have yet to be resolved.

American Hindus

Dr. K. N. Ramaswamy emigrated from India to Atlanta, Georgia, in 1966. He and his wife live in a suburb of the city, where he carries on a successful medical practice. For more than a decade, he has served as a lay leader at the Hindu Temple of Atlanta and has taught classes there as well as participating in many of the temple's other activities. He has witnessed significant growth during this time in the number of Indians who live in Atlanta and who worship at the temple. His story illustrates some of the ways in which Hinduism is now present in the United States.

The Hindu Temple of Atlanta is located in Riverdale, a middle-income community of approximately ten thousand people located thirteen miles south of downtown Atlanta. Across the street is a row of two-story houses, a few small businesses, and an African-American church. Plans for the temple began in1982, land was acquired in 1985, and construction began in 1987. The first services were held in 1990 and images of the deities were installed in 1992; most of the construction was completed in 1996 and final touches were added in 2000.[1] The building, modeled on the Tirumala-Tirupathi temple in south India, which was constructed approximately five thousand years ago, is an imposing white masonry structure that rises majestically above a large parking lot situated on wooded grounds that cover approximately twelve acres. The temple's elaborately detailed tower, or *shikhar*, which rises five stories above the main building, is topped with gold-plated lotus blossoms. The sanctuary or sanctum occupies the main floor, while a lower floor provides ample space for an auditorium, conference rooms, and a bookstore. In keeping with Hindu tradition, the temple represents the body of God and is patterned to correspond with the five layers or aspects of the human body: the physical body, energy, mind, bliss, and consciousness of God. The temple's outer wall is like the physical body, with successive inner spaces corresponding to the other aspects, and deepest inside is the statue representing consciousness of God. It is located in a small space measuring about ten feet on each side, in which only the temple's five priests are allowed. Surrounding it is a large room, the walls of which are decorated with carved forms representing the various aspects of God. People come to the temple from all over the Southeast and even the most actively involved often commute long distances. Dr. Ramaswamy is not atypical: he lives about fifty miles from the temple. Because of the distances, most people do not participate in temple rituals daily, as they might in India. Between twenty and thirty come on weekdays, and this number swells to about three hundred on Saturdays and Sundays. More than seven thousand families are on the temple's mailing list, and more than three thousand donated money toward its construction. The temple's annual budget is approximately $1 million and, unlike many churches and synagogues, its revenue exceeds its expenses.

The Atlanta temple is one of hundreds that have been constructed in recent decades to serve the nation's estimated 1.3 million Hindus.[2] It is one of six in the Atlanta area alone, one of which is a $20 million complex in suburban Lilburn that includes a community center, clinic, youth education facility, and a 40,000-square-foot prayer building modeled on the Shir Swaminarayan temple in London. In Charlotte, North Carolina, the Hindu Center, which was founded in 1981, has grown to a regular membership of some 850, with more than a thousand on festival days. The Hindu Temple and Cultural Center of Littleton, Colorado, also founded in the early 1980s, has grown even more rapidly, now counting 1,500 families as members. One of the largest temples in the United States is the Sri Venkateswara Temple in Pittsburgh, Pennsylvania, which was founded in 1977 and has become an attraction for Hindu and non-Hindu visitors from all over the world.[3] Other sizable Hindu temples can be found in Cleveland, Houston, Sacramento, and Portland; at multiple locations in Los Angeles, Chicago, New York, and Seattle; and in smaller cities such as Allentown, Pennsylvania; Cassellbarry, Florida; Jackson, Mississippi; and Tulsa, Oklahoma.

The main activities at the Hindu Temple of Atlanta include daily rituals, weekly classes, and periodic festivals. The daily rituals, or *pujas*, are performed at 9 A.M. and include prayers, praise of the deities, and a ceremonial conclusion in which devotees receive holy water from the priest and fruits and nuts specially prepared as offerings and given back to devotees as symbols of peace, prosperity, and happiness. At 10 o'clock each day a ritual called *abhishekam* is performed with milk, yogurt, honey mixed with fruits, turmeric, and sandal powder, which symbolize nourishment, welfare, happiness, and gratitude. Rituals are also performed each evening at 6 P.M. and 8:30 P.M. Throughout the day, additional pujas are often performed and special rituals to particular deities are performed on a rotating basis. A wide variety of classes for children and adults are held at the temple, mostly on Sundays. These include classes in some of the sacred texts, such as the Bhagavad Gita, language instruction in Telugu and Sanskrit, yoga, and dance. The festivals occur about once or twice a month and range from full-day to week-long events organized around holidays or in veneration of various deities. The temple also hosts numerous guest lectures and cultural events, such as a presentation of the various dance forms of India, a lecture on meditation by a guest swami from India, and a day of discourses on stress management led by speakers from other U.S. temples.

Dr. Ramaswamy particularly appreciates the daily pujas because they symbolize and sanctify the cycle of ordinary life. In the morning the puja is filled with imagery of waking and preparing for the day. He explains: "The god is treated almost like a child. His teeth are brushed and his face is washed and his feet are washed and then he's given a ceremonial bath and new clothes. Then he's given freshly cooked food as a meal. Then he's given incense sticks as worship and then he's given a lighted candle as worship." In the afternoon the puja reminds people of their need for reverence and sustenance. "Then at night before the door is closed, they do the ceremonial worship with chanting of the verses, putting the god to sleep. This is done every day."

The pujas provide a rich combination of experiential and intellectual elements. At a weekly puja focusing on Lord Rama, for example, devotees participate in reciting a cleansing prayer, watch as the priest lights candles and burns incense, and pass around a picture of Lord Rama. The priest then selects five verses from the Ramayana, chants them in Hindi, and discusses their meaning. He says the verses remind us that we are different from animals, that we must follow moral principles and exercise our mental capacity in order to be humans. Then the participants rise, move to one of the statues and offer a short prayer of thanksgiving. At the end, they partake of cold sweet fruits, praying that their thoughts during the week will also be pure and sweet.

Hindus believe that God (or Brahman) is ultimately beyond human comprehension or experience and thus cannot be accurately spoken of in terms of a person, personal attributes, or other humanly constructed categories. This way of thinking about God is different from the monotheism familiar in Judaism and Islam or the trinitarianism emphasized in Christianity. Were it to be expressed in Western terms, such words or phrases as *ground of being, ultimacy, ultimate reality, holiest, numinous*, or *supreme God* might be used.[4] Some American Hindus draw a sharp distinction between their understanding of God and understandings more familiar to other Americans, whereas other American Hindus are content to speak of God in ways that might connote monotheism while emphasizing the impossibility of adequately describing that deity.[5] Dr. P. Venugopala Rao, a physicist who is a devotee at the Hindu Temple of Atlanta, explains it this way: "Brahman, the ground of all beings, is absolute, beyond all name and form. Whatever our mind can think or imagine cannot describe the Brahman. Brahman is without beginning, undying, unchanging, undifferentiated, and unmanifested."[6]

Within the various traditions of Hinduism a large number of more proximate or knowable deities have been identified over the centuries. These deities are symbolized in statues and pictures of gods and goddesses and in stories about them. It is these symbols and the rituals surrounding them that have provided the occasion for Westerners to describe Hinduism as a religion of idolatry. For this reason, American Hindus are often careful in how they talk about these symbols and rituals. They may speak of gods, goddesses, or idols, but ascribe different meanings to these words than other Americans would. When speaking with non-Hindus, it is common for American Hindus to emphasize that they do not worship these idols in the way a Christian worships God. Rituals that appear to be worship are performed to express gratitude or reverence for the idea or reality represented by the idol and to reinforce consciousness of this reality. Sometimes American Hindus draw parallels between these idols and the ways in which Christians understand such symbols as a cross, loaf of bread, rosary, statue of Jesus, or painting of the Virgin Mary. Choosing his words with care, Dr. Ramaswamy says, "It's not that somewhere there's a god with many forms, but we give form to the gods and we believe that God will bless us when we pray to him in our mind."

One of the more common symbols of these specific deities is a statue of Lord Ganesha, who symbolizes auspicious beginnings and is a patron of learning. Ganesha's elephant-headed shape represents great physical strength, but this strength is tempered by gentleness, wisdom, and peace. Ganesha has four hands, each with symbolic significance: one holds a noose to capture and retain obstacles or difficulties, a second holds a goad to guide the worshipper in the right direction, a third holds a sweet dish that represents the fruit of devotion, and a fourth offers blessings to devotees. Ganesha's right tusk is broken, denoting personal sacrifice to achieve greater things. A mouse at Ganesha's feet symbolizes ego, which can destroy one's will to pursue knowledge just as a mouse can eat away at a storehouse of grain. In other interpretations, the mouse symbolizes divine grace, moving silently and invisibly. Ganesha is one of Dr. Ramaswamy's favorite deities. At the Hindu Temple of Atlanta there is a special service each Sunday in veneration of Ganesha and one part of the sanctum contains the statue of Ganesha. Other services often begin with a prayer to Ganesha because he symbolizes the removal of ambiguities and doubts.

There is also a statue of Sri Venkateswara, popularly known as Balaji, who is one of the manifestations of Vishnu, who in turn is associated with the divine power of sustenance or preservation. Balaji is dark-faced, adorned with garlands of pink and red mixed with other garlands of white and green, and surrounded with elaborate gold carving. Like Ganesha, Balaji has four hands: one holds a *Chakra*, or wheel, which symbolizes the wheel of time; a second holds a *Sankha*, or conch, which signifies the wisdom of the Vedas; a third is directed toward the feet as an indication of the need to surrender difficulties to Balaji; and the fourth rests on Balaji's left thigh as a symbol that the cycle of birth and death is only knee-deep instead of all-consuming. Balaji is venerated each week on Saturdays at the Atlanta temple.

Because of its long history and the vast diversity of local cultures and languages in India, Hinduism is itself quite varied.[7] No single authority figure plays a unifying role such as the pope does in Roman Catholicism and no historical person has the same authority as Jesus in Christianity or Muhammad in Islam. Over the centuries, local heroes have become venerated as avatars, or manifestations of the sacred, and these avatars, along with other icons and rituals, give different temples their distinctive identities. Some of this variation in India has been replicated in the United States. At the Hindu Center in Charlotte, for instance, a majority of the devotees are immigrants from northern India, unlike at the Hindu Temple of Atlanta, which is composed mostly of immigrants from southern India. This means not only that different languages, such as Marathi and Pali, are taught and used in some of the services, but also that the pujas and major festivals are often performed differently. Compared with Balaji, for instance, other incarnations of Vishnu, such as Rama, receive more attention.[8]

Such differences notwithstanding, the immigrant experience has also had a unifying effect on Hinduism in the United States. Although temples such as those in Atlanta and Charlotte reflect distinctive traditions, they also function as pan-Indian centers, bringing together immigrants from the various regions of India and accommodating various deities and styles of worship. In this respect, they resemble Roman Catholic parishes composed of Irish, Italians, Poles, and Mexican Americans, or Protestant megachurches that draw participants from many different denominations. Large urban and suburban Hindu temples, writes the ethnographer Joanne Punzo Waghorne, accommodate diverse immigrant communities as contemporary houses do, "with enough rooms, staircases, twists, and turns . . . to hold a very diverse family made up of gods and humans, men and women, parents and children, Indians and Americans, while giving them all space enough to grow."[9] This process of accommodation is one that typically requires considerable effort and planning.

Ram Datt Utadhaya was head priest for twelve years at the Sri Venkateswara Temple in Pittsburgh. Not liking the cold weather, he eventually decided to relocate to Florida, where he founded and currently serves as head priest at the Hindu Temple of South Florida near Fort Lauderdale. He recalls: "Before I came here, there was no temple and [the various Hindu groups] were fighting each other. They were fighting each other and they didn't have time to go a good way. When I came here as a priest, I went house-to-house for priest services. I gave good talks and I removed all the obstacles and the negative thinking from their minds. Then I told them, 'I came for your religious services. That's why I came here. You have to listen to your priest, and if you don't listen to your priest, that means you're obstructing your priest and that means you're obstructing your religion.' Then they started to listen to me." When plans were drawn up for the temple, elements from all parts of India were included in the design to make all kinds of Hindus feel welcome. The temple includes shrines for six of the more universal deities: Vishnu, Krishna, Shiva, Ganesha, Rama, and Ambaji. Still, it was not able to satisfy everyone. As the Hindu population grew, another temple in the area—the Shiva Vishnu Temple—adopted a more distinctly southern Indian identity, and a third—Shiva Mandir—developed a combination of Caribbean ethnic and Hindu elements.[10]

In most Hindu temples, periodic festivals serve as one of the strongest unifying forces for the various groups who participate. Often held on Saturdays to accommodate American work schedules, the most popular festivals are Diwali, the New Year festival of lights, which occurs in October or November, and the birthday of Krishna, which is celebrated in July or August. Another popular festival is Holi, an event devoted to general merrymaking in February or March. Besides the usual pujas of the day, the festivals include food and brightly colored clothing and are sometimes punctuated with parades, floats, special decorations, and dancing. Music is an especially important part of the festivals, usually performed with tablas, sitars, tambouras, and other instruments.[11]

At Shree Laxmi Narayan Mandir in Sacramento the annual cycle of festivals includes a nine-day celebration for Lord Rama, a twenty-four-hour series of pujas for Lord Shiva, an eight-day celebration for Lord Krishna, a nine-day celebration for Goddess Durga, a one-day event in honor of the birthday of Lord Hanumana, and the five-day festival of lights, which is called Dipawali or simply Diwali. On average, about four hundred people attend these festivals. Pundit Sharma, the head priest, estimates that 80 percent are immigrants from India or Fiji and that the remainder are born in the United States. He says Diwali usually draws people from the wider community as well. It includes an all-vegetarian dinner of curries, tandoori naan, and rasmali; ethnic dancers dressed in bright cottons of red, orange, blue, and purple; and some skits and a fashion show. The lights symbolize goodness and the triumph of truth over falsehood.

As central as the temple is to the lives of American Hindus, the core of Hindu practices takes place in the home. These range from brief acknowledgments of the divine, to reciting or chanting several verses of sacred text, to offering prayers at meals, to longer periods spent in meditation or textual studies. As in all traditions, devotees vary considerably in the amount of time and effort they expend on these practices. One study, conducted by questionnaire among all the members of a medium-sized temple in Illinois, found that 88 percent performed daily pujas at home, 79 percent fasted at least once a month, and 75 percent had a home shrine.[12]

In Atlanta, Dr. Ramaswamy begins his daily cycle of worship as soon as he wakes up, chanting a couple of verses or prayers of gratitude to God. Then, as his feet touch the floor for the first time each morning, he salutes Mother Earth, thanking her for her support and asking for her blessings. After bathing, he goes to his worship room, lights incense, and spends from fifteen minutes to an hour meditating, praying, and chanting. During the day he tries to think of verses that pertain to whatever he is doing, such as traveling or eating, and offers prayers asking for knowledge and guidance. Before going to bed at night, he recites other prayers that ask forgiveness for wrongdoing and blessings while he sleeps. "Everything we do in our daily life should be treated like worship," he says. "Once you have a disciplined life, then you start talking in terms of God and thinking of God. But if you don't have a disciplined life, then you cannot concentrate your mind on what God is."

For most Hindus, a home altar or shrine is an important part of what it means to be Hindu. Dr. Ramaswamy has a special room, but he says most people he knows have a small corner in their house, usually in the kitchen, set apart for this purpose. His room contains pictures or statues representing various aspects of God. Most have special meaning because they were anniversary, birthday, or holiday presents and have been blessed by a priest. A Pakistani woman who came to the United States in 1976 at the age of twenty-one and now lives in Charlotte, North Carolina, says her home altar is the centerpiece of her life. "It keeps me in touch with my own culture. I find a lot of comfort and peace in doing daily worship and being with the Krishna. It just revives me. It gives me strength to go through the day." Her altar has twelve icons, but Krishna is her favorite. She takes it with her whenever she travels.

Besides the various statues and icons, the texts that make up the Hindu tradition also form an important part of daily practice both at home and at the temple. The earliest texts are a collection of hymns called the Vedas, which were compiled around 1500 B.C.E. after having been transmitted orally for many centuries.[13] The Rig-Veda consists of ten books of liturgical chants and sacrificial formulas, totaling more than ten thousand verses, which are central to the Hindu tradition. Other texts include the Upanishads, a collection of philosophical writings compiled in the sixth or seventh century B.C.E., and the massive epics of the Ramayana and the Mahabharata, the latter of which includes the Bhagavad Gita.[14]

Another man who goes regularly to the Hindu Temple of Atlanta works in the computer industry. Born in the United States of immigrant parents from India, he remembers singing Hindu songs as a child and watching his father light an oil lamp every morning and saying short prayers in Sanskrit. When he was in high school, his family started studying the Bhagavad Gita together. He found it satisfying, both as an affirmation of his identity and as a source of inner peace. During college he continued going to the temple and reciting daily pujas at home. At present he does both, focusing increasingly on translating verses from the Vedas and other texts and learning their meaning. He spends at least thirty to forty minutes a day in his "puja room," chanting, lighting candles, and learning new verses. "I chant these scriptures, and it gives me a sense of peace," he says. "I've heard them in the temple in a sacred place with the smell of incense. Reinforcing it at home gives me that same feeling of sanctity."

An elderly woman who lives in Charlotte, North Carolina, and attends the Hindu Center there moved with her husband to the United States fifteen years ago to be closer to their children and grandchildren. They light candles every morning and evening and chant verses from the Vedas together. It is a routine she learned as a child. She says it reminds her each day of how wonderful it is to be alive. "Being born as a human is a great blessing. You can help people, love people, show them compassion only as a human being. Our duty is to realize this." She is teaching her grandchildren the Vedas, translating them into English, so that they will grasp this realization too.

American Hindus are quite conscious of living in an environment in which Hinduism is unfamiliar to the majority of the population. Temple newsletters note with pride the number of non-Indian visitors and encourage devotees to give generously in order to provide more lectures and services to the wider community. Most temples have thrived, not by making converts (which remain few), but because of the steady growth of Hindu immigrants. Because of immigration policies that encourage some kinds of newcomers more than others, Hindu immigrants are overwhelmingly college-educated, many with postgraduate degrees, and a large majority are employed in the professions, science and technology, engineering, and computing.[15] They are thus able to support temple development financially. Temple leaders also report that interest in Hinduism appears to have increased among many immigrants after coming to the United States.[16]

American Buddhists

The Phap Luan Buddhist Culture Center on South Post Oak Road in Houston, Texas, is one of more than thirty Buddhist temples and meditation centers that have been started in Houston since the 1970s. Like nine of the others, it follows the Theravada tradition of Buddhist teachings, and like eight others, it is predominately Vietnamese.[17] Although it is an independent center, it is loosely affiliated with two other organizations: the Vietnamese Theravada Buddhist Songa Congregation and the Vietnamese Unified Buddhist Church. Founded in 1993, it has five monks and approximately eight hundred members. Although as many as 1,500 people come for major celebrations, such as New Year and Buddha's birthday, average attendance at weekly events runs around 150. About twenty of the families live in the immediate vicinity of the center, which is located in a neighborhood that is approximately one-quarter Hispanic and three-quarters African-American. For more than a decade the Vietnamese families met in homes until they could afford to purchase a building that had previously served as a Mormon church. A statue of Buddha occupies the front platform where the altar used to be. Besides the sanctuary, where Buddhist services are now held, several smaller rooms serve as shrines and space for memorials to deceased family members.

Phap Luan is but one example of the recent growth that has occurred in American Buddhism. Some estimates place the total number of Buddhists in the United States, including immigrants and their descendants and native-born converts, at around 4 million, although more conservative estimates put the number closer to 2.5 million.[18] A 1998 study of more than a thousand Buddhist meditation centers, or *sangha*, found that nearly 70 percent had been established since 1985. About 15 percent of those studied followed the Theravada tradition, like Phap Luan, while 42 percent were classified as Mahayana, 35 percent as Vajrayana, and the remainder were eclectic.[19]

The Vietnamese Buddhists at Phap Luan treat it like a community center. They come for weddings and funerals and for less solemn social events. For many of its members, the center has been a source of material and spiritual support during the transition to life in a new country.[20] The monks teach classes in Buddhism and in how to practice meditation. Four times a year one of the monks puts on a meditation retreat, which lasts anywhere from three days to ten days, for people engaged in intensive meditation. The regular weekday and weekend services consist of devotional, or puja, chanting following a style common in Southeast Asia. The longest and best-attended of these services occurs on Sunday mornings. Each service takes between two and two and a half hours. The first forty-five minutes are devoted to chanting. This part begins with the bell being rung and the people gathering in the shrine hall. When the chanting ends, there is silence for about twenty minutes. Then one of the monks gives a *dharma* talk, which is like a sermon or lecture. This usually lasts about an hour and, if there are questions, may extend another twenty minutes. An additional period lasting about forty-five minutes focuses on youth activities or may consist of special prayers for a bereaved family. Many of the people bring food and stay for lunch, which is followed by committee meetings and volunteer work, such as cleaning the building or caring for the grounds.

Unlike most temples, where people sit on mats or cushions on the floor, the people at Phap Luan sit on pews. The monks at Phap Luan also permit lay people to wear shoes in the shrine hall, which deviates from usual Buddhist practice. The chanting that forms the core of their services consists of four main kinds. The most common kind praises Buddha. The second is called *paritta* chanting, which is performed when people ask for blessings because they are ill or facing a difficult time in their lives. The third is chanting for the deceased, which occurs seven weeks after the funeral. And twice a month chanting is done to encourage reflection about one's life and to improve one's conduct. The chanting, like the dharma talks, is usually done in Vietnamese, but is occasionally in English.

The increasing use of English is one of the ways in which the Phap Luan community is adapting to its Houston environment. An increasing percentage of its members are American-born children of Vietnamese immigrants and thus are more comfortable speaking English than Vietnamese. The focus of services has also shifted as a reflection of changing interests. Venerable Jotika, who has served as head monk since the temple's founding, says the people initially focused more on chanting and did so because it was simply part of their familiar customs, but increasingly he senses that they are interested in the dharma talks, which give them a better understanding of Buddhist teachings. He says learning to meditate has also become more popular. In Vietnam, the people were more likely to consider meditation something esoteric that should be done by monks, but in the United States they are more likely to incorporate meditation into their daily lives. They are also more eclectic, drawing on other Buddhist traditions, rather than following purely Vietnamese customs. Venerable Jotika says the monks have learned to adapt as well. "In Vietnam, the people have to keep a distance from the monks and pay their respects to the monks, but here it is different. They are closer to us and we like to be a friend more than just a monk."

The Theravada tradition practiced at Phap Luan originated in ancient India and traces its lineage to the Pali elders, or *Theras*, from which its name derives. The Theravada school traveled to Sri Lanka in the third century B.C.E., thereafter spreading east to Thailand in the thirteenth century and to Laos, Kampuchea, and southern Vietnam in the fourteenth century. Theravada Buddhism teaches that there are three planes of existence: the plane of desire; the material plane, in which desire or sensuousness is reduced through meditation; and the plane of immateriality, which is associated with more serious abandonment of desire through meditation. The specific teachings of Theravada Buddhism focus less on metaphysical questions and more on practices that help the person move beyond desire to a state of worthiness, or *arhat*.[21]

The principal practice by which Theravada Buddhists strive to achieve a state of worthiness is meditation. Venerable Jotika explains: "Buddha says that the truth is within yourself; it's right in front of you. You have to have a clear mind to understand that. We have a way of training to eradicate violence from our minds. When our mind is clear, we're going to understand the truth." The people at Phap Luan typically meditate for about twenty minutes each morning, usually in the presence of a small statue of the Buddha with candles lit and incense burning. They say that chanting frees the mind of external influences and extraneous thoughts, permitting greater concentration and reflection.

Theravada Buddhism has grown rapidly because of immigrants and refugees from Vietnam, Cambodia, Thailand, and Sri Lanka. It has also experienced some growth as a result of converts. *Vipassana* meditation is a form of Theravada Buddhism that emphasizes the importance of purifying one's mind in order to live in harmony with nature and gain ultimate peace, happiness, and freedom. This form of meditation has been adopted by native-born Americans who started visiting Buddhist temples in Asia in the 1970s and subsequently founded "Insight" centers in the United States, such as the Insight Meditation Society in Barre, Massachusetts, and Spirit Rock in Marin County, California.[22] Although the number of people who have learned Vipassana meditation is not known, the number of such centers is said to have grown to approximately seventy by the mid-1980s and then doubled again by the late 1990s.[23] Versions of Vipassana meditation have also been popularized through books such as Sharon Salzberg's *Lovingkindness: The Revolutionary Art of Happiness* and Jack Kornfield's *A Path with Heart: A Guide through the Perils and Promises of Spiritual Life*, and through meditation tapes and guidebooks provided by the same authors.[24] Although these adaptations often bear little resemblance to the Theravada Buddhism practiced among immigrant Buddhists, immigrant temples have also increasingly provided Vipassana meditation to the wider public. At the Buddhist Temple and Meditation Center of Greater St. Louis, for instance, "insight meditation" services are held free of charge for the general public every Saturday evening. Dr. Kongsak Tanpaichitr, a Thai immigrant who is one of the lay leaders of the temple, says the service is attractive to Americans who are leading materially comfortable lives but who want to be reminded of the higher virtues of life.

Compared with Theravada Buddhism, Jodo Shinshu or Pure Land Buddhism has been in the United States longer and has adapted more thoroughly to American culture.[25] Shin Buddhism, as it is often called in the United States, was founded in India in 1224 by a Japanese monk named Shinran Shonin. It came to the United States with Japanese immigrants to California in the 1870s.[26] During World War II, its leaders adopted the name Buddhist Churches of America in response to anti-Japanese sentiments. Shin Buddhism teaches that absolute enlightenment is attained in the Pure Land after death when the finite and limiting qualities of physical being are extinct. In the Pure Land, a person achieves perfect oneness with the wisdom and compassion of Amida Buddha, an aspect of Buddhahood that is often depicted artistically as a standing Buddha with hands held up in a gesture of bestowing blessings on all beings. In the present life, faith is awakened when a person hears the call of Amida Buddha and responds to it. This response, which is the objective of human life, gives insight into the changing conditions of life and enables a person to live with strength, compassion, and inner resolve.[27]

The Denver Buddhist Temple, located in Sakura Square among Japanese businesses in downtown Denver, practices Jodo Shinshu. Founded in 1916, it serves approximately four hundred families in the Denver area and another three hundred families in the wider Rocky Mountain region who participate in its activities through visits to Denver and by periodic trips to their communities by the temple's monks. The temple offers three services on Sunday mornings: a small Japanese-language service, a large service in English for families with children, and a medium-sized service in English for adults. On a typical Sunday about 350 people attend these services. The temple also sponsors a wide range of Japanese cultural events, from singing to the martial arts, sports teams, and dharma lectures. On Sunday mornings, the services begin with traditional ringing of the calling bell, or *konsho*, and lighting of incense. This is followed by chanting a brief section of the Sukavati Sutra in Japanese and by some singing in English. Then there is a dharma talk, or lecture, which lasts about twenty-five minutes, after which brief announcements are read and everyone moves to a reception hall for coffee, punch, and dessert.

The fact that the service closely resembles Sunday morning worship and preaching at Christian churches is no accident. Many Jodo Shinshu services were already conducted in English before World War II and this practice became nearly universal during the internment period. With the adoption of English, many Japanese words were replaced by English words describing Christian customs. As a result, terms such as *church, minister,* and *hymn* came to be associated with Jodo Shinshu. The teachings of Jodo Shinshu often ran parallel to Christian teachings as well, as least in emphasis and interpretation. Both traditions emphasized the absolute depravity of humankind. Both regarded faith as the solution to depravity. If Christianity worshipped an almighty, all-merciful creator God whose existence was eternal, Shin Buddhists recognized the Buddha as an all-merciful and omniscient refuge of endless life and light.[28]

These similarities, however, mask important differences between the two traditions. Mr. Kanya Okamodo, who has been head priest at the Denver Buddhist Temple since 1996, stresses that Shin Buddhists, unlike Christians, do not believe that humans have eternal souls but do believe in an eternal round of rebirths unless one attains salvation. Depravity is regarded less as disobedience to God and more as a result of desire or passions rooted in ignorance. The moment of an awakened faith, which is distinct and consciously known in many Christian interpretations, is unknowable in Shin Buddhism. And, while Christians worship a personal God, Shin Buddhism is nontheistic; nor do Shin Buddhists have anything that resembles the Bible as an absolute statement of divine truth. At the Denver temple, these differences are stressed both in written materials available to members and newcomers and in dharma talks. The Denver temple has also reverted to using more Japanese terms to describe aspects of its services, and leaders wear traditional robes. Still, the temple routinely makes concessions to its fully Americanized clientele; for instance, services that used to extend well into Sunday afternoon now end promptly at noon so that members can make it home to watch the Broncos on television.

While the comparison of Christianity and Shin Buddhism underscores differences in beliefs, lay practitioners of Shin Buddhism are more likely to stress the practical aspects of their religion. Dr. Joy Aoki, for instance, is a woman of Japanese ancestry who goes regularly to services at the Denver temple. She has a home altar where she burns incense and meditates for twenty minutes every day. "It helps calm me," she says. "Sort of clears the mind and keeps me grounded." Setting aside this time gives her an opportunity to reflect, which then helps her during the rest of the day. She regularly does "mini-meditations" that reduce stress when she faces difficult situations. Calming herself this way helps her move past whatever a patient may be saying so she can experience the feelings involved. "Buddhism is very practical," she observes.

A Japanese-American woman who was raised Methodist but converted to Buddhism after living in Japan makes a similar observation. She attends services several times a month at the New York Buddhist Church in New York City.[29] Shin Buddhism appeals to her, even more than Zen (which she practiced for a number of years), because of its emphasis on ordinary life. Her busy schedule as a foundation executive and mother prevents her from meditating every day, but she has a home altar and typically meditates about once a week. She chants several sutras, each of which lasts five to ten minutes. "It carries me to a different level, a different state of mind," she says. "It helps me forget about things that are going on in my daily life and helps me redirect my life. That's why I do it. It's centering, it's focusing, it's settling down."

The Zen Buddhism that this woman was associated with is a cousin to Shin Buddhism. Both derive from the Mahayana tradition, also known as the Great Vehicle, which emerged around 100 C.E. and became dominant in China, Japan, Vietnam, and Korea. Mahayana leaders regarded the Theravada tradition as too narrow and gradually incorporated elements of Hinduism, Taoism, Confucianism, and Shintoism into their practices. Mahayana Buddhism emphasizes the person who aspires to Buddhahood, the *bodhisattva* who seeks to attain wisdom or supreme enlightenment with compassion, and thus is concerned more with the alleviation of suffering than with ultimate liberation from the cycle of life. Zen Buddhism originated within the Mahayana tradition in the thirteenth century through the teachings of Dogen, who traveled to China around 1220 C.E. and founded the Zen Soto school upon returning to Japan. Zen emphasizes meditation, or mental absorption, as a way of attaining enlightenment.

Zen teachers began coming to the United States from Japan in the 1930s, but Zen's most active period of growth was between the late 1940s and early 1970s. Zen Centers were founded in New York in 1945, in Los Angeles in 1947, and in Chicago in 1949. By the early 1960s, more than twenty Zen centers had been founded. Zen was also popularized by writers such as D. T. Suzuki and Alan Watts, the latter an Episcopal priest who had become attracted to Zen as a form of spiritual discipline. Although Zen centers drew immigrants who were already Buddhists, their popularity was mainly among converts. A study conducted in the San Francisco Bay Area in 1973 showed that 30 percent of the Bay Area population was familiar with Zen and, of these, 40 percent had favorable opinions of it and 8 percent had participated in a Zen center. The factors that were most strongly associated with being attracted to Zen were having a college education, being unmarried and geographically mobile, identifying with the counterculture, and being bothered by worries about one's career or work plans.[30] Unlike Shin Buddhism, Zen centers provided a more free-form, individualistic style of spirituality.

At the Zen Buddhist Temple of Chicago, which is located in the suburb of Northbrook, 85 percent of the regular participants are American-born and among the remainder hardly any are Japanese immigrants. The services underwent an Americanization process in the 1980s, but still retain some Japanese elements. A typical service lasts about two hours, beginning at 10 A.M. on Sunday, 2 P.M. on Sunday, or 7 P.M. on Wednesday. Participants wash their hands and remove their shoes before the service begins. They start the service by chanting the Heart Sutra in English, chanting slowly and rhythmically accompanied by a drumlike gong. Then they chant the Four Vows, or bodhisattva vows, first in Japanese, then in English, and again in Japanese. The practitioners then seat themselves on round cushions and assume the proper posture for meditation. After forty minutes of silent meditation a gong sounds and everyone engages in a walking meditation, circling the room one time in a counterclockwise direction. Sitting meditation then resumes for another forty minutes, during which the leader may give a brief talk. After chanting the Heart Sutra again, this time in Japanese, everyone moves forward to the altar—a statue of the Buddha that represents the bodhisattva of compassion—and offers incense.

Although many Zen centers follow the pattern illustrated by the Zen Buddhist Temple of Chicago, there is also considerable variation from one center to another. The Eugene Priory in Eugene, Oregon, provides an example of a more thoroughly Americanized service. It is affiliated with the Order of Buddhist Contemplatives, which grew out of the Shasta Abbey founded in 1970 in northern California by Jiyu Kennett Roshi, one of the first Western women to achieve the title of *roshi*.[31] At the Eugene Priory, meditation services lasting only thirty minutes are held twice daily. On Sunday mornings, the main service comes after the time for meditation. Practitioners rearrange their chairs or cushions (both are used) to face inward rather than toward the wall (as they do during meditation). The prior, or head monk, enters the room, offers incense, and then leads the group in a series of bows and prostrations. Then the group chants the Heart Sutra, which they refer to as the Scripture of Great Wisdom, in English. The words have been set to a Gregorian chant. This is followed by an offering, accompanied by music, and a final series of bows. The whole service lasts about thirty minutes. Afterward, the prior gives a dharma talk or lecture explaining part of the Heart Sutra or some other aspect of Zen teachings.

The other Buddhist tradition that has gained prominence in the United States is Tibetan Buddhism. Like Zen, Tibetan Buddhism is part of the Mahayana tradition. Unlike Zen, which was exposed to modernizing processes over a long period in Japan, Tibetan Buddhism was largely protected from these influences because of Tibet's geographic and economic isolation. It is for this reason more traditional, more influenced by local shamanistic practices, and more focused around the veneration of monks, or lamas, who are sometimes regarded almost as deities.[32] Tibet was occupied by the Chinese in 1950 and an exile Tibetan community was established in India in 1959. Fewer than ten thousand Tibetan exiles live in the United States. The prominence of Tibetan Buddhism among Americans, therefore, is largely a function of the high public profile of the Dalai Lama as an international spokesperson for peace, together with prominent actors and writers and other supporters of the Free Tibet movement, as well as American-born converts or practitioners.

Following the establishment of several prominent centers in the 1960s and 1970s, such as the Tibetan Nyingma Meditation Center in Berkeley, California, and the Tibetan Buddhist Learning Center in New York, Tibetan Buddhism spread to other communities during the 1980s and 1990s. At the Dorje Ling Buddhist Center in Chamblee, Georgia, for example, about thirty-five people meet several times a week for meditation and instruction. Most are American-born, but several are from Taiwan, China, or Malaysia. Other than the head monk, only one is from Tibet. Dorje Ling in Georgia is an offshoot of the Dorje Ling Center in Brooklyn, New York, which was founded in 1991 and claims the distinction of being the first center in the United States following in the seven-hundred-year-old Jonang tradition of Tibetan Buddhism. The Georgia center is an ordinary suburban house that doubles as the head monk's residence. One room is the monk's bedroom, two provide classroom space, and the living room serves as a shrine room for the main services. It includes a large statue of the Buddha, nearly two dozen other statues, and some Buddhist texts. Most of the services are conducted in English, although Mandarin translation is occasionally provided and some of the chanting is in Tibetan. One class gives basic instruction in Buddhist teachings; a more advanced class includes tantric meditation. Services involving tantric meditation often focus on the Green Tara, also known as the Mother of All Buddhas, who embodies female wisdom and is associated with quickness of mind, gener-

osity, fearlessness, and spontaneity. The ritual begins with three prostrations, after which everyone is seated on the floor. The chanting master
then guides participants in about forty-five minutes of meditation using a
text composed by one of the tantric masters in Tibet. Practitioners are
encouraged to visualize the Green Tara in a space above their foreheads
and either to think about the meaning of the words or simply to achieve
mental cleansing and stability through the chanting. The center also puts
on retreats about four times a year and celebrates the New Year and the
Dalai Lama's birthday.

As the Dorje Ling center illustrates, Tibetan Buddhism in the United
States is organized into small subcommunities linked through centers and
teachers to particular Tibetan traditions. The largest of these subcommunities are the Gelugpa, Kagyu, Nyingma, and Sakya schools. The Karma
Thegsum Choling Meditation Center, which was founded in 1997 in
Columbus, Ohio, for instance, is an example of the Kagyu school. Its
abbess, or lama, is Kathy Wesley, a student of Khenpo Karthar Rinpoche
at Karme Ling Retreat Center of Delhi, New York, which is in turn affiliated with Karma Triyana Dharmachakra in Woodstock, New York.[33]
The group in Columbus meets in a former church and follows a schedule
resembling that of many churches. There is an early service of chanting
for more seasoned practitioners, which involves sitting in the meditation
posture, reading from Tibetan transliterated texts, chanting prayers in
praise of compassion, and reciting mantras. After a break, a more general
service follows, which has become the more popular of the two. Participants sit either on cushions or on chairs and engage in silent meditation
for about twenty minutes, followed by a five-minute walking meditation,
and then another twenty minutes of sitting meditation. Afterward, people
are invited to stay for an adult "Sunday school class" focusing on Buddhist
teachings.

American Muslims

Although Muslims have lived in the United States since
the late eighteenth century, the vast majority of Muslim immigration
has occurred within the past half century.[34] It has been difficult to obtain
precise estimates of the Muslim population in the United States, just as it

has been for Hindus and Buddhists.[35] At the start of the twenty-first century, conservative estimates put the number at perhaps two million, while more generous estimates ranged as high as six or seven million, representing a tenfold increase in only three decades.[36] About two-thirds of this number were immigrants and their descendants, the majority of which, contrary to popular belief, did not come from the Middle East, but from Pakistan, India, Bangladesh, Indonesia, Africa, and elsewhere; most of the remainder were African Americans.[37] The largest concentrations of Muslims were in California, New York, Illinois, and New Jersey, followed by Michigan, Virginia, Texas, and Ohio.[38] Muslims worshipped in approximately 3,000 Islamic centers, mosques, and prayer locations, and had established approximately 200 Muslim schools, 500 Islamic Sunday schools, and six schools of Islamic higher education.[39] One study of U.S. mosques showed that 87 percent had been founded after 1970 and nearly two-thirds after 1980.[40]

American Muslims are part of a worldwide community of approximately one billion followers of the teachings of the Prophet Muhammad. Born about 570 C.E., Muhammad became a wealthy merchant, husband and father, and respected citizen of Mecca. He then became dissatisfied with his comfortable life and sought spiritual enlightenment through meditation and contemplation. After a time he began receiving a series of divine revelations, which are recorded in the Qur'an. Faced with hostility and opposition in Mecca, in 622, the Prophet and his followers moved to Medina, where they established a religious community. The Muslim calendar dates from that year. Islam (which in Arabic means submission or obedience) incorporated many of the teachings of Judaism and Christianity and traced its lineage to Abraham through Abraham and Haggar's son Ishmael. It is thus considered one of the Abramic religions and, because of its belief that the Qur'an is God's revelation, is described along with Judaism and Christianity as a "religion of the book."

Muslim belief is expressed most basically in the phrase, "There is no other god but the one great and almighty God."[41] Allah, the personal name of God, is the one whose infinite power and greatness is above all else, defying human comprehension, and uniquely deserving of worship. Muslims believe that other religions that speak of separable aspects or manifestations of God, including Christianity when it emphasizes the trinitarian nature of God (Father, Son, and Holy Spirit) err in diminishing the essential oneness of God. Muslim teachings assert that true belief in the oneness of God discourages narrow-mindedness, enhances self-esteem but tempers it with humility, and reinforces moral behavior and determination. Muslims also believe in angels, who are spiritual beings (but not deities) who carry out God's orders. The sacred text for Muslims is the Qur'an, which is understood to be the last of the divine books revealed by God and therefore exact in a way that previous revelations, such as the Torah and the Christian gospels, are not. Muslim tradition also teaches that God sent messengers or prophets (as many as 124,000) to different peoples at different times. All of these prophets proclaimed the same truth as Muhammad. However, Muhammad was sent for the whole world, rather than to specific peoples, and Muhammad's teachings are complete and free of error in a way that others' were not.

Muslim teachings hold that any act of doing good, or avoiding evil done in the name of God is an act of worship. All of life should be lived in submission to Allah. To assist in achieving this objective, Muslims are encouraged to practice a set of formal acts of worship. The most important of these are the prescribed daily prayers, or *salat*, which are performed five times a day. Salat is understood as an act of submission to God and as a reminder of one's commitments to God. It involves reciting from the Qur'an and asking for God's guidance in order to avoid God's wrath and follow God's path. Salat is not merely a vocal or mental act, but one that involves the entire body and includes a series of ritual bowings and bendings. Muslims also fast from dawn to dusk during the month of Ramadan (the ninth month of the lunar year) as a way of proclaiming the supremacy of God's law.

Agyekum Mahama, an immigrant from Ghana who lives in Washington, D.C., illustrates how Islamic teachings are put into practice in everyday life. Between his responsibilities as a father of three children and as the proprietor of a retail store, Mr. Mahama keeps up a demanding schedule. Yet his day is organized around the performance of salat. "I wake up and wake my wife and my children and then we pray in the morning," he says. "That's how we start our day. Then during the day I'm at work, so that's where I do my noon and mid-afternoon prayers. Then when I come back home in the evening, my family is ready and we do the sunset prayers, if I've not already done them at the Islamic Center. Then just before we go to bed, we also pray the night prayers." His living room, virtually bare except for a carpet, serves as the family's prayer space. He says the best Muslims don't fit the prayers into their schedules but organize their lives around the prayers. "The salat is the defining characteristic of a Muslim. This is how the Muslim performs his primary duty to his creator. We are created as Muslims for the purpose of worshipping God. Salat is the ritual process by which we first establish that worship—in addition, of course, to the other things we do to obey God. But salat is primary."

For Muslims like Mr. Mahama, performing the daily prayers is a constant reminder of the centrality of one's faith. "This is a total way of life," he says. "In Islam we are individually accountable for our salvation. So when we pray, we are submitting to God, and our total devotion and our attention is on God." This awareness gives him a sense of purpose in life—as someone who submits to and worships God, and as someone with responsibilities to do good and avoid evil. "God is good and generous and kind and merciful to us and if we submit to him, only good will come to us. He has blessed us with such beautiful things and with mercy that if we reject his call, then we have ourselves to blame if we are punished." Blessings or punishment happen in the next life as well as in this one. "We Muslims believe that when we die, we will come before our creator and account for our life on earth. If we are found to be worthy as true believers, then we'll inherit paradise. But if we fall short of the grace and mercy of Allah, then we will inherit hell."

Its emphasis on individual salvation notwithstanding, Islam is a deeply family-oriented religion. Its teachings encourage fidelity in marriage and loyalty between parents and children. Muslim parents are encouraged to give their children religious instruction at home and at the mosque and, like Mr. Mahama, to include the whole family in at least some of the daily prayers. Mr. Mahama's account of his own spiritual journey reflects these family influences: "My father and mother were Muslims, so I was raised as a Muslim child. I grew up observing my father and mother living their lives as Muslims. I saw my father's and mother's friends and all the elders in the village trying to live their lives as Muslims. My father taught me the basic tenets of Islam and to practice it with him. As I grew up, I always remembered the teachings and practices of my father and found them to be sound."

Although the Qur'an encourages Muslims to perform salat at the mosque, or *masjid*, as well as at home, mosque attendance is not as common among American Muslims as church attendance is among Christians, at least partly because primary services are held on Fridays rather than Sundays and thus conflict with work schedules. According to surveys, as few as 3 or as many as 14 percent of adult American Muslims attend weekly Friday prayers at mosques or Islamic centers.[42] Mosques vary somewhat in how services are organized, but prayers follow a uniform pattern and a lecture or sermon is generally included. At the Islamic Center in Washington, where Mr. Mahama attends, Friday services begin at noon with a twenty-minute recitation or reading from the Qur'an.[43] Then the center's director gives a sermon, or *khutbah*, first in Arabic and then in English. Each rendering of the khutbah, which typically lasts about thirty minutes, focuses first on the teachings of God concerning the core teachings of Islam and then in the second half on current affairs, such as personal responsibilities, civic duties, or the community. The last part of the service is the salat, after which a free meal of rice, meat, and salad is served. Mr. Mahama especially likes hearing the khutbahs because they make him a better person. "They deal specifically with the daily struggles of a believer and how one can improve one's self," he observes. He says he also prays better at the mosque than at home: "It's a very serene and inviting place of worship."

Located on Massachusetts Avenue in an affluent part of the city near several embassies, the Islamic Center of Washington—one of forty mosques in the greater District of Columbia metropolitan area—is one of the oldest and largest in the United States. Plans for the undertaking began at the Egyptian Embassy in Washington in 1945 and construction began in 1950.[44] Completed in 1957 at a cost of approximately $1 million provided by donations from more than a dozen Islamic countries as well as Muslims in the United States, the building includes a mosque situated at a 60 degree angle to the northeast in order to face the direction of the shortest route to Mecca, as well as an outer courtyard and two wings for an Islamic institute. The minaret rises 160 feet and the main part of the building includes a center courtyard and fountain, Turkish tiles, Iranian carpets, and an Egyptian pulpit. Besides Friday services, the Center offers Islamic studies classes on Sundays, Qur'anic and Arabic language classes on Saturdays and Sundays for adults and children, evening classes, public tours, a library, and a bookstore. Attendance at Friday services typically ranges between one thousand and fifteen hundred. Approximately eighty percent are immigrants, representing more than thirty countries in all, with the majority coming from Africa, India, and Pakistan.

During Ramadan, Muslims not only fast during daylight hours but also come more regularly to the masjid for daily prayers. At the Islamic Center in Washington, the number who come for daily prayers increases from about 150 to approximately 600. Sermons are also given each evening during the thirty days of Ramadan, with an average attendance of about a thousand. The end of Ramadan, which is called Eid al-Fitr, or simply Eid, is a time of celebration marking the end of fasting and symbolizing both the fulfillment of one's responsibility to God and appreciation to God for providing strength. As many as five or six thousand people fill the Center's outer courtyard and spill into surrounding sidewalks and streets. The event begins after the sunset prayer with people saying "Allah Akbar" through the night, meaning that God is greatest and suggesting, as one participant put it, that "we ourselves and our children are winners because we are associated with the greatest power." In the morning, the celebration begins at sunrise with twenty minutes of praise to God followed by a sermon. After a light breakfast, people return to their homes to rest. Then in the evening they return to the Center, wearing their best clothes and bringing the entire family, for a catered feast.

Compared to American Buddhism, Islam in the United States has fewer internal divisions and is practiced more similarly at different locations and among various groups. Yet large mosques like the Islamic Center in Washington represent only a minority of American Muslims. Most attend smaller mosques that are often diverse in their own ways but also reflect local, regional, and ethnic customs. In Brooklyn, New York, two mosques illustrate this variety. Al-Farouq Masjid is a large, six-story mosque that accommodates more than three thousand people. It is the largest of the twenty-seven mosques that have been established in Brooklyn since the early 1970s. Like the Islamic Center in Washington, it follows the dominant Sunni tradition of Islam. Across the street is the Brooklyn Mosque, whose leader, Kadhim Mohamad, is from Iraq and is trained in the Shia tradition. Founded a decade later than Al-Farouq, it remains smaller, seldom drawing more than a hundred people. Ethnically and economically, the two mosques are also quite different: Al-Farouq's members are mostly from the Middle East, have been in the United States longer, and work mostly in the professions; Brooklyn Mosque's are from South Asia and the

Caribbean, have come more recently, and are employed in lower-paying service jobs. Although the basic prayer services are similar, Imam Mohamad says his sermons focus on different needs than those across the street. Similar stories can be found in most major cities, as new waves of immigrants have encouraged the founding of a wider variety of mosques.

Muslim leaders emphasize the unchanging aspects of Islamic practices, and yet it is also evident that change is occurring as a result of being in the American context. Although prayers continue to be said in Arabic, sermons are increasingly given in both Arabic and English, as at the Islamic Center in Washington, or entirely in English. Gender roles are also changing. Nationally, 78 percent of those attending Friday prayer services are men, but the fact that women are routinely present as well is in marked contrast to services in many Muslim societies.[45] A study of mosque governing boards also found that approximately two-thirds permitted women to serve.[46] Governing boards, with an elected board of directors, are themselves a form of accommodation that many American mosques have adopted.[47] Like other immigrant groups, Muslims also experience generational strains between themselves and their children, who may be more fully assimilated into American culture, or with those who remain in their countries of origin. Imam Mumtaz Quasmi, an immigrant from India who heads the Muslim Mosque in Sacramento, California, says these strains are very much in evidence in the community he serves. In India people revered their parents almost like gods, but in the United States immigrants often earn much higher salaries than their parents did and show them little respect except once or twice a year on ceremonial occasions.

The most notable shift, according to Muslim leaders themselves, however, is that Muslim immigrants practice religion more intentionally in the United States than in their countries of origin. At the Islamic Center of the Lehigh Valley in northeast Pennsylvania, for example, Imam Faisal Nabulsi explains the shift this way: "People back home took Islam for granted because everybody around them was Muslim. So they [felt] that everything was okay. Then they come to this country and they must guard Islam because a lot of people around them are not like them." He says back home people felt the government or scholars or someone else would guard Islam. "But here you're alone on the battlefield. So you become more religious. You want to defend what you believe in." Imam Ullah Qazifazl, a Pakistani immigrant who serves as director of religious affairs at the Islamic Center of Northridge in southern California, thinks the turn to religion stems partly from fear. "If we are not committed to our religion," people seem to be saying, "we will lose our family, we will lose our faith, and we will even lose our children."

Other leaders say the impulse to be more religious stems less from wanting to defend Islam and more from finding it valuable when facing the challenges of American life. In Brooklyn, Imam Mohamad, for instance, observes that when Muslims "come here they need their religion to keep their family together and to secure themselves from being away from each other." He says most of the people at his mosque did not pray back home, but "they come here and they start praying." Others point to the permissiveness of American culture, the availability of alcohol and drugs, and even the temptations associated with economic success as challenges that require greater religious commitment. "If one lived in a Christian society that actually practiced the Christian way of life," Mr. Mahama reflects, "a Muslim would feel enlightened and enriched just seeing other people being religious. But there's a lack of emphasis on God in this culture and this is very difficult. So as a Muslim, it becomes incumbent on you to be much more vigilant."

Living among Christians

American Hindus, Buddhists, and Muslims are keenly aware that theirs are minority religions in the United States. To them, the nation is not simply pluralistic or diverse, or even secular and indifferent to religion, but populated largely by Christians. Religion and the religious habits of the culture matter to them a great deal. Their experiences living among Christians are quite varied—functions of race, class, gender, national origin, location, and personality, as well as religion. More than a few say that they have experienced discrimination or felt that they have been treated unfairly. Most assert, however, that living in the United States has been good and argue that the nation's laws and customs provide desired freedom and opportunity. They are often puzzled by the responses of Christian coworkers, neighbors, and clergy—who sometimes try to convert them, often subtly communicate false impressions, or simply treat them with indifference. They are genuinely ambivalent about more active or open engagement with Christians about matters of faith, fearing that Christians would be rigid and uninterested in furthering mutual understanding. They are not, contrary to the opinion of some Christians, dissatisfied with their own religion, secretly longing to become Christians, or incapable of responding to Christians' arguments. What they do want is greater respect and understanding.

Reports of hate crimes and other acts of overt discrimination are disturbing whenever they occur. In Atlanta, Dr. Ramaswamy says that he knows of "dot buster" incidents in which Hindu women have been attacked, sometimes even raped, and the dots on their foreheads scratched off. Narinder Shastri, a priest at the Hindu Temple Society in Los Angeles, says his board regularly discusses hate crimes that have occurred in the area and has felt that zoning ordinances were being unfairly applied to their temple. When the Thai Buddhist temple on Toddville Road in Charlotte, North Carolina, opened, vandals broke in and threw buckets of paint on the murals. At the Denver Buddhist Temple, a priest reports that vandals destroyed one of the statues and left graffiti on a fence. The same thing happened at the temple he previously served in Los Angeles. At the Daar Ul-Islam Masjid in Ballwin, Missouri (near Saint Louis), Imam Muhammad Nur Abdullah says people sometimes sneer at him when they see him on the street in his white robe and yell, "Go home!" At the Islamic Center of Northridge in southern California, Asif Ansari, a Pakistani immigrant who works as an aerospace engineer, thinks it is probably because he looks Middle Eastern, but he says that he has been hassled by airport security and treated rudely in other public places.

Such incidents notwithstanding, the more common responses when Hindus, Buddhists, and Muslims are asked about their experiences in the United States are positive. One of the members of the Hindu Temple of Atlanta says that it has been easier to adjust to American culture than to keep peace within his own family. His parents want him to speak their language, follow traditional Indian customs, and perhaps even consent to an arranged marriage; he thinks it is possible to be a good Hindu without maintaining the Indian culture that went with Hinduism in the past. At the Hindu Center in Charlotte, a woman says that she and her husband, their children, and their grandchildren have all been treated fairly; she has no complaints at all about living in the United States. At the New York Buddhist Church, members say that Buddhists are treated fairly in their community and even in the newspapers and on television. They see a significant improvement in media coverage in the past few years. Kenjitsu Nakagaki, the head priest there, agrees. He says it used to be hard being Buddhist, but thinks the public's impressions are much more positive now. At the Brooklyn Mosque, Imam Mohamad can think of no evidence of prejudice or discrimination against Muslims in his community; indeed, he says that people seem to go out of their way to be nice. At the Islamic Center of North Fulton near Atlanta, Imam Anwar Khan admits that he sometimes feels a little strange being a Muslim in Georgia, but he says that he has never experienced discrimination or prejudice. In Washington, Mr. Mahama tells about incidents in which people have mistreated him because he is African, but he says this is rare; usually there is just a common bond of humanity that transcends racial and cultural differences.

The most frequent exceptions to these general perceptions of good treatment come from parents, especially Muslims, and reflect concerns about their children. In suburban Chicago, a Muslim mother says that her children constantly face problems at school. Her son's teacher taught a lesson on square dancing, which violated his understanding about not dancing with the opposite sex. The public showers after gym class violate Muslim teachings about modesty. The other students make fun of her children for fasting at noon during Ramadan. She has generally been able to negotiate successfully with the school authorities to resolve these problems, although she remains troubled. Another mother who attends the same Islamic center says that her daughter has suffered embarrassment from wearing the traditional scarf, or *hijab*. "There've been a lot of tears rolling down her face because of the children teasing her." Not being able to go on group dates or to swimming parties has also been difficult for her daughter. In southern California, a Muslim man worries about the kinds of values Muslim children are being exposed to in the United States, especially the permissive views about sexuality and the lack of respect for parents. Keeping the daily prayers also becomes more difficult: "Kids want to do all the fun things that other kids do, but if you tell them they've got to wake up at five in the morning and go to the mosque, they say, 'You've got to be out of your mind; my classmates don't do that!'"

Although they generally feel they have been treated well, American Hindus, Buddhists, and Muslims frequently report that they are puzzled by the interaction they have had with Christians. On the one hand, they have usually been confronted at some point in their lives by someone who tried to convert them to Christianity. In Atlanta, a Hindu man says Christians sometimes ask him questions about what he believes and then wind up trying to convert him. A member of the Hindu Temple in Littleton, Colorado, says that people have come to his door a few times "trying to show how Christianity is bigger than any other religion." A New Jersey computer consultant who grew up nonreligious and now attends the New York Buddhist Church, reports that people came to his door, too, talking about Christianity. He thinks that they were Jehovah's Witnesses. In Washington, Mr. Mahama also mentions Jehovah's Witnesses; he says that they are the only ones who have ever tried to get him to become a Christian. Other people report that different methods of evangelism are sometimes used. In suburban St. Louis, Dr. Kongsak Tanpaichitr remembers that a few years ago, when the Wat Pharasriratanaram Buddhist Temple of which he is a board member purchased an Assembly of God church for its meetings, they found messages painted all over the walls and floor telling them that Jesus is the true messiah. In New York, a woman of Japanese ancestry sends her daughter to a Jewish school where, she says, it is fine to be a Buddhist, but her relatives in California tell her that churches there are trying to attract Buddhist children by providing interesting after-school activities. On the other hand, members of non-Christian religions often say that their Christian coworkers and neighbors seem too embarrassed or preoccupied to enter into discussions about religion at all. In Columbus, Ohio, a man who converted from Christian Science to Tibetan Buddhism, muses that nobody has ever tried to persuade him to become a Christian. "I would be surprised if somebody made a concerted effort," he says, "or if they were upset by the fact that me or anybody else was something other than Christian." Another man thinks that you almost have to go out of your way to show that you are a Buddhist; otherwise, people just assume that you are Christian. A Buddhist in Washington, D.C., says that she would actually welcome more conversations about religion with Christians but has been disappointed: "Usually when I say I'm Buddhist, they don't go any further, and the reason, I realized, is they don't understand it. They can't take apart what I believe or try to dismantle it, because they don't comprehend it." A Muslim woman says her Christian neighbors are polite and sometimes ask her questions about Middle Eastern customs but never say much about religion.

The mixed signals they receive in encounters with Christians generate wariness among some American Hindus, Buddhists, and Muslims. Judging from their comments, they figure that someone coming to their door is probably a Jehovah's Witness, in which case they usually give a polite "no" and shut the door. But if someone invites them to church, they are less likely to know how to respond. A Libyan-born Muslim who lives in northeastern Pennsylvania, provides an illustration in describing the only time he consented to attend church with a Christian coworker. The event happened a few years ago when he was working in Kansas. A man there whom he did not know well invited him to go to church. He accepted, thinking that his acceptance would be viewed as a sign of respect for Christianity. "We respect all prophets and all religions," he explains. "We respect Judaism, we respect Christianity, it's part of Islam." But then he discovered that the man had an "ulterior motive." The man was hoping to convert him to Christianity. He says he managed to explain his views and remain friends with the man. But he tells the story as an example of why Christians and Muslims do not always get along.

Apart from specific encounters with Christians, it is troubling to many Hindus, Buddhists, and Muslims to be the object of stereotypes and misinformation. A Pakistani immigrant who runs a day care center says it was difficult starting her business because parents thought she was an atheist. She also recalls that when the Hindu Center in her community opened, the newspaper carried a large photo of shoes piled up outside but said little about what was going on inside. A graphic designer of Japanese ancestry says it bothers him, being a dharma teacher at a Jodo Shinshu Buddhist temple, that the public's impressions of Buddhism seem to be shaped almost entirely by the Dalai Lama or, worse in his view, by celebrities like Tina Turner and Richard Gere. "The Dalai Lama is a gem of a person, but he represents just one small sect within Buddhism." In Denver, Dr. Aoki is also troubled by the public's perceptions of Buddhism. As a child, she was singled out by the other children at school and paraded around the room as a "Buddha head." Nobody quite knew what that was, but regarded her as a curiosity. She thinks the media still purveys this view. "Ooo, weird," she parrots. "You guys sit around and meditate and say 'om' and burn incense. You put dots on your forehead and believe that you can be reincarnated as a dog if you treat your mother poorly." The public must think Buddhists are "really strange cookies," she concludes. At the Ahl-

Al-Beit Islamic Center of Denver, Imam Mohammed Kazerooni worries about equally misguided impressions of Islam: "The American population makes its decision before they see a Muslim for the first time in their life based on what they hear and what they've been told and the way Muslims have been presented. This is one of the problems we have to face." Although they generally dismiss such misinformation, often attributing it to television, people such as these also sense that something deeper and perhaps more troubling about American culture is at issue.

A psychiatrist who immigrated to Pennsylvania from India in 1955, where he was reared in the Jain religion, now attends services at the Hindu Temple Society in his community because there is no Jain temple within convenient driving distance. Although he is a respected member of the community, he and his family have not been free of insults and misunderstanding. When his sons were in college, they were frequently mistaken for Iranians and taunted. During the gasoline shortage in the 1970s, he was turned away because the station attendant thought he was an Arab. More recently, through his continuing contact with other Jains in the United States, he has become concerned about recurrent difficulties purchasing land for temples and acquiring zoning permits. At one level, he understands all this and deals with it philosophically. But at another level, these problems contribute to his conviction that American society is becoming increasingly ignorant, self-interested, and decadent. He remembers thinking when he arrived in the 1950s that America was "the land of milk and honey," but he says "it is not the same country today." Whereas kindness and trust used to be a way of life, now "there is a deterioration in the morals and social fabric of the nation." Pointing to the number of people killed with guns, robberies, rising prison populations, and out-of-wedlock pregnancies, he says that it is shocking to see how the society is tearing apart. "My soul cannot accept this. Some people say this is progress. Hooey. I call it deterioration."

Even if self-interestedness and decadence are not a problem, leaders of new minority religions in the United States see strong barriers to overcome if false impressions are to be corrected. Acharya Kailash Chandra, who heads the Hindu Temple and Cultural Center near Denver, says that Christians have little incentive to understand Hindus in their community: "They have been told that they already have everything. They were taken care of two thousand years ago by the death of Jesus Christ." He thinks that Christian clergy would feel it unworthy of their time to interact with Hindus. At the Hindu Center in Charlotte, Vishnu Moondra is somewhat more optimistic. He says that Christians simply have not had to confront Hindus in the past because there were too few of them in this country; with growing numbers, he feels things will eventually improve. At the Buddhist Vihara in Washington, D.C., Venerable Dhammasiri takes a more cautious view. From personal experience, he believes that Christians and Buddhists can work together; however, he also recognizes that many clergy around the country are reluctant to have anything to do with Buddhists. He thinks this may reflect some insecurity on their part about what they really believe. At the Buddhist Church of Sacramento, which is surrounded by Christian churches, Bob Oshita thinks that the main problem is that pastors are just too busy running their congregations; he has virtually no contact with any of them. In Portland, Oregon, the Muslim Community Center's Muhammad Najieb elaborates the same idea. He says that Muslim, Christian, and Jewish leaders are all working so hard addressing the dysfunctions and temptations among their own people that they have little time to interact. But he is also troubled by the consequences: none of the groups are able to cooperate for larger purposes. Denver's Imam Kazerooni takes a more pessimistic view. He thinks that Christians are inhibited from developing better relations with Muslims by two deeply held assumptions: that "Christianity has a monopoly on the truth" and that Muslims are basically terrorists. He believes that Muslims will have to do the lion's share of the work to bridge the gap.

American Hindus, Buddhists, and Muslims vary considerably in how much they have been exposed formally or informally to the teachings and beliefs of Christianity. At one extreme, they have studied Christianity in school or, as in the case of converts, have participated in Christian Sunday schools and churches. A man in Atlanta, for instance, was sent by his Hindu parents to a Southern Baptist school because they thought he would receive a better education there than in public school. Another woman recalls that she went to Catholic school and attended Baptist summer camps before becoming a Buddhist. Growing up in Ghana, Mr. Mahama also went to Christian schools where he studied the Bible extensively. At the other extreme are Hindus, Buddhists, and Muslims who are recent immigrants from countries in which Christianity was virtually absent and who have had little exposure to churches in the United States. For instance, a Muslim woman says that she has no Christian relatives and, other than a coworker who tried to get her to pray to Jesus one time, has had little contact with Christians who actually talked about their faith. Similarly, a Pakistani immigrant who lives in southern California says that all his relatives still live in Pakistan and his coworkers prefer not to discuss religion; he finds Islam sufficiently engaging that he has little interest in learning more about Christianity on his own. Regardless of how much or how little contact they have had with Christianity, though, Hindus, Buddhists, and Muslims living in the United States are generally aware of ways in which Christianity differs from their own beliefs and practices.

Christianity's apparent claim to be the one true religion is something that most American Hindus, Buddhists, and Muslims have thought about at least a little—enough to have counterarguments at their disposal. A Muslim man says that he knows all about the claim of Christian uniqueness because he has considered it in light of the Qur'an. His understanding is that the Qur'an, as God's perfect and final word, teaches that God accepts all who believe in the oneness of God and in eternal life. Thus it does not bother him that Christians believe only they are God's people; this belief is a distortion of the truth. A Sikh man who practices meditation at the Buddhist Vihara in Washington, D.C., says his first wife was Catholic and both his children are Christian, so he has thought a lot about Christian teachings. He thinks Christians take too much for granted when they argue that only they will go to heaven. "Nobody really knows what heaven and hell are," he asserts. "There may not even be God for that matter, so what is heaven? What is hell? I think that how we live here on this earth is either hell or heaven." A salesman in Chicago who practices Zen Buddhism deflects the question of Christian truth by arguing that behavior is more important than belief. "When I was younger I would argue with people and become just as arrogant in the other direction, insisting that I have all the answers. Now I think it's more important how you live your life, not those types of beliefs." Others simply dismiss the Christian view as a quaint or parochial idea. From his perspective as a Hindu, for instance, a man in North Carolina says the idea that only Christians will go to heaven "amuses" him and "doesn't affect" him at all. In Los Angeles, a Buddhist of Japanese ancestry is equally dismissive: "Catholics, Baptists, Methodists, and all these other iterations, they all have one God," he exclaims. "Yet they can't get their act together. They all say, 'Well, my interpretation of God is much better than yours.' That really bothers me."

Most Hindus and Buddhists (Muslims less so) are also aware that they have often been depicted in Christian teachings as idolaters. At the Buddhist Vihara in Washington, a member describes this view as a straightforward distortion of the truth. "If they think that a Buddhist who bows in front of a statue is worshipping it, that is completely incorrect," she says. "They're just ignorant. If you want to make an argument or dispute something, you'd better know your argument very well or I'm just going to think you're stupid!" A Hindu man remembers learning at the Baptist school he attended that idol worship was evil and being very confused at the time about his Hindu practices. More recently, he says he hears Pat Robertson on *The 700 Club* condemning Hindus for worshipping idols. But he says that he is philosophical about it now. "If Christianity means preaching conversion and speaking against other religions, then I'm not going to condemn them for doing what their scriptures tell them to do." Another man has less patience for such behavior. He recalls a recent episode in which Southern Baptists came to his community and denounced Hinduism as a form of paganism that worshipped thirty million gods. What he found most offensive was simply the Baptists' arrogance in thinking that they knew what Hindus actually believed. A Muslim man says that he has heard similar denunciations of Islam, including being called Satan worshippers. "What really makes you mad," he says, "is that they have no clue what Islam is and then they pass judgment on it."

For Hindus, Buddhists, and Muslims who have had frequent contact with American Christians, one might suppose that Christianity would hold some attraction—at least Christian leaders often argue that it should. Apart from polite acknowledgment of some of Christianity's good points, though, American Hindus, Buddhists, and Muslims seldom give any indication of yearning to become Christians or adopting Christian ideas. Dr. Aoki says that she struggles not to lump all Christians together, but she sees a conservative trend in Denver and in the nation that worries her. She thinks Buddhism encourages tolerance and hopes that some Christians do as well. A Hindu man says living in the United States has taught him that there is good and bad in every culture. But he says that he has met very few Christians who really seem to be living a life of faith. A Muslim man says that being in close contact with coworkers who are Christians has actually reinforced his beliefs as a Muslim. "I can see if you take faith to too high a level of certainty, then you can get into trouble. Even in Islam, there are certain sects that get carried away. So for me it kind of reinforces my own religion when I talk to Christians."

One of the more considered responses to being around Christians is that of Mr. Mahama in Washington. Going to Christian schools in Ghana and subsequently encountering Christians in the United States, including several Christian pastors whom he counts as personal friends, has given him a "better perspective" on being a Muslim. "I had Christian friends who'd tell me they were Christians and for whom going to church wasn't essential. Some of them who did would go to church on Sunday and that was the end of it. But I realized that for me as a Muslim, there were things I had to do, ritualistically and attitudinally, to affirm my being a Muslim on a daily basis, whereas for most of my Christian friends, all they had to do was to say that they were Christians. So I started seeing the differences." He says Islam is a way of life, not just a belief and certainly not just a "private belief" as it is for some Christians. At the same time, he is by no means dismissive of Christian teachings. "If one reads the New Testament, one sees Jesus' total life of devotion to God." He says the New Testament also emphasizes "the good part of a true believer's relationship with his neighbor—that God is love and wants us to be loving also." This, he feels, is common to both Christianity and Islam.

What American Hindus, Buddhists, and Muslims most often report they want from American Christians is simply greater understanding. Some of them would like converts to their religions, but most are more interested in gaining respect. They do not mean this only in a superficial, politically correct way, but in terms of greater familiarity and knowledge. They know that Americans are busy and often acknowledge that the blame is theirs for not reaching out more actively to the wider society. It disturbs them that the mass media have largely defined them. They do not expect Christians to give up being Christians or Christian leaders to fundamentally alter their teachings. But they realize that they are a presence with which Americans are going to have to come to terms. They think it would be better for them if other Americans gained greater familiarity with what they actually believe and practice. They believe better understanding would be good for the rest of the population as well.

Pluralism or Coexistence?

The reflections and experiences of American Hindus, Buddhists, and Muslims indicate clearly that pluralism exists in the United States, broadly enough to embrace the new religious diversity their numbers represent, yet not deeply enough to be genuinely satisfactory. Pluralism is layered, much like our governmental structures, functioning more effectively at some levels than at others. Where it functions best with respect to the members of non-Western religions is in protecting their civil rights. While the occurrence of violence and discrimination shows that these rights are not always respected or upheld, the prevailing assumption—even among those who have been the focus of such incidents—is that these are exceptions that can be adequately handled within existing laws and regulations. This assumption is reinforced in anecdotes that attribute such incidents to deviants and lawbreakers, the misinformed, or extremists. It is also reinforced by responses that regard such incidents as so unusual that they need not be reported at all or that involve seeking legal recourse, negotiating with school authorities or zoning boards, and the like.

Culturally, the situation is much less clear than it is legally. On the one hand, a great deal of assimilation is evident among new immigrant and other non-Western groups, and this assimilation makes pluralism easier by creating commonalities that transcend ethnic and religious subcultures. The great majority have adapted to the norms of American business and professional life, medicine, transportation, and education. First-generation immigrants often complain that their children are becoming too American, abandoning family traditions and ethnic customs, and becoming more like other Americans in their tastes and lifestyles. Individualism and greater gender equality often provide additional markers of assimilation. On the other hand, distinctive values and traditions remain, which become caricatured in stereotypes and misunderstandings. In contrast to interpersonal relationships, which are usually described as polite and congenial, television is regarded as a major source of misinformation. Striving for genuine cultural pluralism is thus a matter of constant negotiation, both to avoid the loss of identity and to combat inappropriate labels.

It is at the religious level that pluralism, as opposed to mere diversity, appears to be weakest. For the most part, American Muslims, Hindus, and

Buddhists are committed to maintaining distinctive practices, rather than moving in the direction of some bland synthesis of all religions, and few show interest in converting to Christianity. If ethnically homogeneous neighborhoods no longer provide the underpinnings for such practices, temples, mosques, sanghas, meditation centers, and other religious organizations do. Although these organizations do not reach everyone, they serve as community and cultural centers for many, providing opportunities for regular worship and special celebrations. Home practices and long traditions of reinforcing these practices through family rituals supplement what takes place outside the home. Yet reports of interaction with Christian organizations suggest a pattern of coexistence rather than pluralism. According to their leaders and lay adherents, the new minority religions exist as enclaves that have very little interaction with the majority religions in their communities.

Judging from what these leaders and lay members say, the heart of the problem is ignorance on the part of the general population about even the rudimentary beliefs and practices of the newer minority religions. Some of this ignorance is no different from that which afflicts the American public about geography, history, and science. Yet it may also reflect the kind of indifference or complacency that stems from the view that Christian truth is sufficient unto itself. However explicit or implicit this view may be, it appears to the adherents of non-Western religions to be narrow-minded, if not symptomatic of religious superficiality. At the very least, adherents of the new minority religions wish to be understood, rather than merely tolerated or treated as if their religious convictions are unimportant. Their growing presence nevertheless poses an important question: Can the majority population, especially those who take their faith seriously, find ways to respond—thoughtfully and meaningfully—to the presence of religious communities whose beliefs and practices are quite different from their own? Or are religious differences so potentially divisive and conflict-ridden that serious interaction and mutual engagement are out of the question?

The Significance of Religious Diversity

WE AMERICANS in the twenty-first century have become so accustomed to diversity that it may be difficult to understand exactly why the growing number of people who belong to religions other than Christianity or Judaism is culturally challenging. Americans of European ancestry can often think of stories about immigrants in their own family histories and conclude that the difficulties faced by recent immigrants are much the same. The melting pot will again prevail. Looking at our neighborhoods and communities, we may also think of religious diversity the same way we do restaurants and convenience stores: the more the better. Greater diversity enriches our options and thereby enhances our freedom to choose. Having variety in our lives gives us opportunities to learn about the world and to gain a better understanding of ourselves.

This positive view of religious diversity is evident in the way Americans respond when asked about its role in our nation's history. In the Religion and Diversity Survey, 86 percent of the public agreed that "Religious diversity has been good for America," while only 12 percent disagreed.[1] Opinions are also generally positive when people talk about whether it is good or bad that the society is becoming more diverse. A woman in Texas says greater religious diversity will be good for the nation because it will "lead people to have more free and open lives." She thinks "more freedom of expression" will result. A similar view is voiced by a woman in California who relishes the growing variety of religions she sees in her community. She explains that this variety "gives people freedom of choice to go and see what they really are looking for."

Freedom is one of our most cherished values. We register its importance in such phrases as "the free world," "land of the free," "personal freedom," and "freedom of expression."[2] When our nation is threatened, leaders emphasize that it is our *freedom* that must be protected (more so than our homes, jobs, or system of government). It is thus easy for us to believe that social change is good if we can associate it with an increase in our basic freedoms. And one of the most basic of these freedoms is the idea that we can choose what to believe. The value of being able to choose leaps immediately to mind for a man in Texas who muses that he "would hate to be in a world where you could only be Roman Catholic or Southern Baptist or something like that." He thinks "just the opportunity to explore other avenues of faith has got to be a positive thing." A man in North Carolina expresses the same idea as he reflects on the fact that "we are a country that is looked upon as a place where people go." In his view, the present diversity strengthens us by encouraging us to promote religious freedom. "In other words, people want to be able to feel free to worship as they wish."

The tendency to view diversity positively is rooted in three long-standing assumptions in American culture. One is respect for individual rights. These rights include the freedom to choose one's beliefs and to live differently from others according to the dictates of one's conscience. A second is the commonsense view of morality that came to America in the eighteenth century through the Scottish Enlightenment. This view works in conjunction with respect for diverse beliefs and lifestyles. It is the conviction that people can readily distinguish good from evil on the basis of their common experience as human beings, regardless of race, ethnicity, nationality, or religion. Respect for individual rights and the commonsense view of morality were cornerstones of the cultural consensus that emerged during and in the decades immediately following the American War of Independence.[3] The third assumption—that diverse choices are like commodities— emerged later, mostly during the last third of the nineteenth century and first quarter of the twentieth century with industrialization and the development of a nationwide consumer market. The commodification of culture that came about during these years taught Americans that diversity is to be welcomed in the marketplace of ideas, just as in the marketplace of goods, because individuals can then more accurately satisfy their particular needs and desires.

Long-standing assumptions notwithstanding, positive views of diversity are tempered by more sober assessments. Many social observers express concern about the adjustments that will be required for the United States to accommodate growing levels of religious and cultural diversity. They understand that diversity may provide opportunities to choose from a larger menu, but see the potential for superficiality and fragmentation as well. Even those who welcome diversity, as many do, understand that social change of this kind necessarily poses significant cultural challenges that will need to be faced in the years ahead.

Ronald Barnes is an attorney in Chicago with more than thirty years of experience in law and government. His view of diversity is more cautious than that usually encountered in the media or on the street. When asked his views about religious diversity, he shakes his head and says that he is worried. "It opens us to new ways of doing business and new ways of solving some of the social problems that we have," he concedes. "But it also creates tremendous pressures as people of different faiths, particularly new immigrants, come to us with different social backgrounds. Existing social programs don't take into account their family or cultural dynamics. Diversity, which is so easily and facilely celebrated, presents all kinds of problems."

The comparative religion scholar Diana Eck, a professor who has spent many years studying world religions abroad and in the United States, writes that "we have the unparalleled opportunity to build, intentionally and actively, a culture of pluralism among the people of many cultures and faiths in America," but she also warns that we may not succeed. "We may find ourselves fragmented and divided with too much *pluribus* and not enough *unum*."[4]

Eck reminds us that the various faiths of which American religion is now composed are not simply alternative paths to the same destination. They exemplify what the political philosopher John Rawls termed a "plurality of conflicting and indeed incommensurable conceptions of the meaning, value and purpose of human life."[5] They may be constrained by a common code of democratic assumptions, as Rawls also suggested. Yet incommensurable beliefs and practices have often in the past resulted in political struggles among contending and hostile factions.

The potential for fragmentation is recognized by a significant minority of the American public. In one survey, 29 percent thought "having many different religions in the United States [makes] it harder to keep the country united."[6] Concerns about divisiveness are particularly on the minds of men and women who live in communities where religious diversity has been increasing in recent years. A woman who lives in a section of suburban Chicago that has witnessed a large increase in Muslims, Hindus, and Buddhists during the past decade says that she hopes for the best but fears the worst. "Some of these groups are like cults that separate people." Increasingly, she predicts, people who are devoted to various religious groups will be bound together by a "terrible need for fellowship," which will encourage them to think negatively about other groups. "I don't think that will be helpful to our society. It will just cause more division." She adds, "I don't think we all need to be the same, and yet I am concerned that the diversity will cause more hatred and more distrust and fear."

Comments like this suggest that greater religious diversity does raise questions about the well-being of our society. But what, more precisely, are these questions? Before we can (in subsequent chapters) consider how Americans have been responding to religious diversity, we need to understand clearly what is at stake. And we need to do this by considering both what ordinary Americans *think* is at stake and what scholars and leaders who are prominent participants in the debates have to say. From interviews and from the published literature, we can identify four distinct arguments about what is at stake. First, there are some who believe that greater diversity poses a threat to democracy itself, especially through the constitutional questions it raises. Second, there is concern that greater religious diversity raises difficult practical questions about fairness and decency. Third, there are those who fear that increasing diversity is undermining long-held American values. And fourth, there is a set of arguments suggesting that the *religious* dimension of religious diversity is itself an important cultural challenge that needs to be taken seriously. My review of these four arguments will suggest that all four are significant, especially because many Americans believe they are and are responding accordingly. I shall also suggest that the first three arguments have sometimes been overstated while the fourth—about religion—has not been considered enough, even though it has the most far-reaching implications.

A Threat to Democracy?

America was profoundly shaped by the distinctive biblical values it imported from western Europe during its formative period. The fact that First Amendment interpretations can still be discussed as matters of *church* and state is one indication of this lasting influence. Another is the habit followed by nearly all recent presidents of ending speeches with "God bless America" (they do not mention Allah, the dharma, or one's "higher power").[7] Our penchant for speaking about the nation's *mission* or its *crusades* is another. So is the assumption signaled by the phrase on our currency: In God We Trust. The framers of that phrase were not concerned with the connotations it might have for Buddhists or Hindus. Previous waves of immigrants such as the Chinese workers who came to California during the Gold Rush and to work on the transcontinental railroad were certainly exceptions—but few enough to have left prevailing national values unchallenged. Now, however, with millions of Americans having been reared in Buddhist, Hindu, or Muslim settings, it is less clear to many that the shared values on which democratic procedures rest can so easily be sustained. Coupled with concerns about racial and ethnic differences, diversity itself raises new questions about the future of democracy. As the political theorist Jean Bethke Elshtain has charged, differences now seem so acute that "it is no longer possible for us to speak to one another." We "inhabit our own little islands of bristling difference," she writes, and sometimes behave as if "no outsiders are welcome."[8]

The possibility that some of the non-Western religious groups could harbor terrorist cells aiming to weaken or overthrow the American government is clearly one of the threats that some people associate with these groups. But this possibility is not the only one. The fact that non-Western religious groups have flourished in parts of the world in which democracy has not fared well is an added source of concern. A community leader who wished not to be identified mentioned that people in his circles are worried about the possibility that their new neighbors might not play by the rules of democracy. He saw this possibility as a potential threat especially in reference to the delicate balance between church and state prescribed in the First Amendment. "If people are Buddhists and come from a totalitarian environment and have a different perspective," he noted, "and if there are large numbers of those people who arrive here, that certainly could affect how we look at the First Amendment." We might be tempted to curb the First Amendment freedoms that are so fundamental to American democracy because we doubt the capacity of practitioners of newer religions to exercise their freedom responsibly.

This leader's concern recognizes the influence of cultural traditions on understandings of democracy. He makes this judgment without expressing thoughts about the compatibility or incompatibility of religious beliefs themselves with good government. For other Americans, this general concern about diversity is compounded by the fact that *Christianity* is, in their view, particularly conducive to the well-being of democracy. A man in Colorado who laments the declining influence of Christianity (which he associates with the rise of other religions) says, "God is the only source of wisdom, and if we look historically, every nation that was great at one time because of its commitment to God suffered all sorts of bad consequences as it began to turn away." A man in Pennsylvania expresses the same view even more strongly. Arguing that "America was based on faith in God" when the nation was founded, he thinks the influx of non-Christians "could lead to the downfall of our society." For these men, religious diversity clearly has implications for how they think about the future of America.

The view that the United States was founded on Christian principles has been questioned by historians, particularly because Enlightenment secularism played such a large role in the philosophical views of many of the founders.[9] It is also possible to sidestep the question of Christianity's centrality to American democracy by arguing, as many social scientists do, that whatever influence Christianity may have had has been transmuted into generic support for morality and decency, which followers of any religion can affirm.[10] Still, the view that American democracy and Christianity go hand in hand is very widely held among the general public. For instance, in the Religion and Diversity Survey, 55 percent of the public agreed that "Our democratic form of government is based on Christianity," and nearly four Americans in five agreed that "The United States was founded on Christian principles" (78 percent) and that "America has been strong because of its faith in God" (79 percent). Whether they agree or disagree with these popular views, some observers fear that Christianity may be so tightly woven into the constitutional fabric that extricating one knot may cause the whole piece to unravel.

As an illustration of this possibility, in 1959 the Ohio legislature adopted as the state's official motto a portion of Matthew 19, verse 26, which asserts, "With God all things are possible." In April 2000, by a two-to-one margin the U.S. Sixth District Court of Appeals ruled that this motto was unconstitutional on the grounds that it was a specific governmental endorsement of Christianity. Writing for the majority, Judge Avern Cohn argued: "No amount of semantic legerdemain can hide the fact that the official motto of the State of Ohio repeats, word-for-word, Jesus' answer to his disciples' questions about the ability to enter heaven, and thereby achieve salvation. As such, to the ears of a reasonable listener, the motto comes directly from the voice of Jesus. To suppress the knowledge that these are the words of Jesus, and to say that they describe something other than the achievement of salvation, is to put a premium on ignorance."[11] Judge Cohn noted further in his opinion that these words of Jesus were not subscribed to by American Jews or Muslims—contrary to the defense's claim that a similar idea could be found in both the Hebrew Bible and the Qur'an.[12]

Critics of the decision argued that it compromised the very basis of American democracy. Television preacher Pat Robertson reportedly denounced the decision as the work of the anti-Christ.[13] A reader of the *Detroit News* opined that it "illustrates the absurd lengths to which American jurisprudes have gone to demonize all practiced faiths."[14] In Ohio, the *Cincinnati Enquirer* termed the ruling "nonsense" and reported that a statewide poll showed 88 percent of the public in disagreement with it.[15] But supporters and critics alike agreed that the First Amendment is in place because of the problems "diverse believers" face in getting along and is thus a barometer of the deep issues that religious diversity poses for our way of government.[16]

A more direct threat to American democracy is foreseen by people who associate fundamentalism and violence with some of the non-Western religions that have grown in recent years. These concerns most often emerge in remarks about Muslims. A woman in California (herself an immigrant) thinks it is generally good for people to have faith because they are more likely to be moral, but she worries about the "fanatical kind" of faith being imported by some immigrant groups. "Is it the Islams or whoever who believe in Allah? And they will kill and murder for Allah because they go straight to heaven if they kill for Allah? That is an extreme bad religion, I think." In another California community a man expresses similar concerns. "I didn't realize a religion could tell people to kill. And then we have all these bombings and terrorist attacks."

An added concern, stemming from the special interests that religious groups represent, is that a greater variety of religious groups will simply overwhelm the legal system, causing American democracy to collapse under the weight of having to deal with particular claims and traditions. One of the clearest expressions of this concern came from Supreme Court Justice Antonin Scalia in a 1990 decision pertaining to whether or not the government should be required to show compelling interest in order to prohibit activities deemed part of the worship services of particular religious groups. Such a requirement, Scalia argued, would be "courting anarchy," a danger that "increases in direct proportion to the society's diversity of religious beliefs." In other words, the government need not protect the free exercise of religion as much as in the past because religious diversity is making it harder to govern effectively—a view that many religious groups regarded as itself being a threat to democracy.[17] "I read Justice Scalia," says Freedom Forum's Charles Haynes, as saying that religious accommodation "is just not practical—not possible in a country committed to sustaining the law. Many of us felt that was a radical decision that gutted the free exercise protection that we assumed was very much a part of what the First Amendment was all about."

On balance, it is probably overstated to suggest that the recent increase in religious diversity is fundamentally a threat to American democracy. Although new questions are being raised about how to apply democratic traditions to a wider variety of religious groups, these traditions appear capable of withstanding the challenge. The American system of government reflects the deep religious divisions that swept across Europe in the century following the Protestant Reformation.[18] Those divisions, erupting in near-fratricidal war between Catholics and Protestants during the Thirty Years War, were in every respect as severe as any of the religious tensions in the world today. John Locke, David Hume, and others to whom America's founders looked for guidance were deeply influenced by these conflicts. American government was deliberately conceived as a system of checks and balances that would prevent any minority—religious or otherwise—from imposing its will on the people while at the same time guaranteeing all minorities freedom in matters of religion, speech, and assembly. The First Amendment embodies these principles.

Much of the litigation concerning the First Amendment rights and privileges of new religious groups in recent years has drawn on precedents from similar cases involving more established religious groups. Constitutional experts generally take the view that this litigation nudges the courts in one direction or another in interpreting the First Amendment but does not pose questions that are very dissimilar to those that have arisen historically concerning religious diversity. Ronald Chen, a professor at Rutgers University Law School who has dealt extensively with constitutional issues related to religious diversity, observes, "Our institutions are pretty well set up to deal with [diversity] and it would be only if the Supreme Court unnecessarily tinkers with the Establishment clause that I would have concerns." Brent Walker, who regularly deals with constitutional issues as executive director of the Baptist Joint Committee, takes a similar view. He believes that increasing religious diversity will focus greater attention on religious liberty, which he regards as a positive contribution to American democracy, but that no new ground will need to be broken. "It's established legal precedents being applied to new groups. The religious liberty battles have always been fought on the edge of things. It's been the Mormons and the Jehovah's Witnesses and the Scientologists and on and on." Nathan Lewin, a Washington-based attorney who has argued a number of cases before the Supreme Court, says vigilance is required, but he also is confident that the underlying principles are right. "The system is able to handle it," he says. "The civil rights revolution put strains on the system. The recognition of gender equality put strains on the system. Various other recognitions of speech rights put strains on the system. But the system was able to tolerate it."

The number of cases involving the First Amendment that reach high courts does seem likely to grow as religious diversity increases. And there will probably be outcries associated with each new ruling about religion either being discriminated against or gaining too much power. Yet the basic principles embodied in the First Amendment, despite differences in interpretation, seem capable of withstanding the challenges posed by added religious diversity. Judge Cohn, reflecting on the Ohio case, for instance, firmly believes that such rulings, whether they stand or are overturned, do not represent a fundamental threat to the nation's system of government. "These things just get recycled in different forms, but they've been here before," he observes. "The legal order that we have can absorb most of this."

The potential for anarchy that worries Justice Scalia may, in the final analysis, be more of a safeguard of democracy than a threat. The historian

Martin Marty has noted the "frightful mess" that has long characterized American religion.[19] Protestants are more of an agglomeration of competing denominations and sects than an established religion. Catholics are divided along ethnic, regional, and theological lines. And Jews have been similarly divided, making it hard for observers to decide whether they are a religious group, an ethnic group, or something else. The new religious diversity simply adds to this messiness. Hindus, Muslims, and Buddhists are all divided by national origins, languages, and traditions. The courts may have their work cut out for them in protecting the rights of everyone. But messiness means that it is unlikely that any single religious group will have the upper hand. Messiness also means that religious diversity will continue to be an issue of public concern. It will be part of discussions about freedom and rights and about the identity of groups, their autonomy, their relationships with other groups, and whether their aims can be accommodated within the established framework of governance.

Fairness and Decency

Apart from the theoretical questions it raises about the future of democracy, religious diversity generates practical concerns about fairness and decency. These are the concerns that Justice Scalia points to in suggesting the possibility of anarchy—issues having to do with dress, dietary restrictions, religious holidays, health standards, building codes, schooling, and the like. Lawmakers and the courts have been called on increasingly to resolve these issues. Neighborhood councils, zoning boards, the police, community leaders, and corporate officials have also been required to address them.

Concerns about religiously distinct dress have been expressed by Muslims, Sikhs, Hasids, and practitioners of other religions in settings such as schools and the military. The workplace has been a particular area of concern. According to a survey conducted by the New York–based Tanenbaum Center for Interreligious Understanding, 76 percent of Muslim respondents were at least somewhat troubled by religious bias at work—the highest rate of concern for any of the religious groups surveyed.[20] Dress is often the issue. Muslim women, for instance, report being pressured by employers not to wear the traditional head scarf, or hijab, and say that doing so has resulted in cold treatment during job interviews.[21] In other cases, members of minority religions have been targets for mistreatment by other employees because of distinctive clothing.[22]

Dietary restrictions raise issues that require increasing attention by the courts as well as by food service providers such as restaurants, hospitals, prisons, and airlines. One of the more notable examples of dietary restrictions having an impact on the wider public occurred when a class-action suit was brought against the McDonald's fast-food chain on behalf of vegetarians when it was discovered that French fries marketed as all-vegetable items contained small amounts of beef flavoring. The discovery, which was said to be particularly offensive to American Hindus, resulted in a public apology and change of practice on the part of McDonald's.[23] An issue that appears to have been resolved more quietly involved the popular candy Gummi Bears. It posed a dietary problem for Jews because of its pork-based substance. With growing numbers of Muslims facing the same problem in the United States and Europe, Haribo (the manufacturer of the candy) developed a new bacteria-based, gelatin-free substance that could be marketed more easily to Jews and Muslims.[24]

With mosques, temples, ashrams, and other religious centers spreading into new areas, building permits and zoning laws have become another matter requiring closer attention. While legally prohibited from discriminating against religious organizations, communities have found creative ways to accommodate the interests of residents upset at the prospect of traffic snarls, broadcasting of public prayers or religious music, and new immigrants moving to their neighborhoods. In one community the zoning board backed away from passing a law preventing the construction of any religious buildings, but enforced building codes so rigorously that members of a new Hindu temple felt that they were being encouraged to leave. Another community paid organizers of a new mosque several hundred thousand dollars to locate elsewhere. In contrast, other communities have rolled out the welcome mat in hopes of attracting upscale Muslims, Hindus, or Buddhists.

Lobbying, pressure groups, accommodation, and creativity in traversing difficult legal terrain have been present in many of these instances. For instance, legislative action in New Jersey that protected consumers from purchasing food falsely labeled as *halal* (meeting Muslim law with respect to dietary codes) was successfully initiated through pressure from Muslim groups, with indirect assistance from Jewish groups that had achieved similar legislation for kosher food, and in a way that avoided being struck down by the courts. Rather than mandating that food distributors follow halal, the legislation only prevented them from advertising food as *halal* if it had not been properly prepared.[25]

Many of the cases that Nathan Lewin, the Washington attorney, has litigated have involved Orthodox Jewish groups. He says these cases raise issues similar to those being voiced by Muslims and Hindus because religion is a way of life for Orthodox Jews and thus spills into the so-called secular realm more readily than it does for Americans who practice their faith privately or only in church. "It's become common in the United States to think of religious rights as being the right to worship at the church of your choice and maybe on the day of your choice and maybe to the God of your choice," he observes. "But there is a lot more to religion as it is practiced in large parts of the world than simply worship. That means various forms of observances, practice, manners of dress, things of that kind." He thinks these issues cannot be resolved only by the courts, but need to be understood better by the public at large and especially by religious leaders.

Litigation involving new immigrant religions has taken place amidst continuing, if not increasing, concerns on the part of more established groups about whether or not they are receiving fair treatment. A suit brought by twenty-seven chaplains against the Navy, for instance, charged that evangelical chaplains were being discriminated against. The suit alleged that the Navy allocates a third of chaplaincies to Roman Catholics, a third to liturgical Protestants (such as Episcopalians and Lutherans), and the remaining third to all other groups, including evangelical Protestants, Jews, and Muslims. Evangelical chaplains said this system underrepresents the numeric prominence of evangelical Protestants in the Navy.[26]

Apart from the sheer difficulty of resolving such issues, there is also the secondary problem of frayed interpersonal relationships. Real or imagined, the administrative problems that arise from accommodating diverse religious practices sometimes weigh heavily on those who do not share these practices. As a case in point, one man expressed concern about how to keep things running smoothly at the office he manages. "You can't just say that people can come from their milk bath ablutions into a work force smelling like rancid milk and the bosses can't do anything about it because it's a religious tradition!"

Hate crimes against religious groups, discrimination, prejudice, and religious violence have occurred in many communities. Following the September 2001 attacks on New York and Washington, hundreds of hate crimes were reported against mosques and individual Muslims.[27] Prior to that, more than a thousand hate crimes against religious groups were already being reported each year to the Federal Bureau of Investigation, a number that was rising despite the fact that crime of many other kinds was declining.[28] The vast majority of these crimes were against Jews, although a growing proportion were against Muslims and other non-Christian groups.[29] And such figures do not include the many incidents—a majority of which may not legally count as hate crimes but which constitute discrimination—that are not reported. In one survey that sought to represent a cross-section of religious groups, 32 percent of American Hindus and 27 percent of American Muslims said that they had experienced discrimination or were personally acquainted with someone who had.[30]

A glimpse of the reality behind these figures is evident in the remarks of Mohammed Kazerooni, an imam at the Ahl-Al-Beit Islamic Center in Denver. When asked if he knew of any incidents of prejudice or discrimination against Muslims, he replied, "We receive complaint after complaint from different people that they are being discriminated against because they have converted to Islam or because they want to practice their faith in a variety of places: in schools against Muslim children, in workplaces against Muslims, in prison against Muslim inmates. It's widespread." The center itself has had stones thrown at it, windows broken, and graffiti painted on its walls.

Leaders and members of other Muslim, Hindu, and Buddhist groups mention problems such as having their buildings broken into or defaced, being hassled by police because of how they are dressed, and being ridiculed for how they pray. As one put it, these are not "what you could go to court" over. They are annoyances that occasionally become full-fledged violations of civil rights. What these members and leaders regret most, though, is simply the lack of understanding that they know exists in the wider public and even in their own neighborhoods.

The fact that followers of non-Western religions represent a relatively small percentage of the population means that many Americans have not been affected personally by the practical questions that have arisen in relation to religious diversity. They simply do not know anyone who practices a religion very different from theirs. Yet the presence of new minority religions has brought to the United States issues that in previous years would have been ignored or treated as purely foreign matters.[31] Questions about dress, dietary restrictions, and religious holidays are all examples of these issues. In a larger sense, religious diversity affects everyone through legislation, regulations in schools and the workplace, and budgets required to enforce such regulations.

The practical questions that are now appearing as a result of increasing religious diversity are far-reaching and need to be taken seriously by lawmakers and public officials. Yet these questions can usually be dealt with by applying precedents from previous cases involving religion, civil rights, and nondiscrimination. Barry Morrison, the Philadelphia region director of the Anti-Defamation League of B'nai B'rith, follows many of these cases as part of his organization's efforts to monitor religious discrimination. He describes the cases with which he is familiar as "a continuation of the interpretation of existing laws with certain new twists, but basically going back to the same fundamental questions and issues." Judge Cohn registers the same view. Referring to a case in which a Sikh brought suit against his employer, who had fired him for wearing Sikh-style headgear, Cohn says that the decision was legally analogous to similar cases involving Jews. He denies that "any fundamentally new legal principles" are likely to be required in the more religiously diverse America of the future.[32]

If practical questions about fairness and decency can be handled within current laws about civil rights and nondiscrimination, they nevertheless forge new symbolic linkages between these laws and religion. Dress, food, buildings, and the right to hold worship services instantiate religion in the culture. Debates about these instantiations send signals about group identities. They force lawmakers and informed members of the public to define their responsibilities as citizens and as individuals toward these religious groups.

Challenges to American Values

Besides the concerns about fairness and decency, the new diversity raises questions about who we are as a nation and as a people. What values should we embrace? Whose values are these? Will they be strong enough to generate conviction and commitment? Inclusive enough to unite us and promote cohesion in our communities? Diversity raises the specter of a frayed society, drawn in different directions by competing life-styles, ethnic identities, national loyalties, customs, and beliefs. But it also evokes new opportunities for rethinking the United States' vision of itself.

These broader cultural challenges come up frequently in discussions about legal and constitutional issues, but go beyond the purely judicial aspects of these issues. Americans United for Separation of Church and State (AU) has been litigating cases involving the free exercise of diverse religious practices since 1947. AU's Robert Boston says the organization expects to see an increase in such cases as a result of the number of minority religions in the United States. Despite this increase, he does not anticipate basic new laws needing to be written. But he does suggest the importance of separating what he calls the *cultural aspect* from the legal issues. "Cultur-ally," he says, "it's difficult to get Americans to understand that small, unpopular, non-Christian groups have the same legal rights as everyone else." He observes that people use the term *cult* and other pejorative terms to imply that there should be a dual system of rights for religious groups: "the well-known groups that everybody feels are okay, and then the unpop-ular groups that government can take steps to curb." He thinks the hardest challenge is "culturally how do we assimilate growing diversity and plural-ism?" The reason this is a cultural challenge is that questions about the *rights* of minority religious groups cannot be divorced from questions about the *legitimacy* of these groups as ways of life.

In the Religion and Diversity Survey, one of the most troubling results was the large number of Americans who were willing to curb the basic rights of non-Western religious groups in the United States. Twenty-three percent of those sampled said they favored "making it illegal for Muslim groups to meet in the United States," and 20 percent said this about Hindu groups and about Buddhist groups. These respondents' definition of basic rights apparently did not extend to freedom of worship for all Americans. An even larger number was willing to countenance government actions that until recently would have been considered inappropriate: 60 percent said they favored "the U.S. government collecting information about Muslim reli-gious groups in the United States," as did 51 percent about Hindu religious groups and 48 percent about Buddhist religious groups. It may not have been prejudice against particular religious groups that caused people to give these responses; indeed, 51 percent also favored the government collecting information "about some Christian groups in the United States." And in view of the fact that the government *had* authorized the Federal Bureau of Investigation to collect information about mosques in relation to concerns about terrorism, it may not be surprising that people felt justified giving these responses. Those who expressed serious worries about terrorism were more likely to give these responses than those who were less worried.[33] Yet the ease with which the public accepted such surveillance was in striking contrast to the past. For instance, concerns about government intrusion in religious affairs still keeps the Census Bureau from asking questions about religious affiliations or the Internal Revenue Service from requiring churches to file the same tax forms as other nonprofit organizations. "Now there is an air of caution," said one of the lay leaders at a mosque in New York. "People are not really as free as they were before. Anybody who says the wrong thing could be wrongly identified or harassed."

Americans generally pride themselves on being tolerant of racial, ethnic, and religious differences, and yet the history of bigotry and exclusion along racial, ethnic, and religious lines should give us pause. As a society, we are at best ambivalent about how welcoming we should be to new immigrants and to new ethnic or religious minorities. In the Religion and Diversity Survey, 64 percent of the public favored "passing a law to reduce the number of immigrants coming into the country." Yet 51 percent said they would welcome "Muslims becoming a stronger presence in the United States," 58 percent said this about Hindus, 59 percent did so about Buddhists, 70 percent did so about Asians, and 73 percent did so about Hispanics. How people reconcile welcoming ethnic and religious minorities with the view that immigration should be reduced is not at all clear. It is evident, though, that Americans are conflicted in their views about social differences. Thus, 46 percent of those surveyed agreed that "foreigners who come to live in America should give up their foreign ways and learn to be like other Americans," while 52 percent disagreed. Now as in the past, putting tolerance into practice is more difficult than ascribing to it as an ideal.

Besides the need for tolerance, which most Americans would at least agree with in principle, there is a sense among some Americans that a religiously diverse society simply makes it harder to sort out one's values. A woman in Ohio says, "It's really difficult raising children in that kind of a society. I think it's harder for them to understand right and wrong."

She recognizes that basic values are inscribed in religious traditions and that these values differ from tradition to tradition. She is among the sizable minority of the public (27 percent) who fear that Christianity itself will become weaker as a result of greater religious diversity.[34]

For those who have been used to living in a more homogeneous context, these cultural concerns may be especially troubling. An older man who has lived in a small town in Texas and attended the Baptist church there all his life asserts, "We're losing the Christian values that this country was founded on. We're moving away from basic Christian principles. The morals of the country are going down." Like a number of other people, he has the uncomfortable feeling that American culture is simply adrift and that an influx of people with diverse religious views is not helping.

But this sense of cultural drift is not limited to the Christian population. Immigrants and people of other faiths sense it, too, and when they express it, they pose another cultural challenge: are native-born Americans willing to listen and learn from the criticisms being voiced by newcomers? It may be one thing for American Christians who have lived in the United States all their lives to suggest that morals are being corrupted; quite another if the same criticism is expressed by a Muslim or Hindu leader who is viewed as an outsider, despite being an American citizen. Outsiders, we might say, should be more respectful.

Dr. Ahmad Moen emigrated in 1973 from Ethiopia to the United States, where he now teaches at Howard University and is a member of the Outreach Committee for Interfaith Dialogue at the Islamic Center in Washington, D.C. He says the United States is "a big country [that] should behave in terms of being fair and understanding its own strength." But he observes that "there are many empires that preceded it [and] became decadent by sheer arrogance." While stopping short of saying that the United States has already become decadent, he warns that it should "learn from the mistakes that other decadent societies" have made. He is especially concerned about the pervasive influences of television and advertising and worries that young people are not being brought up with proper respect for the basic human values taught in all religious traditions. Whether other Americans, even ones who might agree with him, would accept his implied criticism is a difficult question.

Another cultural challenge, though of a more positive sort, is figuring out which values we want to emphasize as we try to learn from the various options set before us by diverse religious traditions. A man in Georgia remarks, "Hindus seem to have strong family beliefs and raise their children the right way." He believes their presence will have a beneficial impact on the United States, but only if non-Hindus strive to learn from their example. Others claim it is more likely that we will have to sort out the values we wish to avoid and perhaps learn from certain religious traditions by negative example. A woman in New York fears that the self-interestedness of American culture may be reinforced by religious diversity unless we take efforts to guard against it. "In a lot of these non-Christian religions the focus is on yourself. It's on how you can change or on what's best for you." She says this cannot be good for the society. "The selfishness and pride that develops can't work for the greater good."

If native-born Americans are having to face questions like these, immigrants whose religious heritage is being reshaped by American society have even more serious cultural challenges to confront. One of the most significant is dealing with negative stereotypes about their group—images that are often reinforced by the mass media. Another is the question of how rapidly or fully to assimilate and what assimilation may mean in terms of potential conflict between first- and second-generation Americans.[35]

A lay member of the Rajdhani Mandir Hindu temple in Washington, D.C., says that he is concerned about both of these questions. The Christian population, he says, harbors several negative impressions of Hindus, including the belief that Hinduism is a "cult" (which he attributes to the high visibility of Hare Krishnas), misunderstandings about "multiple gods," and the perception of "heavy idol worship." For his own community, the question raised by these stereotypes is whether to actively combat them, ignore them, or try to counter them with more positive publicity. He says the generational question comes up because the first generation of immigrants from India was "very much afraid of the Western influence coming on their kids, like an unknown devil," whereas their children (as well as more recent immigrants who were more exposed to Western influences in India) often feel that accommodation between Hinduism and Western values is not problematic.

A different kind of cultural adaptation emerges from the experiences of the Venerable Jotika, the Vietnamese-born monk who directs the Phap Luan Buddhist Culture Center in Houston. For him, the biggest adjustment has been getting used to the growing popularity of Buddhism in the

United States. In Vietnam, he says, meditation was practiced mainly by monks and laity who took the monastic life very seriously; in the United States, people meditate casually because it makes them feel better. Formerly, there was greater respect for monks, more distance between them and people who came to the monasteries to meditate, and more elaborate rituals surrounding food preparation and services. He is not unhappy about these changes because they do not compromise the essential meanings of Buddhism. He does, however, recognize that the Vietnamese community in Houston is undergoing a major cultural transition and he hopes there can be greater learning and mutual respect between people like him and religious leaders in the wider community. "Living in a big city like Houston," he says, "we can see that the tradition of religious practice has been lost, so it's good for us to learn from each other."

In many respects, the cultural questions evoked by religious diversity resemble those raised by racial and ethnic differences and by previous manifestations of religious diversity. We do not have to invent a new language in which to talk about the current religious diversity. We confront questions about values and lifestyles by drawing on the established frames of reference we use to account for our similarities and differences. Among other things, these frames of reference tell us that cultural differences, although real, do not fundamentally separate us from one another. They tell us that differences enrich our lives and are, if anything, of concern because they are being diminished rather than increased.

Race informs nearly all our thinking about diversity. It spills implicitly into the perspectives we bring to bear on religious, ethnic, and national differences, even when these differences have only marginal connections with race itself. Most of us know almost instinctively—by virtue of the messages to which we are exposed in our schools and families and through the mass media—that racial differences are more cultural than biological, real in their consequences, and yet often regrettable. We are taught that racial differences should not matter, especially as far as opportunities are concerned, and if they do, to avoid discrimination on the basis of these differences. Racial diversity is conditioned by powerful norms favoring equality for all. We learn that we should respect the differences in lifestyle, language, and preferences that may be associated with race, but to regard these as a kind of heritage or enrichment, rather than as matters so essential that rights or privileges should be based on them.[36] These understandings about respect, equality, and rights are ones that we can transfer to questions about religious diversity as well.

Thinking about the cultural meanings of diversity is also influenced by the multiplicity of ethnic traditions of which our nation is composed. Ethnicity has, as it were, been tamed or domesticated. The presence of multiple traditions makes for cultural richness, a florid display of customs and colloquial practices. To be sure, the history of rivalry and conflict among ethnic groups has not disappeared, but it has been tempered to the point that cooperation between, say, Italians and Irish or Poles and Germans suggests similar possibilities for more recent immigrants from Pakistan, India, Thailand, or Korea. Ethnic diversity is now experienced as something easily sampled, such as ethnic music, ethnic cuisine, and ethnic festivals. Ethnicity is for many Americans a feature of their identity that they understand as an arbitrary aspect of family history, rather than as a matter of conviction. Although it is to some extent a matter of choice (one can decide whether to emphasize the Italian heritage of one's mother or the Spanish heritage of one's father), it is never entirely an open choice (this same person could not choose to be Asian American) and for this reason, just as with all such choices, a person cannot be held morally accountable for his or her ethnicity.[37] At the deepest level, we hold that Americans of all ethnic backgrounds should be regarded as morally interchangeable with one another: their moral worth is indicated more by the values and behavior they have chosen than by their family heritage.[38]

Besides race and ethnicity, the distinctive characteristics of American religion, particularly its division into many different denominations and confessional traditions, has also had a profound impact on the ways we think about diversity. The historic strength of American religion, we like to tell ourselves, lies in its denominational variety. We can pick and choose, rather than having to live under the rule of a single religion with which we may disagree. What matters is not adherence to any particular creed, but sincere personal conviction. Whatever we may think about religion itself, this heritage gives us reason to believe that cultural diversity is good. We may know that religious divisions have been a source of conflict and violence in other countries, but in our own, we happily assume that many values and perspectives can be reconciled.[39]

Religion as Moral Order

The cultural significance of religious diversity can been seen in the extent to which it generates questions about democracy, about fairness and decency, and about lifestyles and values. To understand religious diversity only in these ways, though, misses the fact that religion itself is an important part of American culture. Religious membership and participation continues to characterize a majority of the population, and nearly everyone claims to have beliefs about God and views on spirituality and religious experience.[40] Religion gives millions of Americans a sense of their place in the cosmos, or at least in their community. An appropriate term for these social and cultural aspects of religion is *moral order*.[41]

A moral order is always culturally constructed. It inheres in the meanings people give to their lives and to the behavior of others. These meanings are shaped by and expressed in language, not only the language of spoken and written words but also the language of gestures, bodily movement, and the arrangement of space. A moral order is more fluid than the idea of order may normally imply, for the meanings of which it is composed are subject to constant negotiation and redefinition. Yet the fluidity of it all is mapped onto an underlying stability. This is the stability that makes things seem not only familiar but right, as if violations were to be interpreted as deviations from social norms.

As moral order, religion is part of how people define themselves individually and in groups. Religion identifies the tradition or traditions from which they derive and serves as a point of personal reference. Religion also provides the narratives through which these identities are communicated and around which mental maps are constructed—narratives from a common stock of biblical stories or the more distinctive narratives of one's denomination, congregation, or spiritual biography. "Religious maps," the historian Robert Orsi writes, "constitute as they disclose to practitioners ways of being in the world, of approaching the invisible beings who along with family members and neighbors make up practitioners' relevant social worlds, and of coordinating an individual's own story with an embracing cultural narrative.[42] This is not to say that religion need be considered important by every single individual for it to serve as a moral order. Not having a religion or not being interested in religion is an identity just as much as having one or having an interest in one. The moral dimension of these identities lies in the fact that religion suggests responsibilities—toward the members of one's own group, toward other groups, and toward oneself—and the enactment of these responsibilities is part of what binds people together. We tell ourselves that *good* people behave in ways that reflect their understandings of moral responsibility. The definition of these responsibilities is, in turn, legitimated by beliefs about the sacred and by the routine practices through which these beliefs are expressed.

Diversity figures importantly in any sense of moral order with which religion is associated. Religious identity is always defined in relation to the *other*. The religious other usually includes a conception of transcendence or sacredness that is set apart from the immediate and the mundane (God as other than human, creator as other than creation, and so on). As we saw in chapter 1, the other is also composed of those who do not belong to one's religious community. The existence of these outsiders is implied in the very definition of community. Either one is part of the community or one is not. And if one is a member, then the existence of nonmembers implies certain responsibilities toward them, such as proselytizing them, curbing their influence, giving them assistance, perhaps learning from them, or at least respecting their rights.[43]

Religious diversity, therefore, raises questions about conceptions of the sacred and about the moral responsibilities that follow from these conceptions. These questions pertain to what people commonly refer to as spirituality. To many social observers, the spiritual aspects of religious diversity pale in comparison with the legal conundrums raised by questions about the rights of various religions to practice freely, and these spiritual aspects seem less important to the well-being of society than questions about ethnicity and diverse ethnic values—especially to writers in the Lockean tradition who believe that religion should, after all, be a matter of inner conviction.[44] Viewed, though, as moral order (for which Locke serves less usefully than Jean-Jacques Rousseau, Émile Durkheim, and Alexis de Tocqueville), religious commitments and identities are always interlaced with the broader practices that give people their sense of meaning and belonging. Diversity thus entails consideration, not only because of the theological questions it may raise, but also because of the moral responsibilities it implies.

The sociologist Peter Berger writes that "the coexistence and social interaction of people with very different beliefs, values and lifestyles . . . influences not so much *what* people believe as *how* they believe."[45] Noting the
high and seemingly constant levels of religious involvement in the United
States, he argues that religious diversity does not necessarily erode levels
of religious commitment. But diversity may result in more subtle changes
in how people think about and practice their faith. For instance, they may
become less sure of their beliefs, less open about sharing their beliefs with
others, and less eager to proselytize. They may downplay traditional doctrines and creeds, interpreting them in relativistic ways that privilege individualistic judgments and personal experience. *Or* they may become more
intransigent in defending their particular beliefs and practices.

Certainly the questions raised by the copresence of different religions
are theological. Theology implies belief and the effort to make sense of
belief. Historically, theology has been an important part of the human
quest for truth. Reflection about the nature of God could not only be
conducted within the bounds of reason, as Kant argued, but could also
contribute to the knowledge that reasonable people were supposed to have
in order to make informed decisions about right and wrong. At present,
though, the quest for truth is frequently subordinated to the accumulation
of information. We go to school to acquire information or to gain technical
certification more than to obtain wisdom. Learning focuses on cultivating
skills, whereas virtue supposedly comes along as a by-product or is simply
there already from early childhood.[46] Truth itself, insofar as it can be found,
is discovered experientially or presumed to exist in the specialized domains
of science, engineering, and perhaps philosophy.

As a society, therefore, we are ill-equipped to consider the differences
and similarities among competing religious traditions theologically. We
have no standards by which to judge whether one tradition is better than
another. Caught as we are in the cultural contexts that we know influence
our judgments, we may feel instinctively that our tradition is best but
realize that this is simply because it is familiar. As we do with difficult
scientific problems, we are content to leave questions about the comparisons among religions to scholarly specialists without taking the time to
make informed decisions about religion ourselves. For the broader society,
theological assumptions are played out in everyday social practices. The
cultural work through which notions of religious identity are expressed

happens in the breach. We make up stories about our religious identities and their relation to other religions without paying much attention to theologians.

Where theology *is* emphasized is in the nation's seminaries and divinity schools, and it is here that we gain some understanding of the particular challenges that religious diversity raises for the leaders of organized religion. Seminaries have been supplementing traditional courses in Christian apologetics with opportunities to reflect on theology within a more thoroughly interreligious context. These new opportunities are encouraging students to rethink the premises of their own convictions. As Professor Timothy Park, who teaches in the School of World Mission at Fuller Seminary in Pasadena, California, explains, being more aware of the pluralistic context in which Christian ministry is taking place is becoming absolutely necessary. As far as theology is concerned, he believes, "We need to ask what is truly essential and what is not. We need to ask some hard questions and not be afraid to think differently. We need some 'paradigm shifts' in our faith." He is not arguing that Christians should abandon their belief in the authority of the Bible, but he does consider it necessary to recast theological arguments in terms of the present context. For instance, he says, "We need a theology of love that embraces differences and [we need to] stand for what we believe to be true."

Few in Christian seminaries would probably disagree. And yet questions remain about how best to structure such opportunities for innovative theological reflection. At the Jesuit School of Theology in Berkeley, California, for instance, Father Thomas Buckley describes a variety of ways in which theological education is being "contextualized" through participation in inner-city ministries, dialogue among ethnic groups, and daily interaction between American-born students and a large number of international students. Most of this effort, though, results in greater awareness of the cultural diversity within Christianity. Little of it brings Christian students into direct contact with practitioners of other world religions in which they may be forced to think more deeply about Christian teachings in an interreligious context.

Besides theology, there are also important questions about how religious organizations should relate to the practitioners of other religions in their communities. Should religious leaders consider the leaders of other religious traditions competitors, like the heads of rival corporations, with whom frank, cooperative relationships are out of the question? Are other religions so alien, so focused on their own constituencies, that the most expedient strategy is simply to ignore them? Individual Americans are increasingly facing questions about what to do religiously in their personal lives, what to think, and how to relate to friends and family members with different religions. These questions are particularly pressing for the growing number of Americans who interact regularly with adherents of other religions through their jobs and in their neighborhoods, let alone for those who share dorm rooms, make friends with, date, or marry people from religious traditions radically different from their own.

Among the thorniest questions that religious diversity poses for all the major religious traditions is whether or not they can sustain their historic claims to being uniquely true or at least better than other traditions in relating people to the sacred. Much of the reason for believers taking an active part in particular denominations or congregations has been the conviction that God could be found best in one theological location rather than in another. Take away this conviction and people have to find other reasons to believe and belong. Such reasons can of course be found: that it makes sense, culturally and socially, to seek spirituality in the tradition in which one has been raised; that God has somehow ordained different paths for different people; or that there should be a kind of emotional "fit" between one's religion and one's feelings about that religion. Reasons of this kind may nevertheless strike some observers as evidence that theology truly does not matter, compared with pragmatic arguments that may in turn be shaped by the self-interestedness that prevails in American culture.

If America is, as some commentators believe, in a kind of spiritual twilight—where "all cats are gray"—then the most reasonable course of all may be for each individual to pick and choose. Exposure to many religions is thus desirable because it enhances one's options. But if this style of highly personalized spirituality is to become the norm, on what grounds is it to be defended rationally and theologically, and are religious leaders going to embrace it or try to demonstrate its inadequacy?

The Reverend Sarah Motley, a chaplain at the University of California, Davis, expresses a view common to many religious leaders currently working with younger Americans. She says there is a long history on her campus of Christian and Jewish students rubbing shoulders with Muslim and Hindu students because the university has actively recruited students from abroad for many years. She sees little evidence of conflict among religious groups or of disagreements among students from the various traditions. Campus religious groups like hers participate in interfaith programs aimed at broadening students' horizons as well. Yet she finds little evidence that students are interested in theology or in the kinds of questions about God, faith, and the religious life with which theology has been concerned. Their approach to spirituality is too personal to be concerned with the larger questions that have animated religious discussions over the centuries. Students are more inclined to believe that all religions are true and, for this reason, take the position that whatever one happens to believe is right.

Reverend Motley thinks this personalized approach to spirituality is problematic. If all religions are true, she says, then it is easy to assume that "on Sunday you can be a Christian, on Monday you can be a Hindu, and on Tuesday you can be a Muslim, and it's all okay." She continues, "I think most religious leaders would say you're not going to plumb the depths of a way to God or receive the benefits of a community or a discipline unless you make a commitment to one." She isn't sure this is a position that has to be defended theologically; it just makes common sense. "The way you're going to discover anything is to commit yourself to something."

This comment suggests that campus ministries have a tall order to fill if they are to persuade young people to think more seriously about religious issues. Nathan Humphrey, reflecting on having taught religion at the middle-school level in a private academy in Washington, D.C., agrees. He says today's adolescents display extraordinary creativity in finding their own solutions to questions of religious diversity. "I'll hear my students, for instance, say that there are four different heavens, one for Muslims, one for Hindus, one for Jews, and one for Christians. Or that there's one God, but God is different for each of them. There's an attempt to kind of square the circle." He thinks young people face much more serious theological questions today as a result of religious diversity than was true of previous generations. "Within a predominantly Christian culture, it was easier simply to think of the great unwashed who were un-Christian and since they were out of sight and out of mind, one could theologically consign them to hell." In contrast, having direct encounters with people from other religions makes that approach more difficult. "You meet Muslim and Jewish people who clearly, at least from all outward appearances, have as strong a relationship with God as a Christian." What is needed, he believes, is an awareness that "Christendom is dead"—meaning that we no longer live in a society where Christianity can be taken for granted as the established religion—and "that's not a bad thing because it challenges us to be even more authentic and to find more authentic expressions of our faith."[47]

Besides the theological issues, religious diversity and the accompanying tendency toward eclecticism also raise difficult ethical issues. Religion has always been thought of as a source of ethical guidance, influencing how people think and behave in matters of personal morality, integrity, and service, as well as broader issues such as peace and justice. This was the view not only of religious leaders themselves, but of social thinkers such as Max Weber, Emile Durkheim, Jane Addams, W.E.B. DuBois, Robert Park, Ruth Benedict, and Margaret Mead. Research among American Christians suggests that religious involvement often does influence how people think and behave, although the same research suggests that people are guided by self-interest, expedience, and relativistic perspectives. When people start taking their cues from several different religious traditions, the ethical influences of any of these traditions may decline. People can pick and choose religious practices that help them do whatever they want but that do not challenge them to behave according to high ethical standards.

A woman who lives in an upscale neighborhood in the San Francisco Bay Area says, only half in jest, that most of her neighbors are nominally Christian but seem to find Buddhist practices much more interesting than traditional Christian teachings. Buddhist meditation, she says, has been helpful for many of the women she knows. Yet when she listens to conversations at the hairdresser's, she wonders if these women have thought much about the moral and ethical implications of Buddhism. Some of them say they admire what the Dalai Lama is doing in Tibet and around the world to promote peace, yet they seem not to have considered how Buddhism could make their marriages work better, let alone how it might challenge them to spend more time helping the poor.

Many Americans seem to hold views that confirm this woman's impressions. Religion, people argue, is generally a good thing, not just because it gives comfort and reassurance, but because it upholds moral and ethical standards, such as loving your neighbor and being kind to the needy. Yet they often do not take any religious practices seriously enough to be able to explain why religion has these ethical implications. When they think about different religious traditions, they assume that all religions pretty much uphold the same ethical ideals. And when they emphasize these good implications of religion, they seldom think much about the negative behavior that might result from religion.

Another challenge is emphasized by the Reverend Mark Edington, chaplain to Harvard College, who thinks the biggest implication of increasing religious diversity will be a sharpened divide between those who think religion is important and those who think it is not. Public leaders over the past fifty years, he feels, have come to believe that religions are so fractious that the better part of wisdom is to ignore them in making major decisions about the direction and governance of our nation. But new immigrant groups composed of Muslims, Hindus, Buddhists, and various kinds of Christians will, in his view, resist this secularizing assumption. To these groups, religion has been important in their countries of origin and will remain so in the United States.

Mark Staver is president and general counsel of Liberty Counsel, an Orlando-based civil liberties education and legal defense organization that deals routinely with cases involving religion. He agrees with Edington. Liberty Counsel has brought suit in a number of instances against school districts and public libraries that denied religious groups access to meeting rooms open to other groups. He understands community leaders' reluctance to deal with religious groups because there are so many with such diverse practices. Yet he argues that leaders "will have to become educated about the role that religion can play and should play."

If Edington and Staver are right, diverse religious groups may band together despite their differences in hopes that preserving any religion is better than living in a world devoid of religion. Staver says he would like to see "religious leaders build a coalition of religious communities capitalizing on their strengths to ultimately benefit their community" rather than "simply focus within their own world." Still, this scenario raises more questions than it answers: Will fundamentalist Baptists join with orthodox Jews and conservative Muslims? Will they do so without regard for the very serious historical and theological differences dividing them? And what of religious people with moderate or progressive inclinations? Will they simply concede to growing secularization or will there be renewed vitality in their ranks—vitality that may depend on closer examination of the distinctive claims of their particular traditions?

For a minority of Americans, the greatest spiritual challenge posed by religious diversity is how to stand up against what they view as false teachings. A woman in Illinois says, "It just scares me to death that there's other religions out there and that they too will be there for people. People may not recognize what I would call the true religion or the Word of God. It really scares me because I think that the devil is very strong out there and he's obviously out to keep as many people as he can away from discovering and learning about the Bible." For people like this, religious diversity requires vigilance, but also a stronger commitment to upholding and sharing what one understands to be spiritual truth—a prospect that worries other believers who think a live-and-let-live attitude is more appropriate.

The antidote to Christian exclusivism may be a more inclusive interpretation of religious truths. Yet leaders who interact regularly with diverse religious groups are reluctant to argue that the price for getting along must be compromise for believers who hold exclusivist views. Robert Boston of Americans United for Separation of Church and State thinks compromise of this kind diminishes the very freedom of religious expression that Americans have always cherished. "There are some faith traditions in the United States where that particular point of view is a very important part of their belief system. It may offend or shock some, but it's something that has historically been embraced by different religious organizations, Christian and non, and I would not want for them to have to dilute that part of their message at all."

Nathan Lewin's affiliation with an Orthodox Jewish synagogue has made him keenly aware of Christian groups that hold exclusivist religious views and attempt to proselytize Jews from that perspective. Yet he does not believe such groups need to give up their convictions in order to live in a religiously diverse society. "I am prepared to accept that most religions would say ours is the true way and yours is not," he says. "The question is what you do as a consequence of that. [If] people are murdered as a result of that view, that's clearly unacceptable and ought to be condemned. But you can say, 'Look, mine is the correct view but I don't believe that I've got to force it on everybody else. I'm not going to behave badly toward somebody else because they don't share that view.' That's perfectly all right."

Striving for that balance is difficult. It requires both clarity about one's religious convictions and willingness to draw the line between conviction and intolerance. Neither is likely to happen unless people spend time thinking about their spiritual orientations and how they fit in a diverse world. Without such thought, the easiest course is probably to act as if religious convictions fall within the same domain as political opinions—matters of personal choice that can perhaps be defended in terms of self-interest but may not have deeper roots in anything other than personal background and ideology.

It is not surprising that spirituality has come to be defined by many Americans as a matter of individual opinion, not mattering in public life and certainly not worth fighting over as long as each individual can believe what he or she wishes. So defined, spirituality seems to let people off the hook as far as having to worry about religious diversity is concerned. In this view, it makes little difference whether there are three, 300, or 300 million different approaches to spirituality. Formal debates about religion can be carried on endlessly by theologians and religious leaders, but in this perspective they matter little because social institutions are governed by different rules. Legal language and civic norms are what really count.

But this view is too easy, as the Ohio motto case, like many others, reveals. In the Ohio decision, the court found it necessary to include in its opinion definitions of Christianity and salvation and a brief account of who Jesus was. It relied on theologians to interpret the biblical passage and called on expert witnesses who testified that clergy, the average college student, and the American public would or would not know the origin of "With God all things are possible." It made claims about the appropriateness or inappropriateness of trying to separate a biblical statement from the religious tradition in which it originated. It took at face value the belief that Jesus was a historical figure who actually uttered the words attributed to him. And it offered opinions about the similarities and dissimilarities among teachings in several of the world's religions.

America's religious traditions often fall short of the ideals they claim to uphold, leaving only a superficial impression on the lives of their adherents. But when these traditions function best, they raise fundamental questions about values and morality, about personal ethics and societal goals. Religious pluralism involves more than the mere coexistence of multiple traditions. At the very minimum, it requires engagement across traditions.

And such engagement necessarily challenges preconceived ideas about beliefs and values.

Daniel Callahan of the Hastings Center suggests that true religious and cultural pluralism would encourage the various groups "to comment on and criticize each other and where necessary to attempt to change by persuasion each other's values when they seem harmful or mistaken." Pluralism of this kind moves beyond wishy-washy acceptance. "All cultures deserve our presumptive respect, but none can claim a moral exemption from scrutiny and evaluation. A serious pluralism should make that acceptable."[48]

If religious and cultural pluralism is taken seriously, it will influence how we think and behave individually. It will also affect our understanding of who we are as a nation. Critical comparisons and efforts to persuade can only happen within the context of discussions about broader principles. In the past, our sense of the destiny we share and the fundamental values we stand for have always been expressed in relation to those we deemed to be different from ourselves. It is not less true today.

Embracing Diversity: Shopping
in the Spiritual Marketplace

A COMMON WAY of thinking about America's religious diversity holds that there are Protestants here and Jews there, Catholics here and Hindus there, Mormons in one place and Muslims in another. Although this view of diversity follows naturally from the geographic patterning that characterized immigration a century ago, it fails to do justice to the complexity of religious life in the United States today. Americans can easily pick up a book about Hinduism one day, see a therapist who teaches them a form of Buddhist meditation another day, talk with a Muslim friend at work the same day, and still attend religious services at a church or synagogue that weekend. Of course some Americans have had more opportunities to do this than others, and some have eagerly embraced the chance to innovate while others have refrained. A place to begin looking, if we are to understand how Americans are responding to the new religious diversity of recent years, therefore, is among those who have been most open to absorbing this diversity into their own beliefs and practices.

The sociologist Robert Bellah provides a convenient description of the internal diversity that has come to typify so many Americans. "We are not fully integrated centers of reflection astonished by the discovery that there are others who see the world differently from ourselves," he writes. "We understand the pluralism of our social context in part because it reflects the variety of ways in which we understand our own experiences." We understand it and yet experience a tension between the scattered loyalties we hold as individuals and the more monolithic identities still assumed within most religious communities. Of Christians, Bellah writes, "The problem of being the church is acute for us not only because we must live side by side with those of other religious communities, but because the church is only one of the communities in which we live. Pluralism is within us as well as without us."[1]

The experience and embrace of multiple communities and beliefs is one of the hallmarks of modern civilization, separating the last several centuries from all that preceded them. Yet there has also been a more recent shift in how Americans think about religious diversity. The tripartite settlement of the mid-twentieth century that permitted most Americans to think of themselves as Christians, reserving a small space in their worldview where Jews could be accommodated, was dramatically rewritten during the 1970s. A new understanding came into being that provided many Americans with ways of accommodating a much wider array of religious diversity. The path to this new understanding was charted by younger Americans who enthusiastically experimented with religious teachings and practices outside the Christian tradition. Some of these younger Americans became converts to what for lack of a better term was referred to as non-Western religions (such as Zen Buddhism, Hare Krishna, and Transcendental Meditation), a designation that classified them less as theological upstarts and more as cultural transplants.[2] The main result of this experimentation, however, was not a post-Christian society, as some observers predicted, in which Christians and non-Christians would have to share the cultural space once reserved for Christianity, but a new outlook on what it meant to be a Christian—or at least a religious—person.[3]

The new approach to religious diversity that emerged during the last quarter of the twentieth century is what we might appropriately term spiritual shopping.[4] The idea of shopping reflects the fact that American religion is shaped by the consumer culture to which all Americans are exposed from early childhood. Shopping connotes making choices and having the freedom to choose according to one's personal tastes and needs. Because many Americans fill up their leisure time with shopping and acknowledge that they shop for pleasure, shopping often conveys a casual, light-hearted approach that strikes some observers as repugnant in the context of spirituality and religion.[5] Shopping can nevertheless be an endeavor that people take quite seriously as well (consider purchasing a new home, for example). Whether casual or more serious, spiritual shopping has become one way of approaching religious diversity. Shopping involves trying out new things, considering whether or not they fit one's lifestyle, and piecing together beliefs and practices from a variety of traditions.[6] The language and experiences of consumption give spiritual shopping legitimacy. Yet the idea that one's religion can be a pastiche of different traditions deviates markedly from adhering to a single tradition. Fabricating a religion of one's own necessitates making sense of what one is doing and why.

Shopping is one of several ways in which the public accommodates religious diversity. It is not the most common response, but in the opinion of many observers it is a kind of bellwether that signals how a growing number of people may think about religious diversity in the future.[7] It is important, therefore, to consider what it means to shop, why some people engage in spiritual shopping and others do not, and what the mentality of spiritual shopping reveals about religious diversity in our society. It will be helpful to start with an example that illustrates the main characteristics of spiritual shopping.

Trev Granger's Story

Trev Granger is an insurance salesman for one of the nation's largest suppliers of automobile, homeowners, and life insurance. A neatly dressed, gray-haired man in his late fifties, he earns a respectable living that covers the expenses he and his wife incur in putting their two daughters through college and maintaining their ranch-style home in suburban Saint Louis. Mr. Granger is intensely interested in spirituality, although he and his wife attend services at a nondenominational church in their neighborhood only several times a year. His interest in spirituality is a lifelong odyssey that has exposed him to a wide variety of religious traditions and practices.

As a child, Trev received virtually no formal religious training. His father was Jewish and his mother Catholic, so they compromised by not taking Trev and his brother to religious services at all. Still, Mr. Granger remembers somehow knowing about God and being convinced of God's existence when he was quite young. During college he read several books about spirituality and meditation, but found it difficult to make sense of them. None of his friends talked about God; they were more interested in dating, going to movies, and figuring out what to do when they graduated. All that changed several years after college when Mr. Granger started dating a young woman who considered herself a born-again Christian. For the first time, he heard evangelical interpretations of the life of Jesus and started thinking seriously about his own relationship to God. Mr. Granger's journey, however, did not result in his becoming a Christian and settling into a Bible-believing church. Neither he nor his girlfriend stayed with Christianity more than a few months. The year was 1968 and, like many of their friends, their lives were profoundly altered by the Vietnam war.

For the next five years, Mr. Granger lived in Canada (he is vague about whether or not he moved there to escape the draft). Earning a living as a semi-skilled worker in construction and logging, he traveled extensively, often sleeping in his van. During his travels he met people like himself who were disillusioned with the war and searching for ways, as they said, to lead an authentic existence. Some of his friends experimented with marijuana and psychedelic drugs and many were interested in spirituality. He avidly consumed works such as the *Tibetan Book of the Dead*, the Upanishads, and every book he could find about Zen Buddhism.

After leaving Canada, Mr. Granger spent several more years on the road, living mostly in Washington, Oregon, California, and Hawaii. By this time, he was a serious spiritual seeker. Still reading, he now practiced meditation every day and on several occasions joined groups of people who were engaged in various non-Western religions. He spent several months at the Zen Center in San Francisco, a summer at the Rajneesh spiritual community in rural Oregon, and many weekends at retreat centers where he learned about Gestalt therapy, kundalini yoga, Aikido, and other spiritual practices.[8] Much of what he experienced is now a blur in his memory, but he recalls teachers and friends along the way who guided him toward new books, new practices, and places to travel: a hitchhiker in western Canada who challenged him to think more seriously about spirituality, a Zen master in Hawaii who dissuaded him from becoming a Zen Buddhist, a Catholic priest in Texas who taught him to pray, and a girlfriend who gave him a copy of the *I Ching*. All played significant supporting roles in his journey to discover the sacred. Eventually, feeling that he was getting to the point where it might be hard to resume a normal lifestyle, he decided it was time to settle down, returned to his boyhood community in Saint Louis, got married, and learned how to sell insurance.

Mr. Granger's story is that of the stereotypical hippie who became alienated from conventional society and pursued a countercultural lifestyle that included experimenting with alternative religions—a familiar story during the 1970s and 1980s. Yet it raises important questions about the ways in which Americans respond to religious diversity. Why do some people respond so enthusiastically to religious diversity, especially that which is outside the traditions of Christianity and Judaism? Why do they embrace a variety of traditions rather than settling into one? How deep or lasting is their encounter with other religious traditions? And, perhaps most important, what does this response to diversity tell us about the ways in which ordinary Americans (those who may not have experienced a bohemian lifestyle like Mr. Granger's) think about religion and spirituality?

Becoming a Spiritual Shopper

In surveys and in personal interviews, most Americans identify themselves as adherents of some Christian denomination or tradition and most claim that they feel most comfortable seeking God through the distinctive beliefs and practices of Christianity. Although there is ample room within the Christian tradition itself to go shopping (to find a particular church to one's liking, for example), few Christians make extensive forays into the beliefs and practices of other world religions. Thus, the spiritual shopper (such as Trev Granger) who seems to be open, even eager, to embrace a wide variety of religions requires some explanation.

Spiritual shopping among a wide variety of religions presupposes exposure to religions other than the faith of one's upbringing. Compared with most people, spiritual shoppers have generally had opportunities to meet practitioners of other religions and to learn about other religious traditions. In Mr. Granger's case, this exposure came during his twenties and early thirties, when he was traveling extensively. Although he was consciously seeking spiritual guidance at this stage in his life, many of his encounters with other religions came through chance meetings with strangers (such as hitchhikers, coworkers, and religious leaders) who happened to tell him about books they had read or retreat centers they had attended. In other cases, exposure comes from growing up in a diverse community where friends and classmates belong to religions other than one's own, from taking courses in college, or from traveling abroad.

A woman who grew up in New York says that she was attuned to other religions from an early age because her best friend was Jewish. A young man from Portland remembers that the youth group at his Methodist church made the rounds one year, visiting local synagogues, mosques, and temples, as well as churches. A woman in Pennsylvania attributes her life-long interest in other religions to a comparative religions course she took in college. A man in Virginia says he was exposed to non-Western religions shortly after college when he traveled extensively in the Middle East and South Asia.

The contact with other religions that characterizes spiritual shopping, although extensive compared to what most people experience, is nevertheless fairly limited in several important respects. Among all who might consider themselves spiritual shoppers, relatively few actually *convert* to one of the other major religious traditions, such as Judaism or Islam. A friend of Mr. Granger's who became so interested in Sufism that he spent several years studying Arabic and eventually converted is an exception. More typical is a woman who described herself as a Methodist Jew, meaning that she was interested in Judaism and had attended some services at a synagogue but, as her Jewish friends said, she was hardly a convert to Judaism. Even those who spend a few weeks learning Zen meditation or traveling in India seldom have sustained exposure to the kinds of non-Western religious communities that characterize many new immigrants. The very idea of shopping (but also of seeking for its own sake) runs counter to settling into another religious tradition long enough to gain a full understanding of it.

A woman, now in her late thirties and still looking for a form of spirituality that suits her, illustrates this point in describing a time in her early twenties when she considered becoming a Hare Krishna. "One of the women took me in the back room and dressed me in a sari, and it was an amazing experience for me. But there was something I could not do, and I think it had to do with commitment. I think I was just afraid of the commitment that it would take."

The religious communities to which spiritual shoppers are exposed limit the likelihood of shoppers becoming converts. These communities make it easy to pick up a spiritual technique here and an insight about the sacred there, rather than commanding loyalty to only one tradition. They differ sharply from the ethnic enclaves in which immigrant religions are embedded. Mr. Granger's experiences are typical in this regard; he had learned a little about Zen Buddhism and had read some Vedic writings, but he had virtually no exposure to other Buddhist traditions or to Islam or Hinduism.

All shopping is brokered, monitored, structured by a network of suppliers who carefully tailor their products for the marketplace—in a word, it is *managed*—and spiritual shopping is no different. The books that Mr. Granger read were readily available in English at American bookstores. Some were English translations of religious texts, others were written by authors (such as D. T. Suzuki and Alan Watts) who distilled the teachings of non-Western religions for a Western audience. The retreat centers and religious communities he visited were established by spiritual entrepreneurs who earned their living selling courses, books, and lectures to spiritual seekers. These courses, books, and lectures mostly emphasized practices that one could learn in a relatively short period of time, although they also included hints at more advanced practices that could be learned if one wanted to be a long-term customer. Practices such as techniques for breathing and meditating are well suited for a consumer market. They can be packaged in ways that beginners can understand and experience. Few of the so-called new religions emphasized weighty philosophical or theological systems that believers had to accept in order to gain some kind of salvation. Most offered simplified teachings and practical advice for daily living; and they were often, as the idea of new religions implied, Americanized versions of non-Western religions that would hardly have been recognized by practitioners of more traditional religions in other parts of the world. Part of what it meant to be an Americanized religion, moreover, was the idea that diversity itself was of value. One woman talks about attending meetings at an organization called "Network of Light," which presented a blend of spiritual paths lightly held together by teachings about the therapeutic virtues of spiritual experience; another remembers going to a shop in her neighborhood that specialized in spiritual potions and healing techniques; it was like a cafeteria, she says.

The religious diversity to which spiritual shoppers in the 1970s and 1980s were exposed was thus a particular kind of diversity—one that usually did not require shoppers to explicitly repudiate Christianity or to buy into one alternative religious tradition exclusively. Few Americans actually became converts to Islam, Buddhism, Hinduism, or Judaism; instead, they learned yoga or Transcendental Meditation as a kind of relaxation technique, practiced Zen meditation in much the same way that other people prayed, or spent free time reading the Upanishads as others read science fiction.[9] The results of this exposure were sometimes profound; like Mr. Granger, thousands of Americans embarked on spiritual quests that led to deeper thoughts about spirituality and more compelling experiences of the sacred than they ever imagined possible. And yet, their encounters were quite different from those of someone who actually lived in another country for an extended period of time or gained extensive understanding of other religious traditions by becoming part of a new immigrant community.

The encounters with religious diversity that people like Mr. Granger experienced in the early 1970s were still relatively amorphous compared with the ways in which spiritual shoppers could experience religious diversity a few years later, but these early encounters were by no means without precedent. From the Transcendentalists and practitioners of the occult in the 1830s and 1840s to the spiritualists during the latter half of the nineteenth century, and from alternative healing practices to psychics and astrologers, not to mention the occasional poet or artist who popularized non-Western religions, the spiritual shoppers of the 1970s could find role models and sources of inspiration if they were needed.[10] In subsequent years, religious diversity could be experienced even more easily, as college courses and popular books provided surveys of old and new religious practices and as holistic health centers, organic food stores, and New Age bookstores became more common.

Rachel Daniels was too young during the 1960s and early 1970s to experience any of the religious experimentation that become such a factor in Mr. Granger's life. An elementary school teacher who lives in Virginia, she illustrates the ways in which the religious diversity that had emerged in the earlier period was sustained, transmitted, and indeed transformed by the late 1970s and 1980s to fit more compatibly with the norms of the marketplace. Her exposure to non-Christian religions began in her late teens. She was searching for ways to express her interest in spirituality after having become dissatisfied with the teachings and practices of the Catholic church she had been attending. The first several years of her explorations, while still in high school, were spent largely in books. Like Mr. Granger, she read avidly about various religions and spiritual practices, but it was easier for her to find books than it was for him: even in the small town where she lived, bookstores stocked shelves of volumes about Taoism, Native American spirituality, Buddhism, Hinduism, and the occult, and the other students at her high school were reading and talking about these books. Then in her early twenties (now living in Washington, D.C.) she started attending meetings for spiritual seekers. Some were sponsored by religious movements that had emerged a decade earlier (such as Scientology and Hare Krishna); others were held at New Age bookstores and holistic health clinics.

Whereas the earlier experimenters were often driven by political alienation or participation in the drug culture of the 1970s, those of Ms. Daniels's generation were more often able to shop for spirituality without experiencing a radical break from the conventional culture. Participating casually in diverse religious traditions had become normalized much in the same way that purchasing herbal remedies and eating at sushi bars was. A Methodist woman who went to college in the 1980s remembers her dormitory as a kind of religious bazaar where hallways were lined with students dabbling in every conceivable spiritual practice. A woman about the same age recalls going to Barnes & Noble, where shelf upon shelf was stocked with books about metaphysics and the occult. Another woman, who now combines Sufism, Native American spirituality, kundalini yoga, goddess worship, and Christianity, says her spiritual awakening began by taking a class in Sufi dancing at a local recreation center. A man who was already in his thirties in the 1980s says his massage therapist introduced him to Native American spirituality. A younger man went to Grateful Dead concerts where hawkers of spiritual practices set up shop in parking lots.

Why some people become spiritual shoppers more readily than others is partly a function of how they were raised. The religious orientations of shoppers' parents are sufficiently diverse to defy easy generalizations: some parents (like Mr. Granger's) displayed virtually no interest in religion while their children were young, while others (like Ms. Daniels's) included either a mother or father (usually a mother) who went regularly to religious services and was quite serious about her or his faith. Nevertheless, most shoppers appear to have been reared by parents who were relatively open-minded about religious diversity and were tolerant of and friendly toward people of different religious convictions, rather than being dogmatically or rigidly committed to Christianity. A woman who says she wanted to be a nun as a child and then started experimenting with mysticism in high school remembers that none of her four parents and step parents were particularly interested in religion themselves but they encouraged her to pursue whatever interested her, including religion. A man in his early fifties who has pursued many different religions as an adult says his "eclecticism" may have been sparked by his father, a devout Catholic who also practiced yoga.

Paradoxically, spiritual shoppers who were raised religiously often report that it was the exclusionary teachings of their childhood churches that led them (or their parents) to adopt an open-minded view of religious truth. For instance, Jan Hobart, a man in his forties who was raised by a Catholic father and a Lutheran mother (and now dabbles in a variety of religions because "Spirit" is in all of them), says he came early to the conclusion that God was somehow above all religions because both the Catholics and the Lutherans claimed God exclusively for themselves and yet it was clearly impossible for both claims to be true. He thinks this realization came less from what either of his parents said than from the fact that he loved both and refused to think that either's religion was better than the other's.

Whether their parents encouraged them or simply ignored what they did, spiritual shoppers generally developed an interest in experimenting with new ideas, experiences, and even lifestyles at some point before they reached adulthood. For the generation that came of age in the early 1970s, the counterculture encouraged a wide variety of experimentation: communes, sex, political movements, drugs, music. Once the counterculture cooled, young people still had ample opportunities to experiment, and some took full advantage of these opportunities. In their own ways, they tested the edges of respectable, conventional social norms and in the process discovered that they could make up their own minds about who they were and what to believe. Sometimes food became the avenue for self-expression. For instance, one woman recounts going through a half dozen popular diets, each of which emphasized a different group; eventually she followed a macrobiotic diet until she nearly starved herself to death. Drugs and alcohol are another common form of experimentation, sometimes encouraging people to dabble in spiritual techniques promising the same sorts of emotional "high."

Experimentation with new spiritual ideas and practices tends to be reinforced by the social contexts in which spiritual shoppers find themselves. College campuses are one of the most influential of these contexts. Virtually everything about campuses is geared toward shopping: from the colorful brochures and professional marketing appeals that seek to lure students to one campus instead of another, to the "activities fair" that greets incoming students, to the smorgasbord of majors from which students are expected to choose, to the unofficial guides that tell students what the really popular courses are. Many spiritual shoppers say they learned that all religions are essentially the same (and thus the value of piecing together their own eclectic spirituality) by taking courses in comparative religions or by participating in campus ministries that included a wide range of religious traditions. Travel is also an important factor in spiritual shopping, but not all kinds of travel encourage it. Being a tourist—someone who visits short-term with an expectation of being stimulated or entertained—is the most conducive form of travel because it produces exposure to religious sites without requiring much in terms of investment or commitment.[11] One man, whose family had toured extensively when he was in high school, offered a good summary of how this kind of travel can change one's attitudes: "You lose the 'us, them' consciousness. You immediately know that people are people everywhere. It really opens you up."

Going to college, traveling abroad, and finding other ways in which to experiment with new lifestyles takes financial resources, and thus it is not surprising that spiritual shoppers tend to come from middle- and upper-middle-class backgrounds rather than from working-class families.[12] Wealth gave some the opportunity to spend a significant amount of time reading religious books or participating in workshops and retreats, the entry fees for which were often steep. But wealth itself was often less important than the personal confidence associated with having been reared in economically secure circumstances. Mr. Granger lived a hand-to-mouth existence for nearly a decade, yet he was a college graduate with family connections who knew that he could easily settle at some point into a middle-class existence. A woman about his age lived in a teepee one winter, nearly freezing at times, but she also knew that friends or relatives would come to her assistance if she needed them.

Despite a reasonably comfortable level of economic security, personal trauma nevertheless plays an important role in the lives of many spiritual shoppers. Usually the trauma consists of an event in one's close social relationships or in one's self understanding that makes it impossible either to live without spirituality or to find spiritual fulfillment through such purely conventional means as attending religious services. A divorced mother in her early twenties who had felt alienated from her father as a child remembers becoming so angry with men that she could no longer believe in the masculine images of God presented at her church; she began at that point shopping for alternatives and quickly discovered a whole new way of thinking about spirituality from reading Merlin Stone's *When God Was a Woman*. A woman in her thirties says that she nearly had a nervous breakdown in her early twenties, recovered as a result of acupuncture, and then embarked on an exploration of Eastern religions to make sense of the relationship between spirituality and healing. Another woman says a close friend committing suicide was what set her to thinking about spirituality. Painful experiences, such as divorce, having an alcoholic or abusive parent, or being in a serious accident, do not in themselves necessitate a spiritual quest, but for people who are already open to new experiences and ideas, the logical way of dealing with trauma is to search for teachings and practices that generate new insights, healing, and greater self-understanding.

If personal trauma encourages spiritual seeking, the seeking that results is usually reinforced by someone who serves as a guide or at least uses his or her authority to legitimate the process of seeking. One kind of guide is the religious leader, author, or personal friend who says, in effect, that he or she has found the answers to life's questions and can impart those answers to any who are willing to listen. Such guides encourage temporary spiritual shopping insofar as a break with one's past may be required, but they ultimately want converts and commitment. The guide who encourages spiritual shopping more explicitly and over the long term is different. This kind of guide offers partial solutions, such as a particular idea or practice, that can be combined with other religious commitments or specifically encourages people to explore a variety of spiritual practices in hopes of arriving at some combination that is personally satisfying. Most spiritual shoppers mention at least several guides who became instrumental at particular points in their lives, providing them with a new insight that helped them overcome a specific problem but that did not require a permanent commitment.

Somewhere along the way, many spiritual shoppers have a significant encounter with the church. They become involved in a local congregation or perhaps in a youth group, prayer fellowship, or Bible study group. Almost like an oasis in the desert, the community of believers provides them with security, answers, and emotional support. For Ms. Daniels, the church became especially meaningful after she fled her parents' home at age fourteen. For two and a half years, she lived with an older sister who was a devout Catholic. Ms. Daniels went regularly to mass and confession, finding the regularity of the rituals and the clarity of the teachings a welcome relief from the confusion she had known all her life. "Everything was really laid out very clearly. There were clear rituals to follow. Boxes, little boxes. You knew exactly what you were supposed to do, what you were not supposed to do. It was very well defined, and at that point in my life, I was just happy to make it through the day."

But the church usually proves to be a temporary stop instead of a permanent spiritual home. Having learned early to be self-reliant, many spiritual shoppers find it difficult to accept the authority with which church teachings and practices are communicated. This uneasiness is aggravated when personal trauma results, as it did for Ms. Daniels, in identifying with a religious community that emphasizes clear, absolute rules. Although such rules may be temporarily comforting, they contrast sharply with the more permissive values with which many spiritual shoppers have been raised. Ms. Daniels remembers leaving the church when she was seventeen. Moving from her sister's to a group home run by a community organization gave her the opportunity to quit attending church services. But she thinks she would have left the church anyway. Its rules were too restrictive; it emphasized guilt, which ran counter to what she was learning in therapy about the sources of her father's abusive behavior; and it taught that God was "over there," as she puts it, instead of nearby as she had believed since childhood.

More generally, the role of the church varies, ranging from providing negative experiences that encourage rebellion to serving as the place where spiritual shopping is actively encouraged. The reasons for rebelling are many, ranging from feeling that the clergy were unable to provide satisfactory answers to one's youthful questions about God, to being treated harshly at a parochial school, to running afoul of church teachings about premarital sex, homosexuality, or divorce. People reconstruct these incidents, often later in life, to explain why they became alienated from the church. But usually the accounts people give have less to do with theology than with human relationships. One woman became disillusioned when her Sunday school teacher was discovered having an affair; a man in his fifties is still struggling to make sense of having been sexually molested by a priest; another man remembers the Baptist pastor of his childhood church haranguing his parents about going to movies. Thus, it is common for spiritual shoppers to have retained some belief in God and some conviction about spirituality even though they reject the idea of any particular religious organization having a monopoly on the truth.

It is easy to understand why someone who has had a falling out with the church might start experimenting with other traditions; harder (or at least more interesting) to know how churches might intentionally encourage spiritual shopping. Yet this is what many spiritual shoppers report. For example, one man recalls being sent by his parents to a Catholic high school run by Jesuits who, he discovered, "were very liberal in their thinking and open to other kinds of values." This was where he started to learn about Buddhism. A woman who now describes herself as a Buddhist Quaker Catholic had a similar experience: during high school, her priest encouraged her to explore the Quaker tradition and from there she moved to yoga, psychotherapy, and Buddhism.

The irony about spiritual shopping is that relatively few spiritual shoppers perceive themselves to be consumers influenced by marketing, advertising, or the attractions of the marketplace; indeed, most feel just the opposite, regarding themselves as purists in search of deeper values than those supplied by commercialism and materialism. Spiritual shoppers are nevertheless products of the culture and social relationships that have been nurtured by the marketplace. Their commitments are relatively short term, they are open to new experiences, and they have enjoyed opportunities to move around, travel, and dabble with diverse lifestyles. Although their encounters with diverse religious traditions are often not as deep or extensive as might be imagined, spiritual shoppers illustrate a kind of mentality that provides a distinct way of managing religious diversity and is thus worth examining more closely.

The Shopping Mentality

Spiritual shoppers are nearly always convinced that God exists—a belief that separates them from people who do not take spirituality seriously at all—and most of them say they have always believed this, even if they were not reared by religious parents. To be sure, they often entertained doubts and questions about specific theological teachings about God but the presence of God in the world was, as Mr. Granger says, "as definite as that of the president of the United States." At the same time, spiritual shoppers are prone to emphasize the mysteriousness of God: denying that God can be fully understood or known through creeds and doctrines. God is instead a spiritual presence that is most tangibly revealed in moments of awe, ecstasy, and wonder. Thus, spiritual shopping generally is not a quest for a coherent set of beliefs but for experiences that serve as affirmations of the goodness and meaningfulness of life. When God is ultimately a mystery, it is easy to assume that all religions contain insights about God but no religion provides a complete understanding of God, and thus one way to increase one's understanding of God is by gleaning ideas from many different religious traditions.

The belief about God that is probably most conducive to spiritual shopping is the sense that God can be experienced directly. Perhaps because they are often raised without intensive exposure to religious teachings, spiritual shoppers do not conceive of God as some distant being who can be known only by holding certain beliefs or engaging in certain liturgical practices. God is simply present or, as Ms. Daniels says, remembering the phrase she used to say over and over to herself as a child while playing under the big oak tree in her backyard, "God is in everything." And if God is truly in everything, then God is in all religions (and in the spaces between religions), meaning that one can freely borrow from various traditions with confidence about being able to find God in one's own way.

Other than their belief that God (or something transcendent) exists and can be experienced directly, spiritual shoppers generally have little interest in the specific doctrines and teachings that have animated Christian leaders over the centuries—about the trinity, original sin, atonement, and the role of sacraments. Those who were raised without religious training had few opportunities to learn that these have been important questions throughout the history of Christianity; those with church backgrounds generally report that they became confused by the theological discussions to which they were exposed, concluded early in life that there were no authoritative answers to such questions, or simply participated in church services without thinking much about what was being taught.

Although they lacked interest in religious teachings while growing up, most spiritual shoppers have nevertheless been attracted by the life of Jesus and have thus had to reconcile the teachings of Jesus with their interests in religious diversity. One man says he could never quite figure out Jesus until he started attending classes at a spiritual guidance center that combines ideas from the various world religions with ideas from contemporary psychology; he now thinks of Jesus as his inner child. A woman whose journey has taken her far afield from her Presbyterian roots remarks, "I believe that Jesus, the Christ that is spoken of in the New Testament, really lived, and that he was a very special person. But just as I am a son of God, he is a son of God. We all are." She adds, "Jesus, I believe, was a very evolved soul. He had evolved to the point where he was able to not only understand but to use the energies which are available to all of us. I believe that energies are like television. If you don't have a television set, you can't do anything with the energies of television. The energies which Jesus used are available to all of us, but we're not evolved enough to know how to use them." A man from a mixed Roman Catholic and Presbyterian background who is married to a former Lutheran, attends a United Church of Christ congregation, and has experimented with Buddhism and Native American spirituality observes, "It may be that the message of what Jesus was preaching is a great message, but whether he was really God or not I don't know that I really care about that any more. It doesn't mean anything to me." Statements such as these reflect a variety of opinions about Jesus, but they also convey an understanding that does not preclude relating to God in ways that do not privilege the role of Jesus. Unlike the Augustinian view that has prevailed throughout most of the history of Christianity, Jesus is not understood as the key source of redemption in a metaphysical drama involving a perfect God and a fallen world. If Jesus is divine, he is so in a way that all people are divine, if only they realized it and if only they were able to draw on the divine power that is already theirs.

Shoppers' views of the Bible are similar to their views of Jesus. The Bible is important, one of many guides from which practical wisdom can be drawn; it is, however, neither particularly authoritative nor the first book to which they might turn to find spiritual guidance. Compared to inspirational books by contemporary writers or popularized versions of texts from other religions, the Bible seems staid, conventional, too strongly associated with Protestant fundamentalism and patriarchal images of God, and not sufficiently oriented toward meditation and religious experience to be an attractive source of spiritual insight. These views may reflect casual opinions that shoppers have picked up from friends or the mass media, but often they are grounded in personal experience. To a much greater extent than the person who expresses polite lack of interest in religion, spiritual shoppers go out of their way to participate in religious groups, to talk with religious people, and to read religious books. Thus, it is hardly surprising that they have often rubbed shoulders with people who take the Bible very seriously. Many spiritual shoppers, for instance, mention having had born-again roommates in college, attending fundamentalist churches with relatives, or being attracted to Bible study groups. Having learned to be open-minded and to patch together ideas from many different sources, spiritual shoppers often feel uncomfortable in these settings. Although they may be interested in reading and studying the Bible, they are put off by the idea, common in many of these settings, that there is one authoritative interpretation of the Bible. They are also likely to be repulsed by the group's insistence that *their* way of life goes hand in hand with believing in the Bible. The idea that the Bible should be viewed metaphorically rather than literally is thus more in keeping with the shopping mentality. A metaphorical interpretation presupposes that there is some truth in the Bible but the Bible does not fully disclose God's nature and intentions. Nor is the Bible the only or best way in which to gain an understanding of God, since God is in all things and capable of being known in some measure through personal experience and intuition. One woman expressed her understanding of the Bible this way: "I have read the Bible a lot of different ways and at a lot of different times in my life. I think that the way that really opens the gates for me is when I read the Bible metaphorically and not literally, that the Bible is kind of a code. It can be a great source for getting in touch with spirituality, rather than simply getting in touch with self-righteous belief systems." A man who in his twenties read the Bible every day for five years but who now spends more time reading Hermann Hesse, James Joyce, and Karen Armstrong offers a similar view of the Bible: "It describes people's experience of what God is or isn't. I don't necessarily think that everything in there is word for word what happened or anything, but it's more the experience of God that has been written down in that way."

Although it might be assumed from these examples that spiritual shoppers take a dim view of religious tradition, the attitude toward tradition that is more typical of spiritual shoppers is ambivalence. On the one hand, tradition connotes subservience to the way in which one was raised or conformity to how other people think and believe, instead of being willing to branch out and learn from new sources. As one woman explains, "I think that you limit yourself if you settle into one religion, because you're limited by what they tell you is the way to understand certain concepts." She does not identify with any religious tradition for this reason. "I feel all religions are equally good, and I think that it just depends on how your particular soul feels like responding. I just feel that religions hold you back. They give you very limited things that you can believe and act on." On the other hand, refusing to identify with one tradition is not the same thing as dabbling. To dabble connotes looking for "a quick fix," as one man put it, engaging enthusiastically in a spiritual quest for a few weeks or even months, but then turning to other pursuits. The same woman who considers tradition limiting, for instance, denies that she is a dabbler: "If I was a spiritual dabbler I would have given up on a lot of these things many, many years ago. I'm very serious about it. I'm intensely serious. I decided I wanted to know why I was here, and that's been a life-long goal. I want to search the truth of why things are happening and why I'm here."

Shoppers vary considerably in how much or how little they seek truth beyond the religious tradition in which they were raised. For many, the search takes them to new venues during early adulthood, after which they settle again in one tradition or another, whereas for others spiritual shopping is like serial monogamy: they take commitment very seriously for a few years and then move on to something else. But for most, tradition is more of a symbol than a reality. They may dislike the idea of religious tradition because it connotes old-fashioned thinking and subservience to clergy authority; yet in practice their explorations usually fall within one, loosely bounded tradition. It may not be a well-defined or centrally organized tradition, such as the Catholic church, but it may well be a blend of Christian or Jewish mysticism, Americanized Buddhism, popular psychology, and therapy, with a touch of Sufism, Hinduism, or the occult thrown in for good measure.

If they owe loyalty to any tradition, spiritual shoppers in the United States are most likely to be rooted in Christianity. Many of their views about God, Jesus, and the Bible suggest that these roots are not deep. But it should not be assumed that all shoppers' relationships with Christianity are superficial. Even though they have deliberately sought insight and inspiration from other traditions, many spiritual shoppers are centrally oriented to Christianity. They grew up feeling most at home with Christian holidays, church services, and biblical stories and they—perhaps almost intuitively and inescapably—frame their spiritual quest in terms of Christian language. One of the best examples of this kind of shopper is Marty Newsome, a woman in California who describes herself as a third-generation mixed religious person whose parents and grandparents were a "mishmash" of Protestants, Catholics, and Jews. She studied Hinduism and Buddhism in college, traveled widely, believes in karma, belongs to a psychosynthesis group, reads books by Deepak Chopra and Thomas More, attends services at a Friends meetinghouse, and participates in a local "spiritual awareness" movement. She believes that God loves and ultimately saves everyone and sees no reason why people of other religions should become Christians. Yet her own journey has been most profoundly influenced by her relationship with Jesus. As a child she was intrigued with Jesus and secretly wished Jesus would visit her in a dream or vision, but he never did. As a young adult, while she was gleaning ideas from other religions, she continued to be interested in Jesus. "I wanted to have a closer relationship with Jesus, because I still had a lot of questions about Jesus and his life and being crucified and a lot of things just didn't make sense to me." She remembers filling her daily journal with a kind of imaginary dialogue, asking Jesus questions (such as, "Why should I trust you?") and writing down the most persuasive answers she could find. Eventually and with the help of church friends, she came to a deeper understanding of Jesus. "I always wondered about the crucifixion, like it didn't make a lot of sense to me," she recalls. "It seemed like we were worshipping God who is victimized." But then she realized that Jesus was not a victim. "His connection with God was so great that the crucifixion was less painful than being separated from his truth of God. That was a big revelation for me, that somebody's connection with God could be that strong." She recognized that she often regarded herself as a victim, but needed to rid herself of that habit. "I got a sense of Jesus. Inside. He said to me, 'Give it over to me.' Inside it was like giving him dirty laundry. It was like taking off dirty clothes and giving him this dirty laundry and he said, 'Yes, I want that. Give that to me.' So I gave him the dirty laundry and poof, it became clean and he gave it back to me clean. I realized that the gift or the sacrifice was to give over the icky stuff to Christ."

Marty Newsome says that she is "definitely Christian" but not a "traditional Christian." She would not pass an orthodoxy exam at most churches and yet she insists that her relationship with God and her understanding of this relationship through Christianity is the core of her spiritual life. She is more committed to the biblical tradition than most spiritual shoppers, but she illustrates an important fact about the relationship between religious tradition and religious diversity: even when people feel that they can pick and choose from any of the religious teachings and practices they may come across, these same people are influenced by the culture in which they live and by the familiar teachings and stories that are part of this culture. This alone is a kind of centripetal force that draws shoppers away from the full flush of religious diversity and requires them to recognize the power of religious tradition.

If they do not dismiss religious tradition out of hand, spiritual shoppers nevertheless pride themselves on having experimented widely enough to be conversant with at least several traditions. Compared with people who have obligingly accepted the teachings of the tradition in which they were raised, there is a kind of hubris about spiritual shopping, an assumption that one's own judgments about various religious teachings are not only valid but productive of insight. A forty-year-old schoolteacher in Brooklyn illustrates this point when she describes her religious preference by asserting, "I've made it my business to sort of look into a number of different faiths and pick a bouquet from them, including ancient pagan beliefs and Christianity and laws and codes that overlap in a lot of different Muslim/ Buddhist/Christian-Judaic laws to live by." When asked if she attends religious services, she says, "No, I make them," explaining that she develops her own ceremonies to commemorate the passing of the seasons or important events in her life by piecing together what she has learned about ancient rituals.

Spiritual shopping is like shopping for television sets, automobiles, or motion pictures insofar as feelings, tastes, and personal preferences play a large role in the selections people make. Although some products may be objectively defective or inferior, the assumption guiding shoppers is generally that most products are reasonable options, and that choices can thus depend on what exactly a person likes and how much he or she is willing to pay. After the fact, a product can be judged in practical terms (does the television get good reception, does the automobile provide reliable transportation), but most products are also evaluated subjectively (do I feel good about my purchase). These kinds of subjective evaluations are common among spiritual shoppers. Some combination of Buddhism, the occult, and Christian meditation simply feels right, often because it generates occasional feelings of being close to the sacred.

The sacred experiences that spiritual shoppers report reflect their views of religious diversity, affirming that diversity is good but also discouraging too narrow an identification with any particular tradition. Shoppers remember times, for instance, when they felt particularly moved during a visit to a service at a synagogue or mosque or feeling that a holy person from a Buddhist monastery communicated an unusual sense of spiritual depth. Memories like this are often recounted to validate the shopper's belief that there is goodness in all traditions and that exposure to these traditions adds richness to one's own spiritual life. At the same time, shoppers' most intense personal experiences of the sacred typically transcend any particular traditions. Feeling close to God, for example, does not take the form of a message from some prophet or guru but simply occurs as an experience of light, peace, bliss, wonder, or numinousness. Implicitly, then, the shopping mentality assumes that different religions provide paths or techniques that facilitate sacred experience, but does not assume that this experience is fundamentally different in the various traditions.

Toward a New Consciousness?

Shopping among diverse religious traditions and spiritual practices is clearly easier for many Americans than was the case fifty or a hundred years ago. Although exposure to non-Western religions is limited and often superficial, the presence of leaders in the United States from some of these traditions and the ease with which Americans can purchase books or travel to remote corners of the world increases the chances that people will come to think of themselves as spiritual shoppers. But is this a trend that will come increasingly to characterize a large majority of Americans, and thus become a major new way of responding to religious diversity, or will it be restricted to the few who because of their upbringing or traumatic personal experiences are shaken from more conventional religious moorings?

Just as in the past, theories of history have been advanced to suggest that something like spiritual shopping (although not by that name) is inevitably the wave of the future. Astrology has again been harnessed to this purpose, especially in arguments (more popular in the 1970s and 1980s) about the spiritual significance of a new Aquarian era.[13] The term *New Age* has been used as a wide umbrella under which to subsume a variety of recently invented self-help, therapeutic, personal discovery, and alternative healing practices, some with weak roots in diverse religious traditions and strong links to the symbolic idea of diversity.[14] Science, too, bringing its own *mythos* of historical progression, has been bent to the cause through arguments from evolutionary psychology about the human brain being hardwired to experience God and thus to supersede the historic divisions among religious traditions.[15]

These theories provide contemporary Americans with ways of making sense of and even encouraging religious diversity. But familiarity with the arguments that have helped Americans to manage diversity in the past should give pause to taking the current arguments at face value. Rather than imagining a new form of religious consciousness being driven by astrological, spiritual, or scientific necessity, a more cautious approach requires paying attention to those aspects of spiritual shopping that are most readily adaptable to present social conditions and cultural assumptions.

One way in which spiritual shopping is altering the present religious landscape is through its effects on mainstream Christian and Jewish orientations toward spirituality. Shopping is reinforced by the presence of non-Western religions that render the idea of religious diversity more compelling and visible, but it is by no means limited to excursions into these other religions. Ordinary churchgoers frequently approach their spiritual journeys as if they were shoppers as well. The books they read may not include Hermann Hesse or the Upanishads, but may range within the space of a few years from Tim LaHaye to J. K. Rowling or from Thomas Keating to Thomas More. They may not be dabblers, in the sense of abandoning the spiritual quest after a few false starts, but they may well be consumers driven by personal tastes, the desire for gratifying religious experiences, and whatever may be advertised in the latest issue of their favorite religious magazine.

The strongest reason for thinking that spiritual shopping may result in a kind of new consciousness is its compatibility with the market system that is so much a part of American culture. The exact nature of this compatibility nevertheless warrants a cautious interpretation. Markets are driven primarily by the desire for profits and by the ability to realize this desire. The profits that have been realized from promoting spiritual shopping among diverse religious traditions have thus far been fairly small in comparison with profits from other consumer goods and in comparison with the contributions and volunteer time still commanded by established religious organizations. The number of conference speakers, lecturers, popular authors, gurus, publishing houses, and Web sites that have made substantial earnings promoting spiritual shopping is meager. The more significant way in which the marketplace encourages spiritual shopping is through the consumer mentality to which most Americans implicitly subscribe. Consumerism emphasizes the needs and desires of the individual. Spiritual shopping caters to the fulfillment of those needs and desires. Spiritual shoppers generally do not identify themselves as loyal members of a community or group, but as individuals who have become alienated from certain communities or groups and have found it necessary to strike out on their own, searching for the sacred by metaphorically going from place to place.

The personalized quests for the sacred that characterize spiritual shopping have contributed to the emphasis that many people now place on the distinction between spirituality and religion. Spirituality refers to an individual's relationship to the sacred, whereas religion connotes organizations, clergy, doctrines, and traditions. The distinction between the two has helped to create a niche in the larger religious marketplace for entrepreneurs claiming to have special insight about spirituality. Thus, much of the present spiritual shopping is guided by authors, speakers, artists, healers, and lay individuals who view themselves as spiritual leaders rather than as religious leaders. Understandably, clergy are often critical of these new competitors and their followers, arguing that spirituality disconnected from religion is inevitably shallow and narcissistic. Yet in another sense this same distinction inadvertently protects established religion from having to deal with religious diversity in larger terms. Spiritual shoppers can be lumped together under a common rubric (such as New Age) and treated as misguided dabblers rather than as representatives of a new form of religious consciousness that embraces diversity in ways that may be fundamentally threatening to traditional understandings of religious exclusivism.

Spiritual shoppers also have a different view of America from the ones that were popular throughout much of the nation's history. America is in their view a diverse mixture of people that includes many different cultures, ethnic groups, and religions, and this diversity is an important reason why life in America is interesting. What makes this view of diversity different from earlier ideas about America as an ethnic melting pot is that it includes Native Americans, both as the starting point for the narrative of American history and as a significant continuing cultural presence, and emphasizes non-Europeans and non-Christians as part of the cultural mix. One woman's comment about diversity provides a good illustration of this view: "Once upon a time it was just Native Americans, and then white people invaded and then brought black slaves, and then Asian people came. Since then there's always been all kinds of people. Diversity is how the creator made things; it's such a great gift. If everything was all exactly the same, that could get pretty boring after a while."

This view of diversity fits naturally with the idea that spiritual shopping is good. The many different faiths and spiritual practices are like different colors of the rainbow or species of plants: they should be experienced and enjoyed. People who stay within their own group and who fear contact with different groups miss out on the richness of life. Indeed, something must be wrong with them (insecurity, for example); otherwise, they would realize the benefits of diversity. The highest form of enjoyment, moreover, is not to live as one species of plant, rooted forever in one's biological makeup, but to rise above particular commitments, spanning them and borrowing from as many as possible for one's edification and pleasure.

Yet, in its more extreme forms, spiritual shopping is self-limiting. The ongoing quest for sacred experiences and spiritual enlightenment is more time-consuming and costly than many people are willing to accommodate. Spiritual shoppers are sometimes hopelessly idealistic, assuming that genuine differences among religions can simply be dissolved by emphasizing their common elements. Shopping depends on the willingness of other people to supply ideas about spirituality, but it ultimately does not contribute very much or very directly to the building of new institutions. Its adherents are too interested in their own pursuits to spend much time creating large organizations and other social structures. In this way, spiritual shopping is a response to religious diversity that celebrates and warmly embraces the idea of diversity, and that even generates added variety of its own, but seems unlikely to bring about a new consciousness that fundamentally alters American religion.

"Many Mansions": Accepting Diversity

WERE A MAP of American religion to be drawn, showing the various Christian denominations and confessional traditions as large centrally located blocks and the various other religions—Judaism, Islam, Hinduism, and Buddhism, among others—occupying smaller peripheral regions, a minority of the American population (perhaps as many as one-quarter) would have to be depicted as spiritual itinerants, moving easily across regions and perhaps heeding the call, as Martin Marty has suggested, to "pay no attention to boundaries" and "invent new responses."[1] Fascinating as they may be, these spiritual shoppers migrate so readily among religious identities and spiritual practices that their impact on established religious institutions may be less profound than that of a second category. This second group, Marty suggests, "seek to choose communal life of a more open character but still respectful of boundaries." They are the churchgoers, the large majority of Americans who continue to identify themselves as Christians and who faithfully adhere to some (perhaps many) of the traditional teachings and practices of Christianity, but who accept religious diversity. Indeed, they do not simply accept this diversity grudgingly as a regrettable but unavoidable fact of life, but accept it eagerly. Not as eagerly, to be sure, as spiritual shoppers. They nevertheless believe that there is truth in other religions besides Christianity, that these religions are legitimate ways of understanding and relating to God, and that there is much to be learned by Christians from gaining familiarity with these other religions.

It all sounds easy, being a good Christian, someone who loves God and neighbor, and thus accepts, even respects, people whose religious views happen to differ. So easy, especially if Christianity means nothing more, as many observers now claim, than a commitment to follow the Golden

Rule, a "religious preference," like a preference for soap or cereal, that says little more about a person than the fact that he or she happens to enjoy attending a particular church. Open-mindedness comes easily then because one's own convictions are shallow.[2] Respecting Buddhists and Hindus is no harder for an inclusive Christian than collegial relationships with Democrats are for moderate Republicans.

But is it really this easy? Religious conviction establishes a view of the world that, in the anthropologist Clifford Geertz's memorable phrase, creates "such an aura of factuality [that] moods and motivations seem uniquely realistic."[3] Entertaining the possibility of other religions being uniquely true can be a dangerous enterprise, as the historian of religions Wilfrid Cantwell Smith argued, for the efficacy of "theirs" conjures up fears about the inadequacy of "ours."[4] Most American Christians profess regularly, as they recite the Nicene Creed or the Lord's Prayer, as they take communion, as they pray and listen to sermons, that Jesus is God, the second person of the trinity, their savior, the central character in the biblical cast. They do not believe the same about Buddha or Muhammad. Yet in one national survey 57 percent of churchgoing Christians said it was true not only that "Christianity is the best way to understand God" *but also* that "All religions are equally good ways of knowing about God."[5] How do serious Christians reconcile these two statements? How does a person say, on the one hand, that Christianity is uniquely true because God sent his son Jesus to die for their sins and, on the other hand, that it doesn't really matter what your religion is because all religions are equally true?

Were the problem simply one of interpreting responses to public opinion polls the solution might be discovered in the fact that people respond without thinking, have only Protestants and Catholics in mind when they say that all religions are equally true, or are registering the same uncanny ability to compartmentalize incompatible views that pollsters find in social and political attitudes. But inclusive Christianity is real. It emerges over and over again when people talk in personal interviews about their faith, just as it does in the understandings of many clergy and in the writings of some Christian leaders. In the heartland of American Christianity, few people are deeply schooled in formal theological arguments, but many have thought about why they are Christians, what it means to believe in God and in Jesus, their reasons for going to church, and how they can personally relate to God. They have not been able to escape the implications of these beliefs for their views of other religions, especially when their neighbors and friends, their coworkers and cousins are increasingly members of other religions.

Inclusive Christianity is difficult—difficult to understand and difficult to practice—because it involves achieving a delicate balance between a commitment to a radically particular way of relating to God and an ability to grapple sympathetically, even appreciatively, with the fact that a large part of the world's population does not relate to God this way at all. The balance required, like walking a balance beam, involves maintaining a fine course between opposing forces, one of which is to veer toward believing that only the Christian way is true after all, the other being the view that what one thinks and does religiously is of little consequence because all religions are the same. Inclusivity is partly a matter of being in the right place, having parents, friends, educational experiences, and church involvements that assist in maintaining a commitment to Christianity and an open mind about other religions. It is much more a matter of the implicit assumptions one learns in these places, assumptions about who God is and what God expects of humans, how to make sense of traditional Christian claims about the unique life and ministry of Jesus, what it means to be spiritual in a Christian way, and why it is important to remain involved in a church. Maintaining an inclusive commitment to Christianity also requires coming to terms with questions about how to relate to people who belong to other religions, especially what to say to them about one's own faith, how much to try to understand the teachings of these other religions, what it means to respect them, and what one may gain from learning about them. This is the cultural work of inclusive Christianity. It is done by the culture, through the informal languages of diversity to which many Americans are exposed in their homes and communities, and it is work performed by individuals themselves as they try to make sense of their convictions and their lives.

Christians who accept religious diversity are thus a particularly interesting group for gaining a clearer understanding of how Americans are responding to religious diversity. Unlike spiritual shoppers, who personalize their spiritual quest to the point that they typically do not identify themselves as Christians or participate actively in churches, inclusive Christians have somehow managed to retain their commitment to Christianity but apparently do not believe in the more exclusionary interpretations that have characterized Christianity in the past. Some of this group accomplish this feat through the same kind of mental flaccidity that permits people who believe firmly in marriage to commit adultery, or that allows zealous liberals to be intolerant of all who oppose them. But some of the open-minded have thought long and hard about their faith and about how it can be reconciled with a world of religious diversity. They hold the key to understanding how a nation that still claims in many ways to be Christian is managing to adjust in its outlooks and practices to the growing reality of religious diversity.

Sandra Michaelson: Beauty in Every Religion

An understanding of the questions that a person who claims to be open-minded about religious diversity is likely to confront can be gained by considering Sandra Michaelson. She is a vivacious woman in her late sixties who retired a few years ago after a long career working for nonprofit health agencies, including the American Heart Association. A few years after her husband died (in the 1970s), she moved from New York to Chicago, but returned a few years later, settling in Greenwich Village, which she adores, ironically, for its "small town" atmosphere. As a child growing up in Florida, she attended worship services and Sunday school at a Methodist church with her mother and six siblings. Although her parents had been Presbyterians before their divorce, her mother joined the Methodist church and went there regularly with the children. Sandra continued attending through high school, but during college "fell away" from the church. In her early twenties she married a man from an Episcopal background who did not attend religious services either. When their first child was born, they tried attending a Methodist church for awhile, but it "didn't click." A decade passed before she became interested in church again. She remembers clearly that a friend gave her a copy of C. S. Lewis's *Screwtape Letters*. Intrigued, she started reading Lewis's other books and found herself being drawn away from the atheism that she had been entertaining and back to "Christianity, or at least theism." For almost another decade, she experimented with reading various authors (she does not elaborate) and going to various churches, ranging from Unitarian to Catholic to Baptist. C. S. Lewis continued to be vitally important as a source of spiritual guidance. She talked occasionally with the pastor at a Methodist church she sometimes attended, she remembers a long conversation with a Baptist minister who explained what it meant to be "born again," and she remembers times when she attended a Unitarian church or did not attend at all. In her late thirties, she joined an Episcopal church but about the same time started attending a prayer group initiated by a group of women who were Catholic charismatics. She and her husband periodically went to revival services with these friends at an independent charismatic church. One evening her husband responded to the altar call at the end of the service and was saved. A month later he died of a heart attack.

Having moved to New York to find a job, Mrs. Michaelson wandered into an Episcopal church one Sunday and was overcome by the sermon ("one of the most powerful things I've ever heard"). She decided to come regularly. Although the church was a "hodgepodge" of people from diverse backgrounds, they seemed to get along and work together effectively. After spending a few years working in Chicago, where she attended a more traditional Episcopal church, she eagerly returned to the church in New York. The church was suffering from growing pains and from internal conflict, but she decided to stay. She met periodically for spiritual direction with one of the women on staff and eventually became a member of the vestry. Even though her spiritual director died a few years ago and the pastor whose sermons she so greatly admired has left, she has no intention of leaving.

Mrs. Michaelson's encounters with religions other than Christianity have been sporadic. As far as she knew, there was only one Jewish student in her school while she was growing up, but she remembers her mother entertaining Jewish friends on several occasions and thinks her mother strongly believed in being tolerant and accepting. She took a course in comparative religions in college and later read books about comparative religions as part of her search to figure out her own beliefs. Through her work, she has traveled in Morocco and in Muslim sections of Eastern Europe, and she has Jewish and Muslim friends in her neighborhood in Greenwich Village. For the past few years, she has been serving on an interfaith women's committee that brings Christians, Jews, and Muslims together in hopes of promoting greater understanding. "I think every religion, every faith system has so much beauty and so much truth to it that there's always something you can take from it," she says.

Although an assertion like this sounds easy (almost breezy), Mrs. Michaelson has had to develop ways of thinking that permit her to remain a dedicated Christian in face of the fact that many of the Christians she knows and many of the Christian teachings she has learned over the years run squarely against the view that all religions are beautiful and true. She makes a point of saying that there is a lot she does not understand about religion. She has never understood, for instance, how a God of love could condemn people who are not Christians. She is unsure whether the Bible is a book of accumulated wisdom or whether it is somehow divinely inspired. Still, she is persuaded that God exists and that the birth, life, death, and resurrection of Jesus are "great spiritual truths." She believes people are saved through their faith in Jesus Christ, but also thinks they can be saved by other means. How has she been able to arrive at this view? How can she be a committed Christian and hold other religions in such respect as well?

Coming to Terms with Diversity

Like spiritual shoppers, church people who are open-minded toward other religions have typically come to this position as a result of social experiences that not only exposed them to people of other faiths but also gave them a way of talking about these faiths in relation to their own commitments to Christianity. For many people, these ways of talking were learned as children. Their parents talked favorably about diversity and encouraged them to take a positive attitude toward other religions, the same as they did toward other races, nationalities, and ethnic groups. Sara Morgan, a government worker in her sixties who grew up Lutheran in California, illustrates this point when she asserts that her parents "accepted all people," "were generous and kind," "never put anybody down," and "lived an example of what was always welcoming, always sharing, always generous, and did not make a distinction between whether or not you had a church background." Sometimes people recall specific phrases or arguments that they learned as children and that have stayed with them whenever they think about religious diversity. J. P. Langford, a retired policeman in Ohio who was raised by his Methodist grandparents (and is now Presbyterian), remembers them teaching him to be "extremely tolerant toward people." They told him that there are "no evil religions per se" and that "God reveals himself in various ways," and, even though "we should share the gospel with everybody, there was that kind of a tolerance built up." In other cases, people remember their parents' actions more than their words. John Edwards, who grew up Presbyterian in Atlanta, recalls, "In terms of faith, my parents were always friends to and had good friends of all faiths. Our next-door neighbor was Mr. Steinberg, who was just a delightful strongly Jewish citizen here in Atlanta and a good friend. There were friendships across religious boundaries." People sometimes remember differences between their mother and father, too. Vivian Swenson, an audiologist who grew up Lutheran in Pennsylvania, remembers that her father ("a good liberal democrat") objected to her brother dating a Catholic, but found himself at odds with her mother, who chided him for being prejudiced; the result, she says, was that "we learned to question things and argue." Of course some people who have become more inclusive as adults look back and realize that their parents were not as open-minded as they are. These people acknowledge that schooling and personal experiences made them more tolerant as they matured, yet they also appear to have thought of reasons why their parents were less tolerant and are thus able to distance themselves fairly easily from their parents' views. For instance, a man who was raised Catholic in California says there was probably some bigotry because the whole neighborhood was Catholic; a woman in Ohio mentions her parents' negative feelings toward the Japanese as an example of their intolerance but says it was because her father fought in World War II.

Unlike spiritual shoppers, whose parents often gave them little childhood exposure to Christianity, the parents of open-minded Christians were usually active church members who took their children to church, taught them to value being at church, and gave them ways of understanding and respecting church teachings. "I was raised in a Methodist family," says Mildred Aiken, a woman in her late seventies from Pennsylvania. "My mother was certainly a good churchgoer, as were her parents. Of course, I went to Sunday school. Started teaching Sunday school when I was sixteen." Melvin Shoemaker, a business manager in his forties who grew up in Texas, gives a similar account of his upbringing: "I've been Catholic all my life. I went from first to eighth grade to a very small Catholic school in central Texas. Did the usual stuff, the first communion and confession and all that sort of thing. I was taught by nuns in the habits, wearing the habits, the traditional thing that you see in the caricatures of Catholic education." Margaret Lanier, a woman in her fifties who grew up as a Presbyterian in Ohio, provides a further illustration: "My parents were very active in the church; in fact they were charter members of a small church that was formed as a mission church after World War II. It was mostly composed of World War II returning veterans who were just setting up their families and moved to kind of a suburb of Youngstown, Ohio, new houses, all of that in the early Fifties." Antonio Diaz, an engineer in his late twenties who grew up in Puerto Rico and now lives in Atlanta, is especially proud of his parents' staunch faith: "My parents have always been very devout people in the faith, in the Catholic faith, but also in their love of God. They were not just doing something as a mechanical thing. They really professed and you see the light of God in them. They are human, imperfect, but they truly show that they have faith in God. They really tried to instill those values in me."

Significantly, most of these people developed close friendships with other children or young people at their churches; faith was thus not so much a matter of learning abstract doctrines or imitating their parents but of experiencing the joy and goodness of human relationships—something that would carry over later to their attitudes about people from other religions. Mrs. Michaelson remembers that her two best friends went to the Methodist church in which she was raised. Mildred Aiken has fond memories of going hiking with friends from her childhood church. Melvin Shoemaker has many memories of his childhood chums who went to the same parochial school, one of the fondest of which is being let out of school for several weeks one year to do odd jobs while the new church was being built. Antonio Diaz remembers being an altar boy with his friends; he draws a connection between these friends and his view that God is essentially his friend.

The combination of respecting others and going to church might still have little to do with religious diversity were it not for the fact that people had opportunities to be exposed directly to other religions. Some of this exposure came during childhood as a result of traveling with parents or meeting parents' friends and coworkers. Compared with spiritual shoppers, people who were exposed to other religions as children often appear to have come to an earlier understanding that other religions were simply a part of ordinary life, rather than being drawn to them as a result of alienation or rebellion. Among older people, these acquaintances were usually Jewish. Mr. Langford, the retired policeman, recalls that starting in seventh grade he had Jewish friends with whom he ran around and studied; he says he felt very honored to have been invited to their houses on several occasions for Passover meals. He thinks these experiences made him "more tolerant and accepting" and persuaded him that "Christianity and Judaism go hand in hand." Sara Morgan knew some Jewish students in high school and then had several Jewish roommates during college. She says they never talked explicitly about religion but she learned to understand some of the Jewish customs by visiting their homes. Fred Strang, an industrial arts teacher who now attends a Calvary Chapel church in Georgia, recalls his best friend in grade school being Jewish and being a victim of prejudice; he thinks this friendship is the reason he now takes a more inclusive attitude toward religion than many of the people at this church. Among younger people, Jewish acquaintances are still more common than acquaintances who belong to any other non-Christian religion, but some who lived in ethnically diverse communities also had Muslim, Hindu, or Buddhist friends. Kimberly Hughes, a woman in her mid-twenties from Los Angeles, for instance, says many of her friends at school were Buddhist. She did not know what to make of their teachings and thinks now that she probably interpreted what she heard through a Christian filter (for example, hearing a Buddhist speaker talking about divine love on one occasion and thinking he must have had some psychic connection with Christ); still, she says it was a positive experience knowing people from other religions because it made her look for the good in all people.

These early encounters with other religions are likely to have continued (for those who went) during college and in early adulthood, now becoming more personal and generating more thoughtful responses in some cases and focusing less on religion at all in other cases. A woman who spent part of her time in college living in the Middle East wound up writing an honors thesis about Muhammad because she was trying to reconcile his claims with her understanding of Christianity. A man who had been raised Lutheran remembers countless "bull sessions" in his college dorm involving debates about God, Jesus, and the Bible with dorm mates who were

Jewish, Christian, or atheist. A woman who attended college in New York says visiting synagogues with friends forced her to examine more carefully why she was a Christian. Several of the Christians who first met Jews in college say they did not discuss religion explicitly because neither they nor their friends were interested in religion at the time; they nevertheless picked up ideas about Judaism and about Jewish customs from things their friends said about their parents or grandparents, from holiday observances, and from conversations about interfaith dating and marriage.

Compared with the exposure that spiritual shoppers experienced at the same stage of life, this exposure is typically less extensive and less intentional. It occurs because a friend happened to belong to another religion, not because the person was actively engaged on a quest for new spiritual experiences. Often this exposure is involuntary (for example, dictated by being assigned a roommate of a different religion in college) or focuses less on religion and more on sports, music, and other interests. In many instances, it nevertheless broadens a person's horizons and reinforces the idea that there are valuable things to be learned from other religions.

Exposure to other religions is only half of the story, though. The other half is the distinctive search for answers that seems to characterize people who turn out as Christians with an inclusive attitude toward other religions. The search typically begins in high school, although in some cases it starts in junior high or even in grade school. Usually it is precipitated by a specific question or event, such as having doubts about the pastor's interpretation of the resurrection, disagreeing with the youth director's stance toward premarital sex, or wondering about the causes of war or racism or gender inequality. It may well be reinforced by larger circumstances, such as a longstanding tension between one's parents about the validity of different denominational traditions or having been taught as a child to question authority. The church itself may encourage questioning. Yet there is also likely to be some frustration, a feeling on the part of the young person that the church was not sufficiently responsive to his or her questions. Mrs. Michaelson is fairly typical in this regard. In retrospect, she says she went around for a long time "asking embarrassing questions" that nobody at the various churches she attended seemed able to answer. Although she is glad that later in life she was able to put some of these questions to rest, she still feels frustrated that it took her so long. "I tried,

I really did try for a long time," she says and then breaks off weeping as she recalls her difficulties in those years.

In contrast to spiritual shoppers, Christians who develop inclusive views of other religions are not as likely to have experienced deep personal trauma that launched them on a spiritual search, and they are less likely to have searched outside of Christianity for answers to their questions. Marla Bolton, a Presbyterian in her fifties who lives in Houston, illustrates this kind of searching. Having attended church and Sunday school through high school, she quit going in college and did not resume until she was in her mid-thirties. Her father's death while she was still a child left her with many unanswered questions. Yet her years away from the church stemmed from lack of interest as much as from frustration in finding answers to her questions. Listening to reggae music eventually started her thinking about spirituality again. Uncomfortable with the idea of simply settling back into a church, she nevertheless looked only at churches, rather than alternative spiritual movements or other religions, and eventually rejoined the same Presbyterian church in which she had been raised.

Tom Polaski provides another instructive picture of the kind of spiritual quest that typifies inclusive Christians. A cabinetmaker in his forties who now lives in southern California, he grew up in a staunch Catholic neighborhood in the Ohio River valley. After years of faithful attendance at mass and at parochial school, he was glad to get away when he went to New York to attend college. Although his parents were tolerant and taught him to respect diversity, the rules at church and at school seemed sufficiently oppressive that he lost interest in attending church. Still interested in spirituality, he remembers talking a lot with his Jewish roommate and with Protestant friends (one of whom became his wife) about religion. Yet he now thinks his interest was more "intellectual" than anything else; at least he was not motivated at the time to explore spirituality in his own tradition or in other traditions. A decade passed and his parents, growing increasingly concerned that their children were losing contact with the church, paid for Mr. Polaski to attend a retreat taught by a monk who was interested in contemplative prayer. The event was a turning point in Mr. Polaski's life. He came home spiritually invigorated and within a few months he and his wife joined a Lutheran church that seemed less rule-bound than the church in which he had been raised and that appealed to his wife's Protestant roots as well.

As these examples suggest, inclusive Christians have often spent part of their lives away from the church, but at some point they return, usually to a congregation that they find stimulating and nurturing as well as open-minded enough to accept their questions and their sense that religions other than Christianity may be true. These inclusive Christians say they are more likely to attend mainline Protestant or liberal Catholic churches than fundamentalist Protestant or conservative Catholic churches. In many instances this difference amounts to little more than the tradition in which a person was raised; however, in a significant number of cases, settling into a liberal congregation has been a deliberate choice—indeed, a choice that has come after trying several other churches, including some time in more conservative settings. Mrs. Michaelson's journey from a more conservative charismatic church to the Episcopal church she now attends in New York City is one example. Will Mathias, a lawyer in his early forties who lives in northern California, is another. He was raised in a Methodist church, occasionally attending Catholic services with his maternal grand-parents, but then during college became active in Campus Crusade for Christ, where he met his wife. For the next five years, he and his wife served as lay leaders in Campus Crusade and attended several different churches, all small and quite conservative theologically. But his wife had been raised Episcopalian and neither she nor he felt entirely comfortable in churches that seemed increasingly to be adopting a fundamentalist stance toward contemporary issues such as women's ordination and abortion. They opted for a large Episcopal church that they have now attended for more than a decade. He finds the church's openness refreshing: "It emphasizes brains. We were given the ability to think. There aren't easy answers and even when you want an easy answer, you may not get it. There are shades of gray. There are questions that you may just not be able to have answered right at the moment. We have clergy who tell you that the answer is going to require some study and some thought and some prayer." He admits that he is not always as tolerant of other points of view as he should be but is pleased that the church encourages him to grow in this direction. "It's great living in a parish that stresses reading and seeking out shades of gray and listening to others and trying to be tolerant."

What keeps people like Mrs. Michaelson and Mr. Mathias involved in their churches is typically not a specific theological position (although theology clearly matters), but some program that sparks their imagination and draws them into an active role in the congregation. For Mrs. Michaelson, it was a shelter and soup kitchen for the homeless; she got involved because helping the needy was "dear to her heart," and through this experience she made friends (one of whom became her spiritual director) and eventually agreed to serve as a member of the vestry. For Mr. Mathias, being part of the church took on new meaning after a couple of years because of the liturgy and because he became involved in one of the ministry teams that handled the church's finances. He says he now has a better understanding of the Eucharist and a clearer sense of how the parish's leaders are guided by their faith. Judging from similar comments from other people, it is probably no accident that liturgy and social ministries were among the strongest attractions in these two cases. Liturgy, as people interpret it in settings like those of Mrs. Michaelson and Mr. Mathias, becomes a pivotal moment in their personal relationship with God. Clearly symbolic, it unites them personally with the sacred and with the gathered community, but also leaves room for personal interpretations of its meaning. Social ministries are hands-on activities that can be justified in broad humanitarian terms and with reference to the service ethic in Christianity whether one happens to believe in particular Christian doctrines or not.

The role of diversity itself as an attraction to such congregations is multilayered. At one level, the congregation's openness to diversity typically makes sense to people who have been raised to appreciate tolerance and inclusiveness. At another level, it may correspond to a person's considered opinion about truth in other religions. But openness to diversity is also a symbol of acceptance—a sign that the person who has never seriously considered joining another religion but who has at times felt estranged from church life will feel at home. For Mrs. Michaelson and Mr. Mathias, the diversity of their present churches provides a welcome contrast with the conservative churches where they felt confined by too many rules. Others point to diversity as proof that their church is caring, friendly, willing to take in people who do not fit elsewhere, and open to new ideas. While an inclusive Christian may talk with pride about his or her church being open toward Jews or Muslims, therefore, the real message may be that there is enough room for diversity among Christians themselves that a person will not feel stifled or constrained.

One thing that inclusive Christians and spiritual shoppers share is an emphasis on the experiential aspects of spirituality. In both cases, feeling close to God or feeling that one is in the presence of the sacred are prized experiences. They affirm that God is real and that the individual has direct access to God. They also affirm the person's worth and validate whatever interpretations of the sacred the person may hold, whether they conform to church traditions or not. But the scripts that inclusive Christians and spiritual shoppers use to interpret their experiences of the sacred differ. Spiritual shoppers less often speak of God, preferring more generic terms, such as Spirit or Power, that might be applicable in any religious tradition (or none). Inclusive Christians are more likely to say that their sacred experiences occurred in church and were facilitated by participating in church services. Their experiences may reinforce their own sense of being in direct contact with God but they also affirm the value of participating in a community of believers.

For many inclusive Christians, then, the strongest social factor encouraging them to remain committed to their faith is the church itself—a congregation that accepts them, gives them an opportunity to serve, offers them a language with which to make sense of their encounters with the sacred, and does not interfere with their conviction that open-mindedness and godliness are kindred. In a word, inclusive Christians have *positive* reasons to embrace Christianity while respecting the truth of other religions. At the same time, these reasons do not preclude the fact that at the end of the day Christianity is the religion of choice for many simply because it is familiar, primal. As Marla Bolton says, she wanted to explore widely in order to find out what she really believed, but always found herself coming back to the faith of her youth: "It just seems right for me. Maybe I'd call it being acculturated, but you just feel more comfortable with what you're raised with when you're young."

How to Be an Inclusive Christian

The social circumstances in which people live—their religious upbringing, exposure to other religions, search for spiritual answers, and participation in tolerant congregations—help explain why someone may be predisposed to be a self-identified Christian who takes an inclusive view of other religions. But inclusive Christians still need to have some sense of what it means to be a Christian and be able to make sense of their faith in a way that does not sharply contradict their conviction that all religions are true. What kind of Christianity is this? What beliefs does it include? And how do these beliefs permit their adherents to be Christian and inclusive at the same time?

Perhaps even more so than spiritual shoppers, inclusive Christians start with the supposition that God exists. (Those who have entertained doubts appear to have moved beyond these doubts less often by finding compelling intellectual arguments and more often by taking a leap of faith and then putting themselves in a church context that reinforced this leap.) But, whereas spiritual shoppers claim to be convinced of God's existence by virtue of having experienced God's presence and by conceptualizing God as a kind of force that is present in all things, inclusive Christians are more likely (understandably) to think of God as a creator or creative being who can at least be imagined to be separate from the realm in which humans exist. The problem of possible separation from God is thus more of an issue for inclusive Christians than it is for spiritual shoppers. It is the kind of problem that at least has to be posited and then answered, however quickly or easily. The answer, given almost universally by inclusive Christians, is that nothing can ultimately separate us from God, where "us" refers most immediately to you and me but by extension, when pressed, to everyone on earth. The justification given for this assertion is typically that God is a thoroughly loving and accepting God; indeed, that love and acceptance are virtually synonymous with God. Mrs. Michaelson illustrates the core elements of this argument in saying that her beliefs can be summarized in these words: "God is love and nothing can separate us from that. No matter what we do, no matter who tries, nobody can separate us from God's love." Tom Polaski, the cabinetmaker, expresses the same idea in somewhat different language: "I believe in an all-powerful, universal, and loving force that is responsible for all life and all expressions of life, an unknowable, ineffable center of everyone's spiritual core." Kimberly Hughes, the Catholic woman in her twenties who lives in California, says that her religious beliefs can be summarized in three words: "God loves you." Kathryn Winters, a retired Presbyterian woman who lives in Illinois, elaborates: "I believe that God in essence is a God of love and healing and presence. I believe that each one of us is individually loved and cared for and treasured by God and that there's a tremendous power and pulling that he has toward each one of us, and wants us very much to respond to that."

When inclusive Christians who believe that God is all-loving and accepting are asked to explain why some people seem not to experience that love or, indeed, suffer horribly from evil and abuse, the most common response is to appeal to the mysterious nature of God. Note, for instance, that Mr. Polaski includes "unknowable" among the words he uses to describe God. Mildred Aiken, the Methodist woman in her seventies who lives in Pennsylvania, offers an interesting version of this idea when she asserts that the Apostles' Creed pretty much sums up her religious beliefs but then immediately backtracks, saying that she does not understand what the creed is trying to express about God and is not sure anyone does: "There are times when the dark blanket has a pinpoint of light in it and I see better, but sometimes it's just all dark." Melvin Shoemaker, the Catholic man in his forties who lives in Houston, expresses the same idea: "I have a lot of uncertainty. I don't know what form God takes. I guess a lot of these things are predicated with 'I don't know.' I have more questions than answers." Others speak of the mysterious presence of God or the need to relate to God with a kind of faith that defies understanding. For instance, Margaret Lanier, the Presbyterian who grew up in Ohio, says she has "a personal respect for the awesome mystery that's out there, and the minute we think we understand it then we're probably really way off."

It is hard to be a Christian, inclusive or otherwise, without believing in some way that Jesus is central to one's faith. Most inclusive Christians do in fact mention something about Jesus when asked to summarize their religious beliefs. Unlike spiritual shoppers who sometimes are willing to classify Jesus among great or wise leaders without further thought, inclusive Christians generally have enough familiarity with the life and teachings of Jesus to offer views about his role that can be reconciled with their views of religious diversity. Most say that Jesus is divine, often referring explicitly to the idea of a trinitarian God in doing so, and yet they also qualify this creedal interpretation of Jesus by acknowledging that the historical record may be biased or that we may be making assumptions about Jesus that are unwarranted. Views range from thinking of Jesus as the essential player in God's plan of redemption to thinking of Jesus as a sage or a great spiritual leader. At one end of the theological spectrum, for instance, a Presbyterian man in his fifties quotes almost verbatim from the Apostles' Creed in describing Jesus as "the Son of God, born of a virgin, raised, died, he's in heaven." At the other end of the spectrum, a Catholic man in his forties says, "I guess I am supposed to espouse a feeling that he was God on earth made human. But again, having looked at the way other religions view him, they all view him as a prophet of one kind or another. Whether he is actually God, I'm open to opinions."

Spirituality is the linchpin in inclusive Christians' interpretations of Jesus and of their own and others' relationship to God. Mr. Langford, the retired policeman, illustrates this view: Jesus, he says, "represents the supreme paradigm for spiritual advancement and seeking; his life is a primary example to any Christian for spiritual advancement." Maria Hernandez, a Catholic from Virginia, also emphasizes spirituality in her description of Jesus as the "most spiritual human being to walk the face of the earth." Marla Bolton, the Methodist woman from Texas, alludes indirectly to the spiritual nature of Jesus: "I believe that he had something that was more advanced or higher than what any of us have and that he had a direct connection to God for whatever reason or was sent directly from God to show us that mankind could obtain God-hood. In other words, it's not something that is outside of our reach, but it is something that is attainable by humans."

Spirituality is not as free-floating or amorphous for inclusive Christians as it is for spiritual shoppers; it focuses specifically on God and involves prayer and efforts to lead a Christian life. But the idea of spirituality also serves several functions for inclusive Christians of which they may not be fully aware. One is to bring God closer, bridging the gap between human and divine, thereby making it possible for people to know and experience God—even if they happen to belong to other religions. Another is to reinforce the idea that God cannot be fully understood through creeds or doctrines, thus diminishing the importance of differences not only among the various Christian traditions but also between Christianity and other religions. The emphasis on spirituality also reinforces an individualistic orientation toward religion, one in which personal striving, sincerity, and experience—all of which may characterize people belonging to any religion—take precedence.

Inclusive Christians typically regard the Bible as God's word and hold it in greater reverence than spiritual shoppers do. They often make a point of saying that they interpret the Bible metaphorically rather than literally—an argument that distances them from fundamentalists but the significance of which is missed if this is all it is interpreted to mean. The key is that inclusive Christians interpose an interpretive step between the context in which the Bible was written and the words that appear in the Bible. Mr. Langford, for example, has been thinking quite a lot about the Bible lately; he expresses the importance of interpretation this way: "Some of the things were probably written by other people and things were added doctrinally that may have fit something in the first century and probably was not really passed on by the original apostles as a teaching of Christ. I just feel that there are basic precepts that are taught in the Bible that can be followed to some degree, but you can't take the Bible literally. When you start doing that, you're dealing with an interpretation based on how you see the language and that's dangerous." He adds: "I think the Bible is God's revelation, but I think the interpretation of it may be somewhat different in different ages." Athough a statement such as this can be viewed as opening the Bible to any and all interpretations, many inclusive Christians bring their emphasis on spirituality to bear on how the Bible is viewed, arguing that a person who has a spiritual relationship with God will be able through God's grace to find divine truth in the Bible. Sara Morgan, the woman in California who grew up Lutheran, makes this connection: "I do believe the Bible can be interpreted by a person who opens themselves to prayer and discussion and thinking. If the Bible says 'Thou shalt not commit adultery,' and I believe that, and I do it, and I'm sorry for it, and I ask forgiveness and I want to start my life over, I believe that I have the opportunity to do that because of love and forgiveness and grace. So the Bible doesn't necessarily mean just one thing, but its meaning is connected with something." This view of the Bible encourages inclusive Christians to look for spiritual truths and practical wisdom in the Bible, but not to treat it as the only authoritative way in which to know God's will. Thus they are free to believe that God may have imparted wisdom through other texts, such as the Qur'an or the Vedic writings, even though they claim the Bible as the scripture that makes most sense to them. Another Lutheran explicitly states this view: "I think the Bible is a unique statement for Western man in this particular period of history. That doesn't mean that the Hindu texts are any less inspired by God. That doesn't mean that Buddhist texts are any less inspired by God." He thinks the Bible is infallible, but only if taken in the right spirit: "If one reads it in an allegorical sense, if one reads it for its spiritual direction, I think you'll find it completely error-free."

Unlike spiritual shoppers, inclusive Christians take the identity of "Christian" seriously enough that they have to give some account of what it means to lead a Christian life and how such a life might differ from that of a person who does not claim to be Christian. The main thing that separates inclusive Christians from spiritual shoppers is the idea of sin: whereas spiritual shoppers seldom mention sin, preferring instead to speak of failure or dysfunction and the possibility of achieving enlightenment or perfection, inclusive Christians usually acknowledge that there is sin in the world and that individuals are affected by sin; they also assert that God still loves people, accepts them, and forgives them unconditionally. The Christian life is thus one of gratefully recognizing God's love and forgiveness, taking a hopeful attitude toward life because of this acceptance, and showing one's gratitude by trying to convey hope to other people through deeds of service. A person who tries to live as a Christian does so, according to this understanding, not as someone who has a special corner on the truth, not by reciting or believing in certain doctrinal principles, but by being a good and decent person who lives in hope and shows love to others. Such a person has a special motivation, a distinct way of describing his or her motives, by virtue of being a Christian; at the same time, this person does not claim to be any more hopeful or loving than someone else who may be motivated by identifying with a different religious belief system. In its underlying logic, this view of the Christian life readily provides Christians with a distinctive identity while leaving room for people of other religions to be faithful in their own ways. In practice, however, this logic often unravels, leaving inclusive Christians with some ambiguity about just how distinctive their identity may be. Mrs. Michaelson, for example, emphasizes her need for forgiveness and her desire to serve the needy through her church, but she also talks about Christianity as being "my path," as if it were quite arbitrary and no better than anyone else's path. A Presbyterian man says being a Christian means "doing no harm" to other people; he trails off, as if there should be more to say about it. A Lutheran man says he mostly tries to love his family and live without fear or anxiety; then, resorting to a more specifically Christian image, he adds, "I try to hold Christ up before me."

Claiming to be Christian also causes inclusive Christians to experience some difficulty—or at least ambivalence—about the idea of trying to convert others to Christianity. On the one hand, being a Christian implies a responsibility or desire to do something for other people, especially those who are obviously hurting, troubled, or searching; doing something may include telling them about Jesus as well as simply trying to love them or convey hope. Inclusive Christians seldom shy entirely away from the idea of being a witness to people who genuinely appear interested in learning more about Christianity. On the other hand, inclusive Christians are usually reluctant to make categorical judgments about other people and are thus unwilling to say that someone who belongs to another religion should convert to Christianity. Mrs. Michaelson says that it worries her, frankly, to see some people (especially atheists) who seem not to know God and who therefore may not be leading as productive or happy lives as they could; yet she sees no reason to actively try to convert such people to Christianity because "God is working with those people" and they may "convert spontaneously." She is especially reluctant to say that Christians should try to convert Jews, Muslims, or Hindus. "That's the path they have chosen to God," she says, "and that's between them and God as far as I'm concerned." Mr. Mathias tries to duck the question of converting people to Christianity by asserting that he does not believe it is right to send missionaries to China to turn people into Episcopalians. When asked what he actually thinks about Christianity, though, he acknowledges that he feels the importance of, in some way, leading an exemplary life—as a father, husband, and neighbor—so that someone watching might be attracted to Christianity. But when he thinks about Muslims or Jews converting to Christianity, he says, no, "we marginalize God when we think that he breaks people down into groups and says only Christians are going to heaven; God is greater than all of that." Marla Bolton also circles around the question of conversion several times, eventually acknowledging that it is something she is still trying to figure out. Her first response is, like Mr. Mathias, to suggest that Christians should be loving and kind so that others may be attracted by their positive lifestyle. She realizes, though, that there is an implicit judgment in suggesting that the Christian way of living may be inherently better than others. She therefore quickly adds that a Christian should somehow refrain from judging others. "I don't believe in condemning other people," she says, or, apparently mimicking what she has heard some Christians say, "I would never say, 'If you don't follow Jesus, you're damned.' " Still, it interests her to think about *how* a person of another faith might come to know God if not through Christ. She ventures that the idea of a savior may be the key: Christians come to God through Jesus; Muslims, through Muhammad; and Buddhists, through Buddha. It bothers her that Jews do not have a comparable savior figure, but she thinks they may have no need for one since they are God's chosen people anyway. "I don't quite understand it all," she says, "I guess maybe I should ask someone who is a religious scholar."

These three examples illustrate three of the most common ways in which inclusive Christians manage the perennial question of whether or not it is appropriate to try to convert members of other religions to Christianity. The first (most evident in Mrs. Michaelson's remarks) emphasizes personal spirituality—the idea of each person having his or her own path. This view is quite similar to that of many spiritual shoppers who assert that every person relates to the sacred in his or her unique way. It differs only in recognizing that individual spiritual quests are likely to be embedded in religious communities and traditions. Spirituality is nevertheless crucial. God somehow works privately in the hearts of individual men and women without respect to differences in religious traditions; some individuals in all traditions are probably close to God and others are not as close, but God ultimately draws everyone into a spiritual relationship. The second (evident in Mr. Mathias's comments) emphasizes the mysteriousness of God. Religious differences seem important to us, but this is because of our limited perspective, perhaps because of the cultural biases to which we have been exposed; they are not important to God, or at least we somehow assume they are not, since we know only that God is unknowable. The third view (illustrated in Mrs. Bolton's ideas) is that different religions operate according to a kind of paradigm that performs similar functions. Thus, even though the average person may not know enough to figure it out, there are probably common, Christian-like elements in all religions, such as something that corresponds to the Christian idea of God and something that serves as a kind of savior. These ways of dealing with the question of conversion are seldom spelled out explicitly and, for this reason, they blend with one another, but they do reflect broader assumptions about spirituality, God, Jesus, and the Christian life that are quite common among inclusive Christians.

The biblical verse that quotes Jesus as saying, "I am the way, the truth, and the life; no one comes to the father except by me," is familiar enough to most inclusive Christians that they have found it necessary to come up with some way of explaining why this statement does not contradict their inclusive views. Mrs. Michaelson reflects the interpretive approach to the Bible that characterizes many inclusive Christians in suggesting that there is no historical proof that Jesus actually said this and that it needs to be understood in its historical context since it appears in the book of John but not in the other three gospels. She nevertheless thinks it represents an important "spiritual truth," probably that Jesus is "a way" and that each person must find his or her own way. A Lutheran woman emphasizes the mysteriousness of God, claiming that she "doesn't claim to comprehend" the statement's meaning; she worries that it leaves non-Christians "in a bit of a squeeze," but quickly sidesteps that concern by avowing that the statement is at least "true for me." A Presbyterian man acknowledges that "this is a hard one," but says he somehow thinks it has to do with Jesus' ethic of love, which is probably common to all religions. Another Lutheran argues that one would have to be a truly spiritual person to properly interpret the verse, meditating on it until one had a "sense" of its divine wisdom; by extension, he thinks "spiritually advanced people" of all religions would probably come to the same conclusions about such verses.

The same ambivalence that characterizes their feelings about conversion also apply to inclusive Christians' views of the church. Although most of them are active in their own churches, there is an element of arbitrariness in their arguments about why it is important to be involved. The most common arguments emphasize the need for community and support and the opportunity to serve. Although these arguments are compatible with Christian teachings, they are seldom justified specifically in relation to Christian teachings. For instance, few people argue that it is pleasing to God for believers to attend church or that Christ is somehow mystically present when Christians gather for worship; it is more common for arguments to be cast in humanistic terms, such as feeling energized by being around other people, enjoying mingling with friends, or being challenged to help the needy. Inclusive Christians do argue that they feel more comfortable worshipping at church than they would in other settings, a view that distinguishes them from spiritual shoppers. But they are like spiritual shoppers in arguing that there is a corrosive quality, an element of inauthenticity about the materialistic society in which we live; thus, the church serves as a kind of counterculture, just as meditating or going on spiritual retreats and participating in holistic health centers do for spiritual shoppers. Also like spiritual shoppers, inclusive Christians often personalize their arguments about churchgoing to the point that there is little reason to think that people outside the church might be better off being there. Churchgoing is depicted as a personal choice, like going to the movies or baking one's own bread; if it happens to give joy and fulfillment, so be it; if it doesn't, do something else. Like their arguments about Christianity, then, inclusive Christians' arguments about churchgoing provide reasons why someone who happens to be a Christian may find it interesting and rewarding to attend church, but these arguments also leave room for people of other faiths (or no faith) to worship and serve in their own ways.

Maintaining a commitment to Christianity while holding an open-minded view of other religions is, in the final analysis, a matter of arriving at a delicate balance between what one may expect to learn from other religions and one's reasons for preferring a single religion. While much of this balancing act is determined implicitly by the assumptions people make about Christianity, it is also something that people think about. They look around at other religions, watch spiritual shoppers, and come up with arguments both in favor of and against trying to benefit by learning about other religions. The arguments in favor are many. One that is voiced frequently is that exposure to other religions, just as experience with any form of cultural diversity, breeds tolerance, acceptance, and perhaps a more cautious hold on what one regards as truth. Another common argument is that exposure to other religions increases one's awareness of diversity itself, thus revealing that God has many faces and that diversity itself is divine. Yet another argument is that a person learns what is truly universal by comparing and contrasting different religions; for instance, if all religions teach that God exists, then one has greater confidence that God really does exist or at least that all humans want God to exist. Strikingly less common are arguments about actually learning something specific from another religion, but such arguments surface occasionally. For example, one woman mentions Gandhi's commitment to nonviolence as something she has learned from Hinduism and observance of the sabbath as a practice she has come to appreciate from Judaism; another woman says that she has learned to meditate more effectively through exposure to Buddhism.

Most of the arguments in favor of learning from other religions do not require much exposure to these religions, only a general awareness that they exist. Inclusive Christians are able to appreciate the *possibility* of learning from other religions without actually devoting much time to trying to understand these religions. In addition, inclusive Christians have strong arguments for limiting their actual exposure to other religions, even though they may be open-minded toward them. The argument most often mentioned is that it is simply too confusing to dabble in too many different belief systems. Another common argument is that depth and dabbling do not go together: one has to be disciplined, spending time in one tradition, to learn it well. People also worry that picking and choosing from various traditions leaves too much room for feelings, whims, and simply taking what suits one's self-interest. Staying true to one tradition, they recognize, forces a person to acknowledge the accumulated wisdom and experience of that tradition.

Envisioning an Inclusive Society

Inclusive Christians typically admit that their knowledge of non-Christian religions is limited. Although they are sufficiently aware of other religions to have crafted or absorbed a view of Christianity that accommodates these religions, their images of Jews, Muslims, and other religions, they say, come as much from the mass media as they do from the few friends they may have had or occasional trips that exposed them to other religions. The idea of diversity, therefore, is often just that—an idea, rather than a feature of life that has been honed by living firsthand in diverse contexts. Even inclusive Christians who attend churches in diverse neighborhoods rarely have significant or extensive contact with people from other religions unless they happen to work in religiously diverse settings; their churches are usually more of an enclave that protects them from exposure than an opportunity to gain greater exposure. But this lack of extensive exposure does not mean that inclusive Christians are devoid of opinions about diversity. Indeed, they often have strong opinions about the virtues of diversity and the prospects for achieving it.

Beside being a fact of American life, diversity is, in the eyes of most inclusive Christians, a good development, and religious diversity is no exception. In this, spiritual shoppers and inclusive Christians are largely agreed: diversity enriches the species, strengthens the gene pool, makes life more interesting, and generates new ideas. On top of that, diversity is probably in keeping with God's plans for the earth. "I just think that new blood, new thinking, new cultures, and new ways of doing things open us up," says Mrs. Michaelson. "That's a great spiritual development." Mr. Polaski, the cabinetmaker in Los Angeles, agrees: "Any time that we can meet and come to know the infinitely deep and varied spiritual expressions of God, I think that we're going to be enriched." A Presbyterian man in Atlanta who compares the present increase in diversity with previous waves of immigration that expanded the American melting pot observes: "There are difficulties involved with it, but I think it's good for people of the world to learn to live together and love each other and respect each other."

As inclusive Christians see it, the growing diversity—religious and otherwise—of American society will generate some problems, but not insuperable ones; indeed, there is a high degree of optimism in their views that God will work out the problems or, if not God, then talented humans themselves. The most commonly mentioned problems are hate crimes (which come to mind because of sensational events publicized by the media but seem not to be perceived as troubles in Christians' own communities), bickering, and petty disagreements. Although regrettable, these problems are thought to be no worse than the troubles caused by previous confrontations with diversity, which the nation dealt with successfully. "We've always handled diversity before," a Methodist woman observes, "so I'm confident we will handle any new conflicts that may arise." Others actually see good coming from such conflicts. For instance, a Presbyterian man, noting that the most serious religious conflicts have occurred in societies with two warring factions, thinks it will be better if the United States has many different religious factions. Or, as a Methodist woman explains, "If you've got a lot of diversity anyway, it's kind of like, 'Well, what's one more religion coming in? We've got so many already.'"

In an inclusive society, religious diversity does mean that achieving consensus and coming together around deeply held common values is likely to be harder than in a more homogeneous setting. Conflicts over different interpretations of honesty, loyalty, the marks of virtue or character, or specific issues such as abortion, gender, and sexual morality, for example, may be exacerbated by religious diversity. Yet, for inclusive Christians, the individualism that pervades their arguments about spirituality (making up one's own mind, following one's own path) is strikingly evident in their views of public morality. They do not worry much about the fact that growing diversity may make it harder to legislate or teach common values; they trust individuals to sort out moral and ethical issues on their own. Mrs. Michaelson says, "My values are my values, and yours are yours, and as long as we can live comfortably with each other within the laws of the land, I don't think we have to have one set of values." Others emphasize the possibility of people from diverse religious traditions still being able to agree on a few basic values, developing what the political philosopher Michael Walzer has termed a "thin consensus."[6] "I think there are some basic evils that can be agreed upon in a diverse society," says a man in Ohio, "and we can function by that kind of agreement without forcing one set of religious values on everyone."

As important as religious diversity is to their outlooks as Christians, these people, like many other Americans, are generally more interested in racial and ethnic diversity and in the diversity of lifestyles connoted by gender and sexual orientation than they are in religious diversity. Whereas religious diversity strikes them as a matter of taste and cultural background that Christians need to be content to live with, it does not conjure up images of inequality and discrimination in the same way that other forms of diversity do. To be sure, religious issues are important in the minds of inclusive Christians, but their thinking about social issues is deeply influenced by what they read in the newspapers, by what they have learned in school, and by a kind of commonsense wisdom about human relationships. Thus, instead of dwelling on the potential for theological or doctrinal conflict among religious groups, they speak of prejudice, fear, and inequality. Vivian Swenson, who belongs to the United Church of Christ, provides a good illustration of this outlook; when asked about religious conflicts, she remarks, "It's really all about economics, about people wanting to have more than someone else."

While they generally favor laws and other programs that protect diverse groups and facilitate diversity, inclusive Christians are more mixed in their views of their own position in a society that is becoming increasingly diverse. Many appear to be so thoroughly involved in their churches and in their open-minded ways of thinking that they can easily imagine themselves to be in a culturally dominant position despite an influx of people who are quite different. Others regard themselves as an enclave, a Christian witness in a post-Christian society, and are happy to assume this role. Being inclined as they are to recognize the potential for religious conflict and yet to avoid confrontation as much as possible, inclusive Christians sometimes opt for a kind of head-in-the-sand outlook that focuses on themselves and their own churches (as does one woman who says, "We just need to pay more attention to participating in our own religious communities and not worry about what other people are doing"). Yet this attitude is tempered by their conviction that a God of love truly wants Christians to reach out in love toward people outside their own group. "We need to inquire more about other people and associate with them more," says one man, "and that way our opinions about other religions will be more informed." A woman who shares his view thinks that "exclusivism" stems mainly from people not having knowledge about other religions; she would like to see children learn more about religious diversity at church and in school. Another woman suggests that religious groups working together on "outreach programs," such as serving in soup kitchens or building low-income housing projects, may be the most effective way to encourage understanding.

At the ground level, then, away from colleges and seminaries where ordinary people of faith live and work and reflect on their lives, inclusive Christianity is an intriguing amalgam of explicit theology and implicit cognitive strategies that have emerged in response to religious diversity. The explicit theology resembles what people hear in the sermons at their churches and runs parallel to the ways in which many clergy have been trained: that the essence of Christianity is love and acceptance, that God is ultimately unknowable but is sufficiently loving and gracious to draw all people into the divine presence without respect to religious traditions, and that Jesus is an example of how to know and serve God. The implicit cognitive strategies are less obvious because they are seldom articulated, but they serve inclusivity well. They reinforce the tolerant attitudes that many people learned from their parents or in school, reconciling tolerance with Christianity by emphasizing divine love and the idea of a common spirituality at the core of all humanity. They give people practical reasons for being active in their churches, reasons that focus less on questions about the absolute truth of Christianity and more on the congregation as a place to serve and find companionship. They offer ways to divert attention from thorny questions about the beliefs and practices of other religions and whether or not Christians should try to convert members of these religions to Christianity.

These cognitive strategies may be viewed within what social scientists have described as an evolutionary (or devolutionary) process of secularization.[7] What was once an arable terrain of formal doctrines and creeds has become an eroded wasteland of relativism and doubt. Each bargain represents a theological compromise. A generation or two later, Christianity itself becomes unrecognizable. "One needs a very long spoon," Peter Berger observes, "if one is to dine with the devil of doubt; without it, one is liable to end up as dessert."[8]

Yet it is not so much doubt as continuing engagement that we see resulting from the cognitive strategies of inclusive Christians.[9] Their cultural work is hardly bargaining at all. It redirects emphasis from the despair of uncertainty to a more positive affirmation of divine mystery. Jesus and the Bible acquire different meanings than among orthodox Christians. At the same time, inclusivity is itself restricted, keeping many of the fences separating religions intact. Wholesale exposure to radically different beliefs is minimized.

If theology and implicit cognitive strategies are important, the extent to which inclusive Christians are absorbed in the life of their local congregations is probably even more important. Although inclusive Christians generally have some firsthand exposure to people from non-Christian backgrounds, they are often so involved in their churches that they have little reason to interact with these other people. Religious diversity poses difficult questions from time to time, but for the most part is an abstraction, a symbol that stands as much for the idea of acceptance as the actual practice of inclusion. At the same time, this involvement means that inclusive Christians take the customs of their own tradition quite seriously, so seriously that they are often more skeptical of spiritual shoppers who seem unwilling to settle into a religious tradition than they are of devout practitioners of other traditions.

Inclusive Christians can, to some extent, be characterized, as the sociologist Nancy Ammerman has suggested, as "Golden Rule Christians"—people who resolve many of the thorny questions of living in a pluralistic society by emphasizing respect, tolerance, and fairness.[10] The inclusive Christians of today stand in a long tradition of people, including Leo Tolstoy, Benjamin Franklin, and Albert Schweitzer, who regarded love of neighbor as the essence of Jesus' teaching. With so many problems in the world needing to be addressed, it seems sensible to these inclusive Christians to roll up their sleeves, as Mother Teresa did, and get to work, putting their faith into practice, rather than worrying about the fate of people following other religions. "Jesus teaches in the Bible to accept everybody no matter what," a hair salon operator in Ohio explains. "No matter what they've done, what they believe. You accept them. You treat them with kindness. You do for them. You help them in time of need."

Yet it is not quite accurate to say that inclusive Christians simply distill their faith into a straightforward rule of unconditional, loving service to the needy. Few come close to living like Mother Teresa. And, more important, those who do believe that the essence of Christianity is love also argue that Christianity is more than this. Doctrines, church traditions, and the sacraments remain important to inclusive Christians, giving them an identity, a reason to love, a way to express their understandings of God. Mr. Shoemaker, the Catholic in Houston, says that Christianity is certainly about love, but "as a religious person you would not reach the fulfillment of your experience unless you at least learn about and appreciate some organized religious structure." Mrs. Winters, the Presbyterian in Chicago, takes the idea a step further, suggesting that love is "pretty tough," requiring "theology" and "ritual" to be fully understood and practiced. Unlike spiritual shoppers, who roam across religious boundaries with relative abandon, inclusive Christians—for all their cultural sophistication—do live then to a much greater extent in a cultural enclave, a Christian subculture. Christianity is meaningful, even though it does not answer all their questions, because it includes an understanding of God's love and God's ineffable presence, as well as an idea of Jesus as an example of how to live spiritually in relation to God. The church programs that draw their interest do not exactly isolate them from the wider world, but do produce a certain amount of insularity. Inclusive Christians are able to maintain their own commitment to Christianity by devising ways to make sense of other religions and thus get along as Christians living comfortably in a world of diversity. Their view of heaven, if the term resonates with their idea of spiritual truth, is that it is a house big enough for all. As one woman remarked, "even Jesus said heaven has many mansions."

"One Way": Resisting Diversity

WHEN THEY STOP to think about people who follow religions other than Christianity, a substantial number of Americans say they have absolutely no doubt that only Christians will go to heaven. Comforted by neither the pluralist vision of the spiritual shopper nor the inclusive hopes of their more liberal-minded fellow Christians, these Americans firmly defend what they regard as an old-fashioned, exclusivist version of the gospel truth. They point to the false teachings of other religions and to the necessity to convert their friends and neighbors to Christianity. Martin Marty says they "turn tribal and exclusive within their boundaries."[1]

But how is it possible to believe that only Christians are saved, to look across the room at one's coworker who may be Jewish or Muslim and murmur to oneself, "Such a shame, she's going to hell"? Do large numbers of Christians actually "turn tribal"—like some archaic group that shows up in the pages of an anthropology journal—or is this a characterization that does them injustice? Are they perhaps tribal more like a warm family who take pride in their kinship, coming together at holidays to share meals and memories, and returning again to live at peace with their coworkers and friends? The difficult (sometimes tortured) mental maneuvering in which spiritual shoppers and inclusive Christians engage suggests that one may be tempted to be an exclusive Christian by default; at least being one would surely be easier. A person could then rely on historical precedent, the centuries of arguments that Christian apologists have given for why they are right and why others must be converted to their view, and thereby avoid having to rethink one's faith to make room for other pathways to God. Particularly if one could truly turn tribal, blocking out troubling impressions of the wider world and its complicated religious mosaic, the weight of historical argument may well prove compellingly real.

Is it truly possible, though, for contemporary Americans to believe that nearly everyone but themselves is destined for eternal damnation? Or is it necessary, even to be an exclusive-minded Christian, to make one's peace with religious diversity, perhaps by inventing new ways of thinking about one's own faith? Virtually everyone now has opportunities to reflect on the religious complexity of their world, whether through personal encounters with people of other religions or through the newspapers and television. And if that is not enough, a person who attends church and thinks very deeply about his or her faith is likely to encounter questions being raised about other religions by clergy and fellow believers. However powerful they may be, the standard theological formulas have to be translated into practical wisdom—verbal scripts that can be recited to oneself and to others—wisdom that makes it possible to believe in the unique, absolute truth of the Christian message in the face of many who clearly believe otherwise.

Like those who become spiritual shoppers or inclusive Christians, Americans who hold to the exclusive truth of Christianity have been subtly encouraged to do so by the particular social circumstances in which they live. Their convictions are in part a reflection of who they know and what they have been taught. Their upbringing, social networks, and even the style of learning to which they become accustomed predispose them to Christian exclusivism. But these experiences are often more ambiguous (even surprising) than at first may be imagined. Exclusive Christians have to work hard, not always consciously of course, but by piecing together a language of faith, a worldview that permits them to believe as they do and yet to meet the challenge of having friends, coworkers, and even family members who believe differently.

Trisha Mobley: "It Is Written"

If anyone should be able to talk persuasively with her friends about their need for Jesus, it ought to be Trisha Mobley. A natural and persuasive talker, she has, for the past sixteen years, been selling Mary Kay Cosmetics—very successfully. She now has more than seven hundred customers whom she services personally and a staff of thirty-six sales-women from whom she derives commissions. Her income has put one son through medical school and is helping to support another son and his wife as missionaries; it is also paying the family bills while her husband, laid off from his firm after thirty-three years, finds a new job. Mrs. Mobley and her husband are dedicated evangelical Christians who attend an ex-panding five-hundred-member nondenominational charismatic church near their home in New Jersey.[2]

Her church and her unwavering conviction that God loves her are the bedrock of her existence. "I just believe that God loved me so much that he wanted me to spend eternity with him," she explains, trying to sum up what she believes in a few sentences, "and the only way that could happen was for Christ to die on that cross, for him to be the price for our sins. That's overwhelming to me that he would give his life. I know that one day I will have that place with him, and I believe that my parents are there, I believe my husband's parents are there, and that one day we will see them and that will be wonderful. But it is not going to be anything in comparison to when I can look at my Lord's face! I know how much he loved me and that I will stand in his presence." Tears start form-ing in the corners of her eyes as she speaks. "We almost laugh about it sometimes, for the last twelve years, something has happened every year. My mom dying, moving, our children growing up and leaving home, something. I just can't imagine going on without having a personal rela-tionship with God."

She believes firmly that Christians should try to convert non-Christians to Christianity. "The only way to heaven is because of Jesus Christ and his death on the cross," she says, "so I want to share that good news with people I come in contact with." In her view, Christianity is the "only promise of eternal security," and not Christianity in the abstract but pro-fessing literally (verbally) one's belief in Jesus as his or her savior. She has no doubts about the need for people who happen to have been raised in other religions to become Christians in order to have salvation. "The Bible tells us that from beginning to end. In the Old Testament, it gave all of the prophesies that Christ was coming and that he would be the savior of the world. The New Testament shows all the ways he is the savior of the world. If I believe that the Bible is the Word of God, and it is the truth, then no matter who I come in contact with, whether it's an atheist, an agnostic, someone who just has never been to church, a Jewish person, or a Muslim, I need to tell them about Jesus."

A bit embarrassed, Mrs. Mobley acknowledges that she does not share her faith in Jesus as often as she should; doing so is somehow difficult. But about a year ago, God spoke to her and said, "I've given you fifteen successful years selling Mary Kay; now I want you to use those networks for me." Mrs. Mobley has been on the lookout since then for people she thinks are especially in need of hearing the gospel—Jehovah's Witnesses, Hindus, atheists, women who have recently gone through a divorce, people who are ill. She tells them Jesus died for them so they can have eternal life. She has also started an organization called Alpha ("a non-threatening way to teach Christianity"), inviting as many of her coworkers, clients, and neighbors as she can. About fifty of them now meet regularly to study the Bible and nourish their souls.

In many ways, it is easy to understand why Mrs. Mobley believes so strongly that Christianity is the one true way and that she should encourage others to discover it. Were it not enough to have heard it from God, she has been told about salvation all her life by her parents, family, pastors, and friends. Her parents started taking her to the Baptist church near their home in North Carolina before her second birthday. When she was six, she "went forward" during the altar call at the end of the Sunday morning service and asked Jesus to come into her heart. She knew immediately "that I would get to go live in heaven with Jesus forever." For the next few months, the pastor came every Saturday morning, sat with her at the kitchen table, his big Bible spread out before him, and talked with her about Jesus. Soon after, she was baptized.

Unlike many of her childhood friends, Mrs. Mobley did not continue in the Baptist church until she grew up, got married, and had children of her own. During her teens, her parents had a falling out with the church, moved to Virginia, and became Episcopalians. She became an Episcopalian, too, for a while at least, but before finishing high school she fell in love with a Methodist, and six months later ran away and got married. They went sporadically to church with his parents and then for several years did not go at all. "I knew I was saved," she recalls, "but wasn't really walking the way God wanted me to." A few years later, when their son was born, they decided it was time to walk right again. Some friends invited them to a Brethren church, which they settled into for the next nine years. Several moves took them to other towns and to other churches, all evangelical. She taught Sunday school and her husband was a deacon. The church they attend now is more lively, teaches the charismatic gifts, and encourages evangelism. Pastor Jack, whom she admires greatly, preaches often about the need for people to come to Jesus. "It's on the name of Jesus that we are saved," Mrs. Mobley explains. "If you don't believe that he's the son of God, and you don't believe what he says, then I don't believe that you can have eternal life."

Yet it would be inaccurate to think of Mrs. Mobley as someone who dogmatically believes in an exclusive view of Christianity because living within her own tribe she has never been exposed to anything else and has no other way of coping with diversity than to assert the truth of her own beliefs. Holding on to her beliefs has been a more challenging, convoluted process than the quick, testimonial-style account of her spiritual journey suggests. She lives in a neighborhood populated by Muslims and Hindus as well as Christians. She grew up with Jewish neighbors, playing with their children and visiting their homes. Before his death, her father quit going to church entirely and her mother, who had been a Catholic early in life, returned to that faith late in life. She and her husband have traveled abroad, and she is aware that the world is much more diverse than the one she has experienced. At times, she wonders if she has "been a Christian too long" and wishes she had been to college or had other opportunities to think more broadly about life. Her best friend is Jewish and it troubles Mrs. Mobley to think that this good woman is eternally condemned. "I love her very, very much; I respect her and what she believes." Her voice cracks and she pauses. "It's just so sad." But then, as if to shore up her own convictions, she asserts: "God says there's one way. He says that. It is written. It's written a million times. One way!"

The Road to Resistance

The standard interpretation of why people who live in diverse settings cling wholeheartedly to what may seem like a narrow interpretation of the world is that they have either never been exposed to people with other views or, if they have been exposed, found themselves threatened to the point of retreating into the safe security of their own beliefs.[3]

The idea of tribalism reflects this interpretation. Tribalists resist the outside world because they do not know any better or because they do know quite well that there are other tribes out there, dangerous ones that need to be guarded against. If there is little contact with the outside world, tribalists live comfortably with their particular view of the world, taking it for granted, and reinforcing one another's assumptions about how the world works by tacitly following these assumptions in the way they speak and act. If there is contact, tribalists (or perhaps their leaders) strengthen the barricades by pointing out how evil the outside world is and encourage people inside to be all the more loyal, interacting with their own kind and mouthing the conventional wisdom. In either case, the plausibility of what might otherwise appear as an implausible worldview is maintained.[4]

Yet the standard interpretation does not sufficiently answer the question, how are worldviews maintained? To suggest that a worldview is plausible implies that people never have to ask questions because they already know the answers; indeed, they may not have to think about what they believe and why they believe it because occasions do not arise in which beliefs are challenged. People like Trisha Mobley show the inadequacy of this interpretation, particularly as it applies to religious diversity. They are quite aware of diversity, both from firsthand acquaintance and from their knowledge of the wider world. They are people like Walt Miller, a member of an African Methodist Episcopal church in Miami, a barber who comes in frequent contact with Muslims in his neighborhood; like Frank Lucas, a federal judge in Chicago who has had Jewish friends all his life; like Heather Badgett, an Episcopalian in Denver who took a class in comparative religions in college; and like Joyce Lee, a Chinese American in Los Angeles whose grandparents are Buddhists. Their lives are not structured to avoid all contact with diversity, but to manage this contact and to supply certain answers to the questions that arise from it.

Like spiritual shoppers and inclusive Christians, Christians who resist accepting religious diversity are heavily influenced by their religious upbringing. Exclusive Christianity is nurtured in exclusive churches where people such as Mrs. Mobley learn early that they are in danger of eternal damnation and accept Jesus as their savior to avoid suffering damnation. They learn that there is one way to heaven and that many people outside of their own group—certainly atheists and followers of other religions but also many self-proclaimed Christians who have not truly turned their hearts to God—will not go to heaven. The unique truth of Christianity fits like a second skin in the many evangelical churches where, according to one study, 96 percent of active members nationally believe that "faith in Christ is the only hope for salvation."[5] It is implicitly reinforced by having close friends in the congregation, feeling accepted, and sensing that Christianity is a religion of love that champions freedom, happiness, individuality, and diversity. Yet the centrality of salvation and the fact that people must choose Christ in order to have salvation necessarily implies that people who have chosen otherwise are not saved. The topic of diversity, whether it is characterized as heresy, heterodoxy, belief in false gods, or simply unbelief, is inescapably connected with any consideration of salvation. The connection is hardly taken for granted; it is reinforced in sermons, through regular altar calls, and in testimonials.

A religious upbringing like this often occurs in a homogeneous setting, such as a single congregation in which a person participates from the time he or she is born until adulthood, a congregation like the Southern Baptist church near Charlotte, North Carolina, to which Jack Otis, a postal worker, went every Sunday until he joined the navy at age nineteen, or like the theologically conservative Methodist church outside Columbus, Ohio, in which Brenda Gilbert, a farmer's wife, and her husband were raised and which they continued attending after they were married. But the image of an isolated enclave does not adequately capture the kind of religious journey that now characterizes a large number of exclusive Christians. Many come from mixed denominational backgrounds and as children were shunted from church to church by their parents' jobs, marital instability, or search for the perfect congregation. As teenagers or adults, they have often searched for spiritual answers and pride themselves on having made a "decision for Christ." They are in their own way spiritual shoppers. Although they do not dabble in esoteric spiritual practices rooted in non-Christian traditions, they often switch churches, fall away, experience conversions and moments of new vitality, and make countless decisions about what to read, who to believe, and how to worship and pray. These choices are typically made in Christian contexts and are guided by Christian pastors, friends, and family members. Yet the very fact of such extensive decision making and the manner in which decisions are made has an important impact on the way in which exclusive Christians understand their faith. In a word, their faith becomes subjective. The ground on which decisions are made increasingly takes the form, as expressed in people's comments, of "just feeling right." And, although it is true that these same people believe firmly that their faith is objectively true (in the sense that God really exists and actually said what is written in the Bible), the role of feelings, of some subjective mood or inclination or emotion, is ever-present.

Mrs. Mobley's story clearly illustrates the relationship between the frequent decisions that many Americans make concerning their faith and the tendency to emphasize feelings as the correct basis for these decisions. In explaining why she and her husband attended one church for a number of years, she says that they just "enjoyed" being there and "felt right" about it; the people were apparently friendly and helpful. Then, when they decided to leave that church, she says that she felt "indifferent," as though she was "drifting." At the new church she started attending, she "had something, had a feeling" and no longer "felt dead." The worship services are geared toward reaffirming these subjective feelings; as Pastor Jack explains, "We worry if people go away having dry experiences; we want them to *feel* God's love, to come away feeling self-actualized."

Basing one's faith decisions on feelings may lead to the kind of personal relativism ("choose your own path") that typifies spiritual shoppers and many inclusive Christians. In the same way that one chooses to believe in Jesus because it feels right, for example, someone else may feel right about being Jewish or Muslim. But the logic works differently for exclusive Christians. For them, the emphasis on feelings tends mostly to undercut rational arguments that might favor a more inclusive perspective and takes the place of intellectual defenses of exclusive Christianity that might at some point prove shaky.[6] Feelings have the power to function in this way because exclusivist Christians do not construe them entirely as personal whims or tastes; instead, they are divinely legitimated feelings—moods interpreted to be evidence of God's leading or of the presence of the Holy Spirit. To the extent that someone considers a choice truly arbitrary (exclusive Christians often recognize that going to one church may be no better than going to any of a dozen other possible choices), the legitimacy of basing one's choice on personal taste is contingent on the fact that the choice is still "within limits." That is, God offers a range of reasonable choices that are acceptable because they do not explicitly violate a biblical teaching. Choosing to switch from one Bible-believing church to another is legitimate; choosing to believe in Vishnu clearly is not.

Besides religious upbringing, exclusive Christians are frequently influenced by having cultivated social relationships in what might be termed restricted networks. Although they may have had friends who belonged to other religions or may have worked or lived in diverse settings, their networks typically include strong emotional or financial ties that induce a kind of dependence on parents, family, or fellow church members. Spiritual shoppers and inclusive Christians also have close friends and for the most part feel warmly toward their parents. But, perhaps because of greater financial security or because their economic well-being depends more on attaining higher education or making connections in business, they are freer to pick and choose, to break ties, and to live at greater distances from relatives. In contrast, exclusive Christians are more likely to live near or in the same household as parents or in-laws, look to parents for babysitting or guidance in raising their children, work for a relative, talk frequently with relatives on the telephone, borrow money from relatives, or have friends in their church with whom they are connected in similar ways.

The Mobleys illustrate what it means to have restricted networks. They have lived in several different states, have always been financially independent, and have traveled, and she has met hundreds of people through her work as a saleswoman; yet she and her husband, having married so young, have always remained closely tied to their parents. For a while, they lived with his parents and close to her parents; when her parents moved to another state, she remembers, "we really missed them" and moved to be near them; for more than a decade, they lived just around the corner from her parents and went to the same church, and after her father died, they moved in with her mother to keep her from being lonely. She credits her parents and her in-laws with giving her stability. They had "strong, stable Christian homes" that she has tried to emulate. Besides her family, she has always sought close, supportive congregations. Although she insists that she and her husband went only to churches that were "Bible-believing," she acknowledges that the most appealing qualities were members being "friendly," "helpful," "supportive," "encouraging," and "accepting."

Restricted networks maintain themselves most of the time, as long as they provide warmth and encouragement and as long as they are not ripped apart by people moving around, seeking jobs, or consciously fleeing from abuse and family dysfunction. For Brenda Gilbert and her husband, inheriting land from his father and farming a few miles from the Methodist church was reason enough to stay loyal. For Ken Hiersma, who now belongs to a new Presbyterian Church in America (PCA) congregation in Denver, spending the first twenty years of his life in a Dutch enclave in Michigan and going to a Christian Reform high school was decisive; "there just wasn't a lot of opportunity to rub shoulders with anybody but people like you," he recalls.

When restricted, supportive networks of this kind fail, the results can be devastating. Mrs. Mobley recalls one such experience: "They were our life. They were our friends. Everything we did revolved around the church and those people. When you leave a fundamental church, you leave it all. They bury you, because they just don't think you're ever supposed to leave." She says the loss of their church friends was like a death in the family, almost as painful as losing her mother. The natural response to such loss is to seek some other tightly knit community that can fill the gap, like the charismatic congregation Mrs. Mobley now attends or like the PCA church that closely resembles the one of Ken Hiersma's youth. Without close relatives to share babysitting and Sunday meals, there may be an acute sense of moral drift, of feeling emotionally lost, at sea, lonely, in need of community (Mrs. Mobley says there was a "big hole" in her heart whenever they switched churches).[7] A new tightly knit church group can provide much-needed emotional support, if not babysitting and an occasional handout as well. If the process involves leaving a supportive church, the bonds have usually been strong enough at some point to overcome whatever sense of alienation may be associated with the shift and thus lead to a search for a new church rather than falling away from the church entirely. The switch includes an explanation that preserves basic commitment to exclusive Christianity, such as feeling a need for something new, a pastor coming or going, or needing a better program for one's children. To the extent that exclusive Christianity is reinforced by spending time in a certain kind of church environment, then, this reinforcement can withstand the migration from church to church that now characterizes many Americans.

The emotional support provided by a tightly knit religious community is often sufficient to keep people actively involved for long periods of time, but in-group loyalty is known to be strengthened by threats to the integrity and values of the group or by other sources of impending danger as well. These threats usually have no direct connection with religious diversity;

for example, they are not fears inspired by worries that one's spouse will convert to another religion or that one's neighborhood is being overrun by people who belong to other religions. They are, however, indirectly related to how people feel toward other religions because they reinforce the view that commitment to the one true faith is essential to the well-being of oneself and one's family. Such perceived threats are sometimes linked to national debates—about abortion, gay rights, or the right to bear arms—and can thus be part of what Christian Smith has termed the "embattled" mentality of some segments of the Christian community.[8] Because these threats are often exploited by political leaders as ways of garnering support for particular candidates or movements, it is safe to say (as Christian Smith, Alan Wolfe, and others have) that the average Christian, even those holding exclusivist views of other faiths, may be more open-minded or conflicted about such issues than media reports and leaders' statements would suggest.[9]

But information obtained from personal interviews, in which people talk freely about their friends and families, indicates that the perceived threats that reinforce commitment to exclusive Christianity are often quite real, much more so than the implied dangers represented by leaders' discussions of political issues, because they are embodied in the life of a family member or close personal acquaintance. The problem may be abortion or homosexuality, but is more likely to be alcoholism, drug use, spousal or child abuse, petty crime, a dysfunctional marriage, the inability to get or keep a job, or some form of despondency or other psychosomatic illness. Mrs. Mobley, for instance, mentions a foster brother her parents always worried about because he seemed uninterested in going to church and unable to hold a steady job; she talks, too, about one of her children having a drug problem, mentioning it in the context of explaining why she has felt it especially important to be part of a Bible-believing church.

Exclusive Christianity is also reinforced by a learning style that is compatible with emotional or financial dependence on a restricted network or tightly knit community. This learning style emphasizes trusting in an authority figure or an authoritative text for answers, submitting graciously to what the Bible, the pastor, one's boss, or one's spouse may say is right.[10] It should not be confused with being brainwashed or exhibiting the extreme traits associated with a so-called authoritarian or fascist personality.[11] Exclusive Christians have inquiring minds and are usually eager to learn, especially when learning is understood as a way of deepening their faith. Yet, in contrast with spiritual shoppers and inclusive Christians, who often insist on creatively personalizing their faith, exclusive Christians are more likely to believe in the existence of a single set of right answers, which a person questions or tampers with at his or her peril. Mrs. Mobley illustrates this orientation by talking about baking a cake. If a person borrows a good cake recipe from a friend, she suggests, it makes no sense to try to improve on it: "If I thought, 'I'm going to doctor this up a little bit,' and I added this and this and this, I wouldn't have that quality cake that she had made at her house."

This attitude toward truth encourages exclusive Christians to feel that they do not have the ability simply to read things entirely of their own choosing, learn by distilling from diverse experiences, or figure out what is right on their own. Teachers and religious leaders see themselves and are seen, not as guides or discussion partners, but as voices of authority whose wisdom should be heeded (as a lay leader at one Baptist church observed, "People here aren't eager to ask questions or discuss; they want to be told the answers"). The distinctiveness of this learning style should not be overdrawn: spiritual shoppers and inclusive Christians are also influenced by peer pressure, by what their friends have read and experienced, and by the idea that some writers or speakers have special wisdom to impart. Yet, in comparison, exclusive Christians appear less likely in many instances to have the cultural capital (education, language skills, experience, wisdom) they feel is needed to make their own choices about what to think and believe; they do not feel that some of life's mysteries are simply beyond human comprehension, but they diminish their own capacity to grapple with such mysteries, compared with other people, by emphasizing that they do not have the requisite training, would need to ask their pastor, or have not had time to think or read about an issue.[12] Although these perceptions of their capabilities reflect the kind of Christian humility that they admire, exclusive Christians also thereby restrict the ideas they think are worth considering to ones found within their own particular religious communities.

In talking about her understanding of Christian teachings, Mrs. Mobley further illustrates the learning style that often characterizes Christians who hold exclusivist views as she does. "He was submissive to the Father," she says, speaking of Jesus, "which I believe is an example for us. He lived here. He lived among people. He loved people. He took people right where they were. If the Bible says it about him, I don't question it. I just take the Bible, I'm not a deep studier. I don't care what it says in the Greek, I don't care what it says in the Hebrew, this is just what it says and it's okay with me." Jesus is her savior, her role model, the center of her life, yet in selecting one attribute of Jesus it is his submissiveness that she emphasizes. Jesus is an example of being subordinate, of doing what someone in authority demands, of not asking too many questions. He came down, not just from heaven to earth, but from his exalted place as king of kings to live among common people (like her). She does not question what the Bible says; she knows that she is not a "deep studier" and that other people (such as her pastor) approach the Bible knowing Greek and Hebrew; she doesn't; she takes things as they are. "I don't read much," she says. "I prefer to sit under teachings, to go hear someone teach." In her case, such comments may well be a reflection of the fact that she was never able to go to college. But other Christians who have had more education sometimes express similar views. Seth Neighbors, a Southern Baptist with a graduate degree in computer engineering, for instance, echoes her view. He says that he "isn't smart enough" to interpret the Bible and figure out what it means; he figures that it is something like gravity, though: "if you step off a building, you're going to fall."

What is at first blush puzzling, given the importance of homogeneous social ties to their lifestyle, is that exclusive Christians typically have some significant exposure to members of other religions as well. They have Jewish friends, as Mrs. Mobley does, grow up in homes where visitors come from other faiths, work among Muslims and Hindus, and travel abroad, where they meet Buddhists, Sikhs, and others. These encounters with other religions, however, are highly structured. Some of them are structured by the church; for instance, by an informational meeting at which a church-sponsored missionary shows slides of people in the Middle East and talks about Muslim customs. The international networks of missionaries and service workers of which many local churches are a part facilitate such encounters.[13] Others occur less formally, but also bear the imprint of the church, such as workplace contacts with members of non-Christian religions that through the encouragement of church-sponsored prayer meetings become defined as opportunities for witnessing. Mrs. Mobley describes a trip to England as one of her most vivid encounters with people who were different from the ones she usually meets at home: atheists, Anglicans, Muslims, Hindus, Sikhs. Yet her visit was arranged by people at her church; she visited with former church members who had moved to England and participated in church meetings that were similar to those at her own church; her contacts with non-Christians were all indirect, arm-length dealings mediated by people who shared her own religious views. Even more intimate encounters can be so thoroughly scripted that they reveal little of someone else's religious views. After discussing religious diversity at great length, Mrs. Mobley suddenly remembered that a young man who was a Buddhist had actually lived with her and her husband for two years. She apparently had forgotten that he was a Buddhist because she had always thought of him as a "Vietnamese refugee" that she and her husband had sponsored through her church. When asked if she had ever talked with him about Buddhism, she said that she and her husband had "talked to him about the Lord" and "got him a Bible," but he didn't speak English very well so all they knew was that he "prayed to Buddha."

The truth is, too, that exclusive Christians seldom go out of their way to learn about other religions, either by talking with people or by reading and taking classes. Although a few acknowledge that it would help in their efforts to convert other people to Christianity to understand the teachings of other religions, most admit little interest in gaining such understanding. Ken Hiersma, the PCA member, says he's "not exposed" and "chooses not to be." Asked to explain, he asserts, "Because I'm convinced that what I believe is right. I have all that I can do just to broaden and understand my own belief system." Sue Carruthers, a Presbyterian who has recently retired from an administrative position at the state capitol in Sacramento, hopes to do a lot of traveling abroad now that she has more time, but she also denies having an interest in learning about other religions. "Somehow I think my plate is pretty full on the Christian end of things," she explains. Bill Jackson, a blue-collar worker in Los Angeles who attends an African-American church, finds support in the Bible for his lack of interest in learning about other religions: "When I look at the Bible, the apostles didn't know all about other people's teaching; they only knew what Christ taught them." Seth Neighbors, the Southern Baptist computer engineer, simply emphasizes the need to make the most effective use of his time: "I don't have time to study what I consider to be the truth," he says, "so I sure don't have time to spend studying something that's out of line."

Comments like this resemble the remark of a married man who said that he did not have much interest in thinking about other men's wives because he was happy with his own. The church has always likened itself to the bride of Christ, reveling in its relationship with the one lover who fully satisfies all that can ever be desired. If being a Christian is a full-time commitment, fulfilled best by mixing only with other Christians, then any time spent studying other religions, even to learn better why others are lost, becomes an act of adultery rather than a way of enriching one's knowledge or deepening one's faith. Yet extending the analogy in the way that Mr. Hiersma and the others do suggests a more acute resistance to diversity, one that might well exclude dating, learning to talk to the opposite sex, or visiting with the neighbors, let alone becoming a marriage counselor or taking a class in comparative cultures.

Maintaining an Exclusivist Worldview

Although the social networks and the church settings in which exclusive Christians interact function in some interesting ways to reinforce an exclusivist worldview, they do not alone provide a sufficient way of understanding the contemporary strength of Christian exclusivism. Christians who reject the validity of other religious traditions have to work at their convictions, making important assumptions about their faith that help to manage their encounters with other religions in a way that seems sensible, credible. These assumptions markedly reflect the official teachings of particular churches, and thus bear the imprint of long-standing theological interpretations. But they are also rooted in the popular culture. They include tacit ways of dealing with diversity and understandings of Christianity that stem from informal conversations with friends and co-workers, television, best-selling books, and the lyrics of mass market music. These tacit ways of managing diversity differ dramatically from the ways in which spiritual shoppers and inclusive Christians view the world; they also sometimes deviate from the formal teachings of exclusive churches, providing church members with mechanisms for living more comfortably with diversity than church leaders (or critics) may suspect.

One of the more notable aspects of exclusive Christians' beliefs is the frequency with which they refer to eternal life. They do not mean some timeless, transcendent, mystical state of being, but a literal place of glory to which Christians go immediately when they die and in which they live for unending eons and eons. Whereas spiritual shoppers and inclusive Christians tend to emphasize a spiritual blending with the sacred, a kind of mystical ooze that happens in this life and somehow transcends it, exclusive Christians speak more explicitly and urgently about the life in heaven to which they will go after death. In contrast with spiritual blending, which is amorphous enough that Christians and non-Christians alike can be imagined attaining it, eternal life is clearly restricted to people who trust in Jesus as their personal savior. Stan Clifford, a restaurant manager in his late thirties who attends an Assembly of God church in New York, explains: "What we must do is repent of our sins, give our lives over to him [Jesus], so that we can live with him eternally. This life is just a vapor. It's just a small period of time. I want to spend my eternity with the Lord." Sheila Lopez, a personnel manager in her early forties who attends a Missouri Synod Lutheran church in Saint Louis, also goes out of her way to stress eternal life: "Without Jesus I'd have eternal damnation and I would have no place to look forward to go." Heather Badgett, the woman who attends an Episcopal church in Denver, dresses up the same idea: "I believe that Jesus is the only way to the Father, salvation, and eternal life. When he died on the cross, that was God's plan and that was the full sacrifice in payment for our sins."

Researchers point out that most Americans believe in some kind of existence beyond this life, a heaven most likely in which angels sing and good people enjoy themselves.[14] But observers note, too, that thoughts about the afterlife are a kind of afterthought, a comforting codicil to Americans' preoccupation with the present. Christians talk about personal fulfillment and happiness, for instance, more than they do about life beyond death, defining salvation as the key to a prosperous life more than to a heavenly kingdom. Salvation of the kind that Jonathan Edwards preached about has been replaced by self-realization, while Christian therapy, dieting, and self-expression have apparently become more urgent than redemption from divine retribution.[15] The frequency with which references to eternal life come up in discussions about religious diversity, therefore, gives reason to suspect that something more may be going on than people simply reporting why their faith is personally meaningful. One possibility is that questions about religious diversity elicit responses reflecting official church positions (and therefore emphasizing eternal life), even though these responses may not be very well integrated with the ways in which people of faith think and behave from day to day. Another possibility is that Christians really do think seriously that non-Christians are destined for eternal damnation, but that this belief does not tell much about Christians' actual behavior toward non-Christians because their behavior is governed more by other aspects of their faith. The two possibilities are not mutually exclusive. Both suggest that exclusive Christians think non-Christians are devoid of eternal life, but may not be sufficiently troubled by this fact to do much about it.

Jesus is central to the grassroots theology of exclusive Christians and, rather than being regarded as a wise spiritual leader, is understood as the sole source of atonement and mediation between humans and God. Inclusive and exclusive Christians largely agree about the divinity of Jesus; where they disagree is that the exclusive view emphasizes a gap between God and humans, a gap created by human sinfulness, that can only be bridged by belief in Jesus. This much resembles historic creedal understandings of Jesus. Yet there is more to it than that. For the contemporary exclusive Christian, God is quite far removed from the human realm: God is wholly pure, righteous, almighty and all-powerful, not a mysterious spiritual essence that may be present in the rocks and trees as well as in all people. This view of God runs contrary to the way in which many exclusive Christians probably think they think about God: it contradicts the idea that God is always near, always present, concerned about the individual, attentive to prayers, and evident in the Holy Spirit if not in miraculous healings and gifts of the spirit. But those ways in which God is near are usually understood in reference to Jesus and the Holy Spirit instead of, in trinitarian terms, God the Father.

The removal of God, in grassroots theology, to a place quite distant from the human realm is crucial to the exclusivist view of other religions. If God were literally present in nature and in humans, as for the inclusivist, then it would be hard to deny believers in other religions the ability to know and experience God. But if God is leagues away, then the need for a bridge of some kind becomes more important and it becomes more conceivable to posit that the Christian bridge is the only one that is truly passable. This means that even if present experiences of closeness to God are desired more than eternal life, Jesus is the answer, the way of being "reconciled back to God," as a member of an African-American church in Los Angeles puts it. Jesus becomes the answer, not just to an intellectual question about the gap between humans and God, but also to such practical problems as how to have an intimate friend who is always there, where to look for guidance in daily living, to whom to pray, and where to find peace and personal happiness. Jesus is the muscular older brother you always wanted to fend off bullies on the playground, the effusive spinster aunt who takes you in for milk and cookies after a bad day, the confidante you can e-mail for instant reassurance.

Joyce Lee, the Asian American (who attends a Christian and Missionary Alliance church in Los Angeles), describes Jesus in a way that illustrates his role in helping her in daily life. She says that she never understood God or trinitarian theology very well growing up and did not experience a great deal of love in her family, but Jesus is her friend: "Everything we need is in Jesus. We look to him. No matter what your problems are, whether it be with children, or your marriage, or your neighbor, whatever it is. Deal with your finances. He's got the way. He will show you the way. You go to him. He'll give you the answers." A Baptist insurance agent in her early thirties who lives in Oregon thinks of Jesus the same way: compassionate, wise, fair, and helpful. And because of how she views Jesus, she thinks that God "wants us to live a life and be blessed by it and wants us to have the fruits of his spirit, the peace and the joy and the love, and he wants us to be successful"; she adds, as if taken aback by her own statement, "Yes, it's okay to be successful. We're not supposed to be poor all of our lives." If Jesus stops short of giving tips on how to make a killing in the stock market, he is at least an alter ego, one's better self, the cheerleader within; as Pastor Jack says, "Jesus wants us to be self-actualized."

In short, Jesus becomes so attractive to the exclusive Christian that he or she finds it difficult to understand why anyone who has heard about Jesus—and most people have, they presume—would not immediately become a Christian. Only the action of a strong evil force, such as the devil, can explain it. This view of Jesus enables exclusive Christians to adopt a familiar stance toward non-Christians: not to feel terribly compelled to evangelize them, because Jesus is too attractive to need much selling, and to imagine that non-Christians probably know (or know about) Jesus, at least from afar, and are trying to find a way to God, but are just missing out on all the good times they could be having with Jesus. Shaking his head, Jack Otis, who lumps Islam and Mormonism together and compares Muhammad to Joseph Smith, says he just can't understand it: "those men have not done anything that makes them anywhere near what Jesus Christ did for us!" He is appalled that some people think of Jesus as just another great prophet, not because Jesus was actually divine but because Jesus is such a good source of peace and happiness. Or, as a hairdresser in her late twenties who attends a Missouri Synod Lutheran church in Denver, explains, "I don't think that Christians should go out and twist people's arms to do something that they're not willing and wanting to do, but there's people out there who are willing and eager to listen and want to know more." With buyers lined up around the block, nobody needs to send out more salespeople to drum up business.

Exclusive Christians ground their understandings of God and Jesus in the Bible. It is, to them, the story of Jesus: how he helped create the world, how God paved the way for Jesus' coming through the struggles and failures of the Israelites, how Jesus fulfilled the Old Testament prophecies, and how his death and resurrection provided redemption and the basis on which the Christian church was founded. Unlike inclusive Christians, exclusive Christians deny that any significant interpretive step is required to understand the Bible. God's literal words are recorded there in the scriptures and done so plainly enough that commonsense applications can be trusted. The preaching and teaching of the Bible that occurs in exclusive Christian churches, therefore, can be understood by members, not as the speaker's interpretation of the Bible, but as an "exposition" of the truth, meaning an amplification and reminder of its applicability to everyday life. This is the reason that exclusive Christians read and study the Bible as often as they do and why they take stock in verses such as the one about Jesus being the way and the truth.

Above all, the Bible provides proof that only Christians can be saved. When asked why they think it is necessary to believe in Jesus to be saved, the most typical response of Christians with an exclusivist worldview is to refer to the Bible, not to elaborate or try to explain why the Bible says what it does, but simply to assert that the Bible is their source as if saying anything more would somehow diminish the flat fact of the Bible's absolute veracity. "That's what it says in God's Word," Seth Neighbors states. "The Bible says it," Mrs. Mobley echoes. Walt Miller, the barber, elaborates only slightly: "The Bible says so—and the Bible is my authority for living."

Because of their emphasis on the Bible, exclusive Christians attach special significance to the rules they find in the Bible for Christian living. In contrast to inclusive Christians, their view of the Christian life encourages behavior that distinguishes Christians from people who follow other religious traditions. This distinctive behavior includes rules about personal morality, such as not engaging in homosexual or extramarital sexual relationships. "As a Christian you need to make choices in your life that aren't as the world would say it's okay to do, but by the standards of what the Bible says," Mrs. Mobley asserts. As examples of behavior to avoid she lists living together before marriage, getting an abortion, watching perverted movies, and slandering your brother.

Many of the rules traditionally associated with sectarian Christianity, such as prohibitions against dancing or the consumption of alcohol, have been relaxed. But spiritual discipline of other kinds is still encouraged; these practices include attentiveness to one's children, praying regularly, avoiding friendships and places of association that might result in temptation, and general honesty and clean living. "It involves your daily living," one woman explains, "such as your language, how you act in your home, how you act with people. Are you angry? Do you have the peace and the joy that you're supposed to have? Are you walking around with a bunch of baggage on you so that you feel like you're hopeless?" And when exclusive Christians say they "respect" people who are committed to other religions, as they often do, they mention their perception that these people uphold some of the same moral and spiritual disciplines (e.g., Jewish devotion to family and Muslim sobriety) that they admire in Christians. A Catholic man who manages a print shop in Pennsylvania and hopes other people will become Christians by being attracted to the way he lives, for example, says that he respects Muslims because "they're very close-knit family people; they are more religious oriented than many Catholics or Protestants; they don't pray once a week, they do it day and night, and they fast."

The most distinctive feature of exclusive Christians' vision of the Christian life, however, is its emphasis on Bible reading and participation in churches that preach and teach the Bible. Whereas inclusive Christians may be drawn to specific church programs that are personally appealing (but also favor broad humanitarian forms of service in which people of all faiths may participate), exclusive Christians believe it is especially pleasing to God to attend church, to serve on church committees, perhaps ladling soup at church dinners or fixing the vestibule roof, and to participate in prayer meetings and Bible studies. Practice follows belief and belief legitimates practice: the tightly knit church communities that structure relationships with people from other religions (or, just as likely, minimize contact) are not merely matters of convenience but divinely ordained. "Be involved with the church," a Baptist woman admonishes, "as the Bible says 'Do not forsake the assembly.' I think that's most important."

Exclusive Christians' assumptions about God, Jesus, and church restrict the amount of contact they have with non-Christians even as they reinforce the view that only Christianity is true. Yet Christianity also encourages evangelism; indeed, any belief system that is not only true but uniquely true is bound to encourage its followers to let other people know about the truth, especially when their immortal souls depend on it. Telling others the "good news" amounts to much more than merely being sociable, like sharing recipes or gardening tips. Thus, it is less surprising that exclusive Christians believe it is right to try to convert others (which media-getting proselytization campaigns invariably emphasize) than that they do not engage more wholeheartedly in such efforts. Some exclusive Christians exempt themselves from proselytizing Jews on theological grounds (arguing that God reserves special treatment for Jews), but nearly all believe it is important to try to make converts of Muslims, Hindus, and Buddhists, and many think this about Jews.

One of the most common ways in which exclusive Christians explain their lack of effort in bringing others to Christ is to emphasize the importance of following God's timing and, for all intents and purposes, letting God do the work. Mrs. Mobley says she wants to share the "good news" that Jesus Christ died for our sins, but she adds: "Do I share it with everybody I come in contact with? Obviously not." When asked to explain, she says, "Do I believe you get in someone's face? No, I don't. I think there has to be a time and a place, and I think God has to appoint that time, and the Holy Spirit has to prepare that person." A Catholic man says non-Christians need to be converted, but prefers to think it is just enough to make them aware of Jesus: "I don't say that you have to do this and you have to do that. I don't believe in that. I think if the spirit moves them to want to know more and through their own choice they decide, that's fine. I don't think it's like I was called that I have to convert somebody that has to be converted because they need to be saved. I'm not out there running around trying to convert everybody."

The idea that a person must be ready to convert and then do so spontaneously fits well with contemporary Christianity's emphasis on the ultimate, unchallenged authority of the individual. Thus, when asked about converting Jews or Muslims, exclusive Christians often say they do not "target any group," but try to relate to individuals no matter what their religion may be. This language is commonly used in public settings to deflect concerns about one religious group proselytizing another (for example, in response to criticisms raised periodically by reports that Southern Baptists are mounting special evangelistic efforts to convert Jews or Hindus). Among individual Christians, it is used as well, especially to emphasize the effectiveness of "friendship evangelism" that occurs only among close personal acquaintances. Since most exclusive Christians know few people of other religions, this strategy effectively minimizes their likelihood of evangelizing many such people (as Mrs. Mobley observes, "The sad thing with so many Christians is because so much of our life is our church and our church family, we don't have too many opportunities outside").

Christians who believe that only Christians are saved also share some of the views that permit inclusive Christians to sidestep some of the hard questions this belief entails. They argue, for example, that only God knows for sure who is saved and who is not saved; as Frank Lucas, the federal judge, explains: "I don't pretend to know these things, even though I wouldn't be sanguine about some of the other world religions. I wouldn't just say because people are good that they're likely to be saved, but I don't have that kind of knowledge. I tend to just leave that to the Lord." Although he believes firmly in the inerrancy of the Bible and understands the Bible to say that non-Christians are unsaved, this man still somehow wants to believe that God makes special deals with each individual, perhaps even deals that permit Muslims or Hindus to be privately regarded as Christians in God's eyes. Another man holds a similar view but articulates it as a possibility of the mysterious working of the Holy Spirit, again in a way that may open avenues for salvation other than explicitly believing in Jesus: "The Holy Spirit draws people to be saved. Whether they make the decision to accept that or not is their choice. I believe that there's millions of people in the world who don't know Jesus and it's not their fault." Stan Clifford, the restaurant manager who attends an Assembly of

God church and says he has had some "interesting conversations" with his Muslim and Jewish friends, also tries to walk a fine line between sticking to his views and not appearing judgmental: "According to the Bible, everybody needs to accept Jesus Christ to attain salvation." But, he hastens to add, "I would be a hypocrite to sit here and say that this person or that person is going to go to heaven or that person isn't going to go to heaven. I can't really honestly sit here and tell you that these different people won't go to heaven. All I can tell you is that the Bible says you have to be born again. Each person's salvation is between him and God. What I believe is that you have to receive Jesus Christ. Now is a really, really devout Jewish or Muslim person who really, really serves God not going to go to heaven? I honestly can't tell you because I'm not God and I don't know. But what the Bible says is you must be born again."

If Christians with exclusivist views of salvation do not for the most part aggressively evangelize people who belong to other religions, they nevertheless hold a number of sharp opinions about other religions and about the people who follow these religions. One common response is to use single words or short phrases, almost like slogans, to characterize the beliefs and practices of other religions. Referring to other religions as cults or in the same breath as devil worship or fanaticism, or associating a complex religious system only with belief in reincarnation or a generalization about polytheism, are examples. Such impressions often include visual images—generated by television far more often than from personal contact—such as those of Muslims kneeling en masse for prayer or beating themselves with chains and Hindus worshipping "idols" at highly adorned altars. Although few of these impressions and images are attributable to explicit discussions about other religions at Christian churches, many of them reflect the view that people who follow these other religions are without salvation. Muslim prayers, for example, are interpreted as "vain works" that mislead people into thinking they can do things to earn salvation instead of realizing that salvation comes only through Jesus. One man who has Muslim friends describes them as "rigid" and "filled with hate"; he says they need the love of Jesus. Another man says Muslims are always "bowing down, like to a king," and need to discover freedom in Christ. A woman who thinks Hindus need the love of Christ says Mother Teresa had to go to India because Hindus don't know how to love those who are suffering.

Another common thread in exclusivist perceptions of other religions is, inadvertently, to turn them into mirrors of one's own problems and concerns. For instance, people who belong to churches that deny women the right to become clergy or to assume other church leadership positions are sometimes especially concerned about the treatment of women in Muslim countries. Mrs. Mobley, for instance, worries that Muslim women are "oppressed," a word she would not use to describe Christian fundamentalists but that might be associated with the submissive gender roles practiced in the churches she has attended. Similarly, Christians whose worldview includes belief in supernatural intervention (in matters such as finding parking places or deciding what to wear) are sometimes especially interested in what they perceive to be superstitious beliefs among the followers of other religions. Another common perception is that people who adhere to other religions are simply shallow, confused, or lacking in commitment. For example, a woman who thinks that a lot of Christians do not really understand and appreciate Jesus attributes the same problem to Jews: if they just studied the Bible, they would realize that Jesus is the Messiah, but "the Jews that I know don't know what they believe or don't believe. They're not really practicing. They go to the synagogue, but they don't really believe. I don't know if they believe in anything."

Yet Christians who hold exclusivist views typically counterbalance negative (or potentially negative) opinions of other religions by affirming the rights of non-Christian groups to worship freely. Conversion should never happen through coercion, they say. Laws should be upheld that permit religious groups to assemble as long as they do so peacefully. It doesn't bother most of them to think that schools should recognize non-Christian religious holidays or, if prayers are said, that some way to accommodate those who object should be found. Ken Hiersma, the Presbyterian man in Denver, puts it well when he says, "People under the democracy that we live in have a right to believe in anything that they want to, they have that right within the limits of the law." Mrs. Mobley shares his view, but her comment is tinged with misgiving: "The founding forefathers were Christians, and they came here so that they could have religious freedom. I think that we've compromised when we've allowed so many other different groups to have their say or to do whatever. But that's a part of the freedom we have in our country. I don't think we can do away with that."

The overall impression of other religions found among most exclusive Christians, therefore, is one of cautious or restrained tolerance mixed with serious misgivings about these other religions. Their tolerance is rooted both in their understanding of the right to religious freedom and in their implicit norms of civility, nonjudgmentalism, and trying to approach people on a one-to-one basis rather than as members of a social category. Their reason for caution ultimately reflects their conviction that the members of other religions are destined for eternal damnation. But it is more immediately rooted in the feeling that these people are simply missing out on some of the happiness that only true Christians can experience. Thus, it is possible for exclusive Christians to say that they respect people of other religions, meaning that they respect their right to worship, respect them as people who are sincerely trying to do what is right, and even respect them as fellow humans whom God loves and would like to save. But this respect is accompanied by a kind of arrogance—arrogance that is by no means restricted to exclusive Christians but that takes a special form among them. This is the arrogance of believing that they are simply happier, less confused, more sure of the truth, and better able to lead good lives than anyone else.

The Social Implications of Christian Exclusivism

Like spiritual shopping and Christian inclusivism, exclusive Christianity offers a way to make sense of the growing religious and cultural diversity in the United States. Because their contact with non-Christians is limited, exclusive Christians do not worry very much from day to day about how diversity may be altering the social landscape; compared to raising their families and watching interesting things on television, thinking about diversity is probably, as one man put it, "just plain boring." Yet they too are sufficiently exposed to diversity that they cannot ignore its implications entirely. Many do not welcome it. They may understand that it is happening and that it will, inescapably, change the composition of their neighborhoods and schools. But they are concerned, certainly more so than inclusive Christians, that its effects will be negative—causing doubts about what to believe and why, creating friction in families, sparking violence, opening the nation to terrorism, and making it more difficult to keep law and order. Indeed, it is not uncommon for exclusive Christians to associate the growth in diversity with some frightening, apocalyptic vision of the end times. This is usually not a vision of violent warfare, disease, terrorism, and nuclear annihilation such as those depicted in motion pictures and best-selling thrillers about the end of the world. It more often is expressed as uncertainty, fear, the feeling that society is becoming so complex and belief systems so fragmented that the whole universe might just go ratcheting out of control, never to right itself until Jesus miraculously intervenes.

Another of the wider implications that exclusive Christians draw from increasing diversity is that tolerance itself may be dangerous—dangerous enough to be viewed skeptically as a kind of bargain with the devil. Although this attitude is probably not shared by a majority of Christian exclusivists, it does temper many of their more positive comments about the importance of respecting others and living up to the pluralist view of rights they associate with American democracy. It may be time to get tough, they say, to take a firm stand against something or someone. More than likely, the stand envisioned is not against Muslims or Hindus, Jews or Buddhists, as long as these groups do not pose an immediate threat to Christians' families and neighborhoods. The threat is more likely to be cast in terms of homosexuality, promiscuous lifestyles, or relativistic values being taught in public schools, any of which may be loosely associated in people's minds with diversity. It surfaces in criticisms of other Christian groups that appear to have lost their moral compass and become too eager to embrace diversity. Getting "back to basics" is a common response. This means studying the Bible, returning to the supposed teachings of the early Christians or the Christian values of the nation's founders, finding security in the Ten Commandments or in comforting slogans such as "In God We Trust."

Mrs. Mobley thinks that diversity is causing people to search harder to find truth but a lot of people she knows do not have a clue about where to find it. "The stuff they believe is just off the wall. I think that the Enemy is busy deceiving. You go into all this other stuff and it just seems so wild to me." She wishes the nation's leaders "had some values," but fears they do not. The basic problem is not other religions, but "our own," Ken Hiersma asserts. He thinks people need to turn back to God; having public prayer in schoolrooms, he says, would help a lot. A Baptist woman claims that "the foundations [of our society] are cracking." People are searching in all the wrong places because they have lost their footing.

Although such expressions of concern about tolerance are conducive to political movements aimed at restoring America to its Christian roots, a more common response to diversity is to retreat into the security of one's local church. Mrs. Mobley says she shrinks from having to think too much about other religions. "Just trying to walk the Christian walk is enough to keep me busy." A Los Angeles housewife who goes faithfully to an Assembly of God church says that the important response to diversity is not social reform but spiritual warfare: "It's got to be constant prayer, constant fellowship. Constant feeding of the Word, being in worship. You have to be just flooded. You have to be surrounded by godly things and godly people" to avoid Satan. "I'm just going to spend my time being a Christian," Jack Otis, the barber, declares. "I don't care if the Hindus come and try to convert me or not."

Still, it would be wrong to envision a future in which Christian exclusivists huddle in homogeneous religious enclaves feeling embattled by the sea of diversity welling up around them. Christians who hold their faith to be exclusively true increasingly go to college, where they learn about diverse ethnic and religious practices and rub shoulders with students from other traditions; they work in a labor force that includes a growing number of new immigrants and others from non-Western and non-Christian backgrounds; they live in a culture that encourages people to broaden their horizons by traveling, reading, watching television, going to the movies, and surfing the Internet. These experiences shape their attitudes, creating tension between the lived realities of their daily life and the Christian exclusivism they learn at their churches.

Many Christian exclusivists are thus genuinely torn, poignantly trying to adhere to the truth as they know it and yet wanting to expand their horizons and perhaps even to find reasons to accept those whose religious views are quite different from their own. Mrs. Mobley vacillates between these extremes. She adamantly argues that everyone who does not "proclaim the name of Jesus" as their savior is hopelessly lost; yet she acknowledges that she does not understand other religions very well and wishes that she were the kind of person who could enjoy learning about them. She tries to pray, when she is with her Jewish friend, in a way that will not be offensive, even though she wonders if she is "denying Christ" in doing so. She chides herself for not witnessing to her Jewish friend, but also ventures that maybe God and her friend will somehow "work it out." And, although she is convinced that her faith in Jesus is more than just an expression of the subculture in which she lives, she does acknowledge that she is ethnocentric in ways that are not entirely healthy. "If you stay in the box where you live," she says, "you think everyone lives in the same kind of box you do. I'm probably very guilty of that. I want everybody to come live in my box."

Mrs. Mobley's remarks illustrate a certain degree of candor and self-awareness that characterize many Christians who believe in the exclusive truth of their own religion. They recognize that what they believe is difficult to defend without seeming to be arrogant, overconfident, and irrational. Consequently, they search for more practical, tentative ways in which to think about their faith. Sheila Lopez, the Lutheran in Saint Louis, backs off ever so slightly from asserting that Christianity *is* the best way for all people to know God, saying instead that she "would want it to be" because it has worked for her. Nellie Johnson, who attends an African Methodist Episcopal church, finds herself puzzled: because Christianity is best, everyone ought to *feel* that it is, yet she knows this isn't true and wonders why. A Baptist man tries to resolve the difficulty he feels in claiming that Christianity is exclusively true by distinguishing "what Jesus taught" from Christianity; he thinks maybe Christianity, as a religion, does not always adequately convey divine truth but that Jesus, through his life and word, is still an ideal expression of the truth.

Other comments reflect similar struggles, as people who believe without any doubts whatsoever that only they and people who profess as they do are going to heaven come face to face with people they love, respect, and know well enough that it is hard to imagine them simply roasting in an eternal hell. Frank Lucas, the judge, thinks Christianity is true for everyone, not just himself; yet he says the reason he thinks this is because of "personal experience," the only thing he can speak from. He wouldn't try to force his beliefs on anyone else, especially the Jews he knows, but would seek "winsome ways" to share his faith. He recognizes that his views have been shaped by living in a diverse society: "It's made me less cocksure of myself. If you'd grown up in a little parochial environment and church, you would think that other Christians weren't going to go to heaven, much less Jews and anyone else in the world. I guess some people could still find my attitude quite narrow, but it's broader than it would have been had I not been exposed to other religions." A woman who has attended a conservative Baptist church most of her life adamantly believes that "Jesus is the only way" and agrees that she should be telling all her friends this "so they won't go to hell"; nevertheless, she is troubled by the attitude at her church that "we are right and they are simply wrong." Ken Hiersma is caught, too, as he describes his views about the truth of Christianity and the falsehood of other religions. "That sounds awfully black and white; when I hear myself saying these things, it doesn't sound like who I really am." Marge Mitchell, a homemaker, just wishes she had more time to figure out what she actually does believe.

This kind of tension cannot easily be resolved. For many people, it results in a tattered view of the world, the pieces of which are held together only by the loosest of logic, if that, and more commonly by retreating into a safe community of like-minded believers where people do not ask vexing questions. The mental bargaining required may be just as severe as that entailed by escaping into a bland pluralistic stew, as many less devout Americans do, where everything floats together on the surface but never truly produces a nourishing mixture of spiritual beliefs and practices. But the tension between exclusivism and diversity can also result in a degree of self-reflection about one's faith that would not likely have been present in less diverse circumstances—self-reflection that does not lead inevitably toward a more inclusive view but that disturbs people's consciences enough to ask God questions they have not considered before.

The Public's Beliefs and Practices

I HAVE SUGGESTED that spiritual shopping, Christian inclusivism, and Christian exclusivism are three ways of responding to the new religious and cultural diversity that now characterizes our society. These are not fixed choices that become stable features of a person's identity in all situations. Indeed, I have suggested that people cobble together responses to religious diversity in ways that often leave them feeling ambivalent. A spiritual shopper may settle into a religious tradition that she accepts and in relation to which she behaves *as if* it were true, even though she may have deep doubts and have repeatedly followed her urge to seek insights in other traditions. So too with Christian inclusivism or exclusivism. The conviction that Christianity represents a superior claim on divine truth may be held tacitly, evidenced more in how a person lives than in how that person may respond to a theological quiz. That conviction may provide certainty against the dark fears one encounters in moments of doubt but matter little in how a person relates to a close friend who, by the logic of this conviction, is eternally damned. To acknowledge the fungibility of these orientations, though, is not to deny their existence.

In the American public it is possible, as we have seen, to identify people who exemplify one or another of these orientations in many of the ways in which their life history has unfolded and in their remarks about what matters most to them spiritually and religiously. Although few Americans are theologians, we are all meaning-makers when it comes to telling our stories and describing our beliefs. We do emphasize certain experiences, and these experiences make sense of our past and guide our thinking about the present and future. None of us is completely the product of the social context in which our experiences and our stories have unfolded. But we are significantly shaped by these contexts. Our convictions cohere, register the opportunities we have enjoyed and the limitations we have faced, and prod us to take action that makes sense within the particular circumstances that have influenced us.

The "public" sometimes behaves in a collective and therefore truly public (i.e., visible) fashion, as when a large number of the population turn out to vote or when there is a general outcry about a political scandal or a collective lament over a national tragedy. We are sometimes interested in aggregating the opinions of private individuals about matters of the heart for this reason: they tell us something of the public "mood" or show the "character" of a people. Religious convictions fall into that category: worrying us that something is lost if these convictions appear to slip over time, or reassuring us that there are reasons for hope and continuing grounds for charitable service and moral deeds. Public opinion is, in this sense, more than the aggregation of private beliefs.

What the American public believes religiously and what it thinks about religious diversity are, I have argued, the result of living in a culture that has a long history of tension between identifying America as a Christian nation and specifying ways to be civil toward one another despite our differences, including differences that run counter to the very notion of America as a Christian nation. Our responses to diversity are further shaped, and indeed challenged, by the fact that the nation has become more diverse in recent years. Contact with people whose beliefs and lifestyles are quite different from our own can generate greater understanding, but such contact can also spark misgivings and lead to conflict. It appears, too, that personal experiences, training, and opportunities for reflection have encouraged some Americans to be more eclectic than others, and have generated ambivalence among those who claim to be Christian about how inclusive or exclusive to be in their views of other religious traditions.

We can now look more systematically at the American public at large, focusing on variations in responses to diversity, and examining the sources of these variations. The results from the Religion and Diversity survey permit us to see how widely shared some of the beliefs and attitudes are that we have considered to this point through the life histories and personal accounts of selected individuals. For the sake of comparison, we will want to identify spiritual shoppers, Christian inclusivists, and Christian exclusivists in the wider public, and examine more closely how they respond to questions about diversity, what their experiences and social backgrounds may tell us, how much contact they have had with various non-Western religious groups, and where they think our nation is headed.

Beliefs about Religious Truth

Among the beliefs and practices that distinguish spiritual shoppers, Christian inclusivists, and Christian exclusivists from one another, their views about religious truth are the most important. A spiritual shopper is, as we have seen, someone who usually does not privilege Christianity and who does regard all religions as equally true. A Christian inclusivist *does* privilege Christianity but also believes there is truth in other religions. A Christian exclusivist believes that only Christianity is ultimately true. With the data from the Religion and Diversity Survey, we can sort people into these three categories by combining their responses to the following statements: "Christianity is the best way to understand God" and "All major religions, such as Christianity, Hinduism, Buddhism, and Islam, are equally good ways of knowing about God."[1] A spiritual shopper is someone who disagrees with the first and agrees with the second. A Christian inclusivist is someone who agrees with both. And a Christian exclusivist is someone who agrees with the first and disagrees with the second. In the survey, 31 percent of the American public qualified by these criteria as spiritual shoppers. Christian inclusivists made up 23 percent of the public. Thirty-four percent fell into the category of Christian exclusivists. Thus, all but 11 percent of the public could be classified in this relatively simple way (we will set aside that 11 percent for purposes of the comparisons at hand). From a follow-up question in the survey, we also know that inclusivists and exclusivists, while agreeing that Christianity is best, differ in how they interpret that statement: 67 percent of the inclusivists said Christianity was best for them personally, whereas only 29 percent said Christianity was best for "everybody"; in contrast, 53 percent of the exclusivists said Christianity was best for everybody, whereas 45 percent said it was best for them personally. This way of defining the three categories of interest has the advantage of being straightforward: we know the responses that located people in each category. We do not have to take at face value that the three groups are different from one another, though,

TABLE 1
Beliefs about Sources of Religious Truth

	Spiritual Shoppers (%)	Christian Inclusivists (%)	Christian Exclusivists (%)	All Respondents (%)
All major religions, such as Christianity, Hinduism, Buddhism, and Islam, contain some truth about God				
Agree	92	89	54	74
Disagree	5	6	33	17
All religions basically teach the same thing				
Agree	68	53	14	42
Disagree	30	44	81	54
Do you think God's word is revealed in any other writings besides the Bible, such as the sacred texts used by Muslims or Hindus?				
Yes	72	50	21	46
No	15	29	60	36
Don't know	12	20	18	18
Would you say that Muslims and Christians pretty much believe in the same things or are their beliefs fairly different?				
Same things	42	25	8	24
Fairly different	48	61	80	64
Don't know	10	13	10	12
Would you say that Buddhists and Christians pretty much believe in the same things or are their beliefs fairly different?				
Same things	27	16	5	16
Fairly different	61	66	80	69
Don't know	11	18	14	15
Number	(897)	(677)	(1,006)	(2,910)

Source: Religion and Diversity Survey.
Note: Weighted data.

or that these simple responses to survey questions can meaningfully distinguish among people whose views are certainly more complex. What we can do is examine how people in these three categories respond to other questions. Doing so, I suggest, will show that spiritual shoppers, Christian inclusivists, and Christian exclusivists do differ in many other ways, and understanding these differences goes a long way toward sorting out the public's responses to religious and cultural diversity.

The figures reported in table 1 are helpful for gauging the public's views about religious truth and for obtaining an initial impression of the differences among spiritual shoppers, Christian inclusivists, and Christian exclusivists in these views. Judging from these figures, it is fairly common in the United States for people to believe that there is at least some divine truth in all major religious traditions. To be specific, among everyone in the survey, three people in four agreed that "all major religions, such as Christianity, Hinduism, Buddhism, and Islam, contain some truth about God," whereas only about one person in six disagreed. This view is shared by almost all spiritual shoppers and Christian inclusivists. Even among Christian exclusivists, a slight majority held this view, whereas only one-third were sure they disagreed with it. Being a Christian exclusivist, it appears, does not require a contemporary believer to regard all other religions besides Christianity as completely false; the exclusivist's God is generous enough to have revealed some truth even to unbelievers.

Americans are much more divided about the possibility that the various religions are fully interchangeable. This is a view, as we have seen in previous chapters, that has been widely discussed over the years. Even today, it is chic in some circles to assert that, well, at the end of the day all religions really teach love or that all religions point to the same God. Yet cursory knowledge of the different teachings and practices of world religions would seem to suggest more diversity than similarity. Thus, when asked in the survey if they thought "all religions basically teach the same thing," 42 percent said they agreed and 54 percent said they disagreed. Agreement or disagreement with this statement was sharply different among shoppers, inclusivists, and exclusivists. More than two-thirds of the shoppers agreed with it, more than four-fifths of the exclusivists disagreed with it, and the inclusivists divided almost squarely down the middle between agreeing and disagreeing.

Another way of thinking about religious truth concerns the possibility of divine revelation in the texts held sacred by different religions. Since most Americans think that there is at least some truth about God in the various religions, we might suppose they would be favorably disposed toward this possibility as well. But not quite half (46 percent) said yes when asked, "Do you think God's word is revealed in any other writings besides the Bible, such as the sacred texts used by Muslims or Hindus?" About a third (36 percent) thought God's word was not revealed in any other writings besides the Bible, and about a fifth (18 percent) said they didn't know what to think. The differences among shoppers, inclusivists, and exclusivists are once again quite strong, though. About three-fourths of the shoppers responded positively to the statement, compared with half of the inclusivists, and only a fifth of the exclusivists.

The remaining two statements shown in table 1 represent, as it were, attempts to force the issue. It may be that people are willing in the abstract to believe that there is truth among the various religions. In the abstract, they may even entertain the possibility that all religions are the same. But knowing something of religion on the ground, it may be harder to take that possibility seriously. Looking at how the followers of various religions actually live and knowing something of the teachings *by which* they live, Americans appear to be more impressed by the differences than by the similarities. Thus, when asked in the survey to compare Muslims and Christians, only 24 percent of the respondents said the two pretty much believe in the same things, while 64 percent thought the beliefs were fairly different. In the comparison between Christians and Buddhists, only 16 percent of the public thought Christians and Buddhists pretty much believe in the same things, while 69 percent thought the two believed in fairly different things. Again, though, shoppers, inclusivists, and exclusivists took different positions. Hardly any of the exclusivists thought Christians and Muslims or Christians and Buddhists believed in the same things, whereas a sizable minority of the shoppers thought they did, and the inclusivists fell in between.

From this information, it appears that most Americans are open to the possibility that divine truth can be found in religions other than their own, but most Americans also recognize differences among the various religions.[2] Yet there is also a certain amount of consistency in the way people answer different questions about religious truth. In the comparisons shown in table 1, spiritual shoppers are always the most likely to see similarities and truth in the various religions, while Christian exclusivists are always the least likely to believe in such similarities, and Christian inclusivists stand squarely in the middle.[3] Other statistical tests show that the more likely people are to respond affirmatively to one of these questions, the more likely they are to respond affirmatively to all the others.[4] The information in table 2 will permit us to look more closely at Americans' beliefs about religious truth.

The questions shown in table 2 pertain to Christianity and to particular ways of understanding Christian teachings. About 80 percent of the public claimed in the survey that they were Christian when asked directly if they were or not. And Christianity is sufficiently familiar in the culture at large that even the remaining 20 percent usually had some opinion about Christian teachings. If how people think about other religions gives us a sense of their openness to religious diversity, their views about Christianity provide a further indication of whether their theological interpretations allow room for divine truth to be found in a variety of ways. As we have suggested, some Christians are more exclusivist than others, and some views about Christianity are also conducive to spiritual shopping.

One of the central doctrines of Christianity, as popularly interpreted, has been the claim that only through belief in Christ can humans find divine salvation (recall Trisha Mobley in chapter 6). If it is less common nowadays, as some of our interviewees cautioned, for people to think about divine salvation in terms of an afterlife in heaven or an escape from eternal punishment in hell, it is still common for people to talk about having a personal relationship with God (either in this life or in an afterlife). One way of thinking about Christianity, therefore, is whether it is or is not the only means through which such a relationship with God may be attained. In the Religion and Diversity Survey, Americans were about evenly divided on this question: 44 percent agreed that "Christianity is the only way to have a true personal relationship with God," and 53 percent disagreed. Like some of the statements we have already considered, this one generated sharply different responses from spiritual shoppers, inclusivists, and exclusivists. Hardly any of the shoppers agreed, nearly all the exclusivists did, and the inclusivists were divided.

How the Bible should be viewed is another topic on which Americans have often disagreed. When asked their opinion of the Bible in the Religion and Diversity Survey, 39 percent of the public said that they believed it was the "actual word of God and is to be taken literally, word for word." A slightly larger number (43 percent) thought that the Bible is the "inspired word of God but not everything in it should be taken literally." Most of the remainder (16 percent) thought that the Bible is an "ancient book of fables, legends, history, and moral precepts recorded by humans."[5] Among spiritual shoppers and Christian inclusivists, and even among exclusivists, there is a range of opinion about the Bible. But exclusivists would seem most likely to take the Bible literally, and indeed 60 percent of them did choose that option in the survey. Among spiritual shoppers, only one person in eight thought that the Bible should be taken literally, about half thought that the Bible was divinely inspired, and about a third thought that it was a book of fables, legends, history, and moral precepts. On this question, inclusivists were more like exclusivists than they were like spiritual shoppers. Nearly half of the inclusivists thought that the Bible should be taken literally, and nearly all of the remainder thought that it was divinely inspired. By this indication, then, Christian inclusivists mostly adhere to one or another of the ways in which Christians have traditionally held the Bible to be a revelation of divine truth.

Views of the Bible are more complex than can be measured by a single survey question, though. We see some of this complexity in the other two questions about the Bible shown in table 2. For instance, one can regard the Bible as divinely (even literally) inspired and still believe that there are other ways of finding God's truth. That is in fact what most Americans believe. In the survey, 79 percent of the public thought that "God's truth is revealed in many ways, such as history, culture, nature, and tradition," while only 18 percent said that the statement "God's truth is fully revealed only in the Bible" was closer to their view. Americans are more evenly divided in how they think about the Bible as a source of spiritual guidance. Almost half (48 percent) said that the statement "I mostly trust the Bible for spiritual guidance" came closer to their view, while almost the same number (46 percent) opted for the statement "I mostly trust my own personal experience for spiritual guidance." Spiritual shoppers, Christian inclusivists, and Christian exclusivists differed dramatically in their responses to these questions. Shoppers were the most likely to feel that God's truth is revealed in many ways and to trust personal experience more than the Bible, followed by Christian inclusivists, while Christian exclusivists more often took the opposing views.

The in-depth interviews we considered in chapters 4, 5, and 6 showed that spiritual shoppers, inclusivists, and exclusivists often differ in their understandings of Jesus. The survey showed that this was also true in the public at large. The traditional teaching—that Jesus "was the only divine son of God who died and rose again to save us from our sins"—is the view held by two-thirds of the public. This proportion, though, dips to about one-third among spiritual shoppers and rises to more than 90 percent among Christian exclusivists. Among those in the public at large who do not share this traditional view, opinion is divided about evenly between the view that "Jesus embodied the essence of divine love and showed us how to attain spiritual union with God" and the view that "Jesus had special insights about God, much in the same way that Muhammad and the Buddha did." Inclusivists were more likely to choose the former, while spiritual shoppers were more likely to choose the latter.

The final question in table 2 was asked only of those who said they were Christians. It sought to determine how many Christians thought it possible "to be a good Christian and a good Buddhist at the same time." Among all self-identified Christians, only 20 percent thought it was "possible to be both," while 66 percent said it was "better to choose between the two," and 13 percent said they didn't know. This was another question on which spiritual shoppers, inclusivists, and exclusivists differed. Half of the Christians who were spiritual shoppers thought it possible to be both a good Christian and a good Buddhist, 18 percent of the inclusivists thought this, and only 5 percent of the exclusivists did.

Like the information in table 1, the information in table 2 shows, then, that the American public is in varying degrees open to interpretations of Christianity that leave room for divine truth to be found in multiple ways. How much room depends on the particular teachings at issue. If adherence to Christianity means belief in the divine inspiration of the Bible and acceptance of long-standing creedal formulations about the divinity and resurrection of Jesus, then a large majority of the public qualifies as Christian. But as more restrictive interpretations are considered, fewer of the public qualifies. Even among self-identified Christians, only a bare majority believe that Christianity is the only way to have a true relationship with God, fewer than a majority believe the Bible should be taken literally, a large minority claim they would trust personal experience more than the Bible for spiritual guidance, and only a fifth believe God's truth is revealed only in the Bible.[6]

We are, in short, a nation divided. We are divided in our views of religious truth, just as we are about many other things—politics, art, public welfare, the economy, abortion, what values to instill in our children, and so on. Our views of religious truth have not been broken into polarized camps by special interest groups or divided along political lines like many of those other issues. But there is, as we have seen, a high degree of consistency in the public's responses to various questions about religious truth: those who are more open to multiple sources of truth on particular questions are more likely to be open on other questions as well. On all the

TABLE 2
Beliefs about Christianity and Christian Teachings

	Spiritual Shoppers (%)	Christian Inclusivists (%)	Christian Exclusivists (%)	All Respondents (%)
Christianity is the only way to have a true personal relationship with God				
Agree	5	62	78	44
Disagree	93	37	18	53
The Bible is:				
Actual word of God and is to be taken literally, word for word	12	48	60	39
Inspired word of God but not everything should be taken literally	52	42	35	43
Ancient book of fables, legends, history, and moral precepts recorded by humans	33	9	3	16
God's truth is:				
Fully revealed only in the Bible	3	18	33	18
Revealed in many other ways	95	80	64	79
For spiritual guidance I mostly trust:				
The Bible	19	57	76	48
My own personal experience	76	39	19	46
Jesus:				
Was the only divine son of God who died and rose again to save us from our sins	35	77	91	65
Embodied the essence of divine love and showed us how to attain spiritual union with God	22	17	6	15
Had special insights about God, much in the same way that Muhammad and the Buddha did	36	4	1	14
Possible to be a good Christian and a good Buddhist at the same time:*				
Possible to be both	48	18	5	20
Better to choose between the two	36	67	84	66
Don't know	14	13	10	13
Number	(897)	(677)	(1,006)	(2,910)

Source: Religion and Diversity Survey.
Note: Weighted data.
* Asked only of self-identified Christians.

questions we have considered, spiritual shoppers are the most open to diverse sources of divine truth, Christian exclusivists are the least open, and Christian inclusivists fall in between.[7] Were we to create a kind of index that simply assigned a point for the more open of the options to each of the twelve questions we have considered in tables 1 and 2, we would see this division even more clearly: among our spiritual shoppers, 75 percent would receive a score of at least "7" on this index; among Christian inclusivists, this proportion would be 24 percent; and among Christian exclusivists, it would be only 2 percent. Conversely, only 2 percent of spiritual shoppers would score low ("3" or less), but this proportion would rise to 20 percent among inclusivists, and then rise further to 79 percent among exclusivists.[8]

Views of America

I have argued in previous chapters that our views about religion and spirituality—private though they may be—are closely connected with our understandings of America as a nation and as a culture. The view that America is a Christian nation has been a projection of personal convictions about Christianity, and these personal convictions have in turn surely been influenced by identifying with a particular conception of America. Having considered how the public responds to questions about the varying sources of religious truth, we can now examine the extent to which these personal convictions are related to our views about America.

Table 3 reports the proportions of the public who *strongly agreed* with some of the statements included in the Religion and Diversity Survey about the Christian roots of American national identity (we considered these statements briefly in chapter 1).[9] About half of the public agreed strongly that the United States was founded on Christian principles. About the same proportion agreed strongly that American has been strong because of its faith in God. These proportions rose to more than two-thirds among Christian exclusivists and fell to less than one-third among spiritual shoppers. Inclusivists were in the middle, although on both questions the proportions who strongly agreed were closer to the proportions for exclusivists than the proportions for shoppers. The numbers who strongly agreed that our democratic form of government is based on Christianity were smaller than for the previous two questions (25 percent among all respondents). But Christian exclusivists were three times more likely to give this response than spiritual shoppers (and inclusivists were only slightly less likely than exclusivists to give it). The next statement—that the United States is still basically a Christian society—evoked strong agreement from 32 percent of the public. This was the one statement to which fewer exclusivists than inclusivists agreed (possibly because exclusivists had in mind a higher standard of what it meant to be a Christian society and thus found the United States wanting). Spiritual shoppers remained the least likely to agree. About a third of the public (31 percent) also agreed that the public schools should teach children the Ten Commandments. This view was shared by two-thirds of the exclusivists, by half of the inclusivists, but by only a fifth of the spiritual shoppers.

The remaining statements in table 3 express in various ways a view of America that emphasizes the nation's special place in the world *and* the need to protect that place against the possible threats of diversity, immigration, and foreignness. Forty-one percent of those surveyed agreed strongly that "Nothing in other countries can beat the American way of life." Nearly two-thirds of the Christian exclusivists did, more than half of the Christian inclusivists did, but only about a third of the spiritual shoppers did. A majority (52 percent) of the respondents strongly agreed that "Religious diversity has been good for America." Shoppers were most likely to say so; exclusivists were least likely. The pattern was roughly the same for strong agreement that "America owes a great deal to the immigrants who came here." Fewer (24 percent) of the respondents strongly agreed that "Foreigners who come to live in America should give up their foreign ways and learn to be like other Americans," but about a third of the exclusivists strongly agreed (and almost as many inclusivists did), while only 12 percent of the spiritual shoppers did.

Clearly there is a relationship between the public's views of religious truth and the public's views of America—whether it has been and is a Christian nation, whether its public schools should teach the Ten Commandments, whether the American way of life is superior to other countries, whether diversity and immigration have been good or bad, and whether foreigners should conform to some ideal standard of what a good American should be like. On nearly all these matters, Christian exclusivists hold different views that spiritual shoppers do, and Christian inclusivists fall at various

TABLE 3
Views about America

	Spiritual Shoppers (%)	Christian Inclusivists (%)	Christian Exclusivists (%)	All Respondents (%)
Percentage who agreed strongly with each statement:				
The United States was founded on Christian principles	30	55	68	50
America has been strong because of its faith in God	28	65	70	52
Our democratic form of government is based on Christianity	12	30	36	25
In the twenty-first century, the United States is still basically a Christian society	23	42	37	32
The public schools should teach children the Ten Commandments	20	51	66	31
Nothing in other countries can beat the American way of life	36	57	64	41
Religious diversity has been good for America	64	55	42	52
America owes a great deal to the immigrants who came here	63	50	48	53
Foreigners who come to live in America should give up their foreign ways and learn to be like other Americans	12	30	32	24
Number	(897)	(677)	(1,006)	(2,910)

Source: Religion and Diversity Survey.
Note: Weighted data.

points along the spectrum in between.[10] We need to be cautious about these conclusions, of course. The differences observed in the table could be a reflection of underlying differences among the people we have classified into various categories. We will want to look at these differences. For now, though, suffice it to say that the observed differences between spiritual shoppers and Christian inclusivists cannot be explained away by taking account of differences in age, education, parents' education, region, gender, race, ethnicity, religious tradition, and religious service attendance; a majority of the differences between Christian inclusivists and exclusivists also remain statistically significant after controlling for these variables.[11]

The Impact of Non-Western Religions

We turn next to the influences that people *say* have shaped their thinking about religion and spirituality, the social factors and experiences that have influenced their views, and the degree to which their views have been affected by contacts with fellow Americans who are adherents of various non-Western religions. This information will give us a basis for answering questions such as: How eclectic are spiritual shoppers in piecing together their perspectives on religion and spirituality? To what extent have Christian inclusivists and exclusivists also been influenced by diverse ideas? Is there a relationship between having certain opportunities for education, travel, and the like and holding certain orientations toward religious truth? And are the greater opportunities many people now have to interact with diverse religious groups a reason for some Americans being more eclectic in their views than others?

The teachings, practices, and other factors that Americans say have had an important influence on their thinking about religion or spirituality are shown in table 4. The items listed refer to what social scientists would call *institutionalized* influences: religious traditions, movements, and other influences such as science, philosophy, and music and the arts. Our concern here is not with the casual conversation one might have with a friend or with the possible influence of a near-accident on the highway. We know those are important to the way people tell stories about their spiritual journeys. But here we are interested in the possible ways in which diverse religious teachings and practices themselves may be shaping the American public. Exposure to Christian and Jewish teachings and practices provides a benchmark. These influences will presumably have been greater than those of religions such as Islam, Hinduism, and Buddhism, which have until recently been further removed from mainstream America. We can compare the extent of these newer influences with some others that have also gained in popularity (at least judging from books published and seminars held) in recent years: Native American and African practices, the New Age movement, and alternative medicine or holistic health practices. As

TABLE 4
Influences on Thinking about Religion or Spirituality

	Spiritual Shoppers (%)	Christian Inclusivists (%)	Christian Exclusivists (%)	All Respondents (%)
Percentage who said each of the following had an important influence on his or her thinking about religion or spirituality:				
Christian teachings or practices	51	75	86	68
Jewish teachings or practices	22	15	14	17
Buddhist teachings or practices	23	8	4	12
Hindu teachings or practices	14	5	2	7
Muslim teachings or practices	17	9	6	11
Native American Indian teachings or practices	32	22	12	21
African spiritual teachings or practices	14	16	10	13
The New Age movement	15	12	10	12
Alternative medicine or holistic health practices	34	22	16	24
Studying or reading about science	47	36	25	36
Studying or reading about philosophy	47	32	24	34
Music, poetry, literature, or art	59	49	47	51
Percentage who selected Buddhist, Hindu, or Muslim teachings	31	14	9	18
Percentage who selected Native American, New Age, or holistic health practices	48	38	28	37
Percentage who selected science or philosophy	60	48	37	48
Number	(897)	(677)	(1,005)	(2,910)

Source: Religion and Diversity Survey.
Note: Weighted data.

further comparisons, the perceived impact of science, philosophy, and music and the arts is also of interest.

Not surprisingly, "Christian teachings or practices" were perceived by the largest number of people in the survey to have influenced their thinking about religion or spirituality. Two-thirds of the whole sample responded affirmatively. Among Christian exclusivists, 86 percent did;

among Christian inclusivists, 75 percent did; and among spiritual shoppers, 51 percent did. I should emphasize that the question asked about *important* influences. As many as half of the remaining third of the sample probably would have said Christian teachings had some influence on their thinking, had they been given a chance. It is worth underscoring, too, that half of the spiritual shoppers felt that Christian teachings or practices had been an important influence on their thinking. Many shoppers were thus starting from a Christian base, either by building on it or rejecting it. Compared with Christianity or even Judaism (about which 17 percent of those surveyed said it had an important influence on them), the impact of Buddhist, Hindu, and Muslim teachings is quite small. Only 12 percent, 7 percent, and 11 percent of the public said these, respectively, had been important influences on their thinking. Those numbers, nevertheless, are considerably higher than estimates of the numbers of Americans who actually *are* Buddhist, Hindu, or Muslim. In each case, the percentage of spiritual shoppers who claim to have been influenced is higher than the corresponding percentage of Christian inclusivists, which is in turn higher than the percentage of Christian exclusivists. If we can take what people say at face value, then, shoppers actually have been influenced to some extent by several different religious traditions, and at least a few Christian inclusivists have, too. Without making too much of the specific numbers, it is also interesting to observe that the perceived influence of Buddhism is relatively large in comparison with that of Islam, given that estimates of the number of Buddhists in the United States are generally quite a bit lower than estimates of the number of Muslims.

The larger impact of non-Western religions, though, must be considered in relation to other religious and cultural influences that also stem from sources outside of Christianity or Judaism (or at least beyond that of clergy and theologians). Nearly all of these other influences have apparently reached more of the American public than Islam, Buddhism, or Hinduism. Leaving aside music and the arts (which may have been church music or Christian poetry), philosophy and science were each selected by a third of the respondents as having had an important influence on their thinking about religion, alternative medicine or holistic health practices were selected by one person in four, Native American Indian teachings or practices were chosen by one person in five, and African spiritual teachings or practices and the New Age movement were included by about one person in eight. It is possible, of course, that people could have been influenced by more than one of these teachings or practices. If we take that possibility into account, though, the impact of non-Western teaching or practices still appears smaller than some of the other influences. Eighteen percent of the respondents said Buddhism, Hinduism, *or* Islam had been an important influence on their thinking; in comparison, 37 percent said this about Native American teachings, the New Age movement, or holistic health practices; and 48 percent said the same about science or philosophy. In each case, spiritual shoppers were more likely than Christian inclusivists or exclusivists to say that they had been influenced; yet, among spiritual shoppers, only about a third had been influenced by non-Western religions, while half had been influenced by the other combinations of teachings and practices.

The point of these observations is not to discount the growing presence of Buddhists, Hindus, and Muslims in the United States or to discredit the possibility that their presence is having a growing impact on Americans' thinking about religion and spirituality. These results do indicate a significant impact, at least as Americans themselves see it. As many as one person in five believes that he or she has been significantly influenced by Buddhism, Hinduism, or Islam. And as many as a third of the spiritual shoppers believe this. Yet, these findings reinforce what we concluded from the qualitative interviews, namely, that spiritual shoppers are generally more open to religious diversity than they are likely actually to have had significant encounters with it. And, as we see here, they are more likely to have been influenced by the more eclectic practices associated with Native American spirituality, the New Age movement, or alternative medicine, or by science and philosophy, than by any of the major non-Western religious traditions. It is notable, though, that being influenced by non-Western religions appears to be more strongly associated with the differences between spiritual shopping, Christian inclusivism, and Christian exclusivism than any of the other influences are; that is, when other factors, such as age and education, are taken into account, the likelihood of being influenced by science, philosophy, the New Age movement, alternative medicine, and Native American practices appears to be more closely associated with those factors, whereas the likelihood of being influenced by non-Western religions remains strongly associated with how open one is to religious diversity.[12] This result suggests two important possibilities: over the long run, greater exposure to non-Western religions is likely to have more of an impact on Americans' attitudes toward religious diversity than exposure to influences such as philosophy and alternative medicine, and in the short term, how Americans respond to non-Western religions is likely to be significantly influenced by how they think about religious truth.

Table 5 provides additional information with which to assess the possible influences of Islam, Hinduism, and Buddhism on the American public. In the Religion and Diversity Survey, respondents were asked how familiar they were with the basic teachings of Christianity, Judaism, Islam, Hinduism, and Buddhism. The table shows the percentages who said that they were very familiar with the teachings of each religion and the percentages who said that they were at least somewhat familiar with each set of teachings. Ninety-five percent of the public claimed to be at least somewhat familiar with the basic teachings of Christianity, and 70 percent said they were very familiar with these teachings. Being somewhat familiar with Christian teachings did not vary between Christian exclusivists and inclusivists or between inclusivists and spiritual shoppers. Christian exclusivists were more likely than the others, though, to say that they were very familiar with Christian teachings. About half the public claimed to be somewhat familiar with Judaism and about one person in seven claimed to be very familiar with these teachings. Spiritual shoppers were the most likely to give this response, and Christian exclusivists were slightly more likely to say that they were very familiar with Judaism than Christian inclusivists. The percentages for Islam, Hinduism, and Buddhism were significantly lower than those for Judaism. Only 5 percent of the public said they were very familiar with the basic teachings of Islam or Buddhism and only 3 percent said this about Hinduism. Still, a substantial minority of the public claimed to have some familiarity with each tradition: 33 percent with Islam, 21 percent with Hinduism, and 29 percent with Buddhism. In each case, spiritual shoppers were more likely than Christian inclusivists or exclusivists to say that they were familiar with these traditions. Christian exclusivists were less likely than inclusivists to say that they were very familiar with each tradition, but were more likely to say they had some familiarity with these traditions.

Whether people who think they are familiar with various religious traditions actually *are* knowledgeable about them is, of course, difficult to know. In the survey we did ask four "knowledge" questions—whether

TABLE 5
Familiarity with Teachings of Selected Religious Groups

	Spiritual Shoppers (%)	Christian Inclusivists (%)	Christian Exclusivists (%)	All Respondents (%)
Percentage who said that they were very familiar with the basic teachings of each religion:				
Christianity	66	65	82	70
Judaism	18	9	12	14
Islam	8	4	3	5
Hinduism	4	3	1	3
Buddhism	8	4	2	5
Percentage who said that they were at least somewhat familiar with the basic teachings of each religion:				
Christianity	96	95	97	95
Judaism	63	39	51	52
Islam	42	24	31	33
Hinduism	31	13	19	21
Buddhism	43	21	23	29
Ever attended services at				
Jewish synagogue	35	19	19	25
Muslim mosque	13	8	4	8
Hindu temple	11	5	4	6
Buddhist temple	19	7	4	10
Attended more than once or twice:				
Jewish synagogue	14	5	0	3
Muslim mosque	3	1	0	2
Hindu temple	2	1	0	1
Buddhist temple	4	1	0	1
Number	(896)	(676)	(1,006)	(2,910)

Source: Religion and Diversity Survey.
Note: Weighted data.

Buddhists believe in the same God that Christians believe in (the correct answer is no), whether Muslims believe in the Ten Commandments (the correct answer is yes), in which religion Ramadan is a special time of fasting and prayer (the correct answer is Islam), and in which part of the Christian Bible the book of Revelation appears (the correct answer is the New Testament). Respectively, the proportion of respondents who gave correct answers were 53 percent, 19 percent, 41 percent, and 54 percent. For the most part, the responses suggested that people who claimed to be more familiar with a particular religion were more likely to give the correct answers than people who said they were unfamiliar with that religion. This was true for the two questions about Islam: those who claimed more familiarity with both Islam and Christianity were more likely to give the right answers. It was also true for the question about the book of Revelation. The exception was the question about Buddhists and Christians believing in the same God. Those who were more familiar with Christian teachings were neither more nor less likely to give the correct answer, while those who claimed more familiarity with Buddhism were *less* likely to give the correct answer.[13]

Table 5 also shows the percentages of the public who said that they had ever attended services (or attended services more than once or twice) at a Muslim mosque, a Hindu temple or center, a Buddhist temple or center, and (for comparative purposes) a Jewish synagogue. Whereas a quarter of the public claimed to have attended a service at a synagogue, only 8 percent, 6 percent, and 10 percent, respectively, had attended services at a mosque, Hindu temple, or Buddhist temple. Three percent claimed to have attended services at a synagogue more than once or twice; 2 percent had done so at a mosque, and 1 percent each had done so at a Hindu or Buddhist temple. Spiritual shoppers were the most likely to have attended in each case, followed by Christian inclusivists.[14]

These results, then, are similar to what we learned from examining the information about influences on people's thinking about religion and spirituality. Only a small proportion of the American public claims to be more than casually familiar with the teachings of Islam, Hinduism, or Buddhism, and the proportions who have attended more than once or twice at a mosque, Hindu temple, or Buddhist temple are also quite small. Still, the extent of casual familiarity with the teachings of these religions and the share of the public who has attended services at mosques or temples needs to be acknowledged as a new and growing influence. Most people who qualify ideologically as spiritual shoppers appear not to have had significant exposure to non-Western religious traditions. But their openness to the possibility of truth in these traditions has apparently been accompanied by some participation and gaining some familiarity—at least more than that of Christian exclusivists or inclusivists.[15]

Social and Cultural Factors

We have now learned enough about the beliefs and attitudes of spiritual shoppers, Christian inclusivists, and Christian exclusivists that it will be helpful to consider the broader social and cultural factors that differentiate the three groups. These factors will help us to interpret *why* some Americans are more open to religious diversity than others and will provide a better way to understand the various opportunities and resources that make it possible for some Americans to be more exposed to the teachings and practices of non-Western religions than others.

In considering these factors, we need to keep in mind that how one thinks about religious diversity is not simply a matter of forming an opinion based on one's thinking or personal experiences. As we have seen, there is an association between openness to diversity and having been influenced by diverse religious teachings and practices. But this is not necessarily a causal relationship and it certainly does not fully explain why some people are more open to religious diversity than others.

The social and cultural factors that are most likely to influence a person's views about religious diversity are of two kinds. One, clearly, is religion itself. Most Americans take their cues from one religious tradition or another, and for the large majority of Americans, these traditions are variants of Christianity. These traditions have taken different stands, explicitly and implicitly, toward religious truth. Some are more exclusive than others; some encourage spiritual shopping and others discourage it. Identifying with one of these traditions means feeling comfortable with its basic teachings—or at least not feeling uncomfortable enough to leave. Having grown up in that tradition, hearing sermons preached from a particular theological orientation, and having friends who think the same way invariably have an influence on one's views. How often one attends and whether one attends religious services in a particular kind of community are also likely to be important factors. Besides the influences of religion, one's thinking about religious diversity is also likely to be shaped by the cultural contexts to which one has been exposed. These include the age cohort in which one participates—younger people are born and reared in a different era, perhaps one in which exposure to and acceptance of diversity is more common, than older people were. One's level of education, including whether one attended college and, if so, what one majored in, as well as the educational level of one's parents, are important factors that expose people to different ideas about diversity. For some, travel may have a formative influence on their ideas about diversity, especially if they have traveled abroad. Whether one lives in an urban or suburban area, in which ethnic and religious diversity may be more common, or in a small town or rural area, in which such diversity may be less common, could be an important factor. The same may be true of living in different parts of the country. And one's gender, race, or ethnic background may also make a difference to one's thinking about diversity.

How spiritual shoppers, Christian inclusivists, and Christian exclusivists compare on these various religious and cultural factors is shown in table 6. In the survey, 30 percent of the respondents claimed to be affiliated with an evangelical Protestant denomination (such as the Southern Baptist Convention or the Assemblies of God). Among Christian exclusivists, this proportion rose to 50 percent; among Christian inclusivists, it was 26 percent; and among spiritual shoppers, it was 14 percent. Thus, we can see that there is, in fact, an affinity between resisting religious diversity and being involved in the kind of churches that may encourage such resistance. Fewer of the respondents belonged to the so-called mainline Protestant churches (such as Presbyterian and Episcopal churches), and there was hardly any difference in the percentages of shoppers, inclusivists, and exclusivists who did (although by a narrow margin Christian inclusivists had the largest proportion of mainline Protestants). Historically black Protestant denominations (such as the African Methodist Episcopal and National Baptist churches) made up 7 percent of the respondents in the survey, and the percentage among inclusivists was slightly higher than among exclusivists or shoppers. Roman Catholics composed 24 percent of the sample. A third of the Christian inclusivists were Catholics and 27 percent of the spiritual shoppers were, compared with only 15 percent of the exclusivists. Nine percent of the sample belong to various other traditions (including Mormons and various Orthodox groups). Slightly more of the spiritual shoppers than of the other two groups fell into this category. Eighteen percent of the sample said that they had no religious preference. This proportion rose to 33 percent among the spiritual shoppers and fell to 6 percent among the Christian exclusivists.

TABLE 6

Religious, Cultural, and Demographic Characteristics

	Spiritual Shoppers (%)	Christian Inclusivists (%)	Christian Exclusivists (%)	All Respondents (%)
Religious preference				
Evangelical Protestant	14	26	50	30
Mainline Protestant	10	15	14	13
Black Protestant	3	11	8	7
Roman Catholic	27	33	15	24
Other	13	5	8	9
None	33	10	6	18
Religious self-identity*				
Fundamentalist	3	10	18	10
Evangelical	2	6	19	9
Religious services				
Attend almost every week	19	48	64	42
Always attend same place**	39	50	57	48
In small town or rural area**	34	38	47	40
In homogeneous area**	50	70	69	56
Age				
18 to 24	22	16	11	16
25 to 44	42	33	39	39
45 to 64	27	32	30	25
65 and over	9	18	20	16
Education				
Postgraduate education	11	4	6	7
College degree	20	12	13	15
Some college	36	29	32	33
Humanities/social science major	10	4	4	7
College-educated parent	40	24	27	31
Travel				
Traveled or lived outside the United States	67	52	54	58
Residence				
Urban	22	22	14	19
Suburban	41	32	33	35
Small town or rural area	36	44	51	44
Region				
Northeast	26	17	12	18
Midwest	24	25	26	25
South	27	40	47	38
West	23	18	15	19
Other				
Female	47	54	57	52
African American	8	17	12	12
Hispanic	11	12	8	11
Number	(896)	(676)	(1,006)	(2,910)

Source: Religion and Diversity Survey.

Note: Weighted data.

* Asked only of Protestants.   ** Asked only of those who attended services.

Researchers have found that people sometimes have religious identities that differ from those of the denominations with which they are affiliated and that these identities are strongly related to how they think about various issues. In the table I have shown the percentages of Protestants who claimed they were fundamentalists or evangelicals. In each case, the percentage of Christian exclusivists who do so is higher than the percentage of Christian inclusivists or spiritual shoppers. It is also worth noting that Christian inclusivists were more likely than exclusivists to have grown up as Christians, whereas exclusivists were more likely than inclusivists to have made a conscious decision to become Christian—a difference that corresponds with popular ideas about converts being prone to be true believers.[16]

Christian exclusivism would probably encourage people to attend religious services faithfully at their particular house of worship, and, as we saw in chapter 5, Christian inclusivists also seem fairly dedicated to their churches. This pattern is evident again in table 6. Nearly two-thirds of the exclusivists said they attended religious services almost every week, if not more often, and half of the inclusivists did. In comparison, only a fifth of the spiritual shoppers attended this often. *Where* one attends also varies among the three groups. Christian exclusivists are the most likely to attend at the same place every time; spiritual shoppers are the least likely to do this. Exclusivists are the most likely to attend a house of worship located in a small town or rural area; spiritual shoppers are the least likely to do this. And exclusivists and inclusivists are equally likely to attend a church in an area where there are no synagogues, mosques, or temples, whereas spiritual shoppers who attend religious services at all are significantly less likely to attend in a religiously homogeneous community.

The differences among spiritual shoppers, Christian inclusivists, and Christian exclusivists continue when other cultural factors are considered. Shoppers are the most likely to be young (age 18 to 24), while exclusivists are the least likely. The differences some scholars have noted in the religious orientations of baby boomers and those younger or older do not seem as evident here. However, exclusivists and inclusivists are more likely to be past the age of retirement than spiritual shoppers are. The three groups also differ in level and type of education. Spiritual shoppers are the most likely to have received a college degree and to have done postgraduate work. They are also the most likely to have majored in the humanities or social sciences and to have been reared by a college-educated parent. Christian inclusivists and exclusivists do not differ from each other on these factors. Travel outside the United States follows a similar pattern.

The other factor on which spiritual shoppers, Christian inclusivists, and exclusivists differ is place of residence. Exclusivists are the most likely to live in small towns and rural areas and least likely to live in urban neighborhoods. Spiritual shoppers are most likely to live in suburban areas and least likely to live in small towns or rural areas. Spiritual shoppers are over-represented (relative to the other two groups) in the Northeast and West, and they are underrepresented in the South. Exclusivists are slightly more likely than inclusivists to live in the South, whereas inclusivists are somewhat more likely than exclusivists to live in the Northeast. Gender, race, and ethnicity do not appear to differ significantly among the three groups, although women are somewhat more represented among the two Christian groups than among spiritual shoppers, and African Americans are somewhat more represented among inclusivists than among the other two groups.[17]

Interreligious Contact and Attitudes

Thus far we have considered the beliefs of spiritual shoppers, Christian inclusivists, and Christian exclusivists and we have examined the teachings and practices that they feel have influenced their thinking and the effects of different religious and cultural experiences. We have yet to consider how much the average American may actually be in contact with members of various minority religious groups and whether this contact is more likely among some Americans than others. In the qualitative interviews we considered in chapters 4, 5, and 6, we saw that encounters between Christians and people of other religions sometimes encouraged Christians to take a more eclectic or inclusive approach to religion; we also saw that Christians' attitudes about religious truth sometimes encouraged them to seek contact with people of other faiths or to avoid such contact.

Table 7 shows the percentages of respondents in the survey who said that they had contact with Muslims, Hindus, and Buddhists, and for comparison, Jews. About half of the public claimed that they had had at least a fair amount of personal contact with Jews, and this proportion rose to two-thirds among spiritual shoppers. Despite the fact that there are presumably about as many Muslims in the United States as Jews, only a

TABLE 7

Contact with Religious and Ethnic Minority Groups

	Spiritual Shoppers (%)	Christian Inclusivists (%)	Christian Exclusivists (%)	All Respondents (%)
Percentage who had a fair amount of personal contact with each group:				
Jews	67	50	49	56
Muslims	32	22	19	24
Hindus	23	11	10	15
Buddhists	23	10	8	14
Percentage who had no contact with each group:				
Jews	7	17	15	13
Muslims	20	39	39	32
Hindus	26	47	49	41
Buddhists	28	52	52	44
Percentage who had any contact with:				
Black Muslims	11	13	10	11
Other Muslims	38	21	23	28
Life-long Buddhists	18	13	11	14
Buddhist converts	22	9	9	14
Among those with any contact, percentage whose contacts with each group were mostly pleasant:				
Jews	80	79	81	80
Muslims	77	64	52	64
Hindus	79	61	55	67
Buddhists	88	72	60	76
Number	(896)	(676)	(1,006)	(2,910)

Source: Religion and Diversity Survey.
Note: Weighted data.

quarter of the public claimed to have had a fair amount of personal contact with Muslims. As with Jews, spiritual shoppers were more likely to have had such contact than either Christian inclusivists or exclusivists. Fifteen and 14 percent of the public, respectively, recalled having had a fair amount of contact with Hindus and Buddhists. Spiritual shoppers were more than twice as likely to have had such contact as Christian inclusivists or exclusivists. If contact of this extent is limited to a relatively small minority of the public, it is nevertheless the case that a much larger share of the public has had at least some contact with these religious groups. The table demonstrates this by reporting the percentages who have had *no* contact: only 13 percent had no contact with Jews, 32 percent had none with Muslims, 41 percent had none with Hindus, and 44 percent had none with Buddhists. So a majority of the public claimed to have had some contact with each of the groups. Exclusivists and inclusivists were equally likely to have had no contact, while only about a quarter of the spiritual shoppers said that they had no contact.[18]

The Religion and Diversity Survey also generated information about the kinds of contact people claimed to have had. Those who said they had had contact with Muslims were asked if this contact had been with black Muslims or with other (presumably immigrant) Muslims. From these responses it was possible to compute that 11 percent of the public claimed to have had contact with black Muslims and 28 percent claimed to have had contact with other Muslims. Spiritual shoppers were more likely than Christian inclusivists or exclusivists to have had contact with other Muslims, but there were no significant differences in the three groups' likelihood of having had contact with black Muslims. Those who had had contact with Buddhists were asked if their contact had been with "people who grew up as Buddhists" or with "people who became Buddhists" (i.e., converts). These responses showed that equal numbers of Americans (14 percent) had had contact with each kind of Buddhists. For both, spiritual shoppers were more likely to have had contact than Christian inclusivists or exclusivists. People who had had contact with each group were also asked if these contacts had mostly been pleasant or had been mixed or unpleasant. By a two-to-one ratio, people said their contacts had been pleasant rather than mixed or unpleasant. Spiritual shoppers were the most likely to say this. And, significantly in view of the fact that the two other groups differed little in the likelihood of having had contact, Christian inclusivists were more likely than Christian exclusivists to say that their contacts with Muslims, Hindus, and Buddhists had been pleasant.

Further analysis of the data showed that contact with immigrant Muslims, Hindus, and Buddhists was more likely among spiritual shoppers than among Christian inclusivists or exclusivists with other social and cultural characteristics of respondents taken into account, and that the differences between inclusivists and exclusivists were not significant. The other factors that increased the likelihood of having had contact with immigrant Muslims, Hindus, and Buddhists were being younger, being better educated, having been raised by college-educated parents, and having traveled outside the United States. Midwesterners and Southerners were more likely than Northeasterners or Westerners to report having had contact with immigrant Muslims. Northeasterners and Westerners were the most likely to report having had contact with immigrant Buddhists and with Hindus. Catholics were less likely than Protestants to have had contact with any of the groups. And men were more likely to have had contact with all of the groups than women.[19]

Table 8 reports the public's perceptions of the Muslim religion, the Hindu religion, and the Buddhist religion. The survey posed the same set of words to respondents for each of the three religions. The words were presented in a randomly rotated order; some words (such as *fanatical, violent,* and *backward*) had negative connotations, whereas others (such as *peace-loving, tolerant,* and *appealing*) had positive connotations. The information shown in the table makes it possible to compare perceptions of Muslims, Hindus, and Buddhists and to compare the perceptions of spiritual shoppers, Christian inclusivists, and Christian exclusivists (we again need to remember that the survey was conducted about a year after the September 11, 2001, attacks on New York and Washington, meaning that perceptions of Muslims were possibly influenced by these events).[20]

In the public at large, negative perceptions of the Muslim religion were significantly more common than negative perceptions of the Hindu or Buddhist religions. Nearly half (47 percent) of the public said that *fanatical* applied to Muslims, whereas only 25 percent said the same word applied to Hindus, and 23 percent said it applied to Buddhists. The public was also more likely to perceive Muslims as "violent," "backward," and "closed-minded" than it was to perceive Hindus or Buddhists thus. About equal percentages, though, thought the word *strange* applied to Muslims, Hindus, and Buddhists. Conversely, words with more positive connotations were associated with Muslims by fewer of the respondents than with Hindus or Buddhists. For instance, 40 percent thought Muslims were peace-loving, compared with 53 percent who thought Hindus were and 63 percent who thought Buddhists were. Some of the differences were small, though. For instance, only 19 percent of the public thought the Hindu religion was "appealing," only slightly more than the 16 percent who thought this about the Muslim religion. The comparisons among spiritual shoppers, Christian inclusivists, and Christian exclusivists show that spiri-

TABLE 8

Perceptions of Religious Minority Groups

	Spiritual Shoppers (%)	Christian Inclusivists (%)	Christian Exclusivists (%)	All Respondents (%)
Percentage who thought each word applied to the Muslim religion:				
Fanatical	37	47	55	47
Violent	27	37	52	40
Peace-loving	55	46	26	40
Backward	23	36	42	34
Closed-minded	45	58	66	57
Tolerant	43	37	20	32
Strange	24	51	58	44
Appealing	22	20	9	16
Percentage who thought each word applied to the Hindu religion:				
Fanatical	16	26	33	25
Violent	9	17	21	16
Peace-loving	72	54	38	53
Backward	16	31	38	29
Closed-minded	25	38	44	35
Tolerant	60	49	32	45
Strange	25	47	57	43
Appealing	31	22	8	19
Percentage who thought each word applied to the Buddhist religion:				
Fanatical	14	25	32	23
Violent	5	14	18	12
Peace-loving	82	61	49	63
Backward	12	31	39	27
Closed-minded	17	34	42	30
Tolerant	75	54	41	56
Strange	23	46	59	42
Appealing	43	25	10	26
Number	(896)	(676)	(1,006)	(2,910)

Source: Religion and Diversity Survey.
Note: Weighted data.

TABLE 9
Views toward Stronger Presence of Religious and Ethnic Groups

	Spiritual Shoppers (%)	Christian Inclusivists (%)	Christian Exclusivists (%)	All Respondents (%)
Percentage who would welcome each group becoming a stronger presence in the United States				
Muslims	71	50	36	51
Hindus	77	58	42	58
Buddhists	82	55	43	59
Jews	86	77	75	78
Christians	87	92	94	90
Asians	84	69	60	70
Hispanics	82	72	66	73
Percentage who would not welcome each group becoming a stronger presence in the United States				
Muslims	23	43	55	42
Hindus	16	34	46	33
Buddhists	12	36	47	32
Jews	8	17	17	15
Christians	7	5	3	6
Asians	11	24	30	22
Hispanics	12	24	26	21
Number	(896)	(676)	(1,006)	(2,910)

Source: Religion and Diversity Survey.
Note: Weighted data.

tual shoppers were more likely than either of the other groups to say that positive words applied to Muslims, Hindus, and Buddhists, and they were the least likely to say that negative words applied. Christian inclusivists were consistently more likely than Christian exclusivists to say that positive words applied to Muslims, Hindus, and Buddhists, and they were consistently less likely to say that negative words applied.

In table 9 another measure of the public's receptivity to Muslims, Hindus, and Buddhists is presented. For each, respondents were asked if they would welcome or not welcome this group becoming a stronger presence in the United States. By a slight majority, the responses were generally favorable toward each of the groups. Fifty-one percent of the respondents said that they would welcome Muslims becoming a stronger presence, as did 58 percent about Hindus and 59 percent about Buddhists. The remainder were sometimes undecided, but in each case a substantial number of respondents said they would not welcome a stronger presence: 42 percent said this about Muslims, 33 percent did about Hindus, and 32 percent did about Buddhists. For comparative purposes, the table also shows responses given to similar questions about Jews, Christians, Asians, and Hispanics becoming a stronger presence in the United States. For these groups, the welcoming responses were much more common than for Muslims, Hindus, or Buddhists, while the unwelcoming responses were much less common. As before, spiritual shoppers were significantly more welcoming toward Muslims, Hindus, and Buddhists than Christian inclusivists, and Christian inclusivists were in turn significantly more likely to be welcoming than Christian exclusivists. The same pattern was evident in the responses about Asians and Hispanics becoming a stronger presence in the United States.

It is worth noting that spiritual shopping, Christian inclusivism, and Christian exclusivism are not orientations that *necessarily* encourage people to be more or less welcoming toward religious minority groups. As I have operationalized these categories here, they refer strictly to people's views about religious truth—whether it is found in all religions and whether Christianity is or is not the best way to understand God. Opinions on those topics may well be obscure and removed from the real world in which people live. Yet it is evident from what we have just considered that Americans' views about religious truth are also strongly related to how likely or unlikely they are to perceive good traits or bad traits among various religions and to how welcoming or unwelcoming they are toward people who follow those religions.

Saying that one would welcome or not welcome Muslims, Hindus, or Buddhists becoming a stronger presence may, of course, be a personal preference that would never affect how people actually behaved. It is thus of interest to consider the responses shown in table 10. These are responses to questions about predispositions to behave in certain ways or to support particular kinds of behavior on behalf of others. The first set of questions concern the public's willingness to abridge the First Amendment right of minority religious groups to meet and to worship freely. The second set concerns intermarriage. And the third focuses on the issue that has arisen

TABLE 10
Acceptance of Minority Religious Groups

	Spiritual Shoppers (%)	Christian Inclusivists (%)	Christian Exclusivists (%)	All Respondents (%)
Percentage who said they favored:				
Making it harder for Muslims to settle in the United States	24	42	46	38
Making it illegal for Muslim groups to meet in the United States	15	27	27	23
Making it illegal for Hindu groups to meet in the United States	12	25	24	20
Making it illegal for Buddhist groups to meet in the United States	12	24	23	20
Suppose you had a child who wanted to marry a Muslim who had a good education and came from a good family.* Would you:				
Object strongly	5	13	43	22
Object somewhat	7	17	22	15
Object a little	14	19	14	15
Not object at all	71	48	16	44
Suppose you had a child who wanted to marry a Hindu who had a good education and came from a good family.* Would you:				
Object strongly	4	9	31	15
Object somewhat	7	18	22	15
Object a little	13	18	21	17
Not object at all	75	50	21	48
Suppose some Muslims wanted to build a large Muslim mosque in your community.* Would this:				
Bother you a lot	6	14	30	18
Bother you a little	16	26	32	23
Not bother you	50	43	29	40
Be something you'd welcome	28	15	6	16
Suppose some Hindus wanted to build a large Hindu temple in your community.* Would this:				
Bother you a lot	4	8	24	13
Bother you a little	12	25	31	22
Not bother you	51	48	37	54
Be something you'd welcome	32	18	4	17
Number	(897)	(677)	(1,006)	(2,910)

Source: Religion and Diversity Survey.
Note: Weighted data.
* Asked of half the sample (randomly selected).

in many communities of residents opposing the construction of a new mosque or temple.

Nearly four Americans in ten (38 percent) would favor making it harder for Muslims to settle in the United States, according to the results shown in table 10. Fewer would go so far as to make it illegal for minority religious groups to meet. But almost a quarter (23 percent) would go that far in the case of Muslims and a fifth would in the case of Hindus or Buddhists. In each case, spiritual shoppers were about half as likely to give these responses as Christian inclusivists or exclusivists. Unlike in the previous tables, inclusivists were just as likely as exclusivists to give these responses. When asked about intermarriage, fewer than half of the respondents said they would not object at all if a child of theirs wanted to marry a Muslim or Hindu who had a good education and came from a good family. More said they would object strongly in the case of marrying a Muslim than in the case of marrying a Hindu, but in both cases about a third said they would object more than a little. Spiritual shoppers were significantly less likely than the other groups to say that they would object; Christian exclusivists were much more likely than Christian inclusivists to say that they would object strongly. The responses to the prospect of Muslims building a mosque or Hindus building a temple in their community was something about which respondents were divided. About four in ten said that they would be bothered by the idea of a mosque being built in their community, about four in ten said they would not be bothered, and about one in six said that they would welcome the idea. The responses to the idea of a Hindu temple were somewhat more favorable, but more than a third said that they would be bothered and only one in six said that they would welcome the idea. Spiritual shoppers were least likely to say that they would be bothered, Christian exclusivists were the most likely to say this, and Christian inclusivists were in the middle.

Interreligious Programs

In our in-depth interviews, we saw evidence of people sometimes being encouraged to think more deeply about other religious groups as a result of interreligious programs at their churches or in their communities and we saw some of the struggles that Christian exclusivists especially were faced with when they thought about efforts to evangelize people of other faiths. We shall want to look more closely at some of the interreligious programs sponsored by churches in chapter 8 and by other organizations in chapter 10. The Religion and Diversity Survey provides some evidence on what the public has been doing and thinks should be done.

One kind of interreligious contact that may come about through the auspices of religious organizations are efforts by Christians to convert people of other faiths to Christianity. Some of these efforts have been widely publicized in newspapers and on television, but scholarly research among the groups most likely to have launched such efforts has cast doubt on journalists' impressions.[21] So did the remarks of the people we discussed in chapters 5 and 6. To obtain additional information, respondents in the survey who said they were Christians were asked if they considered it important for Christians to share their faith with non-Christians (table 11). Sixty percent said this was very important and most of the remainder (26 percent) said it was fairly important. But sharing one's faith apparently means something other than making converts. When asked how important it was for Christians to encourage people from other faiths—such as Muslims, Hindus, or Buddhists—to become Christians, only 36 percent said this was very important. Christian exclusivists were the most likely in both cases to give this response. Fewer thought it important to convert others than thought it important to share their faith, but not many fewer (only 14 percent fewer). In contrast, Christian inclusivists were much less likely to say it was important to make converts than to say it was important to share their faith (34 points less likely). And, although spiritual shoppers who were Christians were less likely in the first place to consider sharing their faith important, they also showed a substantial decline (25 points) when asked about making converts.

About half of the Christians in the survey said that they had talked specifically with someone in the past year who was not a Christian with the intent of persuading that person to become a Christian. One Christian in three claimed to have done this more than once or twice, and only one in eight claimed to have done it "many times." Among the exclusivists, about seven in ten said that they had evangelized in this way at least once during the previous year, among Christian inclusivists half had, and among the spiritual shoppers fewer than one in five had. From these responses,

TABLE 11
Evangelistic Activities (Christians Only)

	Spiritual Shoppers (%)	Christian Inclusivists (%)	Christian Exclusivists (%)	All Respondents (%)
Percentage who said it is very important for Christians to share their faith with non-Christians*	29	63	76	60
Percentage who said it is very important for Christians to encourage people from other faiths to become Christians*	4	29	61	36
Percentage who said they had talked specifically with someone in the past year who was not a Christian to persuade them to become a Christian:				
Many times	2	11	21	13
Several times	5	17	26	18
Once or twice	8	18	21	17
None	82	53	31	52
Percentage who tried to persuade someone who was:**				
Muslim	2	10	10	10
Hindu	2	4	6	5
Buddhist	4	6	8	7
Jewish	10	15	20	17
An atheist	41	44	47	46
Not a churchgoer	78	84	92	88
Number	(550)	(620)	(972)	(2,329)

Source: Religion and Diversity Survey.
Note: Weighted data; asked of the 80 percent of respondents who said they consider themselves "a Christian."
* Asked of half the sample (randomly selected).
** Asked only of those who had tried to persuade someone to become a Christian.

we might suppose that U.S. Christians—at least Christian exclusivists—have been busy evangelizing Muslims, Hindus, and Buddhists. In the bottom panel of table 11, though, we see that this is not the case. Among those who had done any evangelizing in the past year, only 10 percent had tried to persuade a Muslim to become a Christian, only 5 percent had tried to persuade a Hindu, and only 7 percent had tried to persuade a Buddhist. In comparison, 88 percent had tried to persuade someone who was not a churchgoer.[22]

These survey results point to the same conclusion we drew in chapter 6 from listening to Christian exclusivists talk about their experiences with evangelism. Although they thought their non-Christian friends were destined for eternal punishment, few of them were actively engaged in trying to convert their friends. Especially when these friends belonged to another faith, they seemed to be forbidden fruit. Here, it appears that most Christian exclusivists either do not know Muslims, Hindus, or Buddhists or, if they do, they prefer not to talk to them about Christianity. They apparently have enough people who do not attend church to keep them busy.

Evangelism is only one form of possible contact between people of different religions; joint programs, dialogue among leaders, and opportunities for ordinary people to learn about other religions are some of the other possibilities. We should not take it as a given that such programs are desirable. It may be that staying apart is the easiest way to avoid conflict. Yet we have seen that people who do have contact generally feel that their interaction has been pleasant. We have also seen enough indications of misunderstanding and misgiving that there is arguably a need for greater contact and interaction. But is this something the public would support?

Table 12 shows the responses of self-identified Christian church members to five questions in the Religion and Diversity Survey about the desirability of greater interaction and mutual understanding among various religions. By a large margin, Christian church members believe it *is* desirable to have greater cooperation and understanding among the various religions. In the survey, three people in four felt that it was desirable to have "more cooperation among the leaders of the various religions in the United States, such as Christianity, Judaism, Islam, Hinduism, and Buddhism" (40 percent said this was very desirable, only 7 percent said it was very undesirable). When asked about followers, almost as many (73 percent) said it was desirable to have "greater understanding among the followers of different religions, such as between Christians and Jews, Jews and Muslims, and Muslims and Hindus" (32 percent said this was very desirable, while 7 percent said it was very undesirable). An even larger proportion opted for greater understanding when posed with a choice to "learn more about religions other than their own" (80 percent) or "avoid learning too much about other religions." In the context of thinking about the increased levels of religious diversity

TABLE 12
Views about Interreligious Programs

	Spiritual Shoppers (%)	Christian Inclusivists (%)	Christian Exclusivists (%)	All Respondents (%)
Do you feel that more cooperation among the leaders of the various religions in the United States, such as Christianity, Judaism, Islam, Hinduism, and Buddhism, is:				
Very desirable	60	43	31	40
Somewhat desirable	28	38	37	37
Somewhat undesirable	5	12	15	12
Very undesirable	3	5	10	7
Do you feel that greater understanding among the followers of different religions, such as between Christians and Jews, Jews and Muslims, and Muslims and Hindus, is:				
Very desirable	45	30	30	32
Somewhat desirable	41	45	40	41
Somewhat undesirable	8	13	14	13
Very undesirable	4	7	9	7
Do you think: people should learn more about religions other than their own	93	78	76	80
Is it better to avoid learning too much about other religions	4	14	21	16
As a result of increased religious diversity, people will need to think harder about why they believe in their particular faith				
Agree	68	44	81	77
Disagree	30	20	16	20
We all need to learn something about these new groups and their beliefs				
Agree	90	85	79	82
Disagree	9	14	19	16
Number	(279)	(399)	(715)	(1,499)

Source: Religion and Diversity Survey.
Note: Weighted data; self-identified Christians, church members only.

in the United States, most Christians (77 percent) agreed that "people will need to think harder about why they believe in their particular faith," but most (82 percent) also agreed that "we all need to learn something about these new groups and their beliefs."

On the four questions referring to greater cooperation and understanding, spiritual shoppers who were Christian church members remained true to their commitment to religious diversity in being the most likely to feel that greater cooperation and understanding was desirable. Christian inclusivists fell in the middle between spiritual shoppers and Christian exclusivists on these questions. Even among the exclusivists there was generally support for greater cooperation and understanding. Thus, only a quarter of the exclusivists thought it was undesirable to have more cooperation among leaders of different religions, only a fifth thought it was better to avoid learning too much about other religions, and only a fifth disagreed that increased religious diversity means that everyone should learn something about the new groups and their beliefs.

Given the widespread public support for greater cooperation and understanding among different religions, it is of interest to see how many people have actually been involved in programs at their houses of worship that encouraged such cooperation and understanding. We asked Christians who were members of congregations to say if they had personally participated in various kinds of programs that may have involved exposure to leaders of other religions or the teachings of these religions during the year prior to the survey (recall that in the aftermath of the September 11 attacks, interreligious efforts were being encouraged by public officials and the media). The responses are shown in table 13. Only one church member in six said that he or she had participated in "a worship service or other event at your congregation in which a non-Christian leader spoke, such as a Jewish, Muslim, Hindu, or Buddhist leader." Even fewer—one person in nine—had participated in "a class or study group that focused on the beliefs and practices of some other religion besides Christianity or Judaism, such as Islam, Hinduism, or Buddhism." A slightly larger proportion (but still fewer than one person in five) said that they had participated in a "program or activity that was specifically concerned with improving relations between Christians and Jews" or "a service program or volunteer activity sponsored by your congregation

TABLE 13

Participation in Interreligious Programs

	Spiritual Shoppers (%)	Christian Inclusivists (%)	Christian Exclusivists (%)	All Respondents (%)
Percentage who had participated in each of the following during the past year:				
A worship service or other event at your congregation in which a non-Christian religious leader spoke, such as a Jewish, Muslim, Hindu, or Buddhist leader	24	19	13	16
A class or study group that focused on the beliefs and practices of some other religion besides Christianity or Judaism, such as Islam, Hinduism, or Buddhism	12	8	13	11
Any program or activity that was specifically concerned with improving relations between Christians and Jews	12	16	17	16
A service program or volunteer activity sponsored by your congregation that also included people who belong to other religions, such as Muslims, Hindus, or Buddhists	20	18	19	19
A meeting at which a missionary or religious leader spoke about efforts to bring Christianity to people in other countries	35	49	66	54
A class or study group that discussed how to share your faith with others	25	34	59	44
Any organized program to tell people of other faiths—such as Muslims, Hindus, or Buddhists—about Jesus	4	10	19	13
Number	(279)	(399)	(715)	(1,499)

Source: Religion and Diversity Survey.

Note: Weighted data; self-identified Christians, church members only.

that also included people who belong to other religions, such as Muslims, Hindus, or Buddhists."[23] In comparison with activities involving leaders of other religions, it was much more common for church members to hear about missionary or evangelistic efforts—suggesting the possibility that missionaries may still be one of the main ways in which church people learn about other religions through their churches (rather than the mass media). More than half of the church members in the survey said that they had participated in "a meeting at which a missionary or religious leader spoke about efforts to bring Christianity to people in other countries." Nearly that many (44 percent) said that they had participated in "a class or study group that discussed how to share your faith with others." As we saw in the earlier questions about evangelism, though, the number shrank considerably (to 13 percent) when asked if they had participated in "any organized program to tell people of other faiths— such as Muslims, Hindus, or Buddhists—about Jesus."

Spiritual shoppers, Christian inclusivists, and Christian exclusivists differed from one another in their responses to these questions. Among the spiritual shoppers who were church members, a quarter had participated in a worship service or other event at which a non-Christian religious leader spoke; only 13 percent of the Christian exclusivists had done so, and Christian inclusivists fell in between (19 percent). Shoppers and exclusivists were equally likely to have participated in a class or study group about other religions, and inclusivists were the least likely to have done this. We might have supposed otherwise, especially because it would seem that Christian inclusivists would have the most to gain from such studies. Yet, the results suggest that shoppers are probably more likely to participate in such studies because they are more open to truth in other religions, whereas exclusivists may participate because they feel the need to arm themselves against false teachings. Participation in programs to improve relations between Christians and Jews or in service programs involving people of other faiths does not vary much among spiritual shoppers, inclusivists, and exclusivists. Not surprisingly, exclusivists were the most likely to have heard missionaries speak at their churches. They were also the most likely to have participated in classes about evangelism and programs to tell people of other faiths about Jesus.

Conclusions

It is hard to imagine any clearer evidence that religious diversity—and how we think about it—matters. Although the share of the population that is Muslim, Hindu, or Buddhist is quite small, the impact of these groups on American culture is much larger. Millions of Americans who are Christians or Jews come in contact with Muslims, Hindus, and Buddhists through their work, their business dealings, and in their neighborhoods. Millions have visited mosques and temples or traveled to countries in which non-Western religions predominate. Many more Americans have formed opinions about these religions through their reading, what they have heard on television, and their conversations at church or with friends. The American public holds strong views about the teachings and practices of the various religions. Although it is common to give lip service to the value of diversity, many Americans regard religions other than their own as fanatical, conducive to violence, closed-minded, backward, and strange. A large minority (at least a third) of Americans say that they would not welcome these religions becoming a stronger presence in our society. A large minority would not be happy about mosques and temples being built in their neighborhoods, they would not want a child of theirs to marry a Muslim or Hindu, and some would even make it illegal for these religious groups to meet.

How Americans feel about new immigrants with religions different from their own is deeply influenced by their thoughts about religious truth. Seeing how casually people sometimes think about religion and knowing how private people are about their religious convictions, we might not have expected these thoughts about religious truth to matter very much. But they do. American Christians have learned in varying degrees that their faith is special, especially true, and perhaps even the only way to have a true personal relationship with God and to attain eternal salvation. All Americans have been exposed to ideas at their houses of worship, through the mass media, or in classes they may have taken about the truth of various religions. These ideas range from notions about all religions being embodiments of *some* truth to all religions leading to the same God or basically teaching the same things. These are not simply abstract opinions about truth. They are also closely aligned, as we have seen, with how Americans view America itself. Believing that Christianity is exclusively true is strongly associated with believing that Christianity is the source of America's greatness and with feeling that immigrants with different religions are a threat to America's distinctive values and lifestyles. Being more eclectic in one's views about religious truth is associated with a different view of America—one in which Christianity has been less important from the start and in which diversity itself will play a more positive role in the future.

The deep differences that separate Americans from one another in their views about religious diversity are tempered largely by an implicit strategy of *avoidance*. Most people who believe that all religious are the same have not taken the time to gain much familiarity with the various religions and thus to learn how they are different. Most people who believe that it is possible to be a good Christian and to regard all other religions as equally true have not been in classes where they actually learned much about these other religions. The Christians who believe that followers of all other religions are eternally damned avoid confrontation by seldom making any effort to evangelize these followers.

The typical American, then, thinks it is probably a good idea to get the leaders of various religions together. The typical American even acknowledges that he or she should learn more about other religions, should gain a clearer understanding of them, and should work harder to figure out what he or she truly believes about religion. It is thus surprising that so few of those who belong to churches have experienced opportunities to learn more about the teachings and practices of other religions in these contexts. Clergy would surely want to provide these opportunities and find ways to guide the discussion, rather than leaving the public to learn about other religions through CNN and radio talk shows. But clergy have their own stories to tell about interreligious programs, about why some work better than others, and about why they are never easy.

How Congregations Manage Diversity

THE GROWING PRESENCE of other religions in the United States creates a particularly challenging situation for American churches and the clergy who lead these churches. Whereas the average individual may be able to pick and choose, quietly deciding what his or her personal stance will be toward other religions, the Christian church is a public institution. It communicates messages about the sacred through its ministries and its mere presence. What it says and does in response to other religions is inescapably part of its witness, both to the wider community and to its own members. Faced with new neighbors who may be Muslim, Hindu, or Buddhist, clergy can seek ways to tell them about Christianity or can try to find common ground in their diverse traditions, but clergy can hardly pretend that these new neighbors do not exist. To do nothing or say nothing becomes silent testimony to the church's views.[1]

But dealing with other religions in a society as imbued with pluralistic principles as ours is a tricky business for church leaders of almost any persuasion. Some leaders may be willing to proclaim their mandate to "evangelize to people of all religious backgrounds," as one fundamentalist leader did in a *New York Times* opinion piece, on the grounds that evangelization, like war on homosexuality, abortion, and women in the pulpit, is simply "settled by the word of God."[2] Unless one's agenda is deliberately to provoke "the slings and arrows of outraged opponents," as this leader suggests, the task of representing the Christian church in a religiously diverse milieu, however, requires more than bold assertions. If the church's mission includes evangelization, does it carry out this mission by specifically targeting its non-Christian neighbors? Does it find some ground for exempting them, does it take a wait and see attitude, or does it avoid addressing the issue entirely? And if the church in a diverse milieu takes its mission seriously, does it try to learn something about its non-Christian neighbors? Does it study their beliefs and practices? Does it encourage interaction that may lead to greater understanding or even friendships? Or does it busy itself with other preoccupations?

Christian congregations, of which there are currently more than 300,000, represent a powerful force in American life. Scholars increasingly write about the social capital generated through these congregations. Social capital includes the friendships that develop among churchgoers and the relationships linking the church with community organizations, such as coalitions to help the homeless or to serve the needs of inner-city families. Churches promote volunteering and raise money that helps support social programs. Policy makers have even called for closer alliances between government and churches, recognizing the value of so-called faith-based social ministries. Churches are sometimes insular, calling members to retreat from worldly engagement, and yet the churches' presence in local communities is an important fact of community life. Church leaders who ignore this fact do so at their own peril.[3]

The average church, nestled comfortably at the corner of some quiet suburban intersection, may have little sense that the society in which its members live is becoming increasingly diverse. Its members come to church on Sunday mornings presumably because they are already Christians and, if they are the particularly active members whom the pastor or priest happens to know well, their relationships may be largely restricted to other church members. To the extent that they think about diversity, they may do so in terms of the theological views, lifestyles, interests, and racial or ethnic groups represented within their own congregation.[4] Yet it is hard to imagine that these members do not read newspapers or watch television and thus know that much of the world is populated by people who adhere to religions other than Christianity. They may be among the many who have traveled to these parts of the world or whose coworkers, friends, and extended families include people of other religions. Their pastors can scarcely ignore these larger realities. Unless they studiously avoid all topics that concern the wider world, they will have to say something—informed, one hopes—about the church's place in a world of diversity.

Questions about diversity and about how to respond to it are most acute for the growing number of churches situated in religiously diverse neighborhoods. It may be possible to travel long stretches of back roads in rural Kansas or Alabama without seeing a single temple, ashram, or mosque. But those are not the contexts in which most Americans live. A large number of Americans—at least 30 percent—attend churches that are within a few miles of a synagogue, mosque, or some other place of worship besides another church.[5] What happens when Hindus purchase the building down the street, around the block, or next door? Does the church make an effort to welcome them to the community? Does it invite them to an ecumenical service? Does it pretend that they do not exist?

Suppose a pastor does want to respond in some way to the community's increasing religious diversity? Consider the questions that may need to be faced. What kind of event is most appropriate? Should the pastor act alone or plan something to which the congregation is invited? Is it appropriate to invite a rabbi to speak at a church meeting? What about an imam? What should the purpose of such an event be? To break the ice? To cultivate respect and understanding? To acquire information about a potential competitor? Should a busy pastor be contemplating an event of this kind at all? Will congregants understand? Perhaps it would be better to do nothing at all.

It may be difficult, though, to escape having to respond in some way to religious diversity. Suppose the church is invited to join a coalition to help needy families in the community? Does the decision depend on whether the coalition is limited to churches or whether it includes a local synagogue or mosque? What if the church welcomes nonmembers to participate in its service of Holy Communion? Does this invitation extend to non-Christians? Is the pastor willing to perform a wedding between a Christian and a non-Christian? How does the pastor advise a member with Buddhist roots about participating in his or her family's rituals? What does the pastor say when a member of the congregation asserts that all religions are equally true? Or when a newcomer asks if Christianity is uniquely true? Does the church try to address the many questions posed by religious diversity through some specific program or does it wait and hope these questions go away?

For pastors and other church leaders, religious diversity is clearly a subject, then, that requires management. Just as it does to keep the church's finances in order or to ensure that the church grows at a steady pace, it takes thoughtful planning and preparation to respond appropriately to the growing religious diversity that all churches now face in some ways and that many churches face in their immediate neighborhoods. In personal interviews, most clergy recognize that the world in which their ministries take place is becoming more religiously diverse. Yet relatively few have thought through the implications of this diversity for their own churches.

The question needing to be addressed, then, is what *are* clergy doing at the local level to meet the challenges posed by religious diversity? How are they responding and why are they responding as they are? From those who have initiated programs, what can be learned from their experience? From those who have not initiated programs, can something be learned by listening to their reasons for not taking action?

My orientation to these questions as a social scientist is that human behavior often reveals a great deal about our assumptions and beliefs—even more, sometimes, than we realize. Just as individuals do when they talk about religious diversity, church leaders reveal many of their implicit assumptions about the work and mission of the church when they discuss their responses to the religious and cultural diversity in their communities. The ways in which churches are responding to religious diversity send implicit messages about the very meaning of the church in today's culture—how it understands itself, how it has accommodated itself to the culture in which we live, and what it means to be Christian.

What Churches Are Doing

We saw in chapter 7 that relatively few church members (no more than a fifth) claim to have participated personally in any interreligious activities at their congregations. That response suggests that congregations could do a lot better than they currently are in providing interfaith opportunities capable of attracting a significant share of their members. But of course the proportion of congregations that provide these opportunities is probably larger than the proportion of members who take part in them. Some additional evidence about churches' responses to religious diversity comes from a nationally representative survey of the U.S. population (conducted in 2000) in which all members of any kind of religious congregation were asked whether or not their congregation had helped to sponsor "a program or meeting to encourage greater understanding among different religions, such as Christians, Jews, and Muslims." Nationally, 43 percent said their congregation had done this within the past year. To put this figure in perspective, virtually the same percentage said their congregation sponsors a tutoring program, and only a slightly larger proportion (50 percent) said their congregation helps sponsor a shelter for the homeless. In other words, programs to encourage greater understanding among different religions may be about as common as some of the social service activities that have received a great deal of attention in recent years, at least if members' perceptions are accurate.

Some kinds of churches are more likely to sponsor programs or meetings about religious diversity than others. Among evangelical Protestants, only 35 percent say their congregation has helped to sponsor a program or meeting to encourage greater understanding among different religions, whereas the comparable figure among mainline Protestants is 47 percent; among black Protestants, 42 percent; among Catholics, 48 percent; and among Jews, 88 percent. The location and size of churches also make a difference: the highest figures are among mainline Protestants in the Northeast and West and among Catholics in the West (all 53 percent), while the lowest is among evangelicals in the South (32 percent). The figures are higher in churches of more than a thousand members (55 percent) than in churches of three hundred to a thousand members (46 percent), and lowest in churches with fewer than three hundred members (34 percent). The figures are also higher for churches located in the suburbs of large cities (52 percent) than for churches in small towns (42 percent) or rural areas (35 percent).[6]

From such figures, one might conclude that a large number of churches are doing something to take account of religious diversity. Other data challenge this conclusion. In a study of 1,400 congregations conducted by the Hartford Institute for Religion Research, only 7 percent of congregations indicated having held worship services involving people from any other faith and only 8 percent had engaged in interfaith social outreach programs. Catholic and mainstream Protestant congregations were more likely than conservative Protestant congregations to be involved in programs of these kinds. But the low proportions overall were striking, especially because the study found high levels of involvement not only with other Christian congregations but also with secular nonprofit organizations.[7]

The low numbers in the Hartford study might be attributed to the fact that many of the nation's churches remain in rural areas or small towns or are located in suburbs where religious diversity is absent. A study conducted in a religiously diverse section of Chicago, however, also revealed relatively little interaction among different religions. The study's director wrote, "Our research revealed no programs of education about the other religions and ethnoracial groups in the neighborhood, no intergroup visits or exchanges of musicians or instructors. An interfaith Thanksgiving service—a holdover from a period of much less diversity—was the only joint project during the time of our research."[8] This was in a community that included thirty Jewish congregations, twenty-seven Protestant churches, six mosques, five Roman Catholic parishes, four Buddhist temples, a Hindu temple, and a Sikh gurdwara.

Studies like this give mixed impressions of congregational awareness of religious diversity. But they are also limited in the information they provide about what exactly is being done. Actually talking with pastors is a better way of finding out why particular programs do or do not exist and how church leaders address the complexities of ministering in diverse communities. The research on which this chapter is based included in-depth qualitative interviews with more than fifty pastors from around the country who talked at length about their churches' programs as well as their own activities and views. The pastors all served congregations that were within the immediate vicinity of a Jewish synagogue, a Muslim mosque, a Hindu temple, or a Buddhist temple. In short, they were all in contexts where some interaction with people of other religions was possible.

A good example of a church program oriented toward promoting greater understanding between Christians and other religions comes from a Lutheran church in California. Faith Lutheran is a three-hundred-member congregation located in an upper-middle-class suburb that is predominately Jewish. There are four synagogues within a mile of the church. The community has also become more religiously diverse in recent years. Two mosques and two Buddhist temples are only a short drive away and there is a Hindu temple in the community as well. The Reverend Martin Dreisbach believes that his church has an obligation to live in harmony with the other religious organizations nearby. His predecessor started cultivating good relationships some years ago by putting out a sign during Jewish holidays that read "Happy Holidays to Our Jewish Neighbors." Dreisbach tells his congregation that Jews have a covenant relationship with God and thus do not need to convert to Christianity. He believes that Christians and Jews worship the same God and often preaches about the Jewish origins of Christianity. He serves on the board of an organization that brings Christian and Jewish clergy together to combat anti-Semitism through acts such as purchasing copies of *The Diary of Anne Frank* and distributing them to classrooms and school libraries. The congregation has formally adopted a Holocaust survivor who speaks occasionally at the church and organizes tours for church members to the Museum of Tolerance in Los Angeles. The church also teams up periodically with one of the synagogues in the area to sponsor a work day that brings members of both congregations together to work on service projects for the wider community. Beyond its efforts to promote better relationships with its Jewish neighbors, the church sponsors an annual service of tolerance to which members of all religions in the area are invited. Usually about two hundred people attend, including Christians, Jews, Hindus, and Muslims. At the end of the service, people of the various faiths get up and say in their own languages, "God is love and we should love one another." Mr. Dreisbach says his commitment to interfaith reconciliation grows both from his understanding of the Christian gospel and from personal experience. Early in his ministry at Faith Lutheran, someone broke into the church one night and placed a fire bomb under his desk, causing the entire building to burn to the ground. Working for tolerance is his way of showing that love is more powerful than hate.

Other pastors mention a wide variety of activities and programs oriented toward promoting better understanding between Christianity and other religions. A Presbyterian church in suburban Philadelphia hosts a Middle Eastern dinner periodically and invites Jews and Muslims to participate and speak. A Lutheran church in Oregon invites international students (some of whom are Muslim or Hindu) to share meals with members of the congregation. An African-American pastor of a Baptist church in Miami participates in an interfaith social justice organization that includes Muslims. A Catholic parish in Virginia recently hosted a lecture by a rabbi about Judaism. An Episcopal church in Sacramento periodically invites Muslim representatives to speak at its Sunday churchwide forum.

Most of the activities that pastors mention are relatively minor in comparison with their congregations' overall programs of worship, education, and service. Usually interfaith activities happen once or twice a year, are voluntary, and involve bringing one or two representatives of another religion to the church, rather than requiring members to travel to another location, or else they are performed by the pastor in a way that does not involve the congregation at all. Still, these activities are understood by the pastors who initiate them to be a meaningful part of the ministries of some congregations, whereas they are absent in other churches' programs. What accounts for these differences?

The Role of Theology

Although churches are guided by many considerations, including the condition of their finances and the interests of their members, theology is generally the underlying principle that governs the kinds of programs that are considered appropriate or inappropriate. The importance of theology is particularly evident in the following example. First Reformed Church is one of the historic landmarks in its East Coast community. Founded in the mid-seventeenth century, its membership has remained constant in recent years, numbering just below two hundred. The neighborhood is rich in religious diversity. Besides Catholic, Greek Orthodox, and Protestant churches, it includes four synagogues, two mosques, two Hindu temples, and two Buddhist temples. In the past two years, First Reformed has participated in two three-month-long Bible study classes held jointly with a synagogue four blocks down the street. At first, about twenty-five people from the church attended, and then the number grew to around forty. Each week the discussion focused on a passage from the Hebrew scriptures. The pastor and the rabbi led the discussion, but mostly the members of the two congregations just shared their impressions and opinions about the passage. The experience was so positive that the congregation has been considering repeating it and perhaps initiating a similar forum with one of the mosques in the neighborhood. The Reverend Jon Hoekema, now in his twelfth year as pastor at First Reformed, views these interfaith activities as a natural expression of Christ's teachings. The congregation's theological orientation, he says, is firmly trinitarian, mainstream as far as the denomination (Reformed Church in America) is concerned, and conservative. He believes that Christ opens people to a relationship with God that deepens and enriches their lives, and for this reason, he strongly urges people who want a relationship with God to study the Bible and become involved in a community of believers where they can learn about Christ. His understanding of salvation is more positive than negative: those who know Jesus have an abundant, eternal relationship with God; those who resist God's will may in the end also be forgiven or perhaps a merciful God will simply terminate their existence, rather than sentencing them to eternal suffering. Mr. Hoekema says that there is no way to be sure about this, so it is better to focus on other aspects of Christianity. The most important teaching, in his view, is to love one another as God has loved us, and this means loving everyone. "Because of Jesus, I now have a new relationship with every other human being on the face of the earth. They are my brother and sister because God is our father. The way I describe it is because of the exclusive nature of my commitment to Christ I have become a very inclusive person. There is this exclusive nature of Christianity. It is a commitment to Christ which seems to exclude others, but because of my relationship to Christ he has showed me that I am a brother and sister to every other human being on the earth." Thus, in his ministry, he tries to live up to this ideal of inclusivity. He is pleased, for example, that his once all-white congregation is now a melting pot of European Americans, African Americans, Asian Americans, and Puerto Rican Americans and that it helps sponsor a couple of foreign missionaries. He takes an active role in the local clergy council, which includes rabbis as well as pastors, and has been working through this organization to combat hate crimes reflecting the racial, ethnic, and religious tensions in the community.

Over the years, Mr. Hoekema has had ample opportunity to think about the implications of his seemingly paradoxical view about the exclusivity of Christianity being conducive to an inclusive approach to religious diversity. Reared in a predominantly Christian community in the Midwest and having attended a conservative Christian college, he was challenged by some of his college and seminary professors to think hard about his religious assumptions, rather than merely taking them for granted. Traveling in Europe, visiting Holocaust sites, and having close friends who were Jewish and Hindu, as well as his reading, forced him to think about how to be Christian in a religiously diverse environment. It concerns him that some of his friends have decided that there is little reason to be Christian at all because they regard all religions as equally valid and he worries about people who seem to embrace tolerance and pluralism without having thought through the implications of these values for their own faith. His own views are still developing. He says, for example, that he would have no trouble talking to a Muslim about how to become a Christian if that person were interested; at the same time, he thinks there is a kind of devotion and piety in Islam that God probably respects and, indeed, from which Christians could learn. He believes that Jesus is God and is God's revelation to humankind, yet he also believes that people of other religions find God through the way of humility and obedience that Jesus taught even though they may not consciously invoke the name of Jesus. He regards the Bible as God's infallible word, meaning that it is trustworthy, but rejects the idea of biblical inerrancy and insists that the Bible is one of many ways in which God is revealed. His interpretation of Jesus' statement about being the way, the truth, and the life emphasizes the differences between this statement in the gospel of John and those of the other gospel writers; while respecting the teachings of other religions, he also dismisses the notion that all religions are equally true or simply substitutable for one another.

For a person like Mr. Hoekema who takes theology seriously, the reality of other religions—not only in the world but in his immediate neighborhood—poses an opportunity to think more deeply about his faith than otherwise might have been the case. He expects Christianity to become a minority religion in the United States within a generation or two and says that this will probably be a good development. At least those who remain Christians, he hopes, will have a clearer understanding of why they are trying to follow the teachings of Christ. Meanwhile, he acknowledges that he does not have all the answers but believes his God is big enough to encourage Christians to interact on level ground with followers of other religions without fear.

A contrasting view of relating to people of other faiths that reflects a different theological orientation is well illustrated by Jim and Nancy Parsons, co-pastors of a four-hundred-member Assemblies of God church in a large city on the East Coast. Like Mr. Hoekema, they have had plenty of opportunity to think about the relationships between Christians and people of other faiths. Located in a downtown area, their church is within a few blocks of two synagogues, a Hindu temple, and a Buddhist temple, and there is a mosque a little farther away. The congregation itself is quite diverse: more than half of the members are from Puerto Rico, Haiti, the Dominican Republic, and other Central and South American countries, a quarter are African or African American, and the remainder are white Anglos and Asian Americans. Although the members include people of all income groups, ranging from the homeless to wealthy business managers and professionals, the Parsons have also started mission congregations in several other communities to accommodate lower-income families who feel uncomfortable worshipping downtown. All this keeps the Parsons busy enough that they have little time to think about interacting with Jews, Muslims, Hindus, and Buddhists in their neighborhood. They abandoned a small effort to draw Jewish children to some of their programs a few years ago, report that they currently have no contact with Hindus, know only a few Muslims, are critical of an interfaith church in the area that in their view accepts everyone too easily, and now channel most of their own interfaith efforts through a group of Messianic Jews whose ministry they support in a small way. Even if time pressures were not a factor, the Parsons say they would downplay interfaith activities. "In this city that kind of thing has been done to death," Mrs. Parsons explains, "and to be honest, it has not been effective. What usually happens is that you sit down and have people share and emotions get heightened. I'm not saying it shouldn't be done, but we have never seen anything effective. What we focus on with the people is building relationships. What we teach our people is how to win someone to the Lord through relationships. That's the major focus of our ministry."

The Parsons' ministerial focus is an expression of their understanding of the Christian faith. A Christian, in their view, is essentially a person who learns the truths that Jesus set forth in the Bible and who "disciplines your body and your mouth and your mind and your tongue and your living by the standard of the Bible." The Parsons insist that they are not talking about a list of do's and don'ts but standards that God revealed in the Bible to help people lead happier, more loving, and more obedient lives. The main reason for trying to live according to these standards is to please God. Anyone truly interested in pleasing the Lord will, accordingly, spend ample time reading the Bible and attending a church where the Bible is preached. They recognize that many (probably most) people do not seriously try to follow Jesus in these ways and thus it worries them to think about those who stray from God's path. This is the basis for their church's emphasis on evangelism through relationships. "Because we are very relationally based," Mrs. Parsons says, "we try to offer a different answer for every person. We use the 'feel, felt, and found' text. If a person is sick and scared, I've been sick, I've had a bad diagnosis, I know what that feels like, so I can say, 'I know how you *feel*, I've *felt* that same way, and here's what I *found*, that the Lord was able to walk me through this and I would have never gotten through it without his strength.' "

As far as their Jewish, Muslim, Hindu, and Buddhist neighbors are concerned, the Parsons are convinced that they need to hear the gospel of Jesus, come to an understanding that the Bible is the only "standard of truth," and be converted just like an atheist or anybody else. Although this conviction might be expected to lead the Parsons to focus especially on meeting and converting people of other religions, the "feel-felt-found" aspect of their thinking tempers their approach. Using Jehovah's Witnesses as a negative example, they distance themselves from people who aggressively go door to door trying to make converts. In their view, a person has to be in the right spiritual, mental, and emotional place before he or she is willing to seriously consider becoming a Christian, and usually this preparation involves a major personal crisis of some kind, such as losing one's job, coming to terms with an addiction, going through a divorce, or experiencing a serious illness or death in the family. When that happens, it makes no difference as far as the Parsons are concerned whether the person is a Muslim or an atheist; if the person is in enough pain, it becomes possible to talk persuasively to that person about Jesus.

Although they do not aggressively evangelize non-Christians, the Parsons are quite clear that these people do not know God. Their interpretation of Jesus' saying about being the way, the truth, and the life is that this statement leaves open only two options: either Jesus was telling the truth or Jesus was a liar and, since the latter option strikes most people as unattractive, they argue that Jesus really meant it when he said that he was the only way to come to God. Thus, they have little interest in trying to understand the teachings of other religious traditions. They acknowledge that there are well-meaning people who follow these traditions, but these people will not have eternal life unless they believe that Jesus died for their sins.

As these examples suggest, Christian theology and how congregations relate to and think about people of other religions are inextricably interwoven. Pastors like Jon Hoekema who are interested in learning from their Jewish and Muslim neighbors are often somewhat more open in their thinking about such questions as the uniqueness of the Bible than pastors like the Parsons who feel that greater understanding of other religions is less important than engaging in personal evangelism. But theology provides only the broad framework in which pastors' thinking about other religions is shaped. Within these larger frameworks, pastors still struggle with questions about how exactly to think about and relate to people of other religions.

Consider what the Reverend Jim Jimson says about presenting the gospel to Jews or Muslims or Hindus. He is the pastor of a four-hundred-member Southern Baptist Church in a southern city. A seasoned pastor in his midforties, he earned a college degree in English literature before attending seminary at one of his denomination's divinity schools. Since coming to his present congregation, he has had ample reason to think about ministering to people from other religions. The neighborhood, once exclusively white, is now a mixture of blacks, Hispanics, Vietnamese, other Asian Americans, and other recent immigrants. His church is less than a mile away from a Hindu temple, less than three miles from a mosque, and only four miles from a synagogue and a Buddhist organization. He says the church has initiated no programs specifically concerned with evangelizing, or in other ways interacting with, people from these different religions. But he does encourage his congregation to make friends with their non-Christian coworkers and neighbors. The goal of initiating such friendships, he says, is to open the door for opportunities to tell people from other religions about Jesus.

This sounds like straightforward evangelization. But Mr. Jimson's exact words are worth considering more carefully. After acknowledging that he would like his church to be doing more to reach out to people of other faiths, he says, "This is where we kind of get into the difficulties. There's a verse in the Bible where Jesus says, 'I'm the way, the truth and the life, and no one comes to the Father, but by me,' which very much narrows things down, [especially] if you take it that he said those words and meant them just as straight as he said them. There's another one in Acts, and the reason I quote these verses is because like I said, I feel constrained if this really is the Word of God, then I'm constrained to take that perspective, if you will. Peter told some folks, 'There's no other name given under heaven by which men might be saved.' Now if that's the case, if Jesus is the only way to God, then we need to reach out to people of other religious beliefs. I know this sounds . . . ." He trails off somewhat apologetically, saying to the interviewer, "I don't want to make you angry, I hope I'm not doing that."

When the interviewer reassures him that she really wants to know what he thinks, he continues, "I'm not apologizing, but at the same time I want to be . . . ." He searches for the right words: "Yes, then I'm constrained to say there's one way to God and, boy, this sounds . . . ." Again he breaks off. She reassures him again. "Okay," he says. "I just don't want to sound arrogant, because it's not me who's come up with this. If I'm going to be faithful, then I'm constrained to say, then other folks have missed it. I don't want to make it sound like I've come up with this, or I found the way or something."

What this pastor wants to tell people with other religious beliefs is that they must turn to Jesus to be saved. If he ever had the opportunity to talk with a Jew or a Muslim, he says he would like to say something like this: "We're not making fun of your beliefs or anything, but if we have found the only way, we want you to come that way too. Not to join us, but so you can be with God."

The problem that causes him to backtrack and search for the right language is believing that only his religion is true when the culture in which he lives is sufficiently pluralistic to accept more than one view on almost everything and, at a minimum, to discourage people from saying things that seem blatantly arrogant. It helps that he is able to say, in effect, "This isn't really my opinion, but since it's there in the Bible, I have to tell you what the Bible says." Yet that argument, too, runs into difficulty when he has to explain why his view of the Bible is more correct than those of other Christians who regard it differently.

This is just one example of how difficult it is for Christians to find the right way to talk to non-Christians or to imagine talking with them. It does not suggest that the problem is intractable and certainly does not imply that Christians should never engage in dialogue with people of other faiths. It illustrates only that interfaith encounters are not easy; indeed, they are sufficiently difficult that many congregations avoid them as often as they can. But refraining from interfaith activities is itself a decision that reveals some of the challenges that religious diversity brings to Christian communities.

Strategies of Avoidance

One of the main conclusions that emerges from conversations with scores of pastors in various parts of the country is that many churches—probably a majority—are dealing with the growing religious diversity of our society by simply avoiding the issue. They seldom talk specifically about how to relate to their Jewish, Muslim, Hindu, or Buddhist neighbors and they certainly do not sponsor activities that would bring them into contact with these neighbors. Yet these are churches that are located within a few blocks of mosques, temples, or synagogues and their pastors are thoughtful and informed leaders who are clearly aware that other religions are an increasingly prominent reality in today's world. How is it possible for pastors to avoid paying greater attention to other religions?

The pastor of a Southern Baptist church in Texas illustrates one strategy for avoiding contact with people of other religions. He says that his church, a congregation of five thousand members with nine buildings located on a ten-acre campus, would have no problem talking about social and cultural issues with nonmembers living in the surrounding community, but he thinks that his members would resist getting into theological discussions with Jews or Muslims living in the area. He is reluctant to elaborate, but suggests that the congregation is focused on Jesus to the extent that they would be uncomfortable hearing about the teachings of any other religions. The pastor of an independent evangelical church in North Carolina offers a similar explanation: "I think there'd be resistance from the members." A variant on this idea is to suggest that the members, while perhaps not actively resisting interaction, are just not interested. For instance, the pastor of a Baptist church in Sacramento observes that several members of his congregation have vacationed in Israel, but he senses from them that they still have no particular interest in initiating any kind of program at the church to promote better relationships with Jews in their own community. All three of these pastors say they would personally like to do more in the area of interfaith relationships (indeed, most pastors say this). Yet their sense that they should only do things that will not generate resistance—or be met by indifference—from their members gives them a reason for doing nothing.

Another way of explaining their lack of involvement is illustrated by the pastor of an eight-hundred-member Methodist church in Texas that is located within a mile of a synagogue and within five miles of another synagogue, a mosque, a Hindu temple, and a Buddhist temple. His church is a busy place with many educational and service programs for people of all ages, but when asked about activities promoting better relationships with people of other religions, he says that he just wouldn't be interested. "It would just be another thing to do," he sighs. "I'm not feeling like it's an issue." For some pastors, placing relationships with other religions low on their priority list is little more than an admission that one person or even one congregation cannot do everything. For many clergy, though, priorities provide a businesslike way of talking about programs instead of having to defend their choices in theological terms. For instance, a Missouri Synod Lutheran in Saint Louis explained that relating to Jews was a low priority for his church because there were not that many Jews in the community, yet when pressed to say more, he acknowledged that he is not convinced of the value of such activity because "Jesus Christ is the savior of the world" and he worries that "ecumenical efforts" too often involve compromise. An Episcopal priest in Colorado gave a more abbreviated answer: "It's just not in line with what we're trying to do here." A different example that illustrates the same idea comes from the pastor of an evangelical church located just a few miles from a Jewish community center in southern California where a gunman opened fire on a group of children. He says his church has done nothing to promote better understanding between Christians and Jews, but acknowledges that it probably should, now that violence like this has occurred.

The idea that other religions in the community have to be an issue or a problem before interacting with them is warranted comes to the surface in another strategy of avoidance: simply denying that there are people of other religions in the community. A Catholic priest in northern California whose parish is less than a third of a mile from a Muslim mosque asserts that "there just aren't any Muslims around." A Baptist minister in Oregon, whose church is also close to a mosque, explains that Muslims are not "part of the framework of the community." He blames the local newspaper for not publishing stories that would bring their presence to his attention. A variant on claiming that there are no other religious organizations is to acknowledge that there are, but to argue that the members of these organizations prefer to keep to themselves. For instance, one pastor whose church is near a Hindu temple says he hardly ever sees anyone at the temple. Yet another variant is to indicate that one's own congregation is not well positioned to do anything, but to suggest that things are still being done. For example, a Catholic priest in Colorado suggested that the archdiocese took care of these kinds of relationships (although the monsignor, when questioned, said that the archdiocese was still praying about what to do).

Another way in which congregations, at least as their pastors understand it, manage to avoid confronting the religious diversity in their communities is by deflecting attention to other kinds of diversity. Racial and ethnic diversity and diversity among different Christian denominations or different theological orientations are the most common of these topics. One pastor provided a good illustration of this kind of deflection when asked if his congregation ever did anything to promote better understanding between Christians and Jews. "We've done activities not necessarily targeted at Jews, but at anyone to show that we want to have a connection with the community. We don't want to be cut off from the community. We don't want to circle the wagons," he asserted. He then described how the congregation was sharing space with a black congregation and gave several vivid examples of the difficulties in bridging differences in worship styles.

Deflection like this usually does not happen intentionally. Indeed, congregations that have taken significant steps toward addressing one kind of diversity often gain experience that helps them deal with other kinds of diversity. But the tendency for pastors to sidestep questions about religious diversity by focusing on ethnic or interdenominational diversity is instructive. It shows the extent to which addressing diversity has become desirable in our society. Just as universities take pride in recruiting students from diverse backgrounds, religious leaders appear eager to show that they are not insular or unaware of diversity in their communities. If they cannot attest to having done anything about religious diversity, they can speak enthusiastically about the range of ethnic groups in their congregations or about their ability to draw congregants from different denominational backgrounds. Remarks about these other kinds of diversity also show that it does take congregational resources to deal with diversity. Programs have to be planned, the meanings of words sometimes have to be rethought, and misunderstandings may have to be corrected.

This is a way, then, in which the cultural diversity of American society may inhibit more active engagement between Christians and other religious groups, instead of encouraging it. Although it is counterintuitive to suggest that one kind of pluralism may not be conducive to another kind, the reality is that pluralism is a function not only of attitudes but also of programs. The time and energy required to arrange an effective program between a Presbyterian church and a Lutheran church may be the same limited time and energy that would be needed to organize a program to promote understanding between Christians and Muslims.

Strategies for avoiding interaction differ depending on the non-Christian religion at issue. For Muslims, Hindus, and Buddhists, Christian clergy are most likely to deny that they are present in the community at all or, if they are, to assume that they prefer to stay to themselves. Clergy are more likely to have thought about the possibilities for interaction with Jews, undoubtedly because of the shared biblical roots of the two religions. Indeed, a common strategy for avoiding true interfaith contact between Christians and Jews is for clergy to insist that there really are no significant differences worth talking about. For some clergy, both groups are simply seeking God in their own ways. In other instances, clergy point to the fact that their church works with Jews for Jesus or other groups of converted Jews, or, as one pastor did, argue that they themselves are Jewish because they are brothers with Christ.

Strategies of Engagement

The awkwardness of interacting with other religions while holding that one's own religion is uniquely true, coupled with the time pressures that face all church leaders, means that the natural tendency among many congregations is to do nothing to initiate such interaction. Yet there are reasons for congregations to develop contacts across religious lines—reasons ranging from wanting to proselytize, to believing that Christ's teachings about loving one's neighbors extend to people of other faiths, to more pragmatic reasons, such as sharing a parking lot or working together to reduce crime in the neighborhood. To an even greater extent than avoiding contact does, engaging in interfaith relationships requires pastors to develop strategies for doing so. For better or worse, however, these strategies usually work to *minimize* the amount of interaction that actually takes place between churches and other religious organizations as much as they do to justify such interaction.

The vast majority of activities that churches sponsor as ways to promote relationships with Jews, Muslims, and adherents of other religions take what might be termed a *ceremonial* form. Ceremonies are special occasions set apart from ordinary behavior by a particular kind of etiquette and other rituals that define the times, places, and modes of behavior that are considered appropriate. Ceremonies, such as birthday celebrations, funerals, and the festivities surrounding national and religious holidays, play an important role in personal life and in the collective life of families, communities, and societies. They punctuate the workaday routine with occasions that mark the passage of time and that permit special emotions to be expressed. Less obviously perhaps, they allow deviations from normal behavior to take place (Mardi Gras celebrations may be a clear example) without these deviations becoming part of the expectations that pervade other realms of life. Thus, one can dance with strangers, kiss relatives, become inebriated, or tell stories on ceremonial occasions, all in ways that would never do in ordinary circumstances. Yet ceremonies also reflect and reinforce the deepest values of a people or a community, sometimes dramatizing their importance by violating them and sometimes expressing them openly in testimonials and songs.

Congregations' interaction with organizations representing other religions are typically abbreviated, well-defined, ceremonial events that do not occur very often. The annual "service of tolerance" at Faith Lutheran is an example; people saying "God is love" in their various languages is brief, highly structured, and intentionally symbolic. Another example is a Southern Baptist Church in Florida that routinely sends a delegate to an ecumenical organization that includes Jews; the pastor says this simple act helps his congregation understand that they should be nice to Jews. Yet another example is a Catholic church that invited a Jew to speak at an anti-abortion rally on the anniversary of *Roe v. Wade*; the priest acknowledged the symbolic importance of showing that the occasion was of interest not only to Catholics. Other examples include pastors paying cordial visits to the clergy of other religious organizations, almost like a neighbor greeting someone new on the block, or periodically sending an open invitation to a church-sponsored concert or rummage sale to the staff at a neighboring mosque or temple.

Besides events that are actually ceremonies, congregations may also adopt certain practices or affiliate themselves in ways that have symbolic significance similar to that of specific ceremonies. For instance, a Catholic priest in California mentioned his parish holding official membership in an ecumenical organization as the sole example of his efforts to engage other religions, and an Episcopal church in Pennsylvania has a monument tucked away in one corner that the rector says is a token of goodwill toward Jews. A Baptist church in Los Angeles sometimes posts announcements on its bulletin board of events being held at a Buddhist temple nearby. In fundamentalist or evangelical churches, inviting a converted Jew to speak about Judaism or sponsoring a missionary in a Muslim country may serve in similar ways.

Although some of these activities are initiated by congregations themselves, many are initiated by third parties, and some become special occasions only after the fact. In Miami, for instance, one pastor mentioned participating in a public ceremony initiated by the mayor as the only interfaith activity in which he had been engaged. In suburban Philadelphia, a Methodist pastor hosts Children's Sabbath, an initiative of the Children's Defense Fund, at his church. He acknowledges that the brief presence of Jewish and Muslim children at this service once a year does little in itself to promote interfaith understanding, but he emphasizes its ceremonial value by describing it as a way of "sending a signal" both to the congregation and to the wider community that his church is trying to live on good terms with other religions. As an example of something that takes on significance after the fact, a pastor in Charlotte described how synagogue members sometimes used the church's parking lot before they moved into their own structure further away; nobody thought much about it at the time, but in retrospect it has become a story the pastor can tell about good interfaith relationships.

Ceremonies are by no means devoid of content; yet it is noteworthy that many of these events focus more on religious practices or customs than on beliefs and teachings. One congregation occasionally invites Jews in the neighborhood to cook a Seder meal for its members. Another church has put on a "mock wedding" that demonstrates what Christian, Jewish, and Muslim nuptials may include. Other examples include a congregation that has invited a Jewish cantor to sing during a worship service, a special evening service at an Episcopal church that included prayers chanted by an imam, and a slide show at a United Church of Christ of people attending Buddhist and Hindu temples. Activities like these are preferred, some clergy explain, because they avoid thorny theological issues while conveying the idea that people of all faiths engage in worship.

Besides ceremonializing the contact, another way in which congregations structure their interaction with other religions is by drawing a distinction between religion, as they define it, and culture. This distinction emerges most often in pastors' discussions of their interaction with Buddhists and Hindus, although it comes up sometimes with regard to Muslims and Jews as well. The pastor of a Baptist church located near a Buddhist temple in California illustrates this distinction. He says that much of what his Buddhist neighbors do is a reflection of their "family tradition or culture," and that the "religious aspect" is in the background. A distinction like this may have several different implications. For this pastor, it partly makes it easier to interact with his Buddhist neighbors because he can attribute their behavior to custom or tradition rather than to a difference in basic religious beliefs; in short, he can accept them almost as easily as he might a Christian from Korea or Thailand. Yet his acceptance of their cultural traditions also discourages him from taking their religious practices seriously. Indeed, he asserts, "Most do not really even know what Buddhism is; it's just part of their culture and they observe the traditions."

For other pastors, Jewish Seders are interesting ethnic traditions and Islam is scarcely different from Middle Eastern food, rather than either being regarded as something that also has a serious religious dimension. Emphasizing ethnic customs in this way is not surprising; motion pictures, ethnic festivals, and restaurants all contribute to this way of viewing religious differences and, indeed, it is not uncommon for some adherents of any religion to be oriented more toward its ethnic traditions than its specific theological teachings or modes of worship. But such distinctions are also matters of interpretation. Were a non-Christian leader to say that most of what goes on in churches is simply an expression of cultural tradition, Christian pastors would probably object that there was more to it than that. Yet by structuring much of their contact with other religions as a kind of ethnic experience, pastors can more readily maintain the conviction that what they practice is the truth, whereas other religions are just a reflection of culture, or pastors can assume that somehow the underlying truths of Judaism, Islam, Hinduism, or Buddhism are essentially "Christian" even though they are expressed in different cultural packages.

Any formalized contact between churches and other religious organizations may be cumbersome simply because the formality of the occasion means that somehow the church's leaders are acting in an official capacity and thus must gain consensus or the support of a substantial number of their members. Thus, another strategy for managing the contact between churches and other religions is to emphasize individual discretion. This strategy appears to be used most often by pastors in those thorny situations when contact with people of other religions cannot be avoided. These situations include weddings and funerals involving Christians who may have relatives who belong to other religions, and church rituals, such as administering the sacrament of Holy Communion, at which non-Christians may be present. For instance, one pastor talked about counseling members of his congregation about whether they should attend weddings and funerals of their Buddhist relatives and, if so, how actively they should participate. Other pastors noted that a Hindu or Jewish spouse of one of their members is sometimes present when Holy Communion is observed. In every instance, pastors opted for a solution that would avoid any possibility of conflict, embarrassment, or confrontation. They said that if one of their members came for advice about how much to participate in the observances of another religion, they would listen and ask questions but then encourage the person to make up his or her own mind. Some of them suggested that it might be possible for the person to participate by going through the motions but not really meaning what they said or did. Holy Communion was dealt with by Catholic priests who noted that the church's official teaching is that only Catholics can participate, but that there would really be no way of telling who was Catholic and who was not. Among Protestants, most felt that only Christians should participate in Holy Communion, but argued that they were, as one pastor put it, "not the police" and that Buddhists or Jews who somehow decided to participate could do as they pleased.

The ways in which clergy talk about interfaith programs also suggest that managing these contacts often takes the form of treating the other religion as an opportunity for an exotic experience. To say that something is exotic is to suggest that it originates in a foreign country and is a characteristic of foreigners or at least is from the outside. Non-Christian religions are quite literally exotic to most American Christians. Yet exoticism is not just a function of the foreigner; it also depends on how the foreigner is portrayed. A church program concerned with deemphasizing the strangeness of another religion might encourage informal interaction among members, play up similar beliefs and practices, or choose speakers capable of translating ideas from one context to another. Although some programs do adopt these approaches, many inadvertently highlight differences. For instance, one church included a performance by a Sufi dancer but provided no explanation of what the dancer was trying to convey; at another church, members were encouraged to visit a synagogue or mosque but were given no instruction about what to expect. As much as through actual activities, the comments of pastors about other religions also inadvertently play up strangeness. One pastor repeatedly referred to "Jews, Muslims, voodoo worshippers, and cults" in the same breath; another talked about "Hinduism and other strange beliefs"; yet another described Buddhists and Hindus as being "confused by all their strange gods."

None of these strategies is selected because clergy deliberately set out to minimize contact with people of other religions or because church leaders want to stage a ceremony or treat the other religion as some exotic form of behavior. The choices are often made because a particular activity seems workable or even because it is known to have worked in another setting. But the unintended consequences of these choices are to structure the interaction in a way that relatively little happens, as least as far as the potential for conflict is concerned and possibly as far as deeper understanding is concerned as well. If these activities limit contact and understanding, they nevertheless reveal a great deal about the ways in which churches function in our society. Indeed, the strategies of avoidance and the strategies of engagement that clergy resort to as they confront religious diversity are a reflection of the pluralistic cultural norms that presently govern nearly everything that churches do.

The Imprint of Pluralism

The growing presence of non-Christian religions in the United States does not appear to be influencing the programs and teachings of local churches very much in terms of actually bringing Christians and non-Christians together over extended periods of time for soul-searching discussions about the similarities and differences among their respective traditions. But religious diversity is having a powerful effect on local churches insofar as clergy are largely following—and thereby reinforcing—certain cultural scripts about how to be the church, whether they actively interact with other religions or actively avoid such interaction. These scripts honor and uphold the norms of religious pluralism that have become so deeply ingrained in American culture. The underlying rules of pluralism are evident in the strategies that we have just been considering.

The strategy of avoiding contact with other religions for fear of resistance on the part of one's congregation is a case in point. In some societies, the fear of contact would be that one's members might convert to the other religion, but that clearly is not what worries pastors in the United States. Their fear is that some of their members may leave and join a different Christian congregation. Thus, they do not want to engage in any activities that may prove controversial to some of their members. This worry reflects the broader pluralistic climate in which American religion is situated. Pluralism means that there are always competitors waiting to absorb members who may become disgruntled. It also means that slight annoyances can become a reason for switching to another church. Loyalties in pluralistic societies do not run deep. Any alternative that seems slightly more comfortable is sufficient reason to pull up stakes. Paradoxically, then, the very presence of one kind of diversity (among Christian congregations) means that some pastors may be reluctant to embrace the deeper diversity that arises among different religions.

The localistic orientation that encourages pastors to focus on their own congregation rather than on the wider variety of religious organizations in their community is also reinforced by pluralism. In a competitive environment, all organizations try to carve out and protect a distinct niche. If they are large organizations with ample resources (such as a megachurch), they may overpower their competitors with more expansive programs and fancier sanctuaries, but for the average church, avoiding confrontation and preventing one's resources from being spread too thin is the best strategy. Focusing on what happens under the church roof and on what benefits its own members is thus a strategy that may unintentionally lead to a lack of awareness of the presence of a temple or mosque down the street, let alone to expending scarce resources to initiate a joint program with that organization.

The ceremonialized ways in which many churches approach interfaith contacts serve some of the same functions, especially by limiting contact to the point that it does not offend members or use too many scarce resources. Ceremonialized contacts are also characteristic of a pluralistic, competitive society in which display, symbolism, and advertising are common. Automobile manufacturers do not present substantive commercials about their products, but suggestive images that create associations with virility, wealth, and freedom. An occasional interfaith service or the pastor holding membership on an interfaith council serves a similar purpose: it sends a signal (mostly to members) that the church is tolerant or open-minded; the activity may have no more substantive importance than an automobile commercial. Yet this kind of display is nearly inescapable in a pluralistic society. Faced with many different options, people need quick cues to tell them what to like and what not to like. For some, even the briefest ceremonial contact with another religion may be the start of an exploration that leads to a deeper understanding of their own.

It follows that treating religion like an ethnic custom, letting individuals make their own choices about interreligious contact, and even emphasizing the exotic qualities of other religions have become preferred strategies for dealing with religious diversity. These are the strategies of marketers and consumers. If religion is little more than ethnic food and dress, then it is like a preference or taste, similar to the taste that causes some people to prefer one brand of automobile instead of another. Preferences may be very important to individuals for a variety of reasons, including their links to the past and the subcultures in which they have been raised, but they are ultimately matters of individual choice. The best choice may not be the one that is true, but the one that feels most comfortable because it is familiar or meets one's needs. These are the arguments that clergy in a pluralistic society make about why someone should be a Christian. Moreover, gaining temporary exposure to an exotic religion is like taking a vacation to a strange part of the world: one learns just enough to temporarily escape boredom and then desires to return home.

Beyond Insularity?

The evidence considered in this chapter suggests that local church leaders are dealing with the increasing religious diversity of their communities largely by ignoring it or by minimizing their contact with other religions. At least half of the nation's churches appear to be doing nothing to engage directly in interreligious discussions or interaction, while the activities sponsored by the remaining half are fleeting and often more symbolic than substantive. Church leaders appear to be protecting themselves from having to rethink any of their basic theological suppositions or programmatic priorities in light of the fact that a growing number of their neighbors are members of religions other than Christianity. Many church leaders are firmly convinced that Christianity is the only true religion, that all who do not explicitly assert their belief in Jesus as their personal savior are doomed to eternal damnation, and that they have found the only valid answers to living a happy and productive life during their time on earth, yet few of these leaders make any explicit effort to evangelize those in their neighborhoods whom they consider to be lost by virtue of holding membership in a different religion. Many other church leaders seem more willing to accept the validity of non-Christian religions as legitimate ways of reaching God, but these clergy also insulate themselves to the point that they have only a shallow understanding of what these other religions teach or practice.

In neighborhoods where Jews, Muslims, Hindus, and Buddhists have become a significant presence alongside Christian churches, the predominant pattern is thus one of insularity. Each religious organization caters to people who happen to have been raised in the particular religious tradition it represents and occasionally draws new members from people who have recently moved to the community, through natural increase as children mature and take the place of those who die or move away, and from the rare instance in which a spouse from another religion converts or a friend invites someone who has not been attending any religious organization at all. The Christian leaders, as representatives of the majority religion in most communities, have little incentive to initiate relationships with the leaders or members of any of the other religions. Whatever interaction does take place seldom challenges the members of Christian congregations to do anything but affirm what they already believe, whether their beliefs persuade them that tolerance is the best policy or that they have a special corner on the truth.

The insularity and largely ceremonialized contacts that characterize churches' responses to religious diversity go a long way toward explaining why the recent increase of religious diversity has done relatively little to unsettle the idea that America is—or at least should be—a Christian nation. Pastors have unintentionally developed a large repertoire of effective strategies for managing the diversity that has arisen in their communities. They readily recite reasons why they do not have contact with other religious organizations, why they are already busy addressing diversity in other ways, or why the little that they have done is actually quite a lot. They have a somewhat harder time ignoring the Jewish organizations in their communities than the Muslim, Hindu, or Buddhist organizations, since their own tradition is rooted in Judaism, but they have learned mostly to regard Judaism as a kind of quaint subculture with peculiar practices that, after all, has few implications for the ways Christians should think or behave.

There are some negative consequences of all this. Hate crimes, such as swastikas painted on synagogue walls and violence toward Jews and Muslims, break out periodically in nearly every part of the country, but few church leaders have done anything prior to such events to minimize the likelihood of their happening and many church leaders do little afterward except to shake their heads. In communities with large non-Christian populations, the Christian congregations become increasingly marginalized instead of taking leadership positions in wider community affairs. Pastors who have done little to address the religious diversity of their communities are also ill-prepared to assist the parents in their congregations whose son or daughter decides to marry a person of another religion or to counsel members in how to understand and live out their own faith among coworkers and neighbors who belong to other religions.

Yet the situation that has evolved in most religiously diverse communities represents a kind of homeostasis that is comfortable for Christian pastors and their congregations. They may have thought some about their own faith in relation to other faiths during their college and seminary years or as a result of a chance friendship with a Jew or Buddhist, but they are not likely to be putting themselves in harm's way, as it were, by deliberately organizing discussions with leaders of other religions. When such discussions do arise, they take the form of brief excursions into a cross-cultural encounter that can readily be experienced without raising deep questions about the nature of Christianity itself.

For all this, religious diversity nevertheless has an undeniable effect on the ways in which clergy go about the business of leading their congregations. The impact is more implicit than explicit. Knowing that other religions exist, even if there is little direct contact, clergy engage in implicit mental bargains that reduce the dissonance that would likely occur if they took either the position that all non-Christians are eternally damned or the view that all religions are equally valid. They assert that only people who are already deeply immersed in the life of a congregation can truly appreciate Christianity, defend their faith in terms of its value as good therapy or a key to personal happiness, and dismiss other religions by seldom thinking about them, viewing them as curious ethnic subcultures, or proclaiming that these other religions are irrelevant to their own efforts at evangelization.

The result is not a deeper, more informed, intentional, or thoughtful Christianity but a reinforced form of cultural pluralism that has already become the reigning normative outlook of most Americans. Clergy seldom challenge this normative outlook, either by directly calling into question the beliefs and practices of other religions (and following up with dedicated proselytization) or by engaging in the hard, long-term discussions that would be required to identify true areas of agreement and disagreement. Instead, congregations maximize their small niche within the larger pluralistic environment by putting aside difficult questions of biblical interpretation and by focusing nearly all their attention on their own members; by adopting a don't ask, don't tell policy in dealing with their neighbors; and by marketing their programs more like consumer products than matters of ultimate concern. Easy tolerance and limited interaction prevent hackles from being raised when people of one religion meet those of another.

If these norms of pluralistic coexistence prevail, many religious leaders will be happy. For the leaders of non-Christian religions, Christians who insulate themselves from contact may be better neighbors than those who demand confrontation or even more polite forms of engagement. For the secular leaders of local schools, city administrations, and the courts, pluralism of this kind is also desirable. Even a substantially larger number of non-Christian religious organizations in local communities would likely do little to upset the balance. Christian congregations are in many ways admirably adaptable. They can retain their sense that all is well even when the very foundations of their society are undergoing dramatic change.

Negotiating Religiously Mixed Marriages

FEW OPPORTUNITIES for understanding the encounters among different religions and subcultures are as rich as those provided by Americans who have chosen to marry outside their religion. We have seen that spiritual shoppers seldom engage seriously with one of the world's major religious traditions other than Christianity or Judaism. Other Americans typically decide to accept or resist religious diversity without spending much time thinking about it. We have also seen that clergy, even in religiously mixed neighborhoods, expend relatively little effort meeting and attempting to understand practitioners of other faiths. But people who marry outside their religious tradition have to consider what they believe and how they wish to practice their faith in view of having a spouse who believes and practices differently. With religious diversity as part of their daily lives, they are forced to confront difficult questions such as: where shall we attend religious services, which holidays should we celebrate, how shall we raise our children, and what should we say to our family and friends?

Advice columns, counseling handbooks, and study guides published by religious bodies often paint a confusing picture of religiously mixed marriages. On the one hand, these materials argue that interreligious couples face countless conflicts and interpersonal difficulties. Misunderstandings, parents becoming angry or refusing to speak, family members boycotting weddings or christenings, conflicts with clergy, confusion about religious rules and teachings, feelings of shame and disloyalty, and alienation are among the difficulties mentioned. On the other hand, these materials suggest that couples *can* overcome difficulties and achieve happiness in their marriages. Some go further, suggesting that interreligious marriage generates deep spiritual growth, creativity, wonder, and heightened appreciation of one's faith. What these materials seldom illuminate are the

cultural norms governing how partners and spouses in interreligious relationships adapt to their situations and how they actually come to terms
with religious diversity in ways that work satisfactorily from day to day.[1]

The question we need to consider is what exactly happens when people
confront a religious tradition other than their own, interacting with it
seriously, personally, and over an extended period of time. What happens,
not when someone casually takes a course in comparative religions or
meets a stranger from another tradition, but when that person has to make
intimate life-course decisions that require weighing the similarities and
differences between two religious traditions? Do people in such situations
sit down early in their relationship and make informed decisions about
what they are going to believe and practice? Are they guided by conversations with religious officials? Do they adopt a pick-and-choose approach
to their faith and, if so, on what grounds do they pick and choose?

To anticipate my argument, I suggest that we think of interreligious marriage as a process of negotiation that does involve serious questions about
religious differences. In this respect, interreligious marriage offers an opportunity to examine interaction across religious boundaries in concrete settings and thus to gain perspective on the norms governing religious diversity
in real life. But looking closely at interreligious marriage yields some sur-
prises. It reveals that religious pluralism is probably not best envisioned as
a kind of table around which people gather to deliberate the teachings of
their various traditions. Nor is it a black box that we can never hope to
illuminate because of the personal idiosyncrasies involved. A better way of
thinking about it is to emphasize the tacit assumptions, principles, and
categories that guide people in negotiating their differences. In this view, it
becomes important to understand not only that people pick and choose,
but that they do so by following certain implicit guidelines. It is also important to consider how people construct their religious identities and to
notice the underlying reasons they cite for believing that diversity is a good
thing. From these reasons, we can better understand the broader cultural
frameworks that govern how religious diversity is sustained in our society.

Falling in Love

The number of Americans who marry outside their own
religion appears to have grown significantly in recent decades. This growth

is evident in studies of people choosing to cross denominational lines, if they are Protestants, or to marry a Protestant, if they are Catholic, but it is also true that more Christians are married to Jews, Muslims, Buddhists, or Hindus now than in the past.[2] It is impossible to say exactly what the numbers are, but estimates all suggest substantial increases. For instance, research among American Jews that has been conducted over the past thirty years indicates that approximately half of all Jewish marriages now occur between Jews and persons of other faiths—a proportion that is at least twice as high as it was only a few decades ago.[3] The same factors that encourage rising rates of interreligious marriage among Jews—rising levels of education, greater acceptance in the culture at large, working in middle-class occupations, travel, and living in diverse communities—also appear to be contributing to rising rates of interreligious marriage among Muslims, Hindus, and Buddhists.[4]

Robert Orsi in his study of Italian Harlem in the 1930s describes the importance of young people being able to find a space in which to be young, to experiment, and to escape the watchful eye of their mothers and aunts. For young women, these spaces were almost completely absent: going to school, making friends, performing household chores, and finding mates were all performed under the supervision of parents, priests, neighbors, and kin. Young men found places to escape the constant surveillance. They gathered behind vacant buildings, by the railroad tracks, and on street corners near pubs in seedier sections of the community to tell off-color jokes, smoke, and share stories of sexual exploits.[5]

These semipublic, unguarded enclaves have become virtually universal in contemporary society. Young people from different religious backgrounds meet outside of religiously homogeneous neighborhoods, beyond the reach of religious institutions, free of supervision from parents and kin. The most common settings are college campuses, workplaces, tours, and public gatherings such as clubs and parties. A Jewish woman from Kansas tells of meeting her future husband, a Christian, in a class they took together during their junior year abroad. A Christian woman in Texas met her future husband, a Muslim, at the hospital where they worked. A Christian man in Los Angeles met his future wife, a Muslim, at a salsa club frequented by young professionals.

Such settings are frequented by young people from middle-class backgrounds, and in them it is common to find people from all religious traditions. They come knowing that religious differences will not be an obstacle to their involvement. Increasingly, younger Americans also report that they have met spouses while studying, traveling, or living abroad, often in societies where religions other than Christianity prevail. Thus it is not surprising that interreligious marriage has increased. Yet religion continues to be sufficiently important to people that marrying outside one's religion creates significant challenges. Many people who marry outside their faith say the experience has forced them to ponder more deeply than ever before what they truly believe.

One view of what happens when people fall in love and decide to marry outside their religion is that those who are serious about this process engage in sustained reflection about the teachings of the two religious traditions under consideration. In this view, the couple's church, synagogue, mosque, or temple may provide classes or study guides explaining the main teachings of each faith and encouraging the couple to make note of similarities and differences (e.g., about understandings of God, Jesus, heaven, hell, angels, salvation, and good works). The same kind of systematic inquiry may take place in a college course in comparative religions. From study of this kind, the couple may decide that it is more persuaded by the teachings of one religion than by those of the other religion. Alternatively, they may choose teachings on which they can agree and deemphasize points of disagreement. Or they may come to the view that they should not marry because their respective religions hold too many incompatible tenets.

Entering into marriage through a reflective process has been encouraged, especially among middle-class couples, for more than a century. As early as the middle of the nineteenth century, magazines and books provided advice for young people to consider in deciding on marriage partners. These sources took the place of advice supplied by close relatives in homogeneous families as the nation became more mobile, urban, and ethnically diverse. During the twentieth century, marital advice became more sophisticated and professionalized, finding its way into high school home economics courses and college courses about marriage and family.[6] Family counselors and therapists developed tests to determine whether couples were compatible. Pastoral counseling incorporated many of the same ideas. By the 1950s, the major Protestant, Catholic, and Jewish traditions offered premarital counseling involving the study of psychological as well as theological ideas about marriage. Since then, such sessions, classes, and small group discussions have continued and, increasingly, have incorporated ideas about interreligious marriage. Thus, the standard view of how interreligious couples go about resolving their religious differences would suggest that sustained reflection near the beginning of their relationship should be an important part.

A young woman in San Francisco illustrates the rational, reflective approach. She and her fiancé, a Hindu, have been dating for three years and expect to be married in a few months. They met through a mutual friend while living in New York and then started living together when they moved to California. A lifelong Presbyterian, she did not know much about Hinduism, so she began in earnest trying to learn. She read everything she could find on the Internet and had long conversations with her fiancé's mother, who was better versed in traditional Hindu practices than he was. Over the past few months, she and her fiancé have also been attending premarital counseling sessions at her church. These sessions, she says, have been helpful in prompting discussions about child rearing, family finances, communication, and acceptance.

Interreligious couples are generally less reflective about religious differences than this example suggests, however. People fall in love for all kinds of reasons, few having to do with compatible or incompatible religious teachings. Although they may go through the motions of receiving premarital counseling or reading advice books, they are guided more by a romantic ideal of love. Influenced by emotions and focusing on practical questions such as when to marry, where to live, and how to support themselves, they retreat from seriously confronting their religious differences. Once married, however, they have to decide what to believe and practice. At this point, they may seek counsel from clergy, attend classes, read books, and draw up lists of similarities and differences between their respective religions, or simply muddle their way through by making decisions as they go along.

A woman in Michigan recalls meeting her future husband in graduate school at Yale. An active Methodist from Virginia, she had gained some familiarity with Judaism through a college roommate but had never considered marrying a Jew. Indeed, she had no interest in developing a long-term relationship with anyone until she was well-established in her career. However, one thing led to another and she and her future husband saw each other casually, wrote letters, and gradually fell in love. She remembers clearly the evening he gave her a tin of Christmas cookies with a small velvet box inside containing a ring. "It was like, 'Oh my gosh! What am I doing?' But the word 'yes' came out of my mouth and we were engaged and that was the beginning." The beginning, she adds, of "the hard part." Neither family was happy with the engagement. Suddenly the couple had to confront many of the religious issues they had not previously examined. It was the beginning of a long process of negotiation. After a decade of marriage, she and her husband have found common ground around a commitment to human decency and loving God, and they are raising their children in Judaism. But she has also started a support network for interfaith couples because she thinks most of the advice books are unhelpful.

This example illustrates a more down-to-earth view of interreligious marriage and comes closer to what recent studies of love and marriage more generally have shown. The sociologist Ann Swidler, for example, observes that people talk about love quite differently before and after marriage, initially emphasizing romantic, idealistic views and only later coming to terms with the practical realities of day-to-day life.[7] For interfaith couples, no amount of advance preparation seems to take the place of a long, complex, and often subtle process of negotiation. It is this process that yields clues about the cultural norms governing religious diversity.

Negotiating with Religious Authorities

Whether they follow the textbook approach or the more intuitive approach, interfaith couples generally have to deal with clergy. In the textbook approach, clergy enter the scene prior to marriage, helping prospective couples decide whether or not they can reconcile their different beliefs and assisting them in anticipating the decisions they will face. In the more intuitive view, clergy come to be of assistance somewhat later in the process, especially as the romantic period fades and couples start confronting the beliefs and teachings that will carry them though their lives together.

Historically, religious authorities often imposed doctrinal controls and informal pressure to prevent people from marrying outside the faith. If they did marry, these customs encouraged the outsider to convert or children from the marriage to be raised within the religion. This was especially true in Roman Catholicism, but was also the case for many Protestant denominations and for Jews and Muslims. In recent decades, confessional traditions within Christianity have often modified these earlier practices, making it easier, for instance, for children to be baptized despite one or both parents not being church members and recasting the role of church as teacher rather than as doctrinal police. Religious leaders nevertheless continue to be mindful of biblical concerns about believers being "unequally yoked" with nonbelievers, and many religious bodies print booklets and study guides that communicate these considerations to pastors and church members.[8]

At present, religiously mixed couples typically indicate that they have had to negotiate with clergy about who would officiate at their wedding, where the wedding could be held and what statements and activities would be included, and how their children would be raised. While recognizing that clergy may have differing views on these matters, religious bodies encourage clergy to approach them as representatives of distinct theological and confessional traditions.[9] Yet the striking picture that emerges, both from couples themselves and from the remarks of clergy, is one of almost total ineffectiveness as far as the exercise of institutional authority or guidance is concerned.

Christian clergy nearly always acknowledge that it is important to offer counsel to people who are considering marrying outside their faith. Clergy at churches in religiously mixed neighborhoods are especially aware that more people from Christian backgrounds are marrying Jews, Muslims, Hindus, or Buddhists than was true in the past. Yet these pastors admit that they rarely talk with interfaith couples and do not feel very well prepared to counsel them. Indeed, none of the pastors with whom we spoke could suggest anything that might be beneficial for an interfaith couple to read, and none had tried to guide an interfaith couple through the theological thickets of comparing their own beliefs with those of their spouse or fiancé. This is not to say that clergy are completely removed from the scene: some of them offer standard premarital counseling sessions which, if the couple happens to be from different religious backgrounds, may touch on these differences among the longer list of issues about which they are encouraged to think. Sometimes pastors also offer guidance about what should be included in wedding vows. But clergy generally acknowledge feeling awkward and unprepared in such situations.

The pastor of a Church of Christ congregation on the West Coast is fairly typical. He believes that premarital counseling is important and asserts that this is especially the case for religiously mixed couples since religious differences are, in his view, frequently the cause of divorce. He has not talked to many such couples, though, despite the fact that his church is located in a community of Hindus and Jews. He cannot think of anything he has read on the subject of interreligious marriage or anything he could recommend for couples to read. Asked what advice he would give, he suggests only that "good communication" is probably the key.

Couples' experiences are consistent with pastors' reports. Many of the couples we talked to claimed to have good relationships with their pastors, but these relationships were good *despite* not having received helpful instruction, rather than because of such guidance. For instance, a Lutheran woman married to a Jewish man says that she and her husband have enjoyed getting to know the pastor at her church. She says the pastor has been wonderful, accepting, gracious, and helpful. She nevertheless has received no counsel from him about the similarities or differences between Christianity and Judaism, and he strikes her as being reluctant to think about the practical implications of her being married to a Jew.

We can understand these clergy responses better if we recognize that they often reflect one or both of the prevailing models that govern clergy behavior more generally: a managerial model and a therapeutic model.[10] The managerial model—a style of pastoring that emerged toward the end of the nineteenth century as congregations grew larger and as denominations increasingly sought to emulate businesses in efficiency and professionalism—guides pastors' thinking about religiously mixed marriages up to the point that pastors actually begin dealing with a couple contemplating such a marriage. It encourages pastors to be efficient in using their time and to make the most of their particular interests and gifts. Thus, the fact that interfaith couples do not present themselves for counseling very often means that pastors (following the principle of efficiency) spend little time preparing for such requests. They focus on more pressing business, especially those utilizing their talents, such as preparing sermons, visiting the sick, or chairing committees. In theory, they regard interfaith marriage as an important issue, but in practice they minimize its significance. They also follow good managerial practice in making use of the spiritual marketplace, either by actively referring couples to specialists or by simply letting the market dictate where people go to find help. For instance, pastors at large urban churches mention sending couples to counselors or support groups, rather than trying to minister to them directly, and, although they can suggest nothing for interfaith couples to read, they understand that interested couples can probably discover reading material on their own. For a few pastors, the managerial model also takes the form of upholding church rules and finding ways of bending them to fit specific circumstances. Thus, a pastor may indicate that the church has a rule prohibiting the pastor from officiating at an interfaith wedding (not that doing so would be fundamentally wrong), but then refer the couple to another pastor who is willing to conduct the ceremony.

Pastors' comments illustrate the various ways in which the managerial model governs their relationships with religiously mixed couples. A Methodist minister in suburban Chicago says that he recommends such couples "go to a pastoral counselor"; he himself does not try to counsel them. A Catholic priest in a religiously diverse neighborhood in New York says that he explains the church's rule about wanting children to be raised in the church and then encourages the couple to "talk about it" and figure out what *they* want to do. An Episcopal rector in the same neighborhood says that interreligious dating is common in his community, so he encourages such people to find "couples clubs" and support groups that deal with the issues they may face. A Lutheran pastor in Pennsylvania remembers a Christian-Hindu couple phoning not long ago; he directed them to someone else. In all these cases, considerations of expedience and time management keep the pastors from becoming actively involved in discussions about the differences and similarities among religious traditions.

The therapeutic model—which became more prominent around the middle of the twentieth century as clergy began borrowing techniques from professional counselors and therapists—kicks in on those rare occasions when pastors actually have to deal with a religiously mixed couple. This model manifests itself in pastors' attempts to be supportive rather than speaking on behalf of their theological tradition. Frequently, it is as if a pastor deliberately adopts a nonofficial role, saying in effect, "I will now talk with you just as a person, a friend, rather than in my capacity as a representative of the church." The therapeutic model is also evident in the kinds of advice pastors give. Much of this advice emphasizes personal happiness and self-fulfillment, rather than theological principles, and is pitched almost entirely in practical terms. For instance, couples are encouraged to avoid conflict, maintain open channels of communication, show respect, and anticipate what will be beneficial for their children—the same advice other couples receive.

An Episcopal rector in suburban Denver illustrates the therapeutic model when he says that the best thing to do for a religiously mixed couple is to help them turn a "win-lose" situation into a "win-win" relationship. A Presbyterian minister in Ohio says he just tries to help such couples "gain a better understanding" of each other. A United Church of Christ pastor in Illinois mentions counseling a Jewish-Christian couple: the main result was that he himself "felt reassured" about their relationship. By focusing on feelings and by relying on therapeutic models of the family, these pastors avoid confronting deeper theological issues involving the relationships among different religions.[11]

Couples learn quickly to relate to pastors in ways that follow the managerial and therapeutic models. Many couples shop around, avoiding pastors who seem too busy to talk to them or finding ones willing to negotiate the rules. Their questions focus more on rules concerning weddings, baptisms, and related matters than on broad questions about the teachings of various religions. They seek advice more often from friends than from pastors. And when couples do interact with pastors, the responses vary so much from one church to another that they are either confused or able to bargain for what they want.

Michael Bradford, an attorney, is a Roman Catholic whose wife, Nora Stein, is Jewish. After a five-year courtship, which they carried on between Chicago and New York, Michael and Nora were married in a civil ceremony in Connecticut. Although both were active in their respective congregations, negotiations with clergy did not become an issue until their son was born and Michael wanted him to be baptized. Upon consulting a priest near Nora's family home in Westchester, Michael learned that it would be necessary to promise that his son would be raised Catholic. "I don't want to lie to you about this," Michael told the priest. "I'll do my best to see that my son is brought up Catholic, but his mother has some strong feelings about this, too, and it just might not work out." At that point, according to Michael, the priest became intransigent, adding critical remarks about the stubbornness of Jews and his unwillingness to baptize a baby who had a Jewish parent. Michael, in effect, started to negotiate with the priest, pointing out instances of friends in similar situations whose children had been baptized, mentioning a Catholic priest in Chicago who he was sure would perform the rite, and indicating that he might ask an Episcopal rector for assistance if the priest refused. The priest capitulated, agreeing to baptize the baby as long as Michael pledged to "do what he could" to encourage his wife to agree to bringing up their son as a Catholic.

Like Michael, religiously mixed couples generally learn to negotiate—relating to religious institutions instrumentally, expecting (usually with good reason) to find a satisfactory solution to whatever they wish to do as far as wedding plans, child-rearing issues, or other relationships with the church are concerned. Couples do this by shopping in the religious marketplace until they find a member of the clergy willing to do whatever they ask. In the process, couples often become adept at driving down the cost of getting what they want, negotiating until they find the minimum requirement that must be met in order to receive the pastor's blessing. They speak most fondly of pastors who have stepped out of their clergy roles, offering them friendly personal advice or helping them avoid church rules. And they sometimes use geographic distance and impersonality to their advantage—as another episode in Michael's story illustrates.

In the course of negotiating about his son's baptism, Michael ran into an additional hurdle: he had not been married in the Catholic church. The priest asked Michael to secure a document called a cessation as a condition for the baptism. To get this document, Michael had to attend a class about marriage at a Catholic church and have a priest certify that he had attended. Because he was living in Chicago, Michael chose to attend at his parish there. And because his wife was frequently in New York, nobody questioned why she also did not attend. Michael received the cessation without anyone knowing that his wife was Jewish.

Clergy's inability to exercise greater control over intermarriage, or even to provide stronger guidance, usually does not result simply from a failure of nerve on the part of individual pastors or priests. It instead reflects the fact that contemporary religious institutions are themselves thoroughly the products of religious pluralism and function in a religious marketplace. Competition for members, donations, and other scarce resources puts clergy in the position of having to differentiate their ministries from their competitors and often of watering down any teachings or restrictions that

might inhibit people from joining their congregations. Clergy are entre-
preneurial in this respect.

The interaction between religiously mixed couples and clergy, while
often minimal (especially prior to marriage), is nevertheless significant for
what it contributes inadvertently to the ways in which these couples come
to think about religious diversity. The infrequent, abbreviated nature of
this interaction means that couples seldom receive much guidance from
churches. Thus, the very lack of connections with religious officials becomes a significant factor in their lives. They have, as it were, institutional
space in which to figure out their spiritual lives on their own. They realize
that friends, books, and television are more likely to be helpful to their
spiritual quests than clergy. In addition, couples learn to shop around,
going from pastor to pastor or church to church, negotiating and striking
their own bargains.[12] They learn that what matters most in a marriage is
not theology or theological truth, but personal happiness, and they find
clergy dispensing practical advice about achieving happiness more as supportive individuals than as representatives of religious institutions.[13]

The Parsing of Practices

Although institutional flexibility gives them freedom to
negotiate, religiously mixed couples must also decide how to reconcile
their differing traditions. This is the point at which their negotiations
focus less on religious authorities and more on their own beliefs and practices. We have seen in previous chapters that how people think about
religious diversity *is* intimately connected with their theological assumptions. Yet the striking fact about religiously mixed couples is that they
generally behave as if these deeper assumptions *do not* matter. They succeed in relating to someone who does not share their faith, not without
difficulty, but often with remarkable effectiveness and for long periods of
time. They do so by picking and choosing from both partners' religious
traditions, developing their distinctive versions of what observers sometimes refer to as "blended" spirituality. How is this done? What underlying
assumptions make it possible to pick and choose? What implicit principles
emerge when people describe their picking and choosing?

The place to begin is the distinction between religious practice, as a set of activities, and religious belief, as a set of ideas. Although the two are never fully separable in people's lives or in religious institutions, the distinction characterizes people's own understandings of their religious commitments. Among religiously mixed couples, questions about practice surface more readily and more often than questions about belief. This does not mean that belief is unimportant. But practice raises strategic questions about what to do, when to do it, and with whom to do it, all of which evoke some consideration of the couple's relationship with each other and with significant friends and relatives, whereas they usually regard belief as a more private matter.

Religious practices are necessarily intertwined with one another, providing coherence to people's lives and linking them with a community of faith. The philosopher Alasdair MacIntyre writes that this interconnectedness distinguishes practices from mere activities (playing music on a piano as opposed to striking separate keys).[14] In principle, this coherence among practices has been valued in all religious traditions. In reality, it is evident in at least some cases. For instance, a Muslim man says that his children must be raised as Muslims for him to secure eternal life in heaven. In his case, child rearing is part of a larger set of practices that have religious significance. Similarly, a Catholic priest insists that Eucharist should be an integral part of a Christian wedding and a Baptist woman includes the Lord's Prayer at her wedding because it summarizes her beliefs and connects with her religious upbringing. In both cases, practices that are part of ordinary religious services become connected with the wedding ceremony. Thus, it is notable (these examples notwithstanding) that many people parse their religious practices into separate activities. Just as spiritual shoppers do, they simply pick and choose from different traditions. But here the picking and choosing serves specifically to negotiate the terms of religious diversity within an ongoing relationship.

Weddings provide an occasion in which picking and choosing is often evident. A Christian married to a Muslim recalls that he and his wife decided to hold their wedding in a banquet hall at a hotel, rather than in a church or mosque, in order to keep both families happy. A Christian minister officiated, a Muslim leader provided a blessing, and much of the music and food was Persian, giving the ceremony an ethnic flavor. "It was a mixing pot wedding," he says. Similarly, a Christian woman who is planning her wedding to a Hindu says that she wants "a blended ceremony that incorporates cultural as well as religious traditions of both of our faiths." Both couples felt it appropriate to combine elements from different religious traditions. Their comments also suggested that they did not view combining these various elements as a statement about what they really believed.

The parsing strategy that couples adopt for their weddings is evident in subsequent decisions about their religious behavior. A Christian married to a Buddhist has come to appreciate "visual ways of knowing God." Initially she experienced God visually through "dream work" and now she does the same by incorporating Buddhist meditation techniques into her prayers. Her thinking suggests that an activity from one tradition can be inserted into another tradition as long as it serves a useful purpose. The notion of interchangeability is also evident in the remarks of a Christian woman married to a Muslim who says that she fasts from sunup to sundown during Lent as her husband does during Ramadan. She herself does not observe Ramadan, but she considers the two equivalent because of her fasting.

If not strictly interchangeable, religious practices are for many people complementary. The principle of complementarity holds that adding an activity from another tradition is acceptable as long as it fills a gap or somehow enriches one's own tradition. For instance, a couple who are raising their children as Muslims take them to church where they can have fun singing hymns because they feel that "happy music" is lacking in the other tradition. A Christian married to a Hindu says that she meditates and seeks "mindfulness" the way her husband does before she offers her Christian prayers; she feels that this practice enriches her prayer time the same way reading the Bible does. A Jewish man says that he likes reading and hearing the stories in the New Testament: they are comforting and uplifting, compared with the Hebrew stories, which he describes as "violent and vindictive." A Christian married to a Jew says that she has enjoyed celebrating Shabbat every Friday evening because being with family and not answering the telephone reminds her of the simplicity she saw in her grandmother, who observed Sundays the same way. In each of these examples, the person feels that it is just as appropriate to fill the gap he or she experiences by picking an activity from another tradition as it would be to work harder at finding something from his or her own tradition.

In other cases, parsing appears to follow a principle of supplementarity. According to this principle, it is okay (perhaps beneficial, but at least harmless) to add practices as long as they do not take the place of important ones in one's own tradition. For instance, a Christian married to a Buddhist says that he sometimes chants "nam hyoho renge kyo" three times at his wife's request when leaving the house for the day, but he feels more comfortable doing this if he has also said his morning prayers. Several Jewish spouses mention having Christmas trees because this is simply an "add-on" that isn't that distinctively Christian anyway. A Hindu woman says that she celebrates the Christian holidays in addition to her own because they are fun and help her feel more at home in the culture.

Because it is so common, the significance of the blending evident in examples like these can be missed. Within most religious traditions, specific practices do not occur in isolation but in relation to one another. But the assumption in these examples is that practices can be separated, taken out of context, put in new contexts, and combined with other practices from other traditions. Parsing like this depends on several additional assumptions that require closer consideration.

One assumption is that the meanings of a religious practice are limited to the immediate situation in which they occur rather than having more encompassing implications. For this reason, a practice performed in one situation need not be consistent with a practice performed in another situation. Interreligiously married people often invoke this assumption in explaining why it is acceptable to participate in a rite outside of their own tradition. Thus, a Christian spouse might participate in Muslim prayers because they were personally meaningful, not because their meaning was inscribed in a long history of teachings and interpretations. This view, however, would be quite different from that of a Muslim who believed that the daily prayers were the organizing feature of his life.[15] Another assumption is that practices in different religious traditions are relatively equivalent and therefore interchangeable. A Christian woman married to a Hindu, for instance, says that she does not mind praying to Brahma (even though she has trouble with other Hindu gods) because Brahma is the same as her Christian God. This woman recognizes that religious practices are embedded in cultural traditions. But she regards these traditions merely as the vehicles in which the same truth is expressed, rather than thinking that truth itself is different when it is conveyed by different vehicles. An additional assumption is that practices are multivalent and thus can be performed for reasons that may not be fully understood by other people and, indeed, need not be fully disclosed. A Jewish man remembers that he happily included a verse about love from the New Testament in his wedding, not only because it pleased his Christian wife, but because he "liked the sentiment" it expressed. It did not bother him that his Jewish relatives might think he was conceding too much to Christianity. In his view, a practice may reflect a belief that is not evident to other people or may not correspond with belief at all.

Assumptions like these do not pertain only to religion. They function similarly in how we conduct ourselves in business, in public office, in our schools, and in our families. Situationalism, cultural transitivity, and multivalent interpretations are part of what we understand modernity to entail. We do not have to think much about religious diversity because these patterns of thinking and behaving are widely taken for granted.

Where these assumptions sometimes falter is the process of making decisions about children. Although adults are often willing to parse their religious practices in ways that affect children (as some of these examples suggest), many parents in interreligious marriages confront difficult decisions about rearing their children. Some avoid the problem by trying to expose their children to both traditions, but a majority seem convinced that it is necessary to opt for one tradition or the other.

The prospect of having children may be five or ten years in the future, yet couples do indicate that how to raise children—and in which religious tradition to raise them—are questions they have discussed prior to marriage. These discussions are sometimes prompted by church rules that link officiating at weddings to promises concerning child rearing. But these discussions are just as likely to emerge spontaneously as couples decide whether or not their interests are compatible. The guidance couples receive from books and pamphlets, pastoral counseling, and conversations with friends is usually open-ended, offering opinions and advice but leaving the couple to come up with their own reasons for raising children in one tradition or the other (or in both or neither). Consequently, reasons vary considerably from couple to couple, and yet several underlying principles appear tacitly to guide these decisions.

The principle of least resistance emerges frequently in couples' reflections about the religious upbringing of children. They talk about wanting to avoid conflict or go the route that keeps peace with family members or religious institutions; for instance, a Christian woman is raising her children Muslim to keep peace with her in-laws; another couple is waiting and letting the children choose their own religion to avoid conflict with their extended families. Ironically, this principle means that couples actually move in the direction of the force that is exerting the greatest pressure on them. But they often do so half-heartedly—which may be a reason why they are more frequently guided by other implicit principles.

For many couples, the determining factor in how they anticipate rearing children is the principle of relative commitment. That is, they opt to raise children in the tradition to which one spouse has the greater loyalty. The other spouse, in effect, says that he or she cares less about the decision. For instance, a Hindu man says that he feels less strongly about his tradition than his wife does about hers, so he is content to let her raise the children as Christians. Similarly, a Christian woman is raising her children in Judaism because, she says, her faith is not as strong as her husband's. These judgments recognize that it takes considerable time and effort to make sure that the children receive religious training. It usually does not, however, involve either spouse claiming that his or her religion is theologically better or more true.

Besides these, couples often bring in the principle of maximum advantage, opting to raise their children in the tradition that they think will be of greatest benefit to the children. A Muslim man says that he is happy for his children to go to church and Sunday school because they will assimilate better to the dominant culture through having this training. A Catholic married to a Jew says that she and her husband decided to raise the children as Jews in hopes that they will have a more distinct sense of their identity and a stronger feeling of pride in their tradition.

Because none of these principles can be applied with full clarity about the results they are intended to achieve or the grounds on which they are presumed to rest, couples also frequently opt for the principle of optimum flexibility. In some instances, this means involving the children minimally in both traditions, either simultaneously or serially, in order to make use of specific programs or to accommodate parents' changing interests. In other cases, the principle of optimum flexibility involves exposing children to both traditions or to another open-minded tradition in order to let the children decide later for themselves.

In real life, these principles are seldom named or recognized. People know that they have worked out a solution that seems satisfactory to them.

They are less likely to realize that they are following social norms that thousands of other families have followed in similar situations. These are the norms that tell them how to be pluralistic. They have little to do with the content of the various religious traditions under consideration.[16] They function by smoothing the relationships that link people to these traditions. The rationale that governs these relationships emphasizes expedience and efficiency, personal advantage, flexibility, and getting along.

Disaggregating Religious Identities

Scholarship on contemporary religion emphasizes that it is very often guided by considerations of personal identity. People who grow up in homogeneous religious communities necessarily draw their personal identities from these communities. People who are exposed to several religious communities, as so many Americans are, have to make choices about who they want to be. They may opt for a tight-knit religious community as a way of discovering their identity. As they mature, they may repeatedly change or reaffirm their religious identity. Deciding who they are gives them a sense that they are in charge. In all these ways, religion becomes a central part of many people's personal identity—as a reconstructionist Jew, an evangelical Christian, a charismatic Catholic, and so on.[17]

The problem with these understandings of religious identity is that they nearly all pertain to the relationship an individual creates with a religious community. They do not deal adequately with the kinds of issues that individuals confront in relating to others in pluralistic situations, such as in interreligious marriages. In these situations, a surface understanding would suggest that two people interact, each as a representative of his or her respective religious tradition. If that were the case, however, each partner would always be an "other," a symbol of difference, much like the contrasting identities that Americans have ascribed to other nations when thinking of themselves as a Christian people. The reality is that categorical identities like this break down in interreligious marriages. How this happens reveals another dimension of the way religious pluralism actually functions.

Religiously mixed couples adopt discursive strategies—ways of speaking and thinking—that disaggregate religious identities. These strategies break down broad categories, such as Muslim or Jew, so that the spouse in question does not stand as a representative of the larger category. Instead, the spouse's individual identity is emphasized. He or she takes on more personalized characteristics that do not entirely dissociate him or her from the larger religious category but succeed in nuancing that category and demonstrating its internal diversity. Disaggregation can be accomplished in two ways: by emphasizing disagreements between a person and a religious tradition and by emphasizing that the person's religious identity is just one of many competing roles that he or she plays.

Among religiously mixed couples, Christians' descriptions of their spouses' beliefs and practices nearly always point out that the spouse disagrees in some significant way with the tradition in which he or she was raised. A woman married to a Muslim, for instance, says that her husband disagrees with Islamic teachings about women and therefore treats her exceptionally well. A man married to a Jew insists that "everybody has their own belief system, what they choose to believe," which he says means that his wife does not try to convert him and he does not try to convert her. A woman married to a Buddhist says that her husband disagrees with Buddhist temple religion but engages privately in Buddhist meditation because it helps him be more compassionate. What also comes through is a more nuanced picture of the internal diversity within each religious tradition. People emphasize that their spouses do not represent all of Islam or Hinduism, but one strand within this tradition. By implication, it is difficult or impossible to make generalizations about any tradition.

The second strategy—emphasizing multiple roles—is evident in assertions about the spouse being a good husband or wife, a successful physician or businessperson, and a loving father or mother, or having hobbies and doing volunteer work. The spouse's religious identity ceases to be the dominant way in which he or she is viewed. Religion is relativized, its differences transcended by other identities that evoke images of sharing and mutuality. Personality traits also serve in this way. For instance, a Christian married to a Jew says that she and her husband mostly fight about how much or how little to express anger, what it means to be polite, making jokes, and spending money. She attributes these differences to culture, upbringing, and personality rather than religion.

It is interesting that these strategies do not involve arguments about the truth or falsity of religious claims or about fundamental points of agreement among religious traditions. Points of disagreement between individuals and religious traditions are couched in terms of personal experiences and family backgrounds, rendering them relatively arbitrary and subject to situational variations. Emphasizing multiple roles also provides a way to explain such disagreements (for instance, working as a physician may give one a different view of Islam than working as an imam). Thus, the larger significance of these strategies is, as it were, to divide and conquer—dividing religious traditions into smaller, disputable points of view and personalized styles of practice; conquering their traditional authority by suggesting that they are subject to so many variations in interpretation that what ultimately must matter is respecting each other and accepting the validity of one another's interpretations.

The Normalization of Diversity

What is perhaps most surprising about interreligious marriage is the extent to which those involved in it come to see it as *normal*, indeed, as *normative*. One might suppose that interreligious marriage, like any relationship, comes to be normal, taken for granted, just through the familiarity of daily routine, much in the way that a chronic illness can become normal. But interreligious marriage comes to be normalized in a more active way—through the stories people tell about how they got married, why it was right for them, and most revealingly, why marrying someone from another religion is an act that reinforces the deepest values to which any civic-minded, right-thinking person should ascribe.

Religious diversity (and diversity in general) acquires legitimacy through the accounts that interreligious couples give of themselves. Couples do not normalize their behavior by surrounding themselves with other like-minded people, thereby creating what is sometimes referred to as a social "plausibility structure" for themselves.[18] Most are keenly aware that their behavior is *not* normative statistically, and many plainly characterize themselves as deviants or mavericks compared with family and friends. Yet without much difficulty they spin webs of meaning that connect their lives to broadly accepted values about the worth and legitimacy of diversity. For instance, a Maronite Christian married to a Muslim says that he just likes different kinds of people and different kinds of food. He grew up speaking several languages; it would have been "racist" of him to avoid falling in love with someone just because of her religion. His comments suggest that diversity is intrinsically good, a mark of sophistication, and socially desirable. A similarly positive spin on diversity is illustrated by a Christian woman (married to a Muslim) who says that being married to someone of a different religion "keeps things spicy." She adds: "When you're married to someone from a different cultural background or a different faith, you don't take everything for granted." Diversity is thus associated in her mind with being reflective. Another woman (whose husband is Hindu) says her interreligious marriage enriches her quality of life, has a "blossoming effect," and encourages "evolution" in her spiritual life. In these examples, pluralism seems right and good, not because people have resolved their religious differences, but because they have found ways of talking about it that link it to other values that are widely shared in our society.

As they discuss their relationships, people who have married outside their religion tell stories that move beyond explaining how and why they happened to marry the particular person they did. Their accounts implicitly go to some trouble to indicate, "I am normal. I am good. I am even a good Christian. What I have done is not that unusual." The stories they tell stress individuality, uniqueness, and the idiosyncrasies of personal life. Yet they are ultimately not stories of radical individualism, but of connections—to family, friends, sources of cultural authority, and well-accepted social norms.

Another woman who is married to a Hindu tells of meeting her future husband in college and immediately being drawn to the darkness of his skin. Realizing the cultural and religious differences involved, she shied away from dating him at first, but eventually they fell in love. There have been difficulties with both sets of relatives, especially his because they had expected to arrange a marriage for him in India. Still, she paints a bright picture, arguing that it has been good to become more aware of cultural differences. "It's exposed me to racism that I never knew existed. It's helped me to feel on a deeper level what it's like to be in someone else's shoes. It's been a very healthy experience for me." She thinks everyone should get out of the culture in which they have been raised and thus learn to see the world from a new perspective.

In this example, the point is not that the woman has found positive ways of speaking about her relationship. It is rather *how* she chooses to describe it. She links it with such broad cultural values as not being racist, being healthy, and being culturally sophisticated. A woman whose husband is Jewish provides another interesting example. She acknowledges that the Protestant tradition in her family is "pretty deeply in our bones and in our souls," noting that several members of her family are pastors. She was surprised to find herself falling in love with someone from another tradition. She attributes the relationship partly to youthful idealism and acknowledges that there have been difficulties along the way. Early in their relationship, she decided to covert to Judaism. It seemed more authentic to her and helped her circumvent some of the doubts she had encountered with Christianity. She likes the feeling now of having a "deep spiritual connection" with God. Although she would not go so far as to say that her own journey should be followed by others, she does believe that her marriage has resulted in the kind of personal growth to which most people aspire. Thus, personal growth serves as a core value with which she not only associates her own marriage but also makes a normative appeal for the desirability of religious diversity.

What we see in these accounts, then, is that interreligious diversity, even within the context of marital relationships, is possible to sustain and to make sense of, not because religious officials lack the capacity to restrain it, and not simply because people adopt a pick-and-choose approach to their religious practices, but because so much of American culture says that it is fundamentally *right* to engage in diverse relationships. Differences, we say, make us better people, stronger, more thoughtful, more interesting. They enrich our personal lives, stave off boredom, open up possibilities for spiritual growth, and place us at the cutting edge of cultural innovation. But what does all this reveal about the society in which we live?

Ours is in many ways a secular culture. We overwhelmingly claim to believe in God and nearly all of us affiliate with religious organizations to some degree—enough so that interreligious marriages are difficult. Yet when it comes to resolving the tensions that may arise because of such relationships, we are basically guided by civic considerations rather than religious ones. We champion our individual right to make our own choices and to deviate from the majority. We disdain any hint of being influenced by racism or cultural prejudice (although we may admit intellectually to being subject to these very influences). We believe instinctively in compromise, especially if it preserves the collective peace and promotes individual freedom. And we jealously insist on separating what we do in private and the meanings we ascribe to our own behavior from anything public, including what our closest friends and relatives may attribute to us. These are norms that can often be reconciled with religious teachings. Yet it is instructive that we generally do not feel compelled to reconcile them in this way. It is enough just to reference them as if it would defy common sense to think in any other way.

Religious differences, then, are constrained within a rich language embedded in our civic culture. We know that this is true in the public arena when, for example, Methodists and Muslims agree to abide by the laws of the land and go periodically to the polls to participate in democratic elections. It is just as much the case in the highly private decisions people make about dating and marriage. Different rules, perhaps having more to do with religious convictions, are not invoked simply because the decisions are less relevant to the public arena. What we have learned in the public arena applies equally in our private lives. Religion is important enough to worry about and religious differences are of sufficient gravity to require negotiation. But they are not matters of such universal weight that we need to be unbending in our resolve or that we even must resolve them in terms of rich theological understandings of religious traditions themselves.

From Religion to Culture

Western Christianity has long been characterized by a seemingly irrepressible urge toward anticlericalism. Believers think of themselves as having direct access to the divine rather than needing clergy as intermediaries. Nowhere has this emphasis on piety from the bottom up been more evident than in the United States. One of the most interesting conclusions that emerges from considering the widening role of interfaith marriage today, therefore, is that those who are most exposed to interfaith diversity in this way seem surprisingly free of anticlericalism. Nearly everyone has run into roadblocks or faced disappointment in negotiating arrangements about weddings, baptisms, and their role in congregations. Yet hardly anyone seems to have come away profoundly hurt, angry, or disillusioned with clergy. Being able to negotiate the thickets of interfaith relationships on their own terms has worked well for all parties concerned. Couples manage to do pretty much whatever they want to, tailoring their continuing involvement in churches (or their departures) to minimize personal and familial conflict. Christianity is, for them, a fluid, internally variegated tradition that provides sufficient space in which to believe and practice as they choose. Clergy tacitly find this arrangement works well, too. It takes up relatively little of their time, requiring next to nothing in terms of knowledge about other religious traditions and little more than a willingness to be kind to the aliens in their midst, much as they might to stray animals.

As growing numbers of American Christians marry people of other faiths, Christianity will nevertheless be affected. The view that Christianity is a *cultural tradition* will undoubtedly spread. Christianity's historic claim to being the unique repository of divine truth will diminish in the popular mind. People who have been raised believing that Christianity is distinctively true, but who now are in the daily presence of someone outside that tradition, will come to view their tradition as one of many, as a kind of ethnic or linguistic vehicle through which some portion of the human race has tried to make sense of divine mystery. They may still believe in the truth of Christianity, but politely couch this belief in the view, as one young man put it, that "the Christian gospel is true *for Christians*" or with reference to truth being conditioned by personal experience and cultural location. Belief itself will be downgraded relative to spiritual practice—practices of personal prayer and meditation, of charitable service, and of intermittent participation in worship experiences inside or outside of local congregations. With practice rather than doctrine at the core of religious commitment, Christianity may even become a collection of activities, like going to potluck dinners and reading inspirational books, that run the danger of being selected smorgasbord-style in terms of whatever happens to be most gratifying or convenient.

These shifts in how Christians view Christianity will probably be more significant than the impact of the specific teachings of other religions. Even for people who marry and live with persons of other faiths, the direct influence of those faiths on Christianity appears to be relatively minimal. Christian spouses do selectively interpret their tradition to fit comfortably with the diverse lifestyles they have chosen; Christianity comes increasingly to be a religion of love and acceptance, a kind of moral teaching that encourages everyone to be tolerant, open-minded, and willing to see the good in all people. Christian spouses do permit their children to be raised in other traditions (about as often as they raise them in their own), spend some time reading the basic texts of these other traditions, and participate from time to time in other religions' festivals and holidays. But interfaith marriage as a way in which Christians are absorbing particular doctrines and teachings from other religions appears to be relatively inconsequential. Few of the Christian spouses in mixed marriages claim that what they have learned outside their tradition is superior to their own. They taste that which is foreign, as they might at an ethnic restaurant, but seldom adapt their spiritual diet in fundamental ways.

Through intermarriage, then, just as from other sources, American Christianity shows little sign of becoming truly syncretistic as a result of exposure to other religions. In this respect, Christianity retains its dominant position in the culture, influenced by advertising and mass consumption, by the affluence and work lives of middle-class Americans, but remarkably resistant to the other world religions in its midst. Of course there are some exceptions. Christians married to Jews say that they have gained a new appreciation of the Hebrew scriptures, view Christianity less as a fulfillment of Judaism than as an outgrowth from it, and often report greater appreciation of family solidarity. Christian spouses of Buddhists sometimes borrow practices of meditation and relaxation, while those married to Muslims express appreciation of the oneness of God and for this reason view Jesus as a prophet rather than as a savior. These exceptions notwithstanding, Christianity hardly seems in danger of becoming a hodgepodge of borrowings from the diverse traditions to which it is increasingly exposed.

At the same time, the impact of Christianity on other religions through intermarriage also appears limited. Some direct influences are evident, especially in the case of non-Christian spouses who attend church or who agree to have their children baptized and reared in the Christian faith. But these influences are relatively rare because churches seldom offer classes specifically for spouses from non-Christian backgrounds and in most cases seem ineffective at enforcing rules about baptism. Mosques, temples, and synagogues, representing minority religions as they do, are more likely to offer classes for Christian spouses than churches are for non-

Christian spouses, and these classes are more likely to emphasize expectations about loyalty to the minority religion. In any event, active conversion from another religion to Christianity appears to be relatively rare. The more common impact of Christianity, therefore, is to encourage non-Christian spouses to emphasize some of the similarities between Christianity and their own tradition or to borrow certain Christian beliefs. For instance, Buddhists and Hindus married to Christians are sometimes eager to speak about a monotheistic God of love, while Jews married to Christians may betray Christian influences in their thinking about salvation and immortality.[19]

The most significant effect of interreligious marriage will probably be to reinforce the already prevalent view that faith is essentially a private affair. Although interfaith couples do talk about their beliefs and practices with each other, the frequency with which they remain silent on these matters is perhaps even more notable. Each spouse lays claim to his or her religious views, expressing a personalized approach to spirituality that does not require agreement from his or her partner. This kind of privatization is strategic, driven by the simple necessity of getting on with one's life without constantly having to examine large issues about which there is disagreement. It is more deeply rooted in the modern belief that all individuals should be guided in matters of faith by their conscience and for this reason must be free to choose differently even than those closest to them. But few of the people whose comments we have considered actually spoke in the language of conscience. They instead emphasized the *cultural contingencies* of religious practice, easily attributing their differences to the social contexts in which they had been reared and readily assenting to the influence of these backgrounds rather than believing it necessary to work toward an approach to faith that was truly their own. Religious conviction, in these understandings, comes largely to be a matter of personal opinion, an arbitrary manifestation of personal biography (like one's hometown or surname) that is important as a distinguishing aspect of one's identity in a multifaceted social space, rather than an anchor firmly tied to some enduring reality.

Personalized spirituality of this kind does have significant theological implications. It reinforces a kind of religious universalism that assumes that God loves all people equally, whatever their religious or cultural heritage might be. Within the largely Christian context of the United States, it does not appear to diminish belief in God, even for Christians married to spouses whose views of the sacred are quite different from theirs, but it does render authoritative statements about God more difficult. With the silence about deep theological questions that pervades interfaith families, this personalized spirituality encourages people to seek guidance in ways that do not threaten the stability of their daily family routines. Reading inspirational books or novels, talking casually with a friend or coworker, or going alone to a religious service carry few dangers for family stability. But they also may be easier to engage in sporadically as a casual consumer than regularly as a member of a religious community.

Interreligious marriage, then, reveals some of the ways in which we are adapting to the more religiously diverse world in which we live. Religiously mixed couples work out relationships that permit each spouse to live with someone whose religious beliefs and practices are quite different from their own. They do sometimes sit down and ponder these differences, considering the strengths and weaknesses of various teachings as they might when studying a road map or alternative health plans. But this kind of pondering seems rare. What matters more are the ways people learn to negotiate by invoking implicit rules about social relationships that are widely available in our society. People manage to live with religious diversity by keeping religious authorities at bay—a task more easily accomplished because religious authorities themselves follow managerial and therapeutic scripts that diminish conflict and encourage flexibility. People also manage religious diversity by being willing to pick and choose among alternative religious practices and to seek legitimacy for their behavior by referencing values that are part of our civic culture. Tacit negotiation like this makes it possible for people to live in religiously diverse situations. But it also comes at a price as religion becomes more individualistic and privatized and as implicit social norms take precedence over informed choices.

How Pluralistic Should We Be?

THE UNITED STATES is a diverse society religiously, ethni-
cally, and culturally. There is no question about the reality of this diversity
or about the fact that it is increasing. But diversity and pluralism are not
the same. We can be diverse without being truly pluralistic. Pluralism is
our response to diversity—how we think about it, how we respond to it
in our attitudes and lifestyles, and whether we choose to embrace it, ignore
it, or merely cope with it.[1] Some Americans, as we have seen, believe we
are already too diverse. They think we should stand up for our convictions
rather than accepting the values of others. Many welcome diversity but
find it easier to coexist than to engage actively with other groups. They
apparently feel that getting along is better than getting acquainted. As a
nation we therefore face the important question of how pluralistic we
should be.

Officially we are a pluralistic society. Our laws aim to protect the rights
of all citizens regardless of religion or creed, race or ethnicity, gender or
national origin. In the public discourse that manifests itself in journalism
or on the political stage and in the polite language taught in our nation's
schools, we usually try to honor these diverse rights. We practice a language
of respect, and sometimes much more, espousing a code that champions
social diversity as if the future of our species depended on it the way natural
evolution does on biological diversity.

But official discourse is only part of the picture. It often serves as a
veneer, thinly covering the deeper fractures in our society. In our communities and families and in our personal lives, many Americans have rather
different views of diversity than the ones we hear from our national leaders
or in classrooms. When the chips are down, they strike out at people
different from themselves. These are the people who commit hate crimes

and who take a not-in-my-backyard approach to mosques and temples moving into their communities. Others are more tolerant. In fact, despite the range of opinions we have examined among ordinary people and among religious leaders, we have seen that most people adopt a live-and-let-live approach to the religious and cultural diversity in their communities.[2] Yet tolerance, especially of the knee-jerk variety, is not the same as true pluralism, either. It is too casual, too easy. Tolerance of that kind works as long as people can slink off by themselves, avoiding contact, and never facing up to what they truly believe (or think they believe).

Reflective Pluralism

The greatest barrier to pluralism in the United States is not the expansion of differences in our midst but our reluctance to acknowledge the fact that there are indeed *differences*. We want all positions to be equally plausible and any disagreements to be matters of taste. In the case of religion, many Americans blithely assume that all religions are pretty much the same, worshipping God in ways that are only trivially different. As one community leader observed, "There is a kind of shallow understanding that all religions are basically alike. People really don't want to roll up their sleeves and dig because 'Well, if basically all religions are alike, why do I need to study them, why do I need to learn about them?' " But people who have thought seriously about religious differences know otherwise. They know that religions offer fundamentally different claims about how to experience the sacred. Religions have different conceptions of evil and salvation, different teachings about death and immortality, different rituals, dietary habits, holy days, and customs. These differences have been the occasion for prejudice, hate, bloodshed, and war. True pluralism cannot be achieved by merely wishing them away.

Nor can pluralism be achieved in the manner that abstract theories of pluralism sometimes describe. These theories suggest that we can be pluralists collectively but absolutists in our private lives. For instance, a version of this argument has been put forth by the philosopher Nicholas Rescher, who states, "Pluralism holds that it is rationally intelligible and acceptable that others can hold positions at variance with one's own. But it does not maintain that a given individual need endorse a plurality of positions."

He goes on to say, "Pluralism is a feature of the collective group; it turns on the fact that different experiences engender different views. But from the standpoint of the individual this cuts no ice."[3] No ice perhaps. At least if we understand Rescher to be interested in articulating an idea that is only rationally intelligible. What we have seen from how people actually understand pluralism is quite different. They do not blithely accept pluralism at the collective level while remaining insulated from it as individuals. They are inescapably affected by it.

The closest we have to people staking out a position they hold as absolutely true and yet living within the framework of cultural pluralism are those I have described as Christian exclusivists. Pluralists of liberal persuasion express worries about such people. Their firmly held convictions nevertheless are what give pluralists hope that society can be genuinely diverse and still hold together. Yet Christian exclusivists do not merely rely on collective democratic processes to maintain social order while they go on unaffected by living amidst diversity. More so than even they may realize, their beliefs are influenced by their experiences with diversity. They resolve the tension between exclusivism and pluralism, not through a rationally intelligible process of deliberation, but by adopting the languages of avoidance and mediation that we have examined. If they are going to be true to their exclusivist views of Christianity in the future, they have some hard thinking to do. They need to be clearer about why they are exclusivists, what they should be doing to bring their understanding of divine truth to the awareness of others, and how they can do that without engaging in religious warfare.

Inclusive Christians and spiritual shoppers with eclectic religious views, in contrast, are more obviously shaped by diversity, even in their personal lives. They illustrate that it is difficult to live in a pluralist environment without that environment affecting one's beliefs and practices. They also show that coming to terms with pluralism is not simply a matter of sitting down and deciding to be a person of faith without believing that one's views are superior. Instead, they follow the cultural flow. Although some have thought deeply about their faith, implicit strategies of avoidance and a selective emphasis on some religious teachings rather than others are an important part of how they cope with diversity. For them, just as for Christian exclusivists, pluralism happens in the breach. It involves making implicit adjustments in their beliefs and practices. The culture works, almost unwittingly, to smooth the path to diversity without requiring much thought about its effects or what it actually means to be pluralistic. Like Christian exclusivists, these inclusivists have work to do in their churches and in their personal lives. If all religions are true, then some serious theological thinking is in order to say *in what way* Christianity (or any other religion) is true. If they are truly pluralistic, these people also need to get busy and further the task of religious reconciliation. Without their voice, the public arena becomes a stage only for extremists of the fundamentalist and secularist persuasions.

Moving beyond shallow responses to diversity requires engaging in what we might refer to as *reflective pluralism*. For a society truly to make informed decisions about how pluralistic it wants to be, its leaders and citizens must devote time and energy to thinking about the question. In a diverse society, the civic good depends especially on what John Dewey referred to as "habits of mind" or what Robert Bellah and his associates have more recently described simply as "attention"—self-disciplined mindfulness to the social conditions and institutions on which personal and collective well-being depend. [4] Reflective pluralism entails such mindfulness. It involves acknowledging how and why people are different (and the same), and it requires having good reasons for engaging with people and groups whose religious practices are fundamentally different from one's own.

Reflective pluralism moves from the way in which Americans have typically responded to diversity in the past to the more self-conscious, active, and intentional style that will be necessary in the future. The old pattern managed diversity in the same way a person might manage to pay the bills or recover from a bad illness: by doing the best one could, muddling through, making the best of a bad situation. Managing meant dealing with one's neighbors when it was unavoidable, even if they belonged to a different religion; it involved grudgingly adjusting to interreligious marriage among one's kin or tacitly accepting the civil rights of religious newcomers to the community. Reflective pluralism does not shift from this pattern of merely getting by to the kind of management taught in business schools, where managed diversity is like managed health care or managed corporate takeovers, all coordinated by a central agency. Pluralism of that kind would hardly be attractive; it would be imposed and thus seem artificial. The desired alternative suggested by reflective pluralism is more like the managing implied by an earlier understanding of the term, of handling with care and respect, like that of a groom toward a thoroughbred horse.

Pluralism of this kind depends on what an earlier generation of Americans would have called strength of character. It starts with knowing oneself, with knowledge of the principles and practices that are central to one's life, indeed, to one's understanding of what it means to live a good and worthy life. Strength of character means not accepting everything simply because it exists, even though one may strive to live peacefully with those with whom one disagrees. Strength of character means being fully attentive to one's surroundings, engaging them as a person and not simply as a role-player, in order to develop one's self to its fullest potential and to assist others toward achieving the common good.[5]

What are the specific traits that distinguish people who are engaged in reflective pluralism? Few people are consistently pluralistic in all realms of activity, but some provide glimpses of how to move beyond the cultural norms that simply permit diversity to be taken for granted. Among spouses married to people from other religions and among clergy and community leaders, those who have thought most about what it means to be pluralistic exhibit at least some of the following characteristics:

They are interested in the substantive aspects of pluralism. They care about specific issues, teachings, or practices, rather than somehow attempting to rise above such matters. In confronting religious diversity, they have sometimes been able to think grandly about broad comparisons among, say, Buddhism and Christianity and Islam. More typically, though, they have seized on what we might call a "focal issue": a particular teaching or practice that has become especially puzzling to them, often because it symbolizes larger possibilities for agreement and disagreement. Examples include teachings about the afterlife, the question of whether Jesus was divine or a prophet, ideas about reincarnation, concerns about peace and justice, or understandings of God. By focusing on one such issue, they have been able to think concertedly about it, whereas broader comparisons would have been too large to grapple with. They have tried to puzzle through these issues, not only in intellectual terms, but to see what implications they might have for personal and social conduct.

They develop an identity as a "studier," as one woman put it. Unlike people who tacitly assume that religious and other cultural differences are not worth paying much attention to, those who are most reflective about pluralism consciously adopt a stance of inquiry. They understand that religious and cultural pluralism is not easily mastered. They take the view that it may be a long time before they arrive at satisfactory positions on deep questions of belief and value. The quest may never end. Yet they also consider it interesting and worthwhile to make the effort. Being a studier becomes part of how they define themselves. The philosopher Alasdair MacIntyre terms this orientation an "ethics of inquiry."[6] It aims for a deeper understanding of the competing truth claims and concepts of human nature inscribed in alternative religions and civilizations.

They carefully consider what it means to have a "view." On the one hand, they recognize that much of what we claim to know and believe depends on our point of view, which in turn is shaped by the culture in which we live. On the other hand, they acknowledge that viewpoints are not, therefore, simply arbitrary or unconnected from truth. Finding an appropriate middle ground is not something that they can determine once and for all. Rather, they weigh specific issues with recognition that viewpoints need to be examined and compared and with acknowledgment that truth needs to be sought as well.

They consciously seek ways to neutralize objections to pluralism. While it may be surprising to consider this trait, reflective pluralists are usually aware that not everyone is as instinctively open to diversity as they are. They often face resistance from friends, parents, other relatives, neighbors, or fellow members of their congregations. Neutralization comes about by trying to understand the sources of this resistance. For instance, resistance may come from insecurity or from lack of exposure to diversity. Reflective pluralism involves taking account of the reasons for resistance while avoiding regarding one's own position as inherently superior.

They emphasize respect. While it is common to hear statements such as "I respect you even though I know you are wrong," reflective pluralism takes a different view. It recognizes that a person's beliefs (perhaps especially about religion) *are* intimately connected with the person's identity or sense of self. Thus, the two cannot so easily be separated. Respect for the person has implications for how one regards that person's beliefs. One says, in effect, "Because I respect you, and because you hold a particular set of beliefs, I am obligated to consider those beliefs differently than if I simply read about them in a book or considered them in the abstract."

They exhibit a principled willingness to compromise. People who have thought most seriously about pluralism generally do not take the view that one value can simply be traded for another. Compromise does not entail agreeing that one's deepest values are not that important after all. Rather, it involves a conscious decision to give up something in order to arrive at a workable relationship with another person or group. One's comfort level may be sacrificed, for example, in order to move into a social or emotional space in which differences are more common. Or one may agree to forgo the companionship and security that comes from functioning only in familiar surroundings.

As these considerations suggest, reflective pluralism does not involve simply starting with the presupposition that greater interaction and cooperation among diverse groups, religious or otherwise, is a good thing. It begins with a more skeptical attitude. People are busily preoccupied with other things. Many Americans have little daily contact with people whose religions are different from their own. Their circle of friends is deeply fulfilling because it rests on shared values, shared experiences, and shared assumptions about life. People like this have little incentive to reach out to strangers who might challenge these assumptions. For these people, it may be sufficient that the legal system, which they probably understand in barest essentials, provides a guarantee of equal rights to individuals whose views of life are quite different from their own. Among other Americans, the idea of religious and cultural pluralism may be resisted for stronger reasons. Some may oppose it on the grounds that a little knowledge is a dangerous thing; to understand other faiths may be more than anyone has time or interest to do, and for this reason should be left alone. Others will argue especially in the case of religion that greater understanding of other faiths is actually dangerous (in the same way that persistent exposure to falsehoods or half-truths may be). Thus, if more active efforts are to be made to promote interreligious cooperation, good reasons have to be supplied. A case has to be made.

The Case for Cooperation

A small number of religious and community leaders has become persuaded that interreligious cooperation must be actively promoted, given the increasing diversity of American religion and the growing integration of world cultures. They represent interfaith organizations that have been initiated to promote such cooperation, as well as scattered efforts in seminaries, local congregations, and civic or government organizations. These leaders have often thought deeply about the need for interreligious cooperation and, therefore, are good sources to consider in seeking reasons for such cooperation.

A negative reason heads the list. Religious tensions, conflicts, and violence have been so much a part of human history that positive steps need to be taken to prevent or minimize the likelihood of such episodes in the future. A man who has long been active in interreligious efforts gave an example from a meeting with Muslims and Jews: "One of the Muslims was talking about how wonderful the past Mufti of Cairo was. One of the rabbis glared at him and said, 'Nothing good should be said about that man. He separated my grandmother's head from her body.' Yet the rabbi and the Muslim and every other person at that meeting came to a joint declaration about the next steps for resolving the issues in Israel and the occupied territories." For this leader, interreligious cooperation is sorely needed so that personal anguish can be expressed and mutual respect established in the aftermath of conflict and violence. "I'm not interested in this business of 'Oh, we all believe alike,' " he observes. "That is just bullcrap in my opinion."

The leader of another organization told of being especially moved one evening when he attended a joint service of worship and singing for people from Pakistan and India. A Sikh from India remarked about how special the occasion was for him. "We embrace each other here as sisters and brothers, but when I go back home, I can't visit the village I was born in because that village is now in Pakistan and I'm not welcome there." The American said he came away more highly motivated to provide opportunities for people to bridge religious barriers.

The specter of violence among religious factions is reduced by America's democratic system of government. The nation has a long history of immigrant groups learning to live peaceably with one another. Yet there has been enough violence in this history, even in recent years, to suggest a need for continuing vigilance. As one proponent of greater cooperation among religious groups observed, "When we have neighbors who are Muslims or Hindus or Christians or Buddhists or Jews, and if we rest in stereotype and suspicion, we run the real risk of seeing the kinds of tribalism that inflame other parts of the world."

A positive reason for interreligious cooperation emphasizes the goodwill and shared concern for basic human dignity that can be mobilized among the various religious traditions. "You can prospect through the sacred writings of the world's different traditions," says one man who has become involved in interreligious efforts, "and find expressions of something like the Golden Rule everywhere." Others note shared emphases on peace, the sacredness of life, hospitality and respect, caring for the needy, and paying attention to something bigger than ourselves.

If religious people were known for getting along instead of fighting, proponents of religious cooperation argue, people who are now repulsed by religion or indifferent to it would be attracted. Religion itself would benefit and, in turn, society would benefit. As one religious leader observed, "I would love to see a society where religion was not a bad word, where the riches of our religions and spiritual traditions were seen as great gifts for humanity, where we had moved through deepening our religious and spiritual roots into a new stage of being human that reflects Isaiah's vision of a world at peace, where religion is a force to create a moral and ethical society."

The case for interreligious cooperation is also being made on grounds that religions command resources that can be deployed more effectively for common purposes. A small community organization in Easton, Pennsylvania, finds it is better able to provide food and shelter to the needy by uniting the resources of churches and synagogues in the area. An agency in Los Angeles works cooperatively with Muslims, Jews, Christians, and Buddhists because the community it serves is religiously and ethnically diverse. In dozens of other communities, diverse religious groups have banded together to promote healing and reconciliation, to combat violence, and to address community needs.

A related argument holds that interreligious cooperation is worthwhile because of the growing threat of secularism. Leaders worry about narrowly self-interested influences of business, about politicians being guided by quests for power and wealth instead of a commitment to the public good, and about the lure of advertising and consumerism. Others point to environmental concerns, civic disengagement, and the fragmentation of personal identity—what one describes as "the widespread addictive nature of our society" evident in shopping obsessions, substance abuse, racism, classism, and sexism. Against these worries, the teachings and practices of religious traditions may provide welcome alternatives. In these traditions, questions about absolute truth, good and evil, judgment and mercy, love, forgiveness, virtue, and reconciliation are commonly raised.

For some, interreligious cooperation is important because it enriches their own faith. "The more I am in the company of the faithful of any tradition," one man observes, "the more I personally am deepened, challenged, and inspired in my own practice of faith." He adds: "There is an incredible variety of language and God seems to have spoken in a bewildering array of ways to people all over the world and all through history, but the magnificence of that when it's offered openly—when it's aimed at making bridges of understanding that lead to cooperation that will help all life—is the most holy thing I've ever seen."

Yet another argument for interreligious cooperation is that understanding of the human condition itself is at stake. In a society and world that is so clearly diverse in its religious and cultural expressions, these expressions must be taken seriously as part of what it means to be human. It was this curiosity that inspired the comparative study of world religions in the late nineteenth century and was evident well before that in the writings of Jonathan Edwards, Joseph Priestly, and others. Scholars are slowly weaning themselves from the Enlightenment view that religions are simply passé and therefore of less interest than late-breaking developments in science and technology. An educated public, let alone an effective cadre of public leaders, can scarcely consider itself informed if it pays no attention to religion and to the diverse expressions of religion.

An Effort to Promote Understanding

For those persuaded that interreligious understanding is desirable, the question is how best to translate conviction into practice. Throughout our nation's history, Americans have sought to improve civic life through associations. Social observers continue to emphasize their importance, just as Alexis de Tocqueville did in describing how "the circle of public society is extended" by associations in the 1830s.[7] At present, the nation's churches remain one of the most extensive aspects of associational life, as was true in Tocqueville's time. Yet, as we have seen, the typical congregation does relatively little to encourage greater understanding among different religions. Thus, more specialized associations have been experimenting with ways of enhancing interreligious understanding.

One of these associations is the United Religions Initiative (or URI, which executive director Charles Gibbs says is an "ungrammatical message" about sharing). URI came into being in 1995 after several years of planning by San Francisco's Episcopal bishop, William Swing, and a small circle of leaders from religion, business, and government. Swing's interest was sparked when he was asked to host an interfaith event at Grace Cathedral in conjunction with the fiftieth anniversary of the signing of the United Nations charter in San Francisco. Finding it hard to sleep that night, he rose the next morning committed to getting the world's major religious organizations interacting the same way the United Nations had managed to initiate discussions among national leaders.

Swing and his team discovered that reactions to their idea were mixed. Critics observed that religions could not be brought together like the United Nations because the various religions were not organized the way nations were. Critics also observed that it might not be a good idea for religious leaders to interact or, if they did, that the results might be disappointing, just as those of the United Nations often were. Supporters encouraged the bishop to move ahead but cautioned that more than vision and enthusiasm would be needed to make the plan work.

For these reasons, the initial plan was modest. Besides the one-hour interfaith service at Grace Cathedral, Swing and his team organized a gathering of two hundred college-age young people called Rediscovering Justice. Its purpose was to determine if a group of strangers could spend a couple of days talking about their respective faith traditions and come away feeling that the time was well spent. If so, enough of value might be learned to propel the initiative to another level; if not, Swing's team was prepared to call it quits.

Several encouraging things happened. One was that the young people seemed genuinely to enjoy their time together. Many of the participants were international students studying in the United States; the occasion helped them to understand their various cultures and religious traditions. Another was that toward the end of the meeting a spontaneous service of prayer, reading of sacred texts, and sharing of inspirational thoughts emerged. This meeting suggested that the group was beginning to take ownership of itself, actively participating rather than simply waiting for leadership from elsewhere. The group also demonstrated this sense of engagement when it collectively refused to attend the formal event at Grace Cathedral unless one of their number, who had been denied entry by security guards for carrying a ceremonial dagger, was granted access.[8]

Executive director Gibbs recalls that enlisting grassroots participation emerged early as one of URI's strategies. Unlike the United Nations, which brought only leaders together, the organizers of URI felt that its long-term impact would be greater if it could promote direct interaction among ordinary people from the various world religions. Following the small-group or "cell" formula used successfully by such different organizations as the Communist Party and the Methodist Church, URI encouraged the formation of working groups around the nation (and world) whose participants would meet regularly over a period of time to get acquainted and to learn more about one another's religions.

The United Nations served as a model for URI in other respects. Swing felt that a charter was especially important. Working on it would give representatives of the different religions a reason to interact around a specific task, and the result would presumably be a set of statements on which they could all agree. He spent three months during 1995 and 1996 traveling internationally, talking about his idea and inviting religious leaders to come to a conference in San Francisco to draw up a charter.

With the conference only a few months away, Gibbs was still uncertain about what exactly to have the delegates do when they arrived. Then a letter arrived from David Cooperrider, an organizational behavior specialist at Case Western University in Cleveland. Through his work as a management consultant to transglobal organizations, Cooperrider had developed a method called "appreciative inquiry." Unlike problem-solving approaches that emphasize deficits from the past, appreciative inquiry was designed to bring out the positive experiences of the various participants. In sessions of a half hour to an hour, pairs of participants representing different religions would interview each other, asking questions such as: Tell me a story about some cooperative effort you were involved with to make the world a better place, and tell me why was it successful? Or you're a person who has been deeply enriched by your religious or spiritual background, so please tell me what the greatest gifts you've received from your religion are, and if you were to offer that gift to someone else, how would it be offered?

This process worked well. Sixty delegates, including businesspeople, artists and writers, educators, and religious leaders, met in 1996 and worked together to identify positive ideas to further the initiative. They concluded that the top-down structure of the United Nations was less helpful than a bottom-up model such as that used by faith-based community organizing movements.[9] The goal was to forge a globally connected network of people who would be locally rooted and supported. They decided that URI should be more genuinely international than the United Nations. It would not be headquartered in the United States but would come together in regional conferences throughout the world. The delegates also determined that greater gender equality and racial inclusiveness should be a high priority as they moved ahead.

After a number of regional conferences and consultations with heads of other international organizations, URI formally adopted a charter in June 2000. The charter calls people of diverse religions, spiritual expressions, and indigenous traditions "to promote enduring, daily interfaith cooperation, to end religiously motivated violence and to create cultures of peace, justice and healing for the Earth and all living beings."[10] It encourages respect for the uniqueness of each religious tradition but recognition of the value of the various traditions coming together to promote human betterment, healing, and reconciliation. To achieve these objectives, the charter invites local groups of seven or more members representing at least three different traditions to form "Cooperative Circles," which meet to work together on specific projects. Cooperative Circles choose their own projects and can formulate their own rules as long as they are consistent with general URI principles. These principles (twenty-one are listed in the charter) range from encouraging members to deepen their roots in their own tradition, to growing in understanding of other traditions, to honoring gender equality and functioning ethically and with integrity.

URI's present goal is to maintain and expand the number of Cooperative Circles and the projects in which they are engaged. Through a small support staff in San Francisco whose time is covered by private donations, URI keeps in contact with the various circles, offering advice from experience gained in other circles. For instance, one of its circles in Pakistan organized an interfaith group that traveled by bus throughout the country calling on community leaders to work for peace. URI was able to pass along some of the lessons to a circle in Argentina interested in initiating a similar effort. Another interfaith circle in Buenos Aires that works with the terminally ill has received technical advice from URI. Yet another focuses on rights of women and children; not geographically defined, it depends on URI to coordinate its activities on several continents.

Multiple Models

URI's successes remain modest. Despite efforts spanning more than a decade, its leaders acknowledge that the interfaith projects in which the various Cooperative Circles are engaged amount to little more than a drop in an ocean, compared to the activities that take place *within* particular religious traditions. Yet it is clear that URI's efforts have succeeded on a small scale because of its ability to combine two levels of organization: a decentralized array of grassroots groups engaged in specific projects and a relatively centralized but minimal leadership structure that raises funds and provides a mechanism for sharing information.

The Kansas City Interfaith Council provides a sharply contrasting model of how to promote interreligious cooperation. Founded in 1989, it grew from concern about the way religious groups were being portrayed in local newspapers and on television. One of its founders, Reverend Vern Barnett, attended an interfaith conference in another city and came home determined to initiate something to bridge the gap among religions in Kansas City. Most of the Council's work has remained quiet, small-scale, and out of public view. Leaders of Christian, Jewish, Muslim, and Zoroastrian groups have met privately over the years to get better acquainted and to discuss their various religions. Although most are clergy, they do not interact as representatives of their religions but as private persons. Council members then work behind the scenes to help other organizations sponsor public events. For instance, they have encouraged Jewish and Muslim groups to meet to discuss questions about relationships between Israelis and Palestinians and they have met with local journalists to heighten the quality of religious reporting.

Another model of interreligious cooperation is the Interfaith Center of New York, founded in 1997 by Reverend James Morton following his retirement as dean of the Cathedral Church of Saint John the Divine. The Interfaith Center functions primarily as an educational organization. Although it occasionally engages in hands-on community activities, it mostly specializes in hosting events aimed at generating greater understanding of the world's major religions. For instance, it recently sponsored a day-long event on Muslims in New York, which included lectures about Islam, a photo exhibit of mosques in New York, and Middle Eastern music and food. Although similar to a course that might have been offered at Columbia or NYU, the event focused less on the history and formal teachings of Islam and more on practical problems facing New York Muslims and was geared toward increasing understanding of Muslims among local Christians, Jews, Buddhists, and Hindus. Other activities include the Urban Religious Leadership Initiative, which sponsors an annual retreat for New York clergy of all faiths to talk about common problems and interests, such as combating police violence and ministering to people in prison. The Center also sponsors a wide range of interfaith arts and cultural programs. Morton believes these are very important because religious traditions are "not just a head trip, but something you feel in your emotions."

The vast majority of interreligious organizations are local, like these in Kansas City and New York, and they focus on specific community needs or arise in response to local problems and opportunities. The Interfaith Center at the Presidio in San Francisco grew out of an effort to turn the land and buildings near the Golden Gate Bridge that had been used for military purposes into a place where community organizations could meet after the U.S. Army abandoned the site in 1995. Today the Center cooperates with the National Park Commission to hold interfaith worship services periodically in the old chapel. The Thanks-Giving Square Foundation in Dallas devotes its efforts largely to interfaith services held in conjunction with Thanksgiving each November. In Allentown, Pennsylvania, the Interfaith Alliance of the Lehigh Valley emerged from small-scale efforts initiated by the Anti-Defamation League of B'nai B'rith in the 1980s to combat religious and ethnic prejudice. Much of the Alliance's recent work has focused on diversity training for community leaders and hate-crime prevention. These efforts, like dozens of other interreligious groups around the country, have experienced mixed success. None of their leaders claim to have transformed the religious climate of their communities, but their experiences suggest some of the reasons for failure or success.

Why Interreligious Efforts Fail

Many interreligious efforts fail to get off the ground or struggle to stay alive. The main reasons for failure include opposition from other religious groups in the community, indifference, real or perceived concerns about these efforts leading to the formation of new syncretic religions, focusing too much at the start on formal religious doctrines and identities, and financial or administrative difficulties.

John-Brian Paprock, the founder of the Madison Area Interfaith Network (MAIN) in Madison, Wisconsin, provides examples of some of these problems. He recalls that it was an uphill battle to organize an interreligious effort in Madison because a previous effort had provoked strong opposition from conservative churches in the area by inviting a pagan group to participate in a prayer service without securing approval from all participating organizations in advance. There was also skepticism at first because some people in the community thought interreligious cooperation was invariably a first step toward creating a syncretic religion. Their thinking was influenced by having witnessed new religious movements around the University of Wisconsin campus in the 1970s. As MAIN emerged, it also ran into difficulty from generating too much publicity. Paprock had a radio program, which gave him visibility in the community, and he decided it would be valuable at the start to produce a directory listing all the religious groups in the area. The directory, coming as it did without an established groundwork of interpersonal relationships, sparked unexpected concerns, ranging from neopagan groups not wanting to be listed for fear of persecution to churches with differing views about homosexuality objecting to being included in the same list.

Two of MAIN's initial activities experienced limited success, but in retrospect were probably ill-conceived. One was a series of monthly meetings titled "What We Believe" that were held for the public at a local bookstore. The other was an effort to get participants to go as a group to meetings held at various places of worship, including a mosque, a Zen center, a synagogue, and several churches. The purpose of both was to communicate information about the variety of religious beliefs and practices in the Madison area. Both were well-received by the few people who participated. But they also drew criticism and were discontinued. The one focused too much on beliefs rather than on building personal relationships, while the other encouraged thinking about organizations and religious categories instead of the ways in which spirituality is actually practiced.

Within two years of its founding, the Madison effort experienced another set of problems. Although it had experienced some success in organizing conferences and getting diverse people together to talk, its leaders recognized that a more formal structure would be necessary if it were to become an ongoing enterprise. The amount of work needing to be done escalated dramatically. In addition to the events it was used to sponsoring, the organization had to go through the process of filing for tax-exempt status as a 501(c)(3) nonprofit organization, make contacts with potential donors, figure out how it was going to pay expenses, and deal with a larger number of people in the community who had their own ideas about how it should proceed. Papcock did much of the work himself, struggling to keep the organization free of community politics and from being viewed as somehow sponsored by the university, and going into debt to cover the organization's mounting costs. When the work became more than he could handle, he tried to scale back, but by this time others had become dependent on his efforts. Asked to take up the mantle of involvement themselves, a number of his supporters fell away.

Two years later, Paprock himself left the organization after a falling out with some of the other leaders about which activities should receive priority. Although some of the activities have continued, he feels that his own energies are probably better spent working with established interfaith ministries rather than trying to initiate new work. In retrospect, he is more realistic about what it takes to make such organizations succeed and is still surprised by the negative reactions he experienced.

The Madison case is not atypical. It illustrates what leaders in other communities emphasize as well. Religion is something that people care enough about to fight over. Although they may give lip service to interreligious cooperation, barriers must be overcome if such efforts are to succeed. Like any community organization, one of the most significant barriers is the apathy that stems from hectic work and family schedules. People have little time to spend helping their own religious organizations, let alone start something new. In addition, it is easy for skepticism, opposition, and factionalism to mount to the point that even the most dedicated leaders are scared away. Contrary to what one might suppose, confronting similarities and differences among beliefs is probably not the best way to begin. Care must also be taken to prevent public labels from getting in the way of actually promoting cooperation.

How Interreligious Efforts Succeed

Although the interreligious organizations that have succeeded are quite diverse, several factors seem to contribute positively to the successes they have experienced. The leaders of nearly all these organizations emphasize that it is more effective to work interpersonally with interested individuals and local groups than to coordinate formal agreements at the top levels of religious hierarchies. Kansas City's Vern Barnett says that "personal relationships" are key. "When you visit each other, pray with each other, break bread together, and work on projects together, you grow strong." This is a reversal of the thinking behind many of the ecumenical efforts among Christian groups a generation or two ago, when hopes of formal unions and mergers were high. By working locally and informally, interreligious coalitions hope to avoid the divisive theological issues that arise when religious bodies seek formal agreements.

A related point is the need to focus on concrete, task-specific objectives. Usually the stated goal of these organizations is to promote understanding and cooperation among religious groups; yet the best strategy for achieving this goal is not to pursue it directly, but to identify other needs and interests on which to work, letting understanding and cooperation emerge as by-products of these efforts. Usually these activities take the form of humanitarian programs for the whole community, such as disaster relief, medical care, poverty assistance, aid for women and children, reduction in the use of land mines, or the promotion of peace.[11]

Working on shared tasks provides an opportunity for participants to become personally acquainted. "Creating a community of hospitality and respect allows us to deepen our understandings of each other," the leader of one organization explains, "not in an abstract way, but through conversation and building friendships." The process is similar to what we have observed among spouses in religiously mixed marriages. They do not sit down in advance and hammer out an abstract doctrinal credo. Instead, they negotiate with one another over an extended period of time, figuring out what is really important to them, making compromises, taking stands, and getting on with the daily business of their lives. Working together in small groups on interfaith projects establishes relationships that also break down barriers. The people involved cease to be representatives of whole traditions. Personal characteristics become more important and similarities and differences emerge more clearly.

Although some cooperative efforts are needed to address specific instances of conflict, most leaders insist that cooperation works better when it emerges gradually and under less stressful circumstances. "When you're a parent," one leader observes, "you learn that the absolute worst time to try to create a constructive system of boundaries and appropriate behavior is in the middle of a crisis situation. When your kid's throwing a temper tantrum, that's not the time to sit down and have a reasonable conversation. If we wait for flashpoints, we're in trouble." He suggests "enduring, daily cooperation" of the kind that comes from working together and becoming personally acquainted.

An apparent exception to this pattern of working in noncrisis situations is the World Conference of Religion and Peace (WCRP), an international organization founded in 1970 that specializes in bringing multireligious cooperation to bear on the most troubled places in the world. International secretary general William Vendley spends much of his time helping resolve conflicts in war-ridden countries. He says, "The best way to promote an effective understanding of the other person's commitments and cares, animated by their beliefs, is to operationalize those commitments in shared work." For him, the practical is more effective as a starting point than purely intellectual discussions. But he also stresses the personal: despite focusing on crisis situations, WCRP develops long-term relationships among selected religious leaders; thus, there is a basis for cooperation when their assistance is needed.[12]

An emphasis on the practical and personal means, perhaps ironically, that interreligious cooperation succeeds by deemphasizing the basic theological teachings that are central in all religious traditions. URI's Charles Gibbs observes that he and his colleagues "felt from the beginning that it was a non-starter to bring people together to talk about theology and especially theological differences." The reason, he says, was that theological discussions turn too easily into abstract debates about historic arguments, rather than focusing on the lived realities of faith communities. He encourages participants in interfaith efforts to avoid talking about whose God is bigger, but in humility to offer prayers to their own God for guidance and inspiration.

The bottom line is willingness among those involved to grant legitimacy to the various ways in which the world's religions approach the sacred. Without this—without being able to say that different religions all have some access to the sacred—there is little foundation on which to build other cooperative activities. This is not to say that leaders of interreligious efforts necessarily believe that all paths to the sacred are equally true or effective. They may argue vehemently about the importance of believing in God or following the wisdom of particular texts. But they must be willing to grant respect to the other traditions—respect that recognizes the sincerity and seriousness with which followers of other religions practice their faith.

What Else Needs to be Done

Although interreligious organizations can play an important role in promoting reflective pluralism, the front line of American religion is still composed of clergy and lay leaders in local congregations. As clergy minister in religiously diverse neighborhoods and as they deal more often with religiously mixed families, their knowledge of other religions needs to increase. To this end, some seminaries are requiring students to take at least one course in comparative religion or a religion other than Christianity. Seminaries are beginning to supplement regular course offerings by hosting guest speakers with expertise in other religions or in interfaith relationships. Students aspiring to congregational ministries are encouraged to pursue internships in religiously diverse settings, such as interfaith service agencies or hospitals, in addition to the time they may spend in congregations.

J. Dudley Woodberry, who teaches courses in Islam at Fuller Seminary, says the goal to which seminary programs should aspire is understanding and dialogue. Understanding requires study and instruction; dialogue comes about through formal "bridge programs" and informal relationships. "Dialogue," he says, "means willingness to speak and to listen and to learn. It doesn't mean that you give up your own truth claims, although you certainly are open to them being challenged."

Seminary students and clergy might also be encouraged to examine the managerial and therapeutic models that have gained such prominence in pastoral settings. Rather than being guided by administrative considerations or the desire to be personally congenial, clergy might emphasize the theological messages that lie at the heart of their ministries. Too often, the managerial and therapeutic models prove to be the course of least resistance. Stressing theology will lead to questions about the differences among religions, forcing clarity and sharpening comparisons. But difference also leads to discussion, and discussion within the context of supportive congregations and loving families can become a strong bond in itself. Certainly there is interest among many interfaith couples in having opportunities to ponder the differences and similarities among their respective religious traditions.

While representatives of all religions, not just Christianity, would benefit from paying greater attention to religious diversity, Christian clergy have a special obligation to do so. Because of ministering to the majority, they may overlook religious diversity more easily than the leaders of minority religions. The history of Christian exclusivism challenges them to think theologically about their relationships with other faiths. Many may feel that they should focus first on understanding the divisions within Christianity before turning to wider horizons. Yet, as important as the differences are between Methodists and Baptists or Lutherans and Presbyterians, the greater cultural challenge is not here; it is between Christianity and other religions.

Extrapolating to Other Kinds of Diversity

Religious diversity is different from other kinds of diversity: cynically (in the eyes of some) because it matters less than racial or ethnic or gender diversity, or less cynically, in that it involves long-standing beliefs and practices overseen by clergy. Religious diversity is nevertheless closely associated with ethnic and racial diversity and with differences in national origin. The lessons that emerge from considering how the public thinks about religious diversity apply to these other kinds of diversity as well.

What people in interreligious settings have learned about breaking down categorical distinctions clearly applies to other forms of social and cultural difference. Individualism is often maligned in scholarly circles because it seems to focus too much on the self and not enough on social bonds within the community. But pluralism appears to work best when it emphasizes the individual. People learn to relate to one another as unique individuals, rather than as representatives of social categories. Doing so breaks down stereotypes that hinder social interaction and understanding. The process of individuation is as important for overcoming racial and ethnic stereotyping as it is for promoting greater interreligious understanding. Individualism of this kind also promotes character. Rather than falling back on categorical distinctions, people have to focus on individual talents and accomplishments as they interact with others—an emphasis that reinforces considerations of the worth of the individual.

Interreligious relationships also carry broader implications about the limits of assimilation. In recent years much concern has been expressed about the perceived fragmentation of American society. Social critics have worried about the apparent centrifugality of so-called identity politics in which ethnic and racial groups went their own way and in which special interest groups of all kinds were tempted to follow suit. It would be better, some of these critics suggested, if everyone focused on what they had in common, such as their love of freedom or their devotion to family. Religious differences are worth special attention in relation to these arguments. Religious differences may seem so superficial that they should be overthrown in favor of common humanitarian values. Yet religious differences are actually quite deeply rooted. Their strength lies in their distinctive practices, rituals, and teachings. The same is true for many groups defined by ethnic, racial, and regional distinctions. Genuine pluralism will take these differences into account, respecting them and upholding them. Pluralism of this kind stands in opposition to what the philosopher Joseph Raz has called "supermarket liberalism."[13] It resists reducing genuine group differences to a flat set of ideas that encourages all people to be the same.

The complex relationships between religion, race, and ethnicity also need to be considered in thinking about religious pluralism. Many more of the religious leaders we spoke to had thought about racial inequality, for instance, than had spent much time thinking about other religions. Decades of discussion about civil rights and about racial discrimination had made an impression on them. Yet it was also the case that those who had thought most about interreligious relationships had also focused the most attention on racial and ethnic diversity. The two went hand in hand. Leaders who thought it important to reach out in their communities to other religious groups could scarcely ignore the fact that some of these groups were composed of people from different racial or ethnic backgrounds than their own. They were forced to think about prejudice, discrimination, and inequality, and to identify ways of addressing these problems.

The Challenges Ahead

If the argument of this book is correct, pluralism is not so much a matter of how many or how few new immigrants are absorbed into American life or of how different or similar their religious traditions and lifestyles may be but a challenge to all Americans about their sense of identity and their strength of character as individuals and as a people. This may seem like a challenge that does not matter very much, compared with, say, keeping our families intact or securing our borders. But if there is anything to be learned from the historical and the contemporary evidence I have presented here, it is that our identity as a people does matter, and that identity is deeply affected by how we think about religion.

Living in homogeneous enclaves with people from similar backgrounds may be the common experience of people throughout history, but it is no longer the reality of the world in which we live today. We can think of ourselves as Americans who share a great deal—from our unifying governmental structures and laws to our exposure to common advertisements and forms of entertainment. But pluralism demands that we also come to terms with our differences, making choices about who we want to be and how to relate to those who do not share our beliefs and practices. Several challenges loom especially large as we think about these choices.

Religious, Secular, or a Little of Both

Any consideration of religious pluralism must start with questions about how religious or secular we wish to be as a society. Americans have often taken pride in the extent of their religious commitments, especially compared with countries in Europe with exceptionally low rates of religious participation. At the same time, we have jealously sought to protect our way of life from unwanted interference on the part of religious leaders. Both our democratic form of government and our commitment to the principles of a free market economy depend on this freedom from religious interference. At present, we vacillate between wanting to think of ourselves as a religious people and enjoying not having to pay much attention to religious teachings when they do not suit us.

During the nineteenth and twentieth centuries, most Americans resolved the tension between religion and secularity by tacitly accepting the myth that the United States was basically Christian. It was Christian enough to encourage those who wished to attend church faithfully to do so, and it was Christian enough in other respects to acknowledge such tenets of personal morality, honesty, decency, freedom, and neighborliness as were deemed compatible with Christianity. That myth is harder to sustain in the face of ever more apparent religious diversity. We must now confront the more difficult question of how to think about religion in general. Do we, for instance, favor religious groups (all of them) simply because they are religious? Or do we treat religions in the same way we do fraternal organizations, self-help groups, and community associations?

The first option—favoring all religious groups—implies that we think religion is somehow special, either because it contributes importantly to personal and collective life or because we worry about it being in special danger as a result of governmental intrusion. But thinking that religion in all its variety is a category of social life that we need to uphold or protect clearly depends on assumptions about the nature of religion. So does the second option, especially if religion is evaluated chiefly in terms of its contribution to social betterment, rather than being regarded as something intrinsically worthwhile. These alternatives require informed judgments to be made about the nature of religion, the similarities and differences among religious traditions, and the ways in which we judge their contributions to social life.

There are not easy grounds on which to make these judgments. Nevertheless, we have been in recent years in the midst of a growing debate about how much or how little religion should be a part of our public life. People line up as strong defenders of the idea that religion is too important to be excluded from the public arena, and on the other side, argue just as strongly that public life is better conducted in terms of secular understandings of fairness and justice alone. The irony is that none of these discussions pays very much attention to the fact that religion is far more diverse than it used to be. It simply does not work to argue that public displays of religion such as a plaque bearing the Ten Commandments or an appeal to God's blessings are appropriate because all religions believe in the same God. They do not, at least not if we understand that *how we believe* is inscribed in the particularity of our religious traditions. Public leaders, including clergy, need to be held accountable for such arguments.

Reconciling Civic Pluralism and Religious Commitment

One of the main conclusions that emerges from talking extensively with people about religious diversity is that there are two discourses—two languages—in which people are accustomed to speaking, and these discourses often become entangled and confused. The language of civic pluralism is pervasive. It is essentially a language of rights and of tolerance. We emphasize in this discourse the legal way of looking at things. When confronted with people of ethnic or religious backgrounds different from our own, we assert that of course they should have the right to live wherever they want, attend public school, vote, and do whatever they want to as long as it does not threaten public safety. The language of civic pluralism often extends further, suggesting, for instance, that our nation is strong because it has embraced diversity and that we are, each one of us, good people because we can flourish amidst a world of diversity. All this is well and good, contributing to the core culture that holds us together and permits us to live in relative harmony. But it does not always coincide perfectly with our understandings of religion.

The language of religious commitment is for at least a large minority of the public more exclusivistic. It asserts that there is value in being able to share deeply with like-minded people and in passing along particularistic values to one's children. It champions possibilities of truth and of virtues such as goodness or courage or altruism that stand above relativistic conceptions of civic life. For some, religious commitment entails ideas about divinity that are not so easily reconciled with the view that all religions are simply human attempts to express some longing for the sacred. In nearly any conception, religious commitment implies standards by which to judge what is good and bad in one's own tradition and, by implication, the responsibility of being ready to make similar judgments about other traditions that happen to be within one's purview.

The tension between civic and religious discourse is healthy; indeed, American democracy would be diminished without both. But tension implies a willingness to uphold both and to respect the differences between them, rather than opting for an easy blend of the two. Many of us are unwilling to go to the trouble of maintaining this tension. We want an easy least-common-denominator civic culture that prevents us from having to struggle with basic tensions in our values. Or we fear that the alternative is a society riven with factionalism as a result of special interest groups fighting for their views. We need to take the time to reflect more thoughtfully on these matters, whether we do so in educational settings, in civic associations, or in our places of worship.

True-Believing Congregations, Open-Minded Individuals

Greater exposure to the variety of world religions is not for everyone. Many Americans find it is all they can do to be faithful to the God they know through their local congregation, and they would be disappointed if the clergy did not provide a strong rationale for being members of a particular faith. Many others are willing to live in the present, focusing on the daily joys of work and family, and turning to religion in rare moments of crisis and reflection. They too would be surprised if religious institutions offered a little of this and a little of that, rather than being true to their historic understanding of faith. But for the few—the restless souls who have been unable to confine their faith to a single tradition—learning more about other religions will be richly rewarding. Some will be drawn away from the faith in which they were raised. Most will probably discover within themselves a deeper desire to understand their own faith and to serve on the basis of that understanding. Charles Gibbs of URI expresses this view well when he says, "I've been challenged again and again and again to be as faithful a Christian as I've seen people being faithful Muslims or Hindus or Buddhists or Jews or Zoroastrians or Jains."

Open-mindedness is a civic virtue that is highly regarded in democratic societies like ours. Yet it must be weighed carefully against the virtues of faithfulness and truth that are central to religion. In concrete terms, open-mindedness should include respect for those who appear not to be open-minded. Religious pluralism can only remain genuinely respectful of religious diversity if it accepts as legitimate the power of deeply held religious convictions in personal and public life. Some of these convictions may seem narrow or dogmatic to the casual observer. Respect must also extend to those who wish, in a spirit of goodwill and without reliance on coercion or legislation, to share their ideas in hopes of persuading others to join their faith.

Theological Inquiry and Theological Reflection

Within the realm of religion itself, the greatest challenge is finding suitable theological understandings with which to make sense of American Christianity in the context of increasing religious pluralism. Although theological reflection is a dry topic that sparks the typical American's interest far less than discussions of spirituality or intense religious experiences, it remains important. As we have seen, grassroots views of other religions are inextricably entwined in churchgoers' beliefs about God, the Bible, Jesus, churchgoing, conversion, and what it means to lead a Christian life. These grassroots understandings need to be nurtured and deepened. Theological inquiry and reflection are ongoing tasks, linking the traditions of biblical and ecclesiological wisdom to the changing cultural circumstances of each era. It is not surprising, therefore, that theology has not yet come to terms with the challenges of pluralism. But it will be harder for serious theologians to escape these challenges in the future.

Only a few broad outlines of where theological reflection may be headed can be suggested here. One direction that appears promising to a number of religious leaders is paying closer attention to the meanings of the biblical view of God as love. Insofar as love is both divine and human, this teaching suggests that there may be a spirit of love built into the very fabric of the universe—perhaps evident in the restorative cycle of nature itself—or at least as a significant part of human life, including the will to live, the desire to conquer illness and death, and the inevitable longing for nurture and companionship.[14] Love is easily misperceived as a kind of warm, emotionally gratifying feeling. But a nuanced understanding of love also recognizes the destructive forces against which it is pitted. Love is particularly suitable as a focal point for theological reflection amidst pluralism because it suggests the need for openness and understanding in dealing with others of different religious persuasions. In this respect, Christian love and tolerance *properly understood* turn out to have much in common, as Jacques Derrida has reminded us.[15] Yet, as Derrida also observes, the challenge for Christians is to move beyond colonizing the idea of tolerance. Claiming special provenance for tolerance can be a form of Christian imperialism not unlike the associations drawn between Christianity and progress in an earlier era.

For American Christians, an emphasis on divine love cannot be separated from teachings about Jesus and, in turn, understandings of the Bible that give Christians a particular sense of relating to the sacred. One of the more significant developments in interpreting these teachings is to regard them as *sufficient* for salvation rather than necessary. "The Bible represents the word of God and contains all things necessary for salvation" is how one theologian described this interpretation, noting that the Bible and especially the life of Jesus show fully how God relates to humankind. Although this view is clearly a departure from teachings that regard Christianity as the only way to salvation, it preserves a distinctive role for the church at the same time that it makes room for possibilities of knowing God outside of Christianity.

Insofar as theological inquiry focuses on understandings of God in the broadest sense, it must also take into explicit consideration the full range of religious traditions. Perspectives on comparative religions currently emphasize the profound differences among the various traditions, as well as some of their similarities. As familiarity increases, understanding of the variations within traditions also increases. Whereas earlier interpretations stressed the functional equivalence of different religions, more recent views focus on the ways in which religious practices have been influenced by cultural variations. At the same time, this awareness of cultural influences means having to make of life what one has been given, and in that local context choosing to be faithful to the understanding of God that one has attained. Thanks-Giving Square's director, Elisabeth Esperson, illustrates this point when she observes, "I have come to know over many years that there is no way to live except with a desire to do the will of God and to be attentive to that will and to find that will in the opportunities for work and relationships and prayer, both alone and with other people."

In the final analysis, theological interpretation must pay careful attention to both the positive and negative aspects of religion. Although religious traditions may be the special ways in which God is revealed and in which humankind is called into a relationship with God, these traditions have frequently been harnessed to some of the most diabolical impulses in the human spirit. The virtue of American religion, it is often said, is that pluralism permits people to draw comparisons, sorting out the good from the bad, and at least to be more mindful of the options set before them. As pluralism increases, some increase in competitiveness and even conflict among religious traditions may also be expected. Competition alone will not ensure that the best in religion triumphs over the worst. But mindfulness of the comparisons among teachings and practices can generate valuable consideration of their relative strengths and weaknesses. America cannot reap the fullest benefits from the growing religious diversity in its midst by simply accepting it or ignoring it. Religious pluralism will prove most enriching if it results in a practice of sustained critical reflection about the unwavering human desire for transcendence.

NOTES

Introduction. Confronting Diversity

1. Immigration and Naturalization Service, *Statistical Yearbook of the Immigration and Naturalization Service* (Washington, D.C.: Government Printing Office, 2001), table 1. Figure cited in text refers to 1965 through 1999; this figure does not include an estimated seven million undocumented immigrants.

2. Evidence on contact between American Christians and Muslims, Buddhists, and Hindus is presented in chapter 7; the social characteristics of American Muslims, Buddhists, and Hindus are discussed in chapter 2. See also Robert Wuthnow and Conrad Hackett, "The Social Integration of Practitioners of Non-Western Religions in the United States," *Journal for the Scientific Study of Religion* 42 (December 2003): 651–67.

3. H. Richard Niebuhr, *The Social Sources of Denominationalism* (New York: World, 1929), remains the classic statement about this kind of diversity.

4. This was done by using an online mapping service that provides Geographic Information Systems (GIS) locations for each organization and the distances between it and all churches in the area; if no churches were located within one mile of the non-Christian organization, a different non-Christian organization within the same tradition was identified.

5. Members were selected from a list of candidates nominated by pastors, who were asked to provide names of people in their congregations fitting various profiles of age, gender, education level, and level of involvement.

6. Respondents in interreligious marriages were identified through a network sampling method starting with referrals from the Christian clergy and non-Christian religious leaders in the fourteen cities; respondents with eclectic religious practices were identified through a network sampling method starting with informants in two previous research projects who were asked about people who might fit this description.

7. The interviews with local and national leaders lasted from fifteen minutes to an hour; all the other interviews lasted approximately an hour and a half. Material from interviews with local and national leaders is presented mainly in

chapters 1 and 9; with non-Christian leaders and members in chapter 3; with church members in chapters 4, 5, and 6; with Christian pastors in chapter 8; and with interreligious couples in chapter 9.

8. The Religion and Diversity Survey was conducted between September 18, 2002, and February 25, 2003, by SRBI Associates in New York City. Up to nineteen attempts were made to complete an interview at every sampled telephone number; all respondents were offered a ten dollar incentive, and two mailings were sent to nonresponding households. Weighted results are presented whenever descriptive statements from the survey are made; in multivariate analysis, unweighted data are used in order to generate accurate estimates of statistical significance. Most of the questions are reported verbatim in chapter 7 (or elsewhere in the text); the full interview guide is available from the author (*Religion and Diversity Codebook*, Princeton University, Department of Sociology, 2003).

Chapter 1. A Special People in a Diverse World

1. Max Weber, *Sociology of Religion* (Boston: Beacon Press, 1963 [1922]).

2. The point here about societies defining themselves in relation to that which they are not runs parallel to that of Edward W. Said, *Orientalism* (New York: Random House, 1978); however, the Weberian interpretation is quite different from the structuralist and Freudian theory from which Said's argument derives—different in that it assumes neither that an "other" is a society's primary means of self-identification nor that an "other" will be present unless there is also the kind of cosmicizing framework that Weber describes.

3. The notion of America as a chosen people has of course been widely emphasized; e.g., Robert N. Bellah, *The Broken Covenant: American Civil Religion in Time of Trial* (New York: Seabury, 1975), chaps. 2–3; Conrad Cherry, ed., *God's New Israel: Religious Interpretations of American Destiny* (Englewood Cliffs, N.J.: Prentice-Hall, 1971). What has been less emphasized are the implications of this notion for American understandings of religions other than Christianity.

4. Christopher Columbus, *The* Diario *of Christopher Columbus's First Voyage to America, 1492–1493*, abstracted by Fray Bartolomé de las Casas, trans. Oliver Dunn and James E. Kelley Jr. (Norman, Okla.: University of Oklahoma Press, 1991).

5. Donald J. Kagay, "Columbus as Standardbearer and Mirror of the Spanish Reconquest," *American Neptune* 53 (1993): 254–57; John Leddy Phelan, *The Millennial Kingdom of the Franciscans in the New World*, 2nd ed. (Berkeley and Los Angeles: University of California Press, 1970), chap. 2.

6. Pauline Moffitt Watts, "Prophecy and Discovery: On the Spiritual Origins of Christopher Columbus's 'Enterprise of the Indies,' " *American Historical Review* 90 (Fall 1985): 73–102.

7. Columbus, Diario, 69. He was not alone in this view; for instance, Amerigo Vespucci's *Mundus Novus,* published in 1504–5, described the natives of Brazil as being devoid of church or religion; Robert F. Berkhofer Jr., *The White Man's Indian: Images of the American Indian from Columbus to the Present* (New York: Knopf, 1978), 8. Giovanni da Verrazano and Samuel de Champlain also believed the Indians had no religion; Bernard W. Sheehan, *Savagism and Civility: Indians and Englishmen in Colonial Virginia* (Cambridge: Cambridge University Press, 1980), 42; W. L. Grant, ed., *Voyages of Samuel de Champlain, 1604–1618* (New York: Charles Scribner's Sons, 1907), 321; James Axtell, *The Invasion Within: The Contest of Cultures in Colonial North America* (New York: Oxford University Press, 1985), 12–13.

8. Columbus, Diario, 121.

9. Ibid., 127.

10. Ibid., 133, 139.

11. Ibid.,, 143, 184–85.

12. Roger A. Johnson, "To Conquer and Convert: The Theological Tasks of the Voyages of Columbus," *Soundings* 76 (Spring 1993): 19–28.

13. H. R. Trevor-Roper, *The European Witch-Craze of the Sixteenth and Seventeenth Centuries* (New York: Harper & Row, 1967).

14. Protestants sometimes likened Indians' devil worship to that of Catholics; see Karen Ordahl Kupperman, *Settling with the Indians: The Meeting of English and Indian Cultures in America, 1580–1640* (Totowa, N.J.: Rowman and Littlefield, 1980), 64.

15. Francis Jennings, *The Invasion of America: Indians, Colonialism, and the Cant of Conquest* (Chapel Hill: University of North Carolina Press, 1975), chap. 4; Sheehan, *Savagism and Civility,* chap. 2; "Satan knew his friends. He knew that ignoble savages would follow his command in seeking to devour the innocent and the virtuous. Thus Indians became more than dangerous savages in the European imagination; they became the agents of demoniacal ruin" (p. 38). See also Luis N. Rivera, *A Violent Evangelism: The Political and Religious Conquest of the Americas* (Louisville: Westminster / John Knox Press, 1990); and Richard Beale Davis, *Intellectual Life in the Colonial South, 1585–1763* (Knoxville: University of Tennessee Press, 1978), 176–88.

16. Jennings, *Invasion of America,* 53–56.

17. Among early eighteenth-century writers, Father Joseph François Lafitau is a notable example of the belief in common religious origins and degeneracy, writing in *Customs of the American Indians Compared with the Customs of Primitive*

Times (Toronto: Champlain Society, 1974 [1724]), 99, that "from the depths of these religions, vitiated and monstrous as they are, one can draw, as it were, a proof that they are based on the true religion, corrupted and altered so as to be almost unrecognizable."

18. Berkhofer, *White Man's Indian*, 36–38.

19. Kupperman, *Settling with the Indians*, 73–79.

20. Roger Williams, *A Key into the Language of America*, ed. John J. Teunissen and Evelyn J. Hinz (Detroit: Wayne State University Press, 1973 [1643]), 189–200; see also Karen Ordahl Kupperman, *Indians and English: Facing Off in Early America* (Ithaca, N.Y.: Cornell University Press, 2000).

21. Mason I. Lowance Jr., "Cotton Mather's *Magnalia* and the Metaphors of Biblical History," in *Typology and Early American Literature*, ed. Sacvan Bercovitch (Amherst, Mass.: University of Massachusetts Press, 1972), 139–60; Reiner Smolinksi, "*Israel Redivivus*: The Eschatological Limits of Puritan Typology in New England," *New England Quarterly* 63 (September 1990): 357–95; Cecelia Tichi, "The Puritan Historians and Their New Jerusalem," *Early American Literature* 6 (Fall 1971): 143–55.

22. Kenneth Silverman, *The Life and Times of Cotton Mather* (New York: Harper & Row, 1984), 238.

23. Conrad Cherry, "New England as Symbol: Ambiguity in the Puritan Vision," *Soundings* 58 (Fall 1975): 351.

24. Quotation from John Higginson's "Attestation" to Cotton Mather, *Magnalia Christi Americana; or The Ecclesiastical History of New England* (Hartford: Silas Andrus & Son, 1853 [1702]), 7.

25. R. Pierce Beaver, "American Missionary Motivation before the Revolution," *Church History* 31 (June 1962): 216–26; Stephen J. Stein, "Transatlantic Extensions: Apocalyptic in Early New England," in *The Apocalypse in English Renaissance Thought and Literature: Patterns, Antecedents, and Repercussions*, ed. C. A. Patrides and Joseph Anthony Wittreich (Manchester: Manchester University Press, 1984), 266–98.

26. George M. Marsden, *Jonathan Edwards: A Life* (New Haven, Conn.: Yale University Press, 2003), is now the definitive biography of Edwards.

27. Gerald R. McDermott, "The Deist Connection: Jonathan Edwards and Islam," in *Jonathan Edwards's Writings: Text, Context, Interpretation*, ed. Stephen J. Stein (Bloomington: Indiana University Press, 1996), chap. 3; Gerald R. McDermott, "A Possibility of Reconciliation: Jonathan Edwards and the Salvation of Non-Christians," in *Edwards in Our Time: Jonathan Edwards and the Shaping of American Religion*, ed. Sang Hyun Lee and Allen C. Guelzo (Grand Rapids, Mich.: Eerdmans, 1999), pp. 173–202; and Gerald R. McDermott, *Jonathan Edwards*

Confronts the Gods: Christian Theology, Enlightenment Religion, and Non-Christian Faiths (New York: Oxford University Press, 2000).

28. Jonathan Edwards, "Man's Natural Blindness in the Things of Religion," in *The Works of Jonathan Edwards* (Peabody, Mass.: Hendrickson, 1998 [1834]), 2:247–56.

29. Jonathan Edwards, "Mahometanism Compared with Christianity—Particularly with Respect to Their Propagation," in *The Works of Jonathan Edwards* (Peabody, Mass.: Hendrickson, 1998 [1834]), 2:491–93.

30. Jonathan Edwards, *The Miscellanies*, ed, Thomas A. Schafer, vol. 13 of *The Works of Jonathan Edwards,* ed. Harry S. Stout (New Haven: Yale University Press, 1994), 213–14.

31. Earl R. MacCormac, "Jonathan Edwards and Missions," *Journal of the Presbyterian Historical Society* 39 (December 1961): 219–29.

32. M. Darrol Bryant, "America as God's Kingdom," in *Religion and Political Society,* ed. Jurgen Moltmann, Herbert W. Richardson, Johann Baptist Metz, Willi Oelmuller, and M. Darrol Bryant (New York: Harper & Row, 1974), 54–94.

33. Jonathan Edwards, "Importance of a Future State," in *Sermons and Discourses, 1720–1723*, ed. Wilson H. Kimnach, vol. 10 of *The Works of Jonathan Edwards*, ed. Harry S. Stout (New Haven: Yale University Press, 1993), 360. Of natural reason compelling belief in the immortality of the soul, for instance, Edwards writes: "It is not only Christians that own it, but Jews, Mahometans and heathens do all believe it. . . . Even the barbarously ignorant Indians here in America have light enough to believe that, for they do all believe it, and did before ever they heard of Christians."

34. Ronald E. Davies, "Jonathan Edwards: Missionary Biographer, Theologian, Strategist, Administrator, Advocate—and Missionary," *International Bulletin of Missionary Research* (April 1997): 60–67.

35. Sacvan Bercovitch, "The Typology of America's Mission," *American Quarterly* 30 (Summer 1978): 135–55.

36. Bernard Bailyn, *The Ideological Origins of the American Revolution* (Cambridge, Mass.: Harvard University Press, 1967), 32.

37. Ernest Lee Tuveson, *Redeemer Nation: The Idea of America's Millennial Role* (Chicago: University of Chicago Press, 1968).

38. Alan Heimert, *Religion and the American Mind: From the Great Awakening to the Revolution* (Cambridge, Mass.: Harvard University Press, 1966), 59.

39. Harry S. Stout, *The Divine Dramatist: George Whitefield and the Rise of Modern Evangelicalism* (Grand Rapids, Mich.: Eerdmans, 1991).

40. The idea of "theistic perspectivism" is developed particularly in reference to Franklin in Kerry S. Walters, *Benjamin Franklin and His Gods* (Urbana: University of Illinois Press, 1999).

41. Quoted in Charles B. Sanford, *The Religious Life of Thomas Jefferson* (Charlottesville: University of Virginia Press, 1984), 28.

42. Ibid., 11–15.

43. Francis W. Hirst, *Life and Letters of Thomas Jefferson* (New York: Macmillan, 1926), 16.

44. Thomas Jefferson, *The Writings of Thomas Jefferson*, ed. Albert Ellery Berch (Washington, D.C.: Thomas Jefferson Memorial Association, 1905), digital text.

45. Joseph Priestley, *Discourses Relating to the Evidences of Revealed Religion* (Philadelphia: John Thompson, 1796), esp. 56–113.

46. Robert E. Schofield, *The Enlightenment of Joseph Priestley: A Study of His Life and Work from 1733 to 1773* (University Park: Pennsylvania State University Press, 1997), 159–201.

47. Ibid., 72.

48. John Adams, *The Adams-Jefferson Letters*, ed. Lester J. Cappon (Chapel Hill: University of North Carolina Press, 1959), 343–45; Adams, "Letter to Jefferson," in Jefferson, *Writings*, 13: 291–95; also George Washington, *On Religious Liberty and Mutual Understanding*, ed. Edward Frank Humphrey (Washington, D.C.: National Conference of Catholics, Jews, Protestants, 1932).

49. Clifton Jackson Phillips, *Protestant American and the Pagan World: The First Half Century of the American Board of Commissioners for Foreign Missions, 1810–1860* (Cambridge, Mass.: Harvard University Press, 1969), chap. 9. Phillips emphasizes that the missionaries' idea of brotherhood among men was qualified by an explicit repudiation of the idea that "the various systems of paganism are only so many diversified forms of the true religion" (p. 270).

50. William R. Hutchison, *Errand to the World: American Protestant Thought and Foreign Missions* (Chicago: University of Chicago Press, 1987), 1; American Board of Commissioners for Foreign Missions, *Memorial Volume of the First Fifty Years* (Boston: American Board of Commissioners for Foreign Missions, 1861).

51. R. G. Wilder, *Mission Schools in India of the American Board of Commissioners for Foreign Missions* (New York: A.D.F. Randolph, 1861), 11.   ·

52. Quoted in ibid., 12.

53. An earlier example of an optimistic appraisal is M. B. Hope, "An Aspect of the Age with Respect to Foreign Missions," *Princeton Review* 5 (October 1833): 449–62.

54. William Butler, *The Land of the Veda: Being Personal Reminiscences of India* (New York: Carlton & Lanahan, 1872), 56.

55. Edward Thomson, *Our Oriental Missions, vol. 1: India and China* (Cincinnati: Hitchcock and Walden, 1870), 148, 152, 153.

56. On Anderson's pivotal role in American foreign missions, see Paul William Harris, *Nothing but Christ: Rufus Anderson and the Ideology of Protestant Foreign Missions* (New York: Oxford University Press, 1999); and Andrew Porter, "Language, 'Native Agency,' and Missionary Control: Rufus Anderson's Journey to India, 1854–5," in *Missions and Missionaries*, ed. Pieter N. Holtrop and Hugh McLeod (Rochester, N.Y.: Boydell Press, 2000), 81–97.

57. Rufus Anderson, *Foreign Missions: Relations and Claims* (Boston: Congregational Publishing House, 1874), 18: "With our railroads, steamships, and telegraph wires; with our electrotyping and power presses; our sciences, arts, and commerce; with neither Hun, Vandal, nor Moslem to set back the tide of civilization, who does not see that the time for blessing the whole earth with the gospel has come, and that this is the grand business of the churches in our day?"

58. Quoted in Wilder, *Mission Schools in India*, 22.

59. Anderson, *Foreign Missions*, 118–19.

60. Hutchison, *Errand to the World*, 92.

61. Ibid., 91.

62. Roman Catholic writers appeared less confident of Christian progress through American efforts than Protestants did; e.g., T.W.M. Marshall, *Christian Missions: Their Agents and Their Results* (New York: Sadlier, 1864), 2–4.

63. James S. Dennis, *Christian Missions and Social Progress: A Sociological Study of Foreign Missions*, 3 vols. (New York: Fleming Revell, 1897–1906).

64. J. T. Gracey, "The Hindoo and His Reason Why," *Ladies Repository* 2 (December 1875): 540.

65. On this emphasis, including its expression among American sociologists at the turn of the century, see Paul A. Vary, "Motives in Protestant Missions, 1890–1917," in *Modern American Protestantism and Its World: Historical Articles on Protestantism in American Religious Life*, vol. 13, *Missions and Ecumenical Expressions*, ed. Martin E. Marty (Munich: K. G. Saur, 1993), 3–19.

66. Louis Henry Jordan, *Comparative Religion: Its Genesis and Growth* (Edinburgh: T. and T. Clark, 1905), 146.

67. These works are discussed briefly in Sydney E. Ahlstrom, *The American Protestant Encounter with World Religions: The Brewer Lectures on Comparative Religion* (Beloit, Wis.: Beloit College, 1962), chap. 2.

68. James W. Redfield, *Comparative Physiognomy; or, Resemblances between Men and Animals* (New York: Redfield, 1852), 70–71; Orestes A. Brownson, *The American Republic: Its Constitution, Tendencies, and Destiny* (New York: O'Shea, 1866), 27.

69. Susan B. Anthony, *An Account of the Proceedings on the Trial of Susan B. Anthony* (Rochester, N.Y.: Daily Democrat, 1874), 28; Dawson Burns, *The Bases*

of Temperance Reform: An Exposition and Appeal (New York: National Temperance Society, 1873), 207–8.

70. Jefferson, *Writings*, 7: 267.

71. Western interest in Sanskrit developed largely through British rule in India, which, by the treaty of Allahabad in 1765, involved governing Hindu subjects according to Hindu laws. In 1784 the Asiatic Society of Bengal was formed under the direction of William Jones, H. T. Colebrooke, and Charles Wilkins; Jones became particularly interested in the affinities among Sanskrit, Greek, and Latin.

72. Muller's translation of the Rig Veda was funded by the East India Company; Muller's contributions in relation to the missionary movement are discussed in Harvie M. Conn, *Eternal Word and Changing Worlds: Theology, Anthropology, and Mission in Trialogue* (Grand Rapids, Mich.: Academie, 1984), 58–59.

73. F. Max Muller, *Lectures on the Origin and Growth of Religion* (New York: Charles Scribner's Sons, 1899 [originally given in 1878]), 349.

74. Brian Morris, *Anthropological Studies of Religion: An Introductory Text* (Cambridge: Cambridge University Press, 1987), 93.

75. Elman R. Service, "The Mind of Lewis H. Morgan," *Current Anthropology* 22 (February 1981): 25–43.

76. William D. Whitney, "On the So-Called Science of Religion," *Princeton Review*, new series (1881): 451.

77. Charles Hodge, "Early History of Heathenism," *Princeton Review* (July 1865): 321–49; and the survey of literature included in Alice Wayne, "After Babel," *Ladies' Repository* 36 (1876): 401–7.

78. Tomoko Masuzawa, *In Search of Dreamtime: The Quest for the Origin of Religion* (Chicago: University of Chicago Press, 1993), chap. 3; J. Samuel Preus, *Explaining Religion: Criticism and Theory from Bodin to Freud* (New Haven, Conn.: Yale University Press, 1987), chap. 7. Muller's work became the particular focus of criticism by Andrew Lang; see Eric Sharpe, *Comparative Religion: A History* (London: Duckworth, 1975), 58–65.

79. Joseph Campbell, *Hero with a Thousand Faces* (Princeton, N.J.: Princeton University Press, 1972); Joseph Campbell, Bill Moyers, and Betty Sue Flowers, *The Power of Myth* (New York: Doubleday, 1988).

80. Among the many who have written about the World's Parliament, see especially Martin E. Marty, *Modern American Religion*, vol. 1, *The Irony of It All* (Chicago: University of Chicago Press, 1986), 17–31; and Joseph Kitagawa, "The World's Parliament of Religions and Its Legacy," eleventh John Nuveen Lecture (Chicago: University of Chicago Divinity School, 1983), reprinted in *A Museum of Faiths: Histories and Legacies of the 1893 World's Parliament of Religions*, ed. Eric J. Ziolkowski (Atlanta: Scholars Press, 1993), 171–89; quoted in Richard Hughes Seager, "Pluralism and the American Mainstream: The View from the World's

Parliament of Religions," *Harvard Theological Review* 82 (1989): 301–24; see also Marcus Braybrooke, *Pilgrimage of Hope: One Hundred Years of Global Interfaith Dialogue* (New York: Crossroad, 1992), chaps. 1–3.

81. Diana Eck, "Foreword," in *The Dawn of Religious Pluralism: Voices from the World's Parliament of Religions, 1893*, ed. Richard Hughes Seager (Lasalle, Ill.: Open Court Press, 1993), xiv.

82. Quoted in Eric Ziolkowski, "Heavenly Visions and Worldly Intentions: Chicago's Columbian Exposition and World's Parliament of Religions (1893)," *Journal of American Culture* 13 (1990): 11; see also John R. McRae, "Oriental Verities on the American Frontier: The 1893 World's Parliament of Religions and the Thought of Masao Abe," *Buddhist-Christian Studies* 11 (1991): 7–36.

83. Jenny Wiley Legath, "Notes on the World's Parliament of Religions," personal correspondence.

84. Gibbons's participation, although considered a coup by the Parliament's organizers, was reluctant; Dennis B. Downey, "Tradition and Acceptance: American Catholics and the Columbian Exposition," *Mid-America* 63 (1981): 79–92.

85. Swami Vivekananda, "Hinduism," in *The World's Parliament of Religions*, ed. John Henry Barrows (Chicago: Parliament Publishing, 1893), 2: 968–78; Alexander Russell Mohammed Webb, "The Spirit of Islam," in ibid., 2: 989–96; Zitzuzen Ashitzu, "Buddha," in ibid., 2: 1038–40; Virchand A. Gandhi, "The Philosophy and Ethics of the Jains," in ibid. 2:1222–26.

86. See Barrows, ed., *World's Parliament*, vol. 2.

87. Muller's and other responses are discussed in Egal Feldman, "American Ecumenicism: Chicago's World's Parliament of Religions of 1893," *Journal of Church and State* 9 (1967): 180–99.

88. On one of the ensuing controversies over Buddhism, see Larry A. Fader, "Zen in the West: Historical and Philosophical Implications of the 1893 Chicago World's Parliament of Religions," *Eastern Buddhist* 25 (1982): 122–45.

89. Seager, "Pluralism and the American Mainstream."

90. "Christianity and Other Religions," *New York Daily Tribune* (October 1, 1893), 6.

91. From *Following the Equator*, quoted in Stephen Prothero, "Mother India's Scandalous Swamis," in *Religious Practice in the United States*, ed. Colleen McDannell (Princeton, N.J.: Princeton University Press, 2002), 616.

92. Discussed in Prothero, "Mother India's Scandalous Swamis."

93. Robert Ernest Hume, *The World's Living Religions* (New York: Charles Scribner's Sons, 1930), 19.

94. Ibid., 82, 232–33.

95. R. Laurence Moore, *Religious Outsiders and the Making of Americans* (New York: Oxford University Press, 1986), 3–21.

96. Will Herberg, *Protestant-Catholic-Jew: An Essay in American Religious Sociology* (Garden City, N.Y.: Doubleday, 1955).

97. Fred Gladstone Bratton, *The Crime of Christendom: The Theological Sources of Christian Anti-Semitism* (Santa Barbara, Calif.: Fithian Press, 1996); Frederic Cople Jaher, *A Scapegoat in the New Wilderness: The Origins and Rise of Anti-Semitism in America* (Cambridge, Mass.: Harvard University Press, 1994).

98. Gertrude J. Selznick and Stephen Steinberg, *The Tenacity of Prejudice: Anti-Semitism in Contemporary America* (New York: Harper & Row, 1969); Robert Wuthnow, "Anti-Semitism and Stereotyping," in *In the Eye of the Beholder: Prejudice and Stereotyping*, ed. Arthur G. Miller (New York: Praeger, 1982), 137–87.

99. Harry J. Ausmus, *Will Herberg: From Right to Right* (Chapel Hill: University of North Carolina Press, 1987); David G. Dalin, "Introduction," in *From Marxism to Judaism: The Collected Essays of Will Herberg*, ed. David G. Dalin (New York: Markus Wiener, 1989), xiii–xviii; see also Herberg, "After Communism—What?" *The Reconstructionist* 16 (April 7, 1950): 28–32.

100. Franz Rosenzweig was another significant influence on Herberg, causing him to emphasize the "pagan" tendencies in Christianity that he regarded as the true source of Christian anti-Semitism; Herberg, "Rosenzweig's 'Judaism of Personal Existence,' " *Commentary* 10 (December 1950): 541–49.

101. Herberg, *Protestant-Catholic-Jew,* 273; Herberg, "Judaism and Christianity: Their Unity and Difference," in *Jewish Perspectives on Christianity,* ed. Fritz A. Rothschild (New York: Crossroad, 1990), 240–55.

102. Benny Kraut, "A Look from the Outside: Jews and Catholics and the Establishment's Goodwill Movement of the 1920s," in *The Protestant Establishment in the Earlier Twentieth Century,* ed. William R. Hutchison (Cambridge: Cambridge University Press, 1989), pp. 151–69.

103. Benny Kraut, "Towards the Establishment of the National Conference of Christians and Jews: The Tenuous Road to Religious Goodwill in the 1920s," *American Jewish History* 77 (1988): 388–412; Marcus Braybrooke, *Inter-Faith Organizations, 1893–1979: An Historical Directory* (New York: Edwin Mellen Press, 1980), 109–11.

104. James E. Pitt, *Adventures in Brotherhood* (New York: Farrar, Straus, 1955), 29.

105. Gilbert Kollin, "The Impact of the Military Chaplaincy on the American Rabbinate: 1861–1976," in *The American Rabbi,* ed. Gilbert S. Rosenthal (New York: KTAV Publishing, 1977), 23–43; Albert Isaac Slomovitz, *The Fighting Rabbis: Jewish Military Chaplains and American History* (New York: New York University Press, 1999), chaps. 6–7; on interreligious instruction, Pitt, *Adventures in Brotherhood,* 152; on the NCCJ and other efforts during World War II, Wendy L.

Wall, " 'Our Enemies Within': Nazism, National Unity, and America's Wartime Discourse on Tolerance," in *Enemy Images in American History*, ed. R. Fiebig–von Hase and Ursula Lehmkuhl (Berlin: Berghahn Books, 1998), 209–29.

106. I am indebted to Judith Weisenfeld for this connection.

107. H. Richard Niebuhr, *The Social Sources of Denominationalism* (New York: World, 1929).

108. Herberg, *Protestant-Catholic-Jew*, 193.

109. In arguing for greater acceptance of Judaism, Herberg was also an impassioned critic of anti-Catholic sentiment; see, for example, Will Herberg, "The Church and American Politics," *Commentary* 8 (August 1949): 198–200; at the same time, he wrote of worries about antidemocratic tendencies within the American Catholic Church; Herberg, "A Jew Looks at Catholics," *Commonweal* 58 (May 22, 1953): 174–77.

110. For instance, Marshall Sklare, "Third-Generation Religion," *Commentary* 21 (February 1956): 195–96.

111. Seymour Siegel, "Review of *Protestant-Catholic-Jew*," *Judaism: A Quarterly Journal* 5 (Spring 1956): 178–81.

112. S. Joseph Fauman, "Review of *Protestant-Catholic-Jew*," *Jewish Social Studies* 19 (January–April 1957): 83–84; Samuel Sandmel, "For and against Herberg," *Jewish Frontier* 17 (November 1950): 28; Ely E. Pilchik, "Review of *Judaism and Modern Man*," *Jewish Social Studies* 14 (April 1952): 190–91.

113. Mordecai M. Kaplan, "Reflections on the Vatican Communiqué," *The Reconstructionist* 29 (November 29, 1963): 3–4; Arthur Gilbert, "The Council and the Jews," *The Reconstructionist* 29 (January 10, 1964): 6–9.

114. Malcolm L. Diamond, "Catholicism in America: The Emerging Dialogue," *Judaism: A Quarterly Journal* 9 (Fall 1960): 307–18.

115. Herberg, *Protestant-Catholic-Jew*, 257–58.

116. Ibid., 262.

117. Jacob Neusner, "Vatican II on the Jews and Judaism," *The Reconstructionist* 32 (March 4, 1966): 7–12.

118. On the exclusionary aspects of the term *Judo-Christian*, see also Martin E. Marty, "A Judeo-Christian Looks at the Judeo-Christian Tradition," *Christian Century* (October 5, 1986): 858–60.

CHAPTER 2. THE NEW DIVERSITY

1. Derrick Henry, "Hindu Temple of Atlanta," *Atlanta Journal and Constitution*, May 19, 2001, 2B.

2. Felix Hoover, "Local Hindus to Celebrate," *Columbus Dispatch*, August 17, 2001, 1C; Prema Kurien, "Becoming American by Becoming Hindu: Indian Americans Take Their Place at the Multicultural Table," in *Gatherings in Diaspora: Religious Communities and the New Immigration*, eds. R. Stephen Warner and Judith G. Wittner (Philadelphia: Temple University Press, 1998), 37–70.

3. Sri Ventakeswara is the focus of Aparna Rayaprol, *Negotiating Identities: Women in the Indian Diaspora* (New York: Oxford University Press, 1997); see also Diana Eck, *A New Religious America: How a "Christian Country" Has Now Become the Most Religiously Diverse Nation on Earth* (San Francisco: Harper San Francisco, 2001), chap. 3.

4. Herbert Ellinger, *Hinduism*, trans. John Bowden (London: SCM Press, 1995), 10.

5. Lucy G. DuPertuis, "American Adaptations of Hinduism," *Comparative Social Research* 10 (1987): 101–11, emphasizes the tendency in American Hinduism to personify the deity.

6. P. Venugopala Rao, "The Living Sacred Images," *Hindu Temple of Atlanta Consecration Bulletin*, May 24–28, 2000, 15.

7. Hindu leaders often point out that India is more diverse than all of Europe, as a point of reference for thinking about the diversity encompassed by Hinduism.

8. The role of ethnic, language, and regional diversity is also emphasized in Simon Jacob and Pallavi Thaku, "Jyothi Hindu Temple: One Religion, Many Practices," in *Religion and the New Immigrants*, ed. Helen Rose Ebaugh and Janet Saltzman Chafetz (Walnut Creek, Calif.: AltaMira Press, 2000), 229–42.

9. Joanne Punzo Waghorne, "The Hindu Gods in a Split-Level World: The Sri Siva-Vishnu Temple in Suburban Washington, D.C.," in *Gods of the City: Religion and the American Urban Landscape*, ed. Robert A. Orsi (Bloomington: Indiana University Press, 1999), 128–29.

10. On differences among the three temples, see also James D. Davis, "New Hindu Temples Reflect Diversity," *South Florida Sun-Sentinel*, October 28, 1997.

11. Guy L. Beck, *Sonic Theology: Hinduism and Sacred Sound* (Columbia: University of South Carolina Press, 1993), is a wonderful source on the role of music in Hinduism.

12. Raymond Brady Williams, "Swaminarayan Hindu Temple of Glen Ellyn, Illinois," in *American Congregations*, vol. 1, *Portraits of Twelve Religious Communities*, ed. James P. Wind and James W. Lewis (Chicago: University of Chicago Press, 1994), 642.

13. *Veda* can be translated as knowledge or sacred teaching.

14. The word *upanishad* loosely means to sit next to someone, such as a devotee sitting at the feet of a guru; *Bhagavad Gita* is translated as song of the Lord or song of the exalted one.

15. Gerald James Larson, "Hinduism in India and in America," in *World Religions in America*, ed. Jacob Neusner (Louisville: Westminster / John Knox Press, 1994), 177–202, also offers a typology of kinds of Hinduism in the United States.

16. See also Raymond Brady Williams, "Asian Indian and Pakistani Religions in the United States," *Annals of the American Academy of Political and Social Science* 558 (July 1998): 178–95. Some attribute this apparent increase to a shift in the kind of immigrant—from an early majority of men, trained predominately in the sciences and engineering at a time when higher education in India was thoroughly secular, to a wider variety of immigrants more recently and from more diverse backgrounds, including more women with interests in religion; see especially Prema Kurien, "Gendered Ethnicity: Creating a Hindu Indian Identity in the United States," *American Behavioral Scientist* 42 (January 1999): 648–70, which emphasizes the shifting relationship between Indian men and women in this process.

17. Richard Hughes Seager, *Buddhism in America* (New York: Columbia University Press, 1999), places the number of Vietnamese temples in the United States as a whole at approximately 150, and suggests that the majority are located in California.

18. Julie Poppen, "Monument to Buddhism," *Rocky Mountain News*, August 17, 2001, 7A; James W. Coleman, *The New Buddhism: The Western Transformation of an Ancient Tradition* (New York: Oxford University Press, 2001).

19. Don Morreale, ed., *The Complete Guide to Buddhist America* (Boston: Shambhala, 1998).

20. Service provision among similar refugee communities is described in Edward R. Canda and Thitiya Phaobtong, "Buddhism as a Support System for Southeast Asian Refugees," *Journal of the National Association of Social Workers* 37 (January 1992): 61–67. The community center function is also emphasized in a study of His Lai Temple in Los Angeles; Irene Lin, "Journey to the Far West: Chinese Buddhism in America," *Amerasia Journal* 22 (1996): 107–32. On the tendency for Buddhist centers to attract Asian-American "converts," see Carolyn Chen, *Getting Saved in America: Taiwanese Immigrants Converting to Evangelical Christianity and Buddhism* (Princeton, N.J.: Princeton University Press, 2005).

21. Winston L. King, "Theravada in Southeast Asia," in *Buddhist Spirituality: Indian, Southeast Asian, Tibetan, Early Chinese*, ed. Takeuchi Yoshinori (New York: Crossroad, 1993), 79–92.

22. On immigrant and convert Theravada Buddhism, see especially Wendy Cadge, *Heartwood: The First Generation of Theravada Buddhism in America* (Chicago: University of Chicago Press, 2005); see also Paul D. Numrich, *Old Wisdom in the New World: Americanization in Two Immigrant Theravada Buddhist Temples* (Knoxville: University of Tennessee Press, 1996); Gil Fronsdal,

"Theravada Spirituality in the West," in *Buddhist Spirituality: Later China, Korea, Japan, and the Modern World*, ed. Takeuchi Yoshinori (New York: Crossroad, 1999), 482–96; and Gil Fronsdal, "Insight Meditation in the United States: Life, Liberty, and the Pursuit of Happiness," in *The Faces of Buddhism in America*, ed. Charles Prebish and Kenneth Tanaka (Berkeley and Los Angeles: University of California Press, 1998), 163–82.

23. Don Morreale, "Everything Has Changed in Buddhist America," in *The Complete Guide to Buddhist America*, ed. Don Morreale (Boston: Shambhala, 1998), xvi–xvii.

24. Sharon Salzberg, *Lovingkindness: The Revolutionary Art of Happiness* (Boston: Shambhala, 1997); Jack Kornfield, *A Path with Heart: A Guide through the Perils and Promises of Spiritual Life* (New York: Doubleday, 1993).

25. Donald R. Tuck, *Buddhist Churches of America: Jodo Shinshu* (New York: Edwin Mellen Press, 1988).

26. Thomas A. Tweed observes that the U.S. Census of Religious Bodies, conducted in 1906, counted 3,165 Pure Land Buddhists in twelve congregations; Tweed, "General Introduction," in *Asian Religions in America: A Documentary History*, ed. Thomas A. Tweed (New York: Oxford University Press, 1999), 8.

27. Roger J. Corless, "Pure Land Piety," in *Buddhist Spirituality: Indian, Southeast Asian, Tibetan, Early Chinese*, ed. Takeuchi Yoshinori (New York: Crossroad, 1993), 242–74.

28. Alfred Bloom, "The Western Pure Land," *Tricycle: The Buddhist Review* (Summer 1995): 58–63.

29. In 1994, the Buddhist Churches of America counted 17,755 families as members, down from 21,600 in 1977, a decline that leaders attributed to exogenous marriage and other effects of assimilation among descendants of Japanese immigrants; Religious News Service, "Buddhist Group Beset by Membership Drop," *Los Angeles Times*, January 27, 1996, 4.

30. Robert Wuthnow, *Experimentation in American Religion: The New Mysticisms and Their Implications for the Churches* (Berkeley and Los Angeles: University of California Press, 1978), chap. 1.

31. The founding of the Shasta Abbey is described in Charles S. Prebish, *Luminous Passage: The Practice and Study of Buddhism in America* (Berkeley and Los Angeles: University of California Press, 1999), 15–16.

32. Geoffrey Samuel, *Civilized Shamans: Buddhism in Tibetan Societies* (Washington, D.C.: Smithsonian Institution Press, 1995).

33. Karma Triyana Dharmachakra is discussed in Seager, *Buddhism in America*, 125.

34. Muslim explorers from Africa and Spain are thought to have visited the New World in the sixteenth century and Moors from Spain are reported to have lived in South Carolina and Florida in the late eighteenth century; Fareed H. Numan, "American Muslim History: A Chronological Observation" (December 1992), online text www.islam101.com/history/muslim_us_hist.html. Brief accounts of recent Muslim immigration and adaptation are given in Aminah Beverly McCloud, "Islam in America: The Mosaic," in *Religion and Immigration: Christian, Jewish, and Muslim Experiences in the United States*, ed. Yvonne Yazbeck Haddad, Jane I. Smith, and John L. Esposito (Walnut Creek, Calif.: AltaMira Press, 2003), 159–74; and M. A. Muqtedar Khan, "Constructing the American Muslim Community," in ibid., 175–98.

35. See especially Tom Smith, "Religious Diversity in America: The Emergence of Muslims, Buddhists, Hindus, and Others," *Journal for the Scientific Study of Religion* 41, 3 (2002): 577–85; see also Guillermina Jasso, Douglas S. Massey, Mark R. Rosenzweig, and James P. Smith, "Exploring the Religious Preferences of Recent Immigrants to the United States: Evidence from the New Immigrant Survey Pilot," in *Religion and Immigration: Christian, Jewish, and Muslim Experiences in the United States*, ed. Yvonne Yazbeck Haddad, Jane I. Smith, and John L. Esposito (Walnut Creek, Calif.: AltaMira Press, 2003), 217–54.

36. Abdul Malik Mujahid, "Muslims in America: Profile 2001," 2001, online text www.soundvision.com/info/yearinreview/2001/profile.shtml; the 1970 estimate (of five hundred thousand Muslims in the United States) is from Jane I. Smith, *Islam in America* (New York: Columbia University Press, 1999), xii, which is one of the most useful general introductions to the topic.

37. Yvonne Haddad and Adair T. Lummis, *Islamic Values in the United States* (New York: Oxford University Press, 1987), 3ff.

38. Fareed H. Numan, *The Muslim Population in the United States* (Washington, D.C.: American Muslim Council, 1999).

39. Mujahid, "Muslims in America."

40. Mosque Study Project, as summarized in Richard N. Ostling, "Survey of U.S. Muslims Finds a Growing Faith," *Intelligencer Record*, April 27, 2001, B13.

41. Abdul A'la Mawdudi, *Towards Understanding Islam* (Washington, D.C.: Message Publications, 1986), provides a useful introduction to Muslim teachings and beliefs.

42. Mujahid, "Muslims in America," estimates drawn from unpublished studies in Chicago and New York state.

43. This practice of public recitation reflects the Egyptian roots of the Islamic Center; in masjids of Saudi origin the Qur'an is more likely to be read privately prior to the service.

44. Muhammad Abdul-Rauf, *History of the Islamic Center: From Dream to Reality* (Washington, D.C.: Islamic Center, 1978).

45. Ostling, "Survey of U.S. Muslims Finds a Growing Faith."

46. Ibid.

47. Rogaia Mustafa Abusharaf, "Structural Adaptations in an Immigrant Muslim Congregation in New York," in *Gatherings in Diaspora: Religious Communities and the New Immigration*, ed. R. Stephen Warner and Judith G. Wittner (Philadelphia: Temple University Press, 1998), 235–64.

CHAPTER 3. THE SIGNIFICANCE OF RELIGIOUS DIVERSITY

1. These figures and, unless otherwise indicated, other survey results presented in this chapter are from the Religion and Diversity Survey, which was completed in 2003 among a nationally representative sample of 2,910 adults; additional details about the survey were given in the Introduction.

2. I have discussed the changing meanings of freedom in *After Heaven: Spirituality in America since the 1950s* (Berkeley and Los Angeles: University of California Press, 1998), chap. 3.

3. These intellectual assumptions and the contexts in which they emerged are carefully described in Mark A. Noll, *America's God: From Jonathan Edwards to Abraham Lincoln* (New York: Oxford University Press, 2002).

4. Diana Eck, *A New Religious America: How a "Christian Country" Has Now Become the Most Religiously Diverse Nation on Earth* (San Francisco: Harper San Francisco, 2001), 65.

5. John Rawls, "The Idea of an Overlapping Consensus," *Oxford Journal of Legal Studies* 7 (1987): 4.

6. National Religion Survey (April 2002), conducted by Edison Media Research for *Religion and Ethics Newsweekly*; tabulations provided to the author by Bob Abernethy and Missy Daniel; summary results also available online through Lexis-Nexis. Sixty-two percent responded that having many different religions "does not make it harder" and 9 percent responded "don't know." The survey was conducted among 2,002 adults selected to be representative of the population.

7. Constance Hilliard, "Does God Bless More than America?" *USA Today*, September 5, 2003, 13A.

8. Jean Bethke Elshtain, *Democracy on Trial* (New York: Basic Books, 1995), xi; but see also John A. Hall and Charles Lindholm, *Is America Breaking Apart?* (Princeton, N.J.: Princeton University Press, 1999).

9. Mark A. Noll, George M. Marsden, and Nathan O. Hatch, *Search for Christian America* (Chicago: Helmers and Howard, 1989).

10. A classic statement of this argument is Talcott Parsons, "Christianity and Modern Industrial Society," in *Sociological Theory, Values, and Sociocultural Change*, ed. Edward Tiryakian (New York: Free Press, 1963), 385–421.

11. *American Civil Liberties Union of Ohio, et al. v. Capitol Square Review and Advisory Board, et al.* (2000), No. 98–4106, http://pacer.ca6.uscourts.gov/opinions.pdf/00a0148p-06.pdf.

12. The Ohio case is but one of many in recent years that have emphasized the nation's increasing religious diversity as considerations in cases involving church and state; other notable cases have involved public display of the Ten Commandments in Alabama and the "under God" clause in the Pledge of Allegiance; see for instance, Robert Siegel, "Deadline for Ten Commandments Monument to Be Taken Down from Alabama State Judiciary Building," *All Things Considered*, August 20, 2003, online; Christopher Clausen, "Opening Exercises," *American Scholar* 72 (Winter 2003): 35–44.

13. Interview with Judge Avern Cohn; unless otherwise indicated, direct quotations from community leaders and other authorities are from interviews conducted as part of the research for this volume.

14. Tony Snow, "Court Strains Belief with Religion Ruling," *Detroit News*, May 5, 2000, 13.

15. "Ohio—'Illegal' Motto: All Things Are Possible," *Cincinnati Enquirer*, July 19, 2000, A18.

16. Leonard Williams Levy, *Origins of the Bill of Rights* (New Haven, Conn.: Yale University Press 1999), 102.

17. *Employment Division, Department of Human Resources of Oregon, et al. v. Smith et al.*, 1990.

18. The continuing impact of the religious wars on democratic political thought is clearly evident in John Rawls, *Political Liberalism* (New York: Columbia University Press, 1993).

19. Martin E. Marty, "The Frightful, Beneficial Mess of American Religion," *Christian Century* (December 14, 1988): 1150–52.

20. Marc Adams, "Showing Good Faith toward Muslims," *HRMagazine* (November 2000): 52–55.

21. Pat McDonnell Twair, "Who Is That Veiled Woman?" *Sojourners* (May/June 2001): 40–44; Wendy Kaminer, "The Joy of Sects," *American Prospect* (February 12, 2001): 32–33.

22. Tom Robbins, "Unnatural Intolerance in Soho," *Village Voice*, January 23, 2001, 27; see also Marilyn Giorgio-Poole, "The Religious Lives and Ritual Practices of Arab Muslim Women in the United States: A Comparative Study" (Ph.D. diss., University of Pittsburgh, 2002).

23. "McDonald's Apologizes for 'Confusion' over Fries," *Wall Street Journal*, May 25, 2001, B2.

24. "Haribo Launches Kosher and Halal Gummies," *Candy Industry* (April 2001): 18.

25. Richard Turcsik and Jenny Summerour, "Muslim Law," *Progressive Grocer* (August 2000): 12.

26. Ken Walker, "Navy Bias Charged," *Christianity Today* (May 21, 2001): 19.

27. Laurie Goodstein and Gustav Niebuhr, "Attacks and Harassment of Middle-Eastern Americans Rising," *New York Times*, September 14, 2001.

28. Federal Bureau of Investigation, Civil Rights Division, http://www.fbi.gov/hq/cid/civilrights/hate.htm.

29. B. R. Ferrall, "1998–2000 Report on Hate Crimes and Discrimination against Arab Americans," *Journal of Criminal Law and Criminology* 92 (2001): 433.

30. Adams, "Showing Good Faith toward Muslims."

31. Allen D Hertzke and Daniel Philpott, "Defending the Faiths," *National Interest* (Fall 2000): 74–81.

32. I interpret the essays in Nancy Rosenblum's useful collection on religion and First Amendment issues as largely suggesting that religious diversity involving Muslims, Buddhists, Hindus, and Jews does not pose fundamentally new questions that have not been anticipated by the courts in dealing with diversity in cases involving Christians, Mormons, Jehovah's Witnesses, members of the Church of Scientology and the Unification Church, and other groups; see Nancy L. Rosenblum, ed., *Obligations of Citizenship and Demands of Faith: Religious Accommodation in Pluralist Democracies* (Princeton, N.J.: Princeton University Press, 2000).

33. For instance, among those who said they were extremely worried about "the threat of another terrorist attack against the United States," 34 percent favored making it illegal for Muslim groups to meet in the United States, compared with 22 percent among those who were somewhat worried and 20 percent among those who were not very worried or not at all worried.

34. In the Religion and Diversity Survey, respondents were asked, "As you know, many Muslims, Hindus, and Buddhists from other countries have moved to the United States in recent years; as a result, do you think Christianity will become a lot weaker, a little weaker, a little stronger, or a lot stronger?" Five percent said a lot weaker, 22 percent said a little weaker, 31 percent said a little stronger, and 22 percent said a lot stronger.

35. Richard Alba and Victor Nee, "Rethinking Assimilation Theory for a New Era of Immigration," *International Migration Review* 31, 4 (1997): 826–74; Helen Rose Ebaugh and Janet Saltzman Chafetz, "Structural Adaptations in Immigrant Congregations," *Sociology of Religion* 61, 2 (2000): 135–53.

36. On contemporary meanings of race, see especially Cornel West, *Race Matters* (New York: Vintage, 1994); Patricia Hill Collins, *Black Feminist Thought: Knowledge, Consciousness, and the Politics of Empowerment* (New York: Routledge, 2000); and Michele Lamont, ed., *The Cultural Territories of Race: Black and White Boundaries* (Chicago: University of Chicago Press, 1999).

37. Mary C. Waters, *Ethnic Options: Choosing Ethnic Identities in America* (Berkeley and Los Angeles: University of California Press, 1990); Richard Rodriguez, *Brown: The Last Discovery of America* (New York: Viking, 2002).

38. The role of ethnic diversity as an acceptable "gloss" in the United States appears evident in the frequency with which journalists in the U.S. refer to ethnic origins (such as Indian, Arab, or Irish), compared with accounts in England and Canada, which pay more explicit attention to religious labels (such as Hindu, Muslim, or Catholic).

39. Martin E. Marty, *The One and the Many: America's Struggle for the Common Good* (Cambridge, Mass.: Harvard University Press, 1997).

40. For a useful overview of religious statistics, see George Gallup Jr., and D. Michael Lindsay, *Surveying the Religious Landscape: Trends in U.S. Beliefs* (Harrisburg, Pa.: Morehouse, 1999).

41. My conception of moral order has been spelled out in my book *Meaning and Moral Order: Explorations in Cultural Analysis* (Berkeley and Los Angeles: University of California Press, 1987); other treatments of moral order that are congruent with my usage include Robert N. Bellah, "Introduction," in *Emile Durkheim on Morality and Society*, ed. Robert N. Bellah (Chicago: University of Chicago Press, 1973), ix–lv; Alan Wolfe, *Whose Keeper? Social Science and Moral Obligation* (Berkeley and Los Angeles: University of California Press, 1989), esp. chap. 8; and James C. Scott, *Moral Economy of the Peasant: Rebellion and Subsistence in Southeast Asia* (New Haven, Conn.: Yale University Press, 1977).

42. Robert A. Orsi, "Introduction: Crossing the City Line," in *Gods of the City: Religion and the American Urban Landscape*, ed. Robert A. Orsi (Bloomington: Indiana University Press, 1999), 33.

43. Still useful as sociological background is Howard S. Becker, *Outsiders: Studies in the Sociology of Deviance* (New York: Free Press, 1973), and in the religious context, R. Laurence Moore, *Religious Outsiders and the Making of Americans* (New York: Oxford University Press, 1986).

44. For a discussion of the Lockean view, see Stephen Macedo, *Diversity and Distrust: Civic Education in a Multicultural Democracy* (Cambridge, Mass.: Harvard University Press, 2000), esp. 28–36.

45. Peter Berger, "Protestantism and the Quest for Certainty," *Christian Century* (August 26–September 2, 1998): 782.

46. James R. Beniger, *The Control Revolution: Technological and Economic Origins of the Information Society* (Cambridge, Mass.: Harvard University Press, 1989).

47. Humphrey's concept of Christendom follows that of Loren B. Mead, *The Once and Future Church: Reinventing the Congregation for a New Mission Frontier* (Washington, D.C.: Alban Institute, 1993).

48. Daniel Callahan, "Universalism and Particularism," *Hastings Center Report* (January/February 2000): 44.

CHAPTER 4. EMBRACING DIVERSITY: SHOPPING
IN THE SPIRITUAL MARKETPLACE

1. Robert N. Bellah, "At Home and Not at Home: Religious Pluralism and Religious Truth," *Christian Century* (April 19, 1995): 428.

2. The story of new youth movements during the 1960s and 1970s need not be repeated here; see Robert S. Ellwood, *The Sixties Spiritual Awakening: American Religion Moving from Modern to Postmodern* (New Brunswick, N.J.: Rutgers University Press, 1994), and Charles Y. Glock and Robert N. Bellah, eds., *The New Religious Consciousness* (Berkeley and Los Angeles: University of California Press, 1976), among others.

3. Harold Bloom, in *The American Religion: The Emergence of the Post-Christian Nation* (New York: Simon & Schuster, 1992), refers explicitly to this possibility through his book's subtitle but does not, it seems to me, provide supporting historical evidence; in fact, his argument about the tension between American gnosticism and fundamentalism suggests continuity more than it does change.

4. The shopping metaphor is amply explained in Wade Clark Roof, *Spiritual Marketplace: Baby Boomers and the Remaking of American Religion* (Princeton, N.J.: Princeton University Press, 1999), and Richard P. Cimino and Don Lattin, *Shopping for Faith: American Religion in the New Millennium* (San Francisco: Jossey-Bass, 1998).

5. See, for example, Dana Evan Kaplan, "Conversion to Judaism: A Historical Perspective," *Judaism* 48 (Summer 1999): 259–74.

6. While favoring the concept of spiritual seeking over the metaphor of shopping, I have written about the social conditions encouraging what I have described as a spirituality of seeking, contrasting these to the conditions in the 1950s that reinforced a spirituality of dwelling, and I have suggested how casual and more serious forms of spiritual seeking differ; Robert Wuthnow, *After Heaven: Spirituality in American since the 1950s* (Berkeley and Los Angeles: University of California Press, 1998); and Robert Wuthnow, *Creative Spirituality: The Way of the Artist* (Berkeley and Los Angeles: University of California Press, 2001).

7. Keith Yandell, in "Religious Pluralism," *Christians and Scholarship* 2, 3 (1999): 3–6, contrasts exclusivism and inclusivism with "religious pluralism," an unfortunate choice of terms in my view, but one that resembles the spiritual shopping I describe in this chapter; in emphasizing pluralism's rejection of propositional truth about objective realities, however, Yandell misperceives the complexity with which many spiritual shoppers grapple with understandings of truth.

8. On the Rajneesh community, see Frances FitzGerald, *Cities on a Hill: A Journey through Contemporary American Cultures* (New York: Simon & Schuster, 1986), 247–382.

9. A significant exception to this generalization, of course, are African Americans who converted to Islam; see especially Carolyn Rouse, *Engaged Surrender: Consciousness and Empowerment in the Conversion Experience of African-American Muslim Women* (Berkeley and Los Angeles: University of California Press, 2005); and Steven Tsoukalas and Carl F. Ellis Jr., *The Nation of Islam: Understanding the "Black Muslims"* (Louisville: Presbyterian & Reformed Publishing, 2001).

10. On the history of magic and the occult in American religion, see Jon Butler, *Awash in a Sea of Faith: Christianizing the American People* (Cambridge, Mass.: Harvard University Press, 1990), chap. 3.

11. The association between spiritual shopping and tourism is readily suggested by contrasting tourism with other forms of travel, such as migration, military service, conquest, or even religious pilgrimages; see Erik Cohen, "Authenticity and Commoditization in Tourism," *Annals of Tourism Research* 15, 3 (1988): 371–86; Jonathan Culler, "Semiotics of Tourism," *American Journal of Semiotics* 1 (1981): 127–40; James Clifford, *Routes: Travel and Translation in the Late Twentieth Century* (Cambridge, Mass.: Harvard University Press, 1997); and especially Dean MacCannell, *The Tourist: A New Theory of the Leisure Class*, 3rd ed. (Berkeley and Los Angeles: University of California Press, 1999).

12. Robert Wuthnow, *Experimentation in American Religion* (Berkeley and Los Angeles: University of California Press, 1978).

13. Through less commonly than in the 1970s, the term *Aquarian* continues to appear in popular treatments of spirituality; for instance, Wayne Sterba, *The Aquarian Hypothesis: Spiritual Security in a Dot.Com World* (San Francisco: First Books Library, 2001); and Nancy Privett, *Stepping into the Aquarian Age* (New York: Old Lion Publishing, 2001).

14. Paul Heelas, *The New Age Movement: The Celebration of the Self and the Sacralization of Modernity* (Oxford: Blackwell, 1996), offers a valuable overview; see also Wouter J. Hanegraaff, *New Age Religion and Western Culture: Esotericism in the Mirror of Secular Thought* (Leiden: E. J. Brill, 1996).

15. Carol Bausch Albright and James B. Ashbrook, *Where God Lives in the Human Brain* (New York: Sourcebooks, 2001).

CHAPTER 5. "MANY MANSIONS": ACCEPTING DIVERSITY

1. Martin E. Marty, "Revising the Map of American Religion," *Annals of the American Academy of Political and Social Science* 558 (July 1998): 13–27. For an estimate of the proportion of the American public that qualifies as spiritual shoppers, see chapter 7.

2. The shallowness of American religion is a well-established theme in studies of the topic; scholars typically point to this emphasis in Will Herberg, *Protestant-Catholic-Jew: An Essay in American Religious Sociology,* rev. ed. (New York: Anchor, 1960). For a more recent example that draws on opinion polls, see George Barna and Mark Hatch, *Boiling Point: It Only Takes One Degree* (Ventura, Calif.: Regal Books, 2001), esp. chap. 9. The emphasis on Christian love as a kind of least-common-denominator faith has been described in Nancy T. Ammerman, "Golden Rule Christianity: Lived Religion in the American Mainstream," in *Lived Religion in America: Toward a History of Practice,* ed. David D. Hall (Princeton, N.J.: Princeton University Press, 1997), 196–216.

3. Clifford Geertz, *The Interpretation of Cultures* (New York: Basic Books, 1973), 90.

4. Wilfrid Cantwell Smith, "The Christian in a Religiously Plural World," in *Christianity and Other Religions,* ed. John Hick and Brian Hebblethwaite (Philadelphia: Fortress Press, 1980), 98–99.

5. Robert Wuthnow, "Religion and Politics Survey" (Princeton University, machine-readable data file, 2000).

6. Michael Walzer, *Thick and Thin: Moral Argument at Home and Abroad* (Notre Dame, Ind.: University of Notre Dame Press, 1994).

7. Secularization theory is much contested within contemporary social science. Influential formulations include Peter L. Berger, *The Sacred Canopy: Elements of a Sociological Theory of Religion* (New York: Doubleday, 1967), and David Martin, *A General Theory of Secularization* (New York: Harper & Row, 1978); critical perspectives are presented in Jose Casanova, *Public Religions in the Modern World* (Chicago: University of Chicago Press, 1994), and Philip S. Gorski, "Historicizing the Secularization Debate: Church, State, and Society in Late Medieval and Early Modern Europe (ca. 1300 to 1700)," *American Sociological Review* 65 (2000): 138–57. Recent efforts to formulate mediating perspectives include Philip S. Gorski, "Historicizing the Secularization Debate: An Agenda for Research," in *Handbook of the Sociology of Religion,* ed. Michele Dillon (Cambridge: Cambridge University Press, 2003), 110–22, and Christian Smith, ed., *The Secular Revolution: Power, Interests, and Conflict in the Secularization of American Public Life* (Berkeley and Los Angeles: University of California Press, 2004).

8. Peter L. Berger, *A Far Glory: The Quest for Faith in an Age of Credulity* (New York: Free Press, 1992), 42. Berger's argument has sometimes been associated with an empirical literature debating whether or not religious diversity leads to decreased religious participation; see Mark Chaves and Philip S. Gorski, "Religious Pluralism and Religious Participation," *Annual Review of Sociology* 27 (2001): 261–81. One of the more recent contributions to this debate suggests that there is no relationship between religious pluralism and religious participation, and shows that relationships reported in previous research are statistical artifacts; see David Voas, Alasdair Crockett, and Daniel V. A. Olson, "Religious Pluralism and Participation: Why Previous Research Is Wrong," *American Sociological Review* 67 (2002): 212–30. This research has generally defined religious pluralism in terms of denominational diversity within the Christian context and thus does not bear directly on the issue here of how Christians make sense of their faith in relation to other religious traditions. I share Berger's view that the effects of religious diversity are of greatest interest in *how* people understand and experience spirituality, matters that are not well expressed in rates of church attendance.

9. Insofar as inclusive Christianity is associated with mainline Protestantism, see Michael Hout, Andrew Greeley, and Melissa J. Wilde, "The Demographic Imperative in Religious Change in the United States," *American Journal of Sociology* 107 (2001): 468–500, for an account of the decline in membership among mainstream Protestant denominations, which was previously thought to have been an instance of secularization rooted in a lack of commitment to strict religious beliefs, for example, in Dean M. Kelley, *Why Conservative Churches Are Growing: A Study in the Sociology of Religion* (New York: Harper & Row, 1972). See also Robert Wuthnow and John H. Evans, eds., *The Quiet Hand of God: Faith-Based Activism and the Public Role of Mainline Protestantism* (Berkeley and Los Angeles: University of California Press, 2002), for evidence on the stabilization of membership and participation in mainline churches during the 1990s.

10. Ammerman, "Golden Rule Christianity."

CHAPTER 6. "ONE WAY": RESISTING DIVERSITY

1. Martin E. Marty, "Revising the Map of American Religion," *Annals of the American Academy of Political and Social Science* 558 (July 1998): 27.

2. Although evangelical Christians are more likely to believe in the exclusive truth of Christianity than mainline Protestants or Catholics, I do not mean to equate the two. On the broader meanings of evangelicalism in the contemporary United States, see especially Christian Smith, *American Evangelicalism: Embattled*

and Thriving (Chicago: University of Chicago Press, 1998), and Christian Smith, *Christian America? What Evangelicals Really Want* (Berkeley and Los Angeles: University of California Press, 2000); and on the kind of nondenominational church to which Mrs. Mobley and her husband belong, see Donald E. Miller, *Reinventing American Protestantism: Christianity in the New Millennium* (Berkeley and Los Angeles: University of California Press, 1997).

3. The standard interpretation finds expression in much of the social science literature on religion and modernity; see especially Peter L. Berger, *The Homeless Mind* (Garden City, N.Y.: Doubleday, 1974); Richard Hofstadter, *The Paranoid Style in American Politics and Other Essays* (Cambridge, Mass.: Harvard University Press, 1996); and James Davison Hunter, *American Evangelicalism: Conservative Religion and the Quandary of Modernity* (New Brunswick, N.J.: Rutgers University Press, 1983).

4. The language of "plausibility" and worldview maintenance here is taken from Peter L. Berger, *The Sacred Canopy: Elements of a Sociological Theory of Religion* (Garden City, N.Y.: Doubleday, 1967); see also Peter L. Berger, *Facing Up to Modernity: Excursions in Society, Politics, and Religion* (New York: Basic Books, 1977), chap. 1.

5. Smith, *American Evangelicalism*, 23.

6. For further discussion of the roles of feelings and rational arguments, see Robert Wuthnow, *Meaning and Moral Order: Explorations in Cultural Analysis* (Berkeley and Los Angeles: University of California Press, 1987).

7. The sense of loss and moral drift that people having left tightly knit religious communities describe resembles that of the flood victims studied in Kai T. Erikson, *Everything in Its Path: Destruction of Community in the Buffalo Creek Flood* (New York: Simon & Schuster, 1976).

8. Smith, *American Evangelicalism*, chap. 5.

9. Smith, *Christian America?*; Alan Wolfe, *One Nation after All: What Americans Really Think about God, Country, Family, Racism, Welfare, Immigration, Homosexuality, Work, the Right, the Left and Each Other* (New York: Viking, 1998).

10. R. Marie Griffith, *God's Daughters: Evangelical Women and the Power of Submission* (Berkeley and Los Angeles: University of California Press, 1997); Matthew P. Lawson, "Struggles for Mutual Reverence: Social Strategies and Religious Stories," in *Contemporary American Religion: An Ethnographic Reader*, ed. Penny Edgell Becker and Nancy L. Eiesland (Walnut Creek, Calif.: AltaMira Press, 1997), 51–78.

11. Theodor W. Adorno, Else Frenkl Brunswick, and Daniel J. Levinson, *The Authoritarian Personality* (New York: John Wiley & Sons, 1964).

12. On cultural capital, see Pierre Bourdieu, *Distinction: A Social Critique of the Judgment of Taste*, trans. Richard Nice (Cambridge, Mass.: Harvard University

Press, 1984); Michele Lamont, *Money, Morals, and Manners: The Culture of the French and the American Upper-Middle Class* (Chicago: University of Chicago Press, 1992); and Paul DiMaggio, "Cultural Capital and School Success: The Impact of Status Culture Participation on the Grades of U.S. High School Students," *American Sociological Review* 47 (1982): 189–201. More on the social and cultural characteristics of Christian exclusivists is presented in chapter 7.

13. The extent to which many tightly knit churches are involved in international networks suggests a caveat to earlier research that found a strong association between localistic orientations and negative attitudes toward other religions. See especially Wade Clark Roof, *Community and Commitment: Religious Plausibility in a Liberal Protestant Church* (New York: Elsevier, 1978); besides a localistic orientation, it is probably just as significant to have wider contacts that nevertheless are highly structured by the religious community.

14. Andrew M. Greeley and Michael Hout, "Americans' Increasing Belief in Life after Death: Religious Competition and Acculturation," *American Sociological Review* 64 (December 1999): 813–35.

15. E. Brooks Holifield, *A History of Pastoral Care in America: From Salvation to Self-Realization* (Nashville, Tenn.: Abingdon Press, 1983); Marsha G. Witten, *All Is Forgiven: The Secular Message in American Protestantism* (Princeton, N.J.: Princeton University Press, 1993).

CHAPTER 7. THE PUBLIC'S BELIEF AND PRACTICES

1. Fifty-eight percent of the respondents in the Religion and Diversity Survey said they agreed that "Christianity is the best way to understand God" (40 percent agreed strongly). Fifty-four percent agreed that "All major religions, such as Christianity, Hinduism, Buddhism, and Islam, are equally good ways of knowing about God" (24 percent agreed strongly). Compared with other questions about Christianity and other religions (shown in tables 1 and 2) on which most people either agreed or disagreed, these questions, then, discriminated between roughly equal proportions of the population. The two questions were negatively associated ($r = -.325$), but only moderately so, meaning that a significant proportion of the population fell into each of the three main categories of interest.

2. It may be of interest to some readers to know how Christians responded to these questions. When asked directly if they considered themselves to be Christian, 80 percent of the respondents said yes. Among this 80 percent, the proportions who agreed with each of the statements in table 1 were as follows: 74 percent agreed that all religions contain some truth, 50 percent agreed that all religions are equally true, 38 percent agreed that all religions teach the same thing, 44

percent agreed that God's word is revealed in other sacred texts besides the Bible, 22 percent agreed that Muslims and Christians believe the same things, and 15 percent agreed that Buddhists and Christians believe the same things. In short, these percentages are quite close to those for the total sample.

3. For the items shown in table 1, separate likelihood-ratio chi-squares for the differences between shoppers and inclusivists show that all are significant at the .001 level, except for the first item, which is significant at the .05 level; and for the differences between inclusivists and exclusivists, all are significant at the .001 level (I use likelihood-ratio chi-squares rather than Pearson chi-squares because the likelihood-ratio chi-squares are additive and thus can be parsed for comparisons among pairs of categories in the sample).

4. Cronbach's alpha, which varies between 0 and 1, is a convenient summary measure of the degree to which the five items shown in table 1 and the question about all religions being equally true fit together. For those six items, Cronbach's alpha is .732.

5. The wording of this question was taken from Gallup surveys; e.g. George Gallup Jr. and D. Michael Lindsay, *Surveying the Religious Landscape: Trends in U.S. Beliefs* (Harrisburg, Pa.: Morehouse Publishing, 1999), p. 35. In a 1998 Gallup survey, 33 percent of the public opted for the literalist response, 47 percent said the Bible was inspired but should not be taken literally, and 17 percent said it was a book of fables, legends, history, and moral precepts. According to other recent surveys (available online through Lexis-Nexis), the proportions choosing the literalist response generally range from 29 percent to 37 percent; the nonliteralist response from 48 percent to 53 percent; and the third response from 12 percent to 15 percent.

6. Among the 80 percent of the public that identified itself as Christian, the results were much the same: 52 percent thought Christianity is the only way to have a relationship with God, 44 percent took a literalist view of the Bible (while 45 percent thought it was inspired and 9 percent regarded it as a book of fables and history), 77 percent thought God's truth was revealed in many ways (20 percent only in the Bible), 56 percent said they were guided by the Bible (38 percent were guided by personal experience), and 75 percent took the traditional view of Jesus while 15 percent opted for Jesus as an example of divine love and 7 percent said Jesus merely had a special relationship with God.

7. Likelihood-ratio chi-square tests for the differences between shoppers and inclusivists and for the differences between inclusivists and exclusivists showed that all differences in table 2 were significant at the .001 level. Cronbach's alpha for the six items in the table was .701.

8. The index assigned respondents a point for the more inclusive response to each of the twelve items shown in tables 1 and 2; scores of 0 through 3 were

considered low, between 4 and 6 were considered moderate, and 7 through 12 were considered high. In the total sample, 36 percent scored low, 31 percent scored moderate, and 33 percent scored high (the index thus divides the sample in approximately the same way that the simpler measure used to distinguish among shoppers, inclusivists, and exclusivists does). The strong relationship between the index and the shopper, inclusivist, exclusivist taxonomy (r = .633) provides an indication of the validity of the taxonomy.

9. Agreeing *strongly* seemed to matter more than simply agreeing, since most people did agree at least somewhat with most of the statements.

10. Likelihood-ratio chi-squares for all differences between spiritual shoppers and Christian inclusivists are significant at the .001 level, as are all differences between Christian inclusivists and exclusivists except for the item about American owing a great deal to immigrants.

11. To determine if any of the relationships shown in the table were spurious, I examined multivariate logistic regression models for each dependent variable using unweighted data. The independent variables were dichotomous variables for spiritual shopping and Christian exclusivism, meaning that Christian inclusivism was the excluded referent category. A dummy variable was included for the 11 percent of respondents who did not fall into any of the three main categories of the independent variable. The following control variables were included in each model: age (dummy variables for 25 to 44, 45 to 64, and 65 and over, meaning that 18 to 24 was the referent category), education (dummy variables for some college, college graduate, and postgraduate, meaning that high school or less was the referent category), parents' education (at least one parent with a college degree), region (Midwest, South, and West, with Northeast as the referent category), gender (male), race (black), ethnicity (Hispanic), religious tradition (evangelical Protestant, mainline Protestant, black Protestant, Catholic, Jewish, other tradition, with no affiliation as the referent category), and religious service attendance (weekly, monthly, a few times a year, with never as the referent category). In all of the models, the coefficient for spiritual shoppers was significant at or beyond the .05 level, indicating significant differences between shoppers and inclusivists. The coefficients for exclusivists indicated significant differences between exclusivists and inclusivists at the .05 level for all items except the second, sixth, and ninth, and at the .08 level for the eighth.

12. From logistic regression analysis of each of the dependent variables in table 4, all differences between spiritual shoppers and inclusivists are statistically significant (except for influences of New Age and science) and all of the differences between inclusivists and exclusivists are statistically significant (except for New Age), controlling for age, education, parents' education, region, gender, race, ethnicity, religious tradition, and religious service attendance.

13. Books about Buddhism clearly portray the differences in basic teachings between Buddhism and Christianity; I recognize, though, that some variants of American Buddhism stress the similarities more than the differences (as discussed in chapter 3).

14. Likelihood-ratio chi-squares for the differences between spiritual shoppers and Christian inclusivists being very familiar with the teachings of Islam and Buddhism were significant at the .01 level (the difference for familiarity with Hinduism was not significant). The differences between spiritual shoppers and Christian inclusivists for having attended services at a mosque, Hindu temple, or Buddhist temple were all significant at the .01 level. The differences between Christian inclusivists and exclusivists for being very familiar with the teachings of Hinduism and Buddhism were significant at the .05 level (the difference for familiarity with Islam was not significant). The difference between Christian inclusivists and exclusivists for having attended services was significant at the .05 level for a mosque or Buddhist temple but was not significant for a Hindu temple.

15. In logistic regression models that controlled for age, education, parents' education, region, gender, race, ethnicity, religious tradition, and religious service attendance, the effect of spiritual shopping (versus Christian inclusivism) was statistically significant and positive for five of the six dependent variables (being very familiar with each of the non-Western religions and having attended services at these religions' houses of worship); the exception was being very familiar with Hinduism. The effect of Christian exclusivism (versus Christian inclusivism) was statistically significant and negative for five of the six dependent variables; the exception was being very familiar with Islam.

16. Among those who said they were Christians, 56 percent of the inclusivists said they were "a Christian because you were raised that way," compared with 36 percent of the exclusivists, while 38 percent of the exclusivists said they "decided to become a Christian," compared with 22 percent of the inclusivists.

17. When all the variables in table 6 are examined simultaneously in logistic regression models, those that have positive and statistically significant effects on the likelihood of being a spiritual shopper rather than a Christian inclusivist are: some college, college graduate, post-college education, parents' education, travel, and being Jewish; those that have a negative and statistically significant effect are: being age 45 to 64, being age 65 and over, living in any region other than the Northeast, being male (marginally significant), being black (marginally significant), identifying with any of the Protestant or Catholic traditions (as opposed to being nonreligious), and attending religious services more often. The variables that have positive and statistically significant effects on the likelihood of being a Christian exclusivist rather than a Christian inclusivist are: being age 25 to 44 or age 65 or over (rather than age 18 to 24), having post-college education, being

evangelical Protestant, and attending religious services weekly; the variables that are negatively associated with being a Christian exclusivist rather than a Christian inclusivist are: being black (marginally significant) and being Catholic.

18. Besides the comparison provided by contact with Jews, the Religion and Diversity Survey also asked about contact with Latinos and Asians. Among non-Latinos, the proportions who claimed to have had at least a fair amount of contact with Latinos was 77 percent among spiritual shoppers, 58 percent among Christian inclusivists, 60 percent among Christian exclusivists, and 65 percent for all non-Latino respondents; among non-Asians, the comparable figures for contact with Asians were 70, 47, 46, and 54, respectively.

19. These results are from logistic regression analysis in which all the variables mentioned were included simultaneously. Frequency of religious service attendance was also included and showed inconsistent results (taking account of all the other variables): monthly churchgoers were the most likely to have had contact with immigrant Muslims, churchgoers (regardless of frequency) were more likely than those who did not attend to have had contact with immigrant Buddhists (possibly because of refugee resettlement programs sponsored by churches?), and those who attended seldom or never were the most likely to have had contact with Hindus.

20. The Religion and Diversity Survey assessed the possibility that perceptions of Muslims had been influenced by the concerns following September 11, 2001, by asking respondents how worried they were about the threat of another terrorist attack against the United States. Those who said that they were worried were slightly more likely to express negative views of Muslims than those who were less worried. For instance, 45 percent of those who said that they were extremely worried said the word *violent* applies to Muslims, compared with 37 percent of those who said they were not very worried; similarly, 47 percent of the former said they would not welcome Muslims becoming a stronger presence in the United States, compared with 36 percent of the latter. A detailed analysis of public opinion toward Muslims between 1991 and 2002 showed that opinions of Muslims became both more favorable and more unfavorable (i.e., fewer people said that they had no opinion) in the weeks following September 11, 2001, and that opinion stabilized a few months after the attacks at about the same levels as before; see Ismail Royer, "U.S. Public Opinion toward Islam and Muslims after the Sept. 11 Attacks," April 2, 2002, online at www.islamtoday.net.

21. As an example of journalistic coverage, see Laurie Goodstein, "Seeing Islam as 'Evil' Faith, Evangelicals Seek Converts," *New York Times*, May 27, 2003, online; for more systematic research, see Christian Smith, *Christian America? What Evangelicals Really Want* (Berkeley and Los Angeles: University of California Press, 2000), and Alan Wolfe, *One Nation after All: What Americans Really Think about*

God, Country, Family, Racism, Welfare, Immigration, Homosexuality, Work, the Right, the Left and Each Other (New York: Viking, 1998).

22. These figures mean that nationally fewer than 4 percent of the public had tried to persuade anyone who was a Muslim to become a Christian, fewer than 3 percent had done this with a Buddhist, and fewer than 2 percent had with a Hindu. Because of the small percentages, I created a single variable that gave respondents a "1" if they had tried to persuade a Muslim, Hindu, *or* Buddhist to become a Christian and then examined the correlates of this variable using logit regression analysis. Spiritual shoppers were significantly less likely to have proselytized than inclusivists or exclusivists, with all other variables taken into account. Several of the variables associated with having had greater contact with non-Western religions showed positive effects here as well: youth, higher education, parents with college degrees, travel, and being male. Frequent church attendees were much more likely to have proselytized than less frequent attendees, but taking account of the other factors, evangelical Protestants were not significantly more likely than mainline Protestants or Catholics to have proselytized.

23. The question referred specifically to activities that were part of respondents' congregations, but respondents may have included other activities in which their congregation was only peripherally involved (and perhaps ones in which they themselves did not interact directly with people of other faiths).

CHAPTER 8. HOW CONGREGATIONS MANAGE DIVERSITY

1. I have written about the manifest and latent ways in which congregations give messages about the sacred in my book *Producing the Sacred: An Essay on Public Religion* (Urbana: University of Illinois Press, 1994).

2. R. Albert Mohler Jr., "Against an Immoral Tide," *New York Times*, June 19, 2000.

3. On social capital and churches, see especially Robert Putnam, *Bowling Alone: The Decline and Renewal of American Communities* (New York: Simon & Schuster, 2000). Valuable studies of congregations include Mark Chaves, *Congregations in America* (Cambridge, Mass.: Harvard University Press, 2003); Cynthia Woolever and Deborah Bruce, *A Field Guide to U.S. Congregations: Who's Going Where and Why* (Louisville: Westminster / John Knox, 2002); Carl S. Dudley, Nancy T. Ammerman, and Loren B. Mead, *Congregations in Transition: A Guide for Analyzing, Assessing, and Adapting in Changing Communities* (San Francisco: Jossey-Bass, 2002); and Nancy Tatom Ammerman, *Congregation and Community* (New Brunswick, N.J.: Rutgers University Press, 1997).

4. Diversity within congregations is treated in Penny Edgell Becker, *Congregations in Conflict: Cultural Models of Local Religious Life* (Cambridge: Cambridge University Press, 1999), and Michael O. Emerson and Christian Smith, *Divided by Faith: Evangelical Religion and the Problem of Race in America* (New York: Oxford University Press, 2000). Popular treatments oriented toward clergy and lay audiences are illustrated by Tim Matovina, "Building Multicultural Parishes Requires More than Sensitivity," *National Catholic Reporter,* July 27, 2001, 20; John Dart, "Hues in the Pews," *Christian Century* (February 21, 2001): 16–19; and Eleanor Scott Meyers, "The Church in the City," *Interpretation* (January 2000): 23–35.

5. Among church members in the Religion and Diversity Survey, 30 percent said yes when asked, "Does the neighborhood in which your congregation is located have any synagogues, mosques, Hindu temples, or Buddhist temples?" The figures varied from 42 percent in the Northeast and 38 percent in the West to 25 percent in the South and 24 percent in the Midwest.

6. Robert Wuthnow, Religion and Politics Survey (Princeton University, machine-readable data file, 2000); my analysis.

7. Carl S. Dudley and David A. Roozen, *Faith Communities Today: A Report on Religion in the United States Today* (Hartford: Hartford Institute for Religion Research, 2001), see esp. table 4.20; also available as an online text.

8. Lowell W. Livezey, "Communities and Enclaves: Where Jews, Christians, Hindus, and Muslims Share the Neighborhoods," *Cross Currents* 51 (Spring 2001): 45–70. Livezey observed that most of the religious congregations he studied were homogeneous "ethnoracial enclaves" and that even the most cosmopolitan ones were internally divided and did little to bridge differences in the community, despite providing valuable services and a sense of belonging for their own participants.

CHAPTER 9. NEGOTIATING RELIGIOUSLY MIXED MARRIAGES

1. The proliferation of advice books is an interesting indication of the growing importance of interreligious marriage; see for example, Mary Helene Rosenbaum, Stanley Rosenbaum, and Ned Rosenbaum, *Celebrating Our Differences* (New York: White Mane, 1999); Joel Crohn, *Mixed Matches: How to Create Successful Interracial, Interethnic, and Interfaith Relationships* (New York: Fawcett Books, 1995); Donna E. Schaper, *Raising Interfaith Children: Spiritual Orphans or Spiritual Heirs?* (New York: Crossroad, 1999); and Brenda Lane Richardson, *Guess Who's Coming to Dinner: Celebrating Interethnic, Interfaith, and Interracial Relationships* (Tucson: Wildcat Canyon Press, 2000).

2. Egon Mayer, *Love and Tradition: Marriage between Jews and Christians* (New York: Plenum Press, 1985); Dean R. Hoge and Kathleen M. Ferry, *Empirical Research on Interfaith Marriage in America* (Washington, D.C.: United States Catholic Conference, 1981).

3. Jack Wertheimer, "Surrendering to Intermarriage," *Commentary* (March 2001): 25–32.

4. As far as I have been able to determine, survey questions have not been asked consistently enough at different times to show precisely how attitudes toward interreligious marriage have changed; however, Gertrude J. Selznick and Stephen Steinberg, *The Tenacity of Prejudice: Anti-Semitism in Contemporary America* (New York: Harper & Row, 1969), show in a major national study that attitudes toward marrying Jews were closely related with other indicators of anti-Semitism which, in turn, were associated negatively with cosmopolitanism and cultural sophistication and negatively with higher education and youth, thus suggesting the likelihood of greater acceptance of interreligious marriage as the society became more highly educated and populated by people born more recently. In that survey, conducted in 1965, 42 percent of the public said they would object if they "had a child who wanted to marry a Jew who had a good education and came from a good family"; the identical question, asked in 1981, found that only 28 percent said they would object (Anti-Semitism in the United States, survey conducted by Yankelovich, Skelly and White; reported on Public Opinion Online, available through Lexis-Nexis).

5. Robert Anthony Orsi, *The Madonna of 115th Street: Faith and Community in Italian Harlem, 1880–1950* (New Haven, Conn.: Yale University Press, 1985).

6. For a useful historical overview, see Beth L. Bailey, *From Front Porch to Back Seat: Courtship in Twentieth-Century America* (Baltimore: Johns Hopkins University Press, 1988).

7. Ann Swidler, *Talk of Love: How Culture Matters* (Chicago: University of Chicago Press, 2001).

8. Examples include *Interfaith Marriage: A Resource by Presbyterian Christians* (Louisville: Global Mission Ministry Unit, Office of Ecumenical and Interfaith Relations, Presbyterian Church, U.S.A., 1989); Judy Petsonk and Jim Remsen, *The Intermarriage Handbook: A Guide for Jews and Christians* (New York: William Morrow, 1988); and Paul Cowan and Rachel Cowan, *Mixed Blessings: Marriage between Jews and Christians* (New York: Doubleday, 1987).

9. Writing from a Lutheran perspective, for instance, Samuel Sandmel, *When a Jew and Christian Marry* (Philadelphia: Fortress Press, 1977), 28, asserts that wedding rites should "reflect the theological stance of the denomination, not just the personal views of the clergyman," adding, "to deviate or omit any part of the

wedding service may present a clergyman with difficult questions beyond simply words, phrases, or sentences."

10. On the managerial model, see Peter Stanford, "God's Managers," *Management Today* (April 1999): 72–77; on the therapeutic model, see E. Brooks Holifield, *A History of Pastoral Care in America: From Salvation to Self-Realization* (Nashville: Abingdon, 1983).

11. Compared with Christian clergy, the Muslim and Jewish clergy we interviewed (Buddhist and Hindu clergy less so) claim to provide more extensive counsel about how the ceremony is to be performed, the religious duties of each spouse, and requirements concerning the religious upbringing of children.

12. As one Jewish man observed, if your own rabbi won't perform the service, you can usually find a "rent-a-rabbi" who will.

13. This pattern appears to be more common among Christian clergy than among their Jewish, Muslim, Hindu, or Buddhist counterparts. Compared with the managerial and therapeutic language in which Christians speak, the other leaders we interviewed spoke more plainly of theological principles. Though there are differences, these other religious leaders often refer to the Qur'an or to Jewish law or argue that it is consistent with Hinduism or Buddhism to accept people of other faiths.

14. Alasdair MacIntyre, *After Virtue*, 2nd ed. (Notre Dame, Ind.: University of Notre Dame Press, 1984), 187.

15. As Mr. Mahama does (see chapter 2).

16. The content of different religious traditions does matter in terms of the particular issues religiously mixed couples face. In our interviews, Jewish spouses were most likely to say that they worried about having betrayed their tradition; Christian-Hindu couples most often reported conflicts about family traditions; Buddhists mentioned cultural differences more often than religious differences; Muslims denied that religious differences were important but expressed concerns about the lack of respect from Christians.

17. Particularly perceptive studies of religion's role in constructing identities include Lynn Davidman, *Tradition in a Rootless World: Women Turn to Orthodox Judaism* (Berkeley and Los Angeles: University of California Press, 1991); Eileen Barker, *The Making of a Moonie: Choice or Brainwashing?* (New York: Basil Blackwell, 1984); and R. Marie Griffith, *God's Daughters: Evangelical Women and the Power of Submission* (Berkeley and Los Angeles: University of California Press, 1997).

18. Peter L. Berger, *Facing Up to Modernity: Excursions in Society, Politics, and Religion* (New York: Basic Books, 1977), chap. 1.

19. Bruce A. Phillips, *Reexamining Intermarriage: Trends, Textures, Strategies* (New York: American Jewish Committee, William Petschek National Jewish Family Center, and the Susan and David Wilstein Institute of Jewish Policy Studies, 1997).

CHAPTER 10. HOW PLURALISTIC SHOULD WE BE?

1. Wendy Freedman Katkin, Ned Landsman, and Andrea Tyree, eds., *Beyond Pluralism: The Conception of Groups and Group Identities in America* (Urbana: University of Illinois Press, 1998).

2. This conclusion is similar to that drawn in Alan Wolfe, *One Nation after All: What Americans Really Think about God, Country, Family, Racism, Welfare, Immigration, Homosexuality, Work, the Right, the Left and Each Other* (New York: Viking, 1998).

3. Nicholas Rescher, *Pluralism: Against the Demand for Consensus* (Oxford: Clarendon Press, 1993), 89.

4. John Dewey, *Democracy and Education* (New York: Macmillan, 1916), chap. 7; Robert N. Bellah, Richard Madsen, William M. Sullivan, Ann Swidler, and Steven M. Tipton, *The Good Society* (New York: Knopf, 1991), 254–56. Bellah and his coauthors emphasize "mindfulness" as described in Buddhist as well as in Christian practices.

5. For a helpful discussion of character, see James Davison Hunter, *The Death of Character: On the Moral Education of America's Children* (New York: Basic Books, 2000).

6. Alasdair MacIntyre, "Moral Pluralism without Moral Relativism," in *Ethics*, vol. 1 of *The Proceedings of the Twentieth World Congress of Philosophy*, ed. Klaus Brinkmann (Boston: Philosophy Documentation Center, 1999), 1–19.

7. Alexis de Tocqueville, *Democracy in America* (New York: Vintage, 1945), 2: 227; see also Mark E. Warren, *Democracy and Association* (Princeton, N.J.: Princeton University Press, 2001).

8. The security guards reluctantly granted this request.

9. Interest in faith-based community organizing has been examined in Mark R. Warren, *Dry Bones Rattling: Community Building to Revitalize American Democracy* (Princeton, N.J.: Princeton University Press, 2001); Stephen Hart, *Cultural Dilemmas of Progressive Politics: Styles of Engagement among Grassroots Activists* (Chicago: University of Chicago Press, 2001); and Richard Wood, *Faith in Action: Religion, Race, and Democratic Action in America* (Chicago: University of Chicago Press, 2002). These studies emphasize not only grassroots action but also the importance of discussing religious values and developing strategies for contestation and compromise among different perspectives.

10. United Religions Charter, online.

11. Examples of interreligious organizations that focus on specific issues include the Interfaith Action Food Bank in Columbus, Georgia; the Interfaith Re-Employment Group in Pittsburgh, Pennsylvania; and the Interfaith Day Care

Center in Columbia, Maryland. Larger, multipurpose interreligious organizations generally have Web sites describing their mission and activities.

12. See www.wcrp.org.

13. Joseph Raz, "Multiculturalism: A Liberal Perspective," *Dissent* (Winter 1994): 67–79.

14. Among theologians, the work of David Tracy has been especially concerned with the meanings of love in the context of pluralism; see, for instance, his *Plurality and Ambiguity: Hermeneutics, Religion, Hope* (Chicago: University of Chicago Press, 1994).

15. Jacques Derrida, "Faith and Knowledge: The Two Sources of 'Religion' at the Limits of Reason Alone," in *Religion: Cultural Memory in the Present*, ed. Jacques Derrida and Gianni Vattimo (Stanford, Calif.: Stanford University Press, 1996), 21–22.

SELECTED BIBLIOGRAPHY

Abdul-Rauf, Muhammad. *History of the Islamic Center: From Dream to Reality.* Washington, D.C.: Islamic Center, 1978.

Abusharaf, Rogaia Mustafa. "Structural Adaptations in an Immigrant Muslim Congregation in New York." In *Gatherings in Diaspora: Religious Communities and the New Immigration,* edited by R. Stephen Warner and Judith G. Wittner, 235–64. Philadelphia: Temple University Press, 1998.

Adams, John. *The Adams-Jefferson Letters.* Edited by Lester J. Cappon. Chapel Hill: University of North Carolina Press, 1959.

Adams, Marc. "Showing Good Faith toward Muslims." *HRMagazine,* November (2000): 52–55.

Adorno, Theodor W., Else Frenkl Brunswick, and Daniel J. Levinson. *The Authoritarian Personality.* New York: John Wiley & Sons, 1964.

Ahlstrom, Sydney E. *The American Protestant Encounter with World Religions: The Brewer Lectures on Comparative Religion.* Beloit, Wis.: Beloit College, 1962.

Alba, Richard, and Victor Nee. "Rethinking Assimilation Theory for a New Era of Immigration." *International Migration Review* 31, 4 (1997): 826–74.

Albright, Carol Bausch, and James B. Ashbrook. *Where God Lives in the Human Brain.* New York: Sourcebooks, 2001.

American Board of Commissioners for Foreign Missions. *Memorial Volume of the First Fifty Years.* Boston: American Board of Commissioners for Foreign Missions, 1861.

Ammerman, Nancy Tatom. *Congregation and Community.* New Brunswick, N.J.: Rutgers University Press, 1997.

———. "Golden Rule Christianity: Lived Religion in the American Mainstream." In *Lived Religion in America: Toward a History of Practice,* edited by David D. Hall, 196–216. Princeton, N.J.: Princeton University Press, 1997.

Anderson, Rufus. *Foreign Missions: Relations and Claims.* Boston: Congregational Publishing House, 1874.

Anthony, Susan B. *An Account of the Proceedings on the Trial of Susan B. Anthony.* Rochester, N.Y.: Daily Democrat, 1874.

Ashitzu, Zitzuzen. "Buddha." In *The World's Parliament of Religions*, vol. 2, edited by John Henry Barrows, 1038–40. Chicago: Parliament Publishing, 1893.

Ausmus, Harry J. *Will Herberg: From Right to Right*. Chapel Hill: University of North Carolina Press, 1987.

Axtell, James. *The Invasion Within: The Contest of Cultures in Colonial North America*. New York: Oxford University Press, 1985.

Bailey, Beth L. *From Front Porch to Back Seat: Courtship in Twentieth-Century America*. Baltimore: Johns Hopkins University Press, 1988.

Bailyn, Bernard. *The Ideological Origins of the American Revolution*. Cambridge, Mass.: Harvard University Press, 1967.

Barker, Eileen. *The Making of a Moonie: Choice or Brainwashing?* New York: Basil Blackwell, 1984.

Barna, George, and Mark Hatch. *Boiling Point: It Only Takes One Degree*. Ventura, Calif.: Regal Books, 2001.

Barrows, John Henry, ed., *The World's Parliament of Religions*, vol. 2. Chicago: Parliament Publishing, 1893.

Baybrooke, Marcus. *Inter-Faith Organizations, 1893–1979: An Historical Directory*. New York: Edwin Mellen Press, 1980.

Beaver, R. Pierce. "American Missionary Motivation before the Revolution." *Church History* 31, June (1962): 216–26.

Beck, Guy L. *Sonic Theology: Hinduism and Sacred Sound*. Columbia: University of South Carolina Press, 1993.

Becker, Howard S. *Outsiders: Studies in the Sociology of Deviance*. New York: Free Press, 1973.

Becker, Penny Edgell. *Congregations in Conflict: Cultural Models of Local Religious Life*. Cambridge: Cambridge University Press, 1999.

Bellah, Robert N. "At Home and Not at Home: Religious Pluralism and Religious Truth." *Christian Century*, April 19 (1995): 423–28.

———. *The Broken Covenant: American Civil Religion in Time of Trial*. New York: Seabury, 1975.

———. "Introduction." In *Emile Durkheim on Morality and Society*, edited by Robert N. Bellah, ix–lv. Chicago: University of Chicago Press, 1973.

Bellah, Robert N., Richard Madsen, William M. Sullivan, Ann Swidler, and Steven M. Tipton. *The Good Society*. New York: Knopf, 1991.

Beniger, James R. *The Control Revolution: Technological and Economic Origins of the Information Society*. Cambridge, Mass.: Harvard University Press, 1989.

Bercovitch, Sacvan. "The Typology of America's Mission." *American Quarterly* 30, Summer (1978): 135–55.

Berger, Peter L. *Facing Up to Modernity: Excursions in Society, Politics, and Religion*. New York: Basic Books, 1977.

————. *A Far Glory: The Quest for Faith in an Age of Credulity.* New York: Free Press, 1992.

————. *The Homeless Mind.* Garden City, N.Y.: Doubleday, 1974.

————. "Protestantism and the Quest for Certainty." *Christian Century,* August 26–September 2 (1998): 782–96.

————. *The Sacred Canopy: Elements of a Sociological Theory of Religion.* Garden City, N.Y.: Doubleday, 1967.

Berkhofer, Robert F., Jr. *The White Man's Indian: Images of the American Indian from Columbus to the Present.* New York: Knopf, 1978.

Bloom, Alfred. "The Western Pure Land." *Tricycle: The Buddhist Review,* Summer (1995): 58–63.

Bloom, Harold. *The American Religion: The Emergence of the Post-Christian Nation.* New York: Simon & Schuster, 1992.

Bourdieu, Pierre. *Distinction: A Social Critique of the Judgment of Taste.* Translated by Richard Nice. Cambridge, Mass.: Harvard University Press, 1984.

Bratton, Fred Gladstone. *The Crime of Christendom: The Theological Sources of Christian Anti-Semitism.* Santa Barbara, Calif.: Fithian Press, 1996.

Braybrooke, Marcus. *Inter-Faith Organizations, 1893–1979: An Historical Directory.* New York: Edwin Mellen Press, 1980.

————. *Pilgrimage of Hope: One Hundred Years of Global Interfaith Dialogue.* New York: Crossroad, 1992.

Brownson, Orestes A. *The American Republic: Its Constitution, Tendencies, and Destiny.* New York: O'Shea, 1866.

Bryant, M. Darrol. "America as God's Kingdom." In *Religion and Political Society,* edited by Jurgen Moltmann, Herbert W. Richardson, Johann Baptist Metz, Willi Oelmuller, and M. Darrol Bryant, 54–94. New York: Harper & Row, 1974.

Burns, Dawson. *The Bases of Temperance Reform: An Exposition and Appeal.* New York: National Temperance Society, 1873.

Butler, Jon. *Awash in a Sea of Faith: Christianizing the American People.* Cambridge, Mass.: Harvard University Press, 1990.

Butler, William. *The Land of the Veda: Being Personal Reminiscences of India.* New York: Carlton & Lanahan, 1872.

Cadge, Wendy. *Heartwood: The First Generation of Theravada Buddhism in America.* Chicago: University of Chicago Press, 2005.

Callahan, Daniel. "Universalism and Particularism." *Hastings Center Report,* January/February (2000): 37–44.

Campbell, Joseph. *Hero with a Thousand Faces.* Princeton, N.J.: Princeton University Press, 1972.

Campbell, Joseph, Bill Moyers, and Betty Sue Flowers. *The Power of Myth*. New York: Doubleday, 1988.

Canda, Edward R., and Thitiya Phaobtong. "Buddhism as a Support System for Southeast Asian Refugees." *Journal of the National Association of Social Workers* 37, January (1992): 61–67.

Casanova, Jose. *Public Religions in the Modern World*. Chicago: University of Chicago Press, 1994.

Chaves, Mark. *Congregations in America*. Cambridge, Mass.: Harvard University Press, 2003.

Chaves, Mark, and Philip S. Gorski. "Religious Pluralism and Religious Participation." *Annual Review of Sociology* 27 (2001): 261–81.

Chen, Carolyn. *Getting Saved in America: Taiwanese Immigrants Converting to Evangelical Christianity and Buddhism*. Princeton, N.J.: Princeton University Press, 2005.

Cherry, Conrad. "New England as Symbol: Ambiguity in the Puritan Vision." *Soundings* 58, Fall (1975): 351–64.

———, ed. *God's New Israel: Religious Interpretations of American Destiny*. Englewood Cliffs, N.J.: Prentice-Hall, 1971.

Cimino, Richard P., and Don Lattin. *Shopping for Faith: American Religion in the New Millennium*. San Francisco: Jossey-Bass, 1998.

Clausen, Christopher. "Opening Exercises." *American Scholar* 72, Winter (2003): 35–44.

Clifford, James. *Routes: Travel and Translation in the Late Twentieth Century*. Cambridge, Mass.: Harvard University Press, 1997.

Cohen, Erik. "Authenticity and Commoditization in Tourism." *Annals of Tourism Research* 15, 3 (1988): 371–86.

Coleman, James W. *The New Buddhism: The Western Transformation of an Ancient Tradition*. New York: Oxford University Press, 2001.

Collins, Patricia Hill. *Black Feminist Thought: Knowledge, Consciousness, and the Politics of Empowerment*. New York: Routledge, 2000.

Columbus, Christopher. *The* Diario *of Christopher Columbus's First Voyage to America, 1492–1493*. Translated by Oliver Dunn and James E. Kelley Jr. Abstracted by Fray Bartolomé de las Casas. Norman, Okla.: University of Oklahoma Press, 1991.

Conn, Harvie M. *Eternal Word and Changing Worlds: Theology, Anthropology, and Mission in Trialogue*. Grand Rapids, Mich.: Academie, 1984.

Corless, Roger J. "Pure Land Piety." In *Buddhist Spirituality: Indian, Southeast Asian, Tibetan, Early Chinese*, edited by Takeuchi Yoshinori, 242–74. New York: Crossroad, 1993.

Cowan, Paul, and Rachel Cowan. *Mixed Blessings: Marriage between Jews and Christians.* New York: Doubleday, 1987.

Crohn, Joel. *Mixed Matches: How to Create Successful Interracial, Interethnic, and Interfaith Relationships.* New York: Fawcett Books, 1995.

Culler, Jonathan. "Semiotics of Tourism." *American Journal of Semiotics* 1 (1981): 127–40.

Dalin, David G. "Introduction." In *From Marxism to Judaism: The Collected Essays of Will Herberg,* edited by David G. Dalin, xiii–xviii. New York: Markus Wiener, 1989.

Dart, John. "Hues in the Pews." *Christian Century,* February 21 (2001): 16–19.

Davidman, Lynn. *Tradition in a Rootless World: Women Turn to Orthodox Judaism.* Berkeley and Los Angeles: University of California Press, 1991.

Davies, Ronald E. "Jonathan Edwards: Missionary Biographer, Theologian, Strategist, Administrator, Advocate—and Missionary." *International Bulletin of Missionary Research,* April (1997): 60–67.

Davis, James D. "New Hindu Temples Reflect Diversity." *South Florida Sun-Sentinel,* October 28, 1997.

Davis, Richard Beale. *Intellectual Life in the Colonial South, 1585–1763.* Knoxville: University of Tennessee Press, 1978.

Dennis, James S. *Christian Missions and Social Progress: A Sociological Study of Foreign Missions, 3 vols.* New York: Fleming Revell, 1897–1906.

Derrida, Jacques. "Faith and Knowledge: The Two Sources of 'Religion' at the Limits of Reason Alone." In *Religion: Cultural Memory in the Present,* edited by Jacques Derrida and Gianni Vattimo, 1–78. Stanford: Stanford University Press, 1996.

Dewey, John. *Democracy and Education.* New York: Macmillan, 1916.

Diamond, Malcolm L. "Catholicism in America: The Emerging Dialogue." *Judaism: A Quarterly Journal* 9, Fall (1960): 307–18.

DiMaggio, Paul. "Cultural Capital and School Success: The Impact of Status Culture Participation on the Grades of U.S. High School Students." *American Sociological Review* 47 (1982): 189–201.

Downey, Dennis B. "Tradition and Acceptance: American Catholics and the Columbian Exposition." *Mid-America* 63 (1981): 79–92.

Dudley, Carl S., Nancy T. Ammerman, and Loren B. Mead. *Congregations in Transition : A Guide for Analyzing, Assessing, and Adapting in Changing Communities.* San Francisco: Jossey-Bass, 2002.

Dudley, Carl S., and David A. Roozen. *Faith Communities Today: A Report on Religion in the United States Today.* Hartford: Hartford Institute for Religion Research, 2001.

DuPertuis, Lucy G. "American Adaptations of Hinduism." *Comparative Social Research* 10 (1987): 101–11.

Ebaugh, Helen Rose, and Janet Saltzman Chafetz. "Structural Adaptations in Immigrant Congregations." *Sociology of Religion* 61, 2 (2000): 135–53.

Eck, Diana. *A New Religious America: How a "Christian Country" Has Now Become the Most Religiously Diverse Nation on Earth.* San Francisco: Harper San Francisco, 2001.

———. "Foreword." In *The Dawn of Religious Pluralism: Voices from the World's Parliament of Religions, 1893,* edited by Richard Hughes Seager, xiii–xvii. Lasalle, Ill.: Open Court Press, 1993.

Edwards, Jonathan. "Importance of a Future State." In *The Works of Jonathan Edwards,* vol. 10, edited by Wilson H. Kimnach, 360–62. New Haven: Yale University Press, 1993.

———. "Mahometanism Compared with Christianity—Particularly with Respect to Their Propagation." In *The Works of Jonathan Edwards,* 2: 491–93. Peabody, Mass.: Hendrickson, 1998 [1834].

———. "Man's Natural Blindness in the Things of Religion." In *The Works of Jonathan Edwards,* 2: 247–56. Peabody, Mass: Hendrickson, 1998 [1834].

———. The *"Miscellanies."* Vol. 13 of *The Works of Jonathan Edwards,* edited by Thomas A. Schafer. New Haven: Yale University Press, 1994.

Ellinger, Herbert. *Hinduism.* Translated by John Bowden. London: SCM Press, 1995.

Ellwood, Robert S. *The Sixties Spiritual Awakening: American Religion Moving from Modern to Postmodern.* New Brunswick, N.J.: Rutgers University Press, 1994.

Elshtain, Jean Bethke. *Democracy on Trial.* New York: Basic Books, 1995.

Emerson, Michael O., and Christian Smith. *Divided by Faith: Evangelical Religion and the Problem of Race in America.* New York: Oxford University Press, 2000.

Erikson, Kai T. *Everything in Its Path: Destruction of Community in the Buffalo Creek Flood.* New York: Simon & Schuster, 1976.

Fader, Larry A. "Zen in the West: Historical and Philosophical Implications of the 1893 Chicago World's Parliament of Religions." *Eastern Buddhist* 25 (1982): 122–45.

Fauman, S. Joseph. "Review of *Protestant-Catholic-Jew.*" *Jewish Social Studies* 19, January–April (1957): 83–84.

Feldman, Egal. "American Ecumenicism: Chicago's World's Parliament of Religions of 1893." *Journal of Church and State* 9 (1967): 180–99.

Ferrall, B. R. "1998–2000 Report on Hate Crimes and Discrimination against Arab Americans." *Journal of Criminal Law and Criminology* 92 (2001): 432–36.

FitzGerald, Frances. *Cities on a Hill: A Journey through Contemporary American Cultures.* New York: Simon & Schuster, 1986.

Fronsdal, Gil. "Insight Meditation in the United States: Life, Liberty, and the Pursuit of Happiness." In *The Faces of Buddhism in America,* edited by Charles Prebish and Kenneth Tanaka, 163–82. Berkeley and Los Angeles: University of California Press, 1998.

———. "Theravada Spirituality in the West." In *Buddhist Spirituality: Later China, Korea, Japan, and the Modern World,* edited by Takeuchi Yoshinori, 482–96. New York: Crossroad, 1999.

Gallup, George, Jr., and D. Michael Lindsay. *Surveying the Religious Landscape: Trends in U.S. Beliefs.* Harrisburg, Pa.: Morehouse, 1999.

Gandhi, Virchand A. "The Philosophy and Ethics of the Jains." In *The World's Parliament of Religions,* vol. 2, edited by John Henry Barrows, 1222–26. Chicago: Parliament Publishing, 1893.

Geertz, Clifford. *The Interpretation of Cultures.* New York: Basic Books, 1973.

Gilbert, Arthur. "The Council and the Jews." *The Reconstructionist* 29, January 10 (1964): 6–9.

Giorgio-Poole, Marilyn. "The Religious Lives and Ritual Practices of Arab Muslim Women in the United States: A Comparative Study." Ph.D. dissertation, University of Pittsburgh, 2002.

Glock, Charles Y., and Robert N. Bellah, eds. *The New Religious Consciousness.* Berkeley and Los Angeles: University of California Press, 1976.

Goodstein, Laurie. "Seeing Islam as 'Evil' Faith, Evangelicals Seek Converts." *New York Times,* May 27, 2003, online.

Goodstein, Laurie, and Gustav Niebuhr. "Attacks and Harassment of Middle-Eastern Americans Rising." *New York Times,* September 4, 2001.

Gorski, Philip S. "Historicizing the Secularization Debate: An Agenda for Research." In *Handbook of the Sociology of Religion,* edited by Michele Dillon, 110–22. Cambridge: Cambridge University Press, 2003.

———. "Historicizing the Secularization Debate: Church, State, and Society in Late Medieval and Early Modern Europe (ca. 1300 to 1700)." *American Sociological Review* 65 (2000): 138–57.

Gracey, J. T. "The Hindoo and His Reason Why." *Ladies Repository* 2, December (1875): 536–40.

Grant, W. L., ed. *Voyages of Samuel de Champlain, 1604–1618.* New York: Charles Scribner's Sons, 1907.

Greeley, Andrew M., and Michael Hout. "Americans' Increasing Belief in Life after Death: Religious Competition and Acculturation." *American Sociological Review* 64, December (1999): 813–35.

Griffith, R. Marie. *God's Daughters: Evangelical Women and the Power of Submission*. Berkeley and Los Angeles: University of California Press, 1997.

Haddad, Yvonne, and Adair T. Lummis. *Islamic Values in the United States*. New York: Oxford University Press, 1987.

Hall, John A., and Charles Lindholm. *Is America Breaking Apart?* Princeton, N.J.: Princeton University Press, 1999.

Hanegraaff, Wouter J. *New Age Religion and Western Culture: Esotericism in the Mirror of Secular Thought*. Leiden: E. J. Brill, 1996.

Harris, Paul William. *Nothing but Christ: Rufus Anderson and the Ideology of Protestant Foreign Missions*. New York: Oxford University Press, 1999.

Hart, Stephen. *Cultural Dilemmas of Progressive Politics: Styles of Engagement among Grassroots Activists*. Chicago: University of Chicago Press, 2001.

Heelas, Paul. *The New Age Movement: The Celebration of the Self and the Sacralization of Modernity*. Oxford: Blackwell, 1996.

Heimert, Alan. *Religion and the American Mind: From the Great Awakening to the Revolution*. Cambridge, Mass.: Harvard University Press, 1966.

Henry, Derrick. "Hindu Temple of Atlanta." *Atlanta Journal and Constitution*, May 19, 2001, 2B.

Herberg, Will. "After Communism—What?" *The Reconstructionist* 16, April 7 (1950): 28–32.

———. "The Church and American Politics." *Commentary* 8, August (1949): 198–200.

———. "A Jew Looks at Catholics." *Commonweal* 58, May 22 (1953): 174–77.

———. "Judaism and Christianity: Their Unity and Difference." In *Jewish Perspectives on Christianity*, edited by Fritz A. Rothschild, 240–55. New York: Crossroad, 1990.

———. *Protestant-Catholic-Jew: An Essay in American Religious Sociology*. Garden City, N.Y.: Doubleday, 1955.

———. *Protestant-Catholic-Jew: An Essay in American Religious Sociology*, rev. ed. New York: Anchor, 1960.

———. "Rosenzweig's 'Judaism of Personal Existence.'" *Commentary* 10, December (1950): 541–49.

Hertzke, Allen D., and Daniel Philpott. "Defending the Faiths." *National Interest*, Fall (2000): 74–81.

Higginson, John. "Attestation," in *Magnalia Christi Americana; or The Ecclesiastical History of New England*, by Cotton Mather, 13–18. Hartford: Silas Andrus & Son, 1853 [1702].

Hilliard, Constance. "Does God Bless More than America?" *USA Today*, September 5, 2003, 13A.

Hirst, Francis W. *Life and Letters of Thomas Jefferson*. New York: Macmillan, 1926.

Hodge, Charles. "Early History of Heathenism." *Princeton Review,* July (1865): 321–49.

Hofstadter, Richard. *The Paranoid Style in American Politics and Other Essays.* Cambridge, Mass.: Harvard University Press, 1996.

Hoge, Dean R., and Kathleen M. Ferry. *Empirical Research on Interfaith Marriage in America.* Washington, D.C.: United States Catholic Conference, 1981.

Holifield, E. Brooks. *A History of Pastoral Care in America: From Salvation to Self-Realization.* Nashville, Tenn.: Abingdon Press, 1983.

Hoover, Felix. "Local Hindus to Celebrate." *Columbus Dispatch,* August 17, 2001, 1C.

Hope, M. B. "An Aspect of the Age with Respect to Foreign Missions." *Princeton Review* 5, October (1833): 449–62.

Hout, Michael, Andrew Greeley, and Melissa J. Wilde. "The Demographic Imperative in Religious Change in the United States." *American Journal of Sociology* 107 (2001): 468–500.

Hume, Robert Ernest. *The World's Living Religions.* New York: Charles Scribner's Sons, 1930.

Hunter, James Davison. *American Evangelicalism: Conservative Religion and the Quandary of Modernity.* New Brunswick, N.J.: Rutgers University Press, 1983.

———. *The Death of Character: On the Moral Education of America's Children.* New York: Basic Books, 2000.

Hutchison, William R. *Errand to the World: American Protestant Thought and Foreign Missions.* Chicago: University of Chicago Press, 1987.

———. *Religious Pluralism in America: The Contentious History of a Founding Ideal.* New Haven: Yale University Press, 2003.

Immigration and Naturalization Service. *Statistical Yearbook of the Immigration and Naturalization Service.* Washington, D.C.: Government Printing Office, 2001.

Jacob, Simon, and Pallavi Thaku. "Jyothi Hindu Temple: One Religion, Many Practices." In *Religion and the New Immigrants,* edited by Helen Rose Ebaugh and Janet Saltzman Chafetz, 229–42. Walnut Creek, Calif.: AltaMira Press, 2000.

Jaher, Frederic Cople. *A Scapegoat in the New Wilderness: The Origins and Rise of Anti-Semitism in America.* Cambridge, Mass.: Harvard University Press, 1994.

Jasso, Guillermina, Douglas S. Massey, Mark R. Rosenzweig, and James P. Smith. "Exploring the Religious Preferences of Recent Immigrants to the United States: Evidence from the New Immigrant Survey Pilot." In *Religion and Immigration: Christian, Jewish, and Muslim Experiences in the United States,* edited by Yvonne Yazbeck Haddad, Jane I. Smith, and John L. Esposito, 217–54. Walnut Creek, Calif.: AltaMira Press, 2003.

Jefferson, Thomas. *The Writings of Thomas Jefferson*. Edited by Albert Ellery Berch. Washington D.C.: Thomas Jefferson Memorial Association, 1905.

Jennings, Francis. *The Invasion of America: Indians, Colonialism, and the Cant of Conquest*. Chapel Hill: University of North Carolina Press, 1975.

Johnson, Roger A. "To Conquer and Convert: The Theological Tasks of the Voyages of Columbus." *Soundings* 76, Spring (1993): 19–28.

Jordan, Louis Henry. *Comparative Religion: Its Genesis and Growth*. Edinburgh: T. and T. Clark, 1905.

Kagay, Donald J. "Columbus as Standardbearer and Mirror of the Spanish Reconquest." *American Neptune* 53 (1993): 254–57.

Kaminer, Wendy. "The Joy of Sects." *American Prospect*, February 12 (2001): 32–33.

Kaplan, Dana Evan. "Conversion to Judaism: A Historical Perspective." *Judaism: A Quarterly Journal* 48, Summer (1999): 259–74.

Kaplan, Mordecai M. "Reflections on the Vatican Communiqué." *The Reconstructionist* 29, November 29 (1963): 3–4.

Katkin, Wendy Freedman, Ned Landsman, and Andrea Tyree, eds. *Beyond Pluralism: The Conception of Groups and Group Identities in America*. Urbana: University of Illinois Press, 1998.

Kelley, Dean M. *Why Conservative Churches Are Growing: A Study in the Sociology of Religion*. New York: Harper & Row, 1972.

Khan, M. A. Muqtedar. "Constructing the American Muslim Community." In *Religion and Immigration: Christian, Jewish, and Muslim Experiences in the United States*, edited by Yvonne Yazbeck Haddad, Jane I. Smith, and John L. Esposito, 175–98. Walnut Creek, Calif.: AltaMira Press, 2003.

King, Winston L. "Theravada in Southeast Asia." In *Buddhist Spirituality: Indian, Southeast Asian, Tibetan, Early Chinese*, edited by Takeuchi Yoshinori, 79–92. New York: Crossroad, 1993.

Kitagawa, Joseph. "The World's Parliament of Religions and Its Legacy." In *A Museum of Faiths: Histories and Legacies of the 1893 World's Parliament of Religions*, edited by Eric J. Ziolkowski, 171–89. Atlanta: Scholars Press, 1993.

Kollin, Gilbert. "The Impact of the Military Chaplaincy on the American Rabbinate: 1861–1976." In *The American Rabbi*, edited by Gilbert Rosenthal, 23–43. New York: KTAV Publishing, 1977.

Kornfield, Jack. *A Path with Heart: A Guide through the Perils and Promises of Spiritual Life*. New York: Doubleday, 1993.

Kraut, Benny. "A Look from the Outside: Jews and Catholics and the Establishment's Goodwill Movement of the 1920s." In *The Protestant Establishment in the Earlier Twentieth Century*, edited by William R. Hutchison, 151–69. Cambridge: Cambridge University Press, 1989.

————. "Towards the Establishment of the National Conference of Christians and Jews: The Tenuous Road to Religious Goodwill in the 1920s." *American Jewish History* 77 (1988): 388–412.

Kupperman, Karen Ordahl. *Indians and English: Facing Off in Early America.* Ithaca, N.Y.: Cornell University Press, 2000.

————. *Settling with the Indians: The Meeting of English and Indian Cultures in America, 1580–1640.* Totowa, N.J.: Rowman and Littlefield, 1980.

Kurien, Prema. "Becoming American by Becoming Hindu: Indian Americans Take Their Place at the Multicultural Table." In *Gatherings in Diaspora: Religious Communities and the New Immigration,* edited by R. Stephen Warner and Judith G. Wittner, 37–70. Philadelphia: Temple University Press, 1998.

————. "Gendered Ethnicity: Creating a Hindu Indian Identity in the United States." *American Behavioral Scientist* 42, January (1999): 648–70.

Lafitau, Joseph François. *Customs of the American Indians Compared with the Customs of Primitive Tribes.* Toronto: Champlain Society, 1974 [1724].

Lamont, Michele, ed. *The Cultural Territories of Race: Black and White Boundaries.* Chicago: University of Chicago Press, 1999.

————. *Money, Morals, and Manners: The Culture of the French and the American Upper-Middle Class.* Chicago: University of Chicago Press, 1992.

Larson, Gerald James. "Hinduism in India and in America." In *World Religions in America,* edited by Jacob Neusner, 177–202. Louisville: Westminster / John Knox Press, 1994.

Lawson, Matthew P. "Struggles for Mutual Reverence: Social Strategies and Religious Stories." In *Contemporary American Religion: An Ethnographic Reader,* edited by Penny Edgell Becker and Nancy L. Eiesland, 51–78. Walnut Creek, Calif.: AltaMira Press, 1997.

Levy, Leonard Williams. *Origins of the Bill of Rights.* New Haven, Conn.: Yale University Press, 1999.

Lin, Irene. "Journey to the Far West: Chinese Buddhism in America." *Amerasia Journal* 22 (1996): 107–32.

Livezey, Lowell W. "Communities and Enclaves: Where Jews, Christians, Hindus, and Muslims Share the Neighborhoods." *Cross Currents* 51, Spring (2001): 45–70.

Lowance, Mason I., Jr. "Cotton Mather's *Magnalia* and the Metaphors of Biblical History." In *Typology and Early American Literature,* edited by Sacvan Bercovitch, 139–60. Amherst, Mass.: University of Massachusetts Press, 1972.

MacCannell, Dean. *The Tourist: A New Theory of the Leisure Class,* 3rd ed. Berkeley and Los Angeles: University of California Press, 1999.

MacCormac, Earl R. "Jonathan Edwards and Missions." *Journal of the Presbyterian Historical Society* 39, December (1961): 219–29.

Macedo, Stephen. *Diversity and Distrust: Civic Education in a Multicultural Democracy.* Cambridge, Mass.: Harvard University Press, 2000.

MacIntyre, Alasdair. *After Virtue*, 2nd ed. Notre Dame, Ind.: University of Notre Dame Press, 1984.

———. "Moral Pluralism without Moral Relativism." In *Ethics*, vol. 1 of *The Proceedings of the Twentieth World Congress of Philosophy*, edited by Klaus Brinkmann, 1–19. Boston: Philosophy Documentation Center, 1999.

Marsden, George M. *Jonathan Edwards: A Life.* New Haven, Conn.: Yale University Press, 2003.

Marshall, T.W.M. *Christian Missions: Their Agents and Their Results.* New York: Sadlier, 1864.

Martin, David. *A General Theory of Secularization.* New York: Harper & Row, 1978.

Marty, Martin E. "The Frightful, Beneficial Mess of American Religion." *Christian Century*, December 14 (1988): 1150–52.

———. "A Judeo-Christian Looks at the Judeo-Christian Tradition." *Christian Century*, October 5 (1986): 858–60.

———. *Modern American Religion*, vol. 1, *The Irony of It All.* Chicago: University of Chicago Press, 1986.

———. *The One and the Many: America's Struggle for the Common Good.* Cambridge, Mass.: Harvard University Press, 1997.

———. "Revising the Map of American Religion." *Annals of the American Academy of Political and Social Science* 558, July (1998): 13–27.

Masuzawa, Tomoko. *In Search of Dreamtime: The Quest for the Origin of Religion.* Chicago: University of Chicago Press, 1993.

Mather, Cotton, *Magnalia Christi Americana; or The Ecclesiastical History of New England.* Hartford: Silas Andrus & Son, 1853 [1702].

Matovina, Tim. "Building Multicultural Parishes Requires More than Sensitivity." *National Catholic Reporter*, July 27, 2001, 20.

Mawdudi, Abdul A'la. *Towards Understanding Islam.* Washington, D.C.: Message Publications, 1986.

Mayer, Egon. *Love and Tradition: Marriage between Jews and Christians.* New York: Plenum Press, 1985.

McCloud, Aminah Beverly. "Islam in America: The Mosaic." In *Religion and Immigration: Christian, Jewish, and Muslim Experiences in the United States*, edited by Yvonne Yazbeck Haddad, Jane I. Smith, and John L. Esposito, 159–74. Walnut Creek, Calif.: AltaMira Press, 2003.

McDermott, Gerald R. "The Deist Connection: Jonathan Edwards and Islam." In *Jonathan Edwards's Writings: Text, Context, Interpretation*, edited by Stephen J. Stein, chap. 3. Bloomington: Indiana University Press, 1996.

———. *Jonathan Edwards Confronts the Gods: Christian Theology, Enlightenment Religion, and Non-Christian Faiths*. New York: Oxford University Press, 2000.

———. "A Possibility of Reconciliation: Jonathan Edwards and the Salvation of Non-Christians." In *Edwards in Our Time: Jonathan Edwards and the Shaping of American Religion*, edited by Sang Hyun Lee and Allen C. Guelzo, 173–202. Grand Rapids, Mich.: Eerdmans, 1999.

McRae, John R. "Oriental Verities on the American Frontier: The 1893 World's Parliament of Religions and the Thought of Masao Abe." *Buddhist-Christian Studies* 11 (1991): 7–36.

Mead, Loren B. *The Once and Future Church: Reinventing the Congregation for a New Mission Frontier*. Washington, D.C.: Alban Institute, 1993.

Meyers, Eleanor Scott. "The Church in the City." *Interpretation*, January (2000): 23–35.

Miller, Donald E. *Reinventing American Protestantism: Christianity in the New Millennium*. Berkeley and Los Angeles: University of California Press, 1997.

Mohler, R. Albert, Jr. "Against an Immoral Tide." *New York Times*, June 19, 2000.

Moore, R. Laurence. *Religious Outsiders and the Making of Americans*. New York: Oxford University Press, 1986.

Morreale, Don, ed. *The Complete Guide to Buddhist America*. Boston: Shambhala, 1998.

———. "Everything Has Changed in Buddhist America." In *The Complete Guide to Buddhist America*, edited by Don Morreale, iii–xvii. Boston: Shambhala, 1998.

Morris, Brian. *Anthropological Studies of Religion: An Introductory Text*. Cambridge: Cambridge University Press, 1987.

Muller, F. Max. *Lectures on the Origin and Growth of Religion*. New York: Charles Scribner's Sons, 1899 [originally given in 1878].

Neusner, Jacob. "Vatican II on the Jews and Judaism." *The Reconstructionist* 32, March 4 (1966): 7–12.

Niebuhr, H. Richard. *The Social Sources of Denominationalism*. New York: World, 1929.

Noll, Mark A. *America's God: From Jonathan Edwards to Abraham Lincoln*. New York: Oxford University Press, 2002.

Noll, Mark A., George M. Marsden, and Nathan O. Hatch. *Search for Christian America*. Chicago: Helmers and Howard, 1989.

Numan, Fareed H. *The Muslim Population in the United States*. Washington, D.C.: American Muslim Council, 1999.

Numrich, Paul D. *Old Wisdom in the New World: Americanization in Two Immigrant Theravada Buddhist Temples*. Knoxville: University of Tennessee Press, 1996.

Orsi, Robert A. "Introduction: Crossing the City Line." In *Gods of the City: Religion and the American Urban Landscape*, edited by Robert A. Orsi, 1–78. Bloomington: Indiana University Press, 1999.

———. *The Madonna of 115th Street: Faith and Community in Italian Harlem, 1880–1950*. New Haven, Conn.: Yale University Press, 1985.

Ostling, Richard N. "Survey of U.S. Muslims Finds a Growing Faith." *Intelligencer Record*, April 27, 2001, B13.

Parsons, Talcott. "Christianity and Modern Industrial Society." In *Sociological Theory, Values, and Sociocultural Change*, edited by Edward Tiryakian, 385–421. New York: Free Press, 1963.

Petsonk, Judy, and Jim Remsen. *The Intermarriage Handbook: A Guide for Jews and Christians*. New York: William Morrow, 1988.

Phelan, John Leddy. *The Millennial Kingdom of the Franciscans in the New World*. 2nd ed. Berkeley and Los Angeles: University of California Press, 1970.

Phillips, Bruce A. *Reexamining Intermarriage: Trends, Textures, Strategies*. New York: American Jewish Committee, William Petschek National Jewish Family Center, and the Susan and David Wilstein Institute of Jewish Policy Studies, 1997.

Phillips, Clifton Jackson. *Protestant America and the Pagan World: The First Half Century of the American Board of Commissioners for Foreign Missions, 1810–1860*. Cambridge, Mass.: Harvard University Press, 1969.

Pilchik, Ely E. "Review of *Judaism and Modern Man*." *Jewish Social Studies* 14, April (1952): 190–91.

Pitt, James E. *Adventures in Brotherhood*. New York: Farrar, Straus, 1955.

Poppen, Julie. "Monument to Buddhism." *Rocky Mountain News*, August 17, 2001, 7A.

Porter, Andrew. "Language, 'Native Agency,' and Missionary Control: Rufus Anderson's Journey to India, 1854–5." In *Missions and Missionaries*, edited by Pieter N. Holtrop and Hugh McLeod, 81–97. Rochester, N.Y.: Boydell Press, 2000.

Prebish, Charles S. *Luminous Passage: The Practice and Study of Buddhism in America*. Berkeley and Los Angeles: University of California Press, 1999.

Preus, J. Samuel. *Explaining Religion: Criticism and Theory from Bodin to Freud*. New Haven, Conn.: Yale University Press, 1987.

Priestley, Joseph. *Discourses Relating to the Evidences of Revealed Religion*. Philadelphia: John Thompson, 1796.

Privett, Nancy. *Stepping into the Aquarian Age*. New York: Old Lion Publishing, 2001.

Prothero, Stephen. "Mother India's Scandalous Swamis." In *Religious Practice in the United States*, edited by Colleen McDannell, 618–32. Princeton, N.J.: Princeton University Press, 2002.

Putnam, Robert. *Bowling Alone: The Decline and Renewal of American Communities*. New York: Simon & Schuster, 2000.

Rao, P. Venugopala. "The Living Sacred Images." *Hindu Temple of Atlanta Consecration Bulletin*, May 24–28, 2000, 15.

Rawls, John. "The Idea of an Overlapping Consensus." *Oxford Journal of Legal Studies* 7 (1987): 1–25.

———. *Political Liberalism*. New York: Columbia University Press, 1993.

Rayaprol, Aparna. *Negotiating Identities: Women in the Indian Diaspora*. New York: Oxford University Press, 1997.

Raz, Joseph. "Multiculturalism: A Liberal Perspective." *Dissent*, Winter (1994): 67–79.

Redfield, James W. *Comparative Physiognomy; or, Resemblances between Men and Animals*. New York: Redfield, 1852.

Religious News Service. "Buddhist Group Beset by Membership Drop." *Los Angeles Times*, January 27, 1996, 4.

Rescher, Nicholas. *Pluralism: Against the Demand for Consensus*. Oxford: Clarendon Press, 1993.

Richardson, Branda Lane. *Guess Who's Coming to Dinner: Celebrating Interethnic, Interfaith, and Interracial Relationships*. Tucson: Wildcat Canyon Press, 2000.

Rivera, Luis N. *A Violent Evangelism: The Political and Religious Conquest of the Americas*. Louisville: Westminster / John Knox Press, 1990.

Robbins, Tom. "Unnatural Intolerance in Soho." *Village Voice*, January 23, 2002, 27.

Rodriguez, Richard. *Brown: The Last Discovery of America*. New York: Viking, 2002.

Roof, Wade Clark. *Community and Commitment: Religious Plausibility in a Liberal Protestant Church*. New York: Elsevier, 1978.

———. *Spiritual Marketplace: Baby Boomers and the Remaking of American Religion*. Princeton, N.J.: Princeton University Press, 1999.

Rosenbaum, Mary Helene, Stanley Rosenbaum, and Ned Rosenbaum. *Celebrating Our Differences*. New York: White Mane, 1999.

Rosenblum, Nancy L., ed. *Obligations of Citizenship and Demands of Faith: Religious Accommodation in Pluralist Democracies*. Princeton, N.J.: Princeton University Press, 2000.

Rouse, Carolyn. *Engaged Surrender: Consciousness and Empowerment in the Conversion Experience of African-American Muslim Women*. Berkeley and Los Angeles: University of California Press, 2005.

Royer, Ismail. "U.S. Public Opinion toward Islam and Muslims after the Sept. 11 Attacks." *Islam Today,* April 2 (2002), online.

Said, Edward W. *Orientalism*. New York: Random House, 1978.

Salzberg, Sharon. *Lovingkindness: The Revolutionary Art of Happiness*. Boston: Shambhala, 1997.

Samuel, Geoffrey. *Civilized Shamans: Buddhism in Tibetan Societies*. Washington, D.C.: Smithsonian Institution Press, 1995.

Sandmel, Samuel. "For and against Herberg." *Jewish Frontier* 17, November (1950): 24–33.

———. *When a Jew and Christian Marry.* Philadelphia: Fortress Press, 1977.

Sanford, Charles B. *The Religious Life of Thomas Jefferson*. Charlottesville: University of Virginia Press, 1984.

Schaper, Donna E. *Raising Interfaith Children: Spiritual Orphans or Spiritual Heirs?* New York: Crossroad, 1999.

Schofield, Robert E. *The Enlightenment of Joseph Priestley: A Study of His Life and Work from 1733 to 1773*. University Park: Pennsylvania State University Press, 1997.

Scott, James C. *Moral Economy of the Peasant: Rebellion and Subsistence in Southeast Asia*. New Haven: Yale University Press, 1977.

Seager, Richard Hughes. *Buddhism in America*. New York: Columbia University Press, 1999.

———. "Pluralism and the American Mainstream: The View from the World's Parliament of Religions." *Harvard Theological Review* 82 (1989): 301–24.

Selznick, Gertrude J., and Stephen Steinberg. *The Tenacity of Prejudice: Anti-Semitism in Contemporary America*. New York: Harper & Row, 1969.

Service, Elman R. "The Mind of Lewis H. Morgan." *Current Anthropology* 22, February (1981): 25–43.

Sharpe, Eric. *Comparative Religion: A History.* London: Duckworth, 1975.

Sheehan, Bernard W. *Savagism and Civility: Indians and Englishmen in Colonial Virginia*. Cambridge: Cambridge University Press, 1980.

Siegel, Robert. "Deadline for Ten Commandments Monument to Be Taken Down from Alabama State Judiciary Building." *All Things Considered,* August 20, 2003, online.

Siegel, Seymour. "Review of *Protestant-Catholic-Jew.*" *Judaism: A Quarterly Journal* 5, Spring (1956): 178–81.

Silverman, Kenneth. *The Life and Times of Cotton Mather.* New York: Harper & Row, 1984.

Sklare, Marshall. "Third-Generation Religion." *Commentary* 21, February (1956): 195–96.

Slomovitz, Albert Isaac. *The Fighting Rabbis: Jewish Military Chaplains and American History.* New York: New York University Press, 1999.

Smith, Christian. *American Evangelicalism: Embattled and Thriving.* Chicago: University of Chicago Press, 1998.

———. *Christian America? What Evangelicals Really Want.* Berkeley and Los Angeles: University of California Press, 2000.

———, ed. *The Secular Revolution: Power, Interests, and Conflict in the Secularization of American Public Life.* Berkeley and Los Angeles: University of California Press, 2004.

Smith, Jane I. *Islam in America.* New York: Columbia University Press, 1999.

Smith, Tom. "Religious Diversity in America: The Emergence of Muslims, Buddhists, Hindus, and Others." *Journal for the Scientific Study of Religion* 41, 3 (2002): 577–85.

Smith, Wilfrid Cantwell. "The Christian in a Religiously Plural World." In *Christianity and Other Religions*, edited by John Hick and Brian Hebblethwaite, 98–99. Philadelphia: Fortress Press, 1980.

Smolinski, Reiner. "*Israel Redivivus:* The Eschatological Limits of Puritan Typology in New England." *New England Quarterly* 63, September (1990): 357–95.

Snow, Tony. "Court Strains Belief with Religion Ruling." *Detroit News*, May 5, 2000, 13.

Stanford, Peter. "God's Managers." *Management Today,* April (1999): 72–77.

Stein, Stephen J. "Transatlantic Extensions: Apocalyptic in Early New England." In *The Apocalypse in English Renaissance Thought and Literature: Patterns, Antecedents, and Repercussions*, edited by C. A. Patrides and Joseph Anthony Wittreich, 266–98. Manchester: Manchester University Press, 1984.

Sterba, Wayne. *The Aquarian Hypothesis: Spiritual Security in a Dot.Com World.* San Francisco: First Books Library, 2001.

Stout, Harry S. *The Divine Dramatist: George Whitefield and the Rise of Modern Evangelicalism.* Grand Rapids, Mich.: Eerdmans, 1991.

Swidler, Ann. *Talk of Love: How Culture Matters.* Chicago: University of Chicago Press, 2001.

Takeuchi, Yoshinori, ed. *Buddhist Spirituality: Indian, Southeast Asian, Tibetan, and Early Chinese.* New York: Crossroad, 1993.

Thomson, Edward. *Our Oriental Missions*, vol. 1, *India and China.* Cincinnati: Hitchcock and Walden, 1870.

Tichi, Cecelia. "The Puritan Historians and Their New Jerusalem." *Early American Literature* 6, Fall (1971): 143–55.

Tocqueville, Alexis de. *Democracy in America*, vol. 2. New York: Vintage, 1945.

Tracy, David. *Plurality and Ambiguity: Hermeneutics, Religion, Hope.* Chicago: University of Chicago Press, 1994.

Trevor-Roper, H. R. *The European Witch-Craze of the Sixteenth and Seventeenth Centuries.* New York: Harper & Row, 1967.

Tsoukalas, Steven, and Carl F. Ellis Jr. *The Nation of Islam: Understanding the "Black Muslims."* Louisville: Presbyterian Reformed Publishing, 2001.

Tuck, Donald R. *Buddhist Churches of America: Jodo Shinshu.* New York: Edwin Mellen Press, 1988.

Turcsik, Richard, and Jenny Summerour. "Muslim Law." *Progressive Grocer,* August (2000): 12.

Tuveson, Ernest Lee. *Redeemer Nation: The Idea of America's Millennial Role.* Chicago: University of Chicago Press, 1968.

Twair, Pat McDonnell. "Who Is That Veiled Woman?" *Sojourners,* May/June (2001): 32–33.

Tweed, Thomas A. "General Introduction." In *Asian Religions in America: A Documentary History,* edited by Thomas A. Tweed, 1–12. New York: Oxford University Press, 1999.

Vary, Paul A. "Motives in Protestant Missions, 1890–1917." In *Modern American Protestantism and Its World: Historical Articles on Protestantism in American Religious Life,* vol. 13, *Missions and Ecumenical Expressions,* edited by Martin E. Marty, 3–19. Munich: K. G. Saur, 1993.

Vivekananda, Swami. "Hinduism." In *The World's Parliament of Religions,* vol. 2, edited by John Henry Barrows, 968–78. Chicago: Parliament Publishing, 1893.

Voas, Davis, Alasdair Crockett, and Daniel V. A. Olson. "Religious Pluralism and Participation: Why Previous Research Is Wrong." *American Sociological Review* 67 (2002): 212–30.

Waghorne, Joanne Punzo. "The Hindu Gods in a Split-Level World: The Sri Siva-Vishnu Temple in Suburban Washington, D.C." In *Gods of the City: Religion and the American Urban Landscape,* edited by Robert A. Orsi, 103–30. Bloomington: Indiana University Press, 1999.

Walker, Ken. "Navy Bias Charged." *Christianity Today,* May 21 (2001): 19.

Wall, Wendy L. " 'Our Enemies Within': Nazism, National Unity, and America's Wartime Discourse on Tolerance." In *Enemy Images in American History,* edited by R. Fiebig–von Hase and Ursula Lehmkuhl, 209–29. Berlin: Berghahn Books, 1998.

Walters, Kerry S. *Benjamin Franklin and His Gods.* Urbana: University of Illinois Press, 1999.

Walzer, Michael. *Thick and Thin: Moral Argument at Home and Abroad.* Notre Dame, Ind.: University of Notre Dame Press, 1994.

Warren, Mark E. *Democracy and Association.* Princeton, N.J.: Princeton University Press, 2001.

Warren, Mark R. *Dry Bones Rattling: Community Building to Revitalize American Democracy.* Princeton, N.J.: Princeton University Press, 2001.

Washington, George. *On Religious Liberty and Mutual Understanding.* Edited by Edward Frank Humphrey. Washington, D.C.: National Conference of Catholics, Jews, and Protestants, 1932.

Waters, Mary C. *Ethnic Options: Choosing Ethnic Identities in America.* Berkeley and Los Angeles: University of California Press, 1990.

Watts, Pauline Moffitt. "Prophecy and Discovery: On the Spiritual Origins of Christopher Columbus's 'Enterprise of the Indies.' " *American Historical Review* 90, Fall (1985): 73–102.

Wayne, Alice. "After Babel." *Ladies' Repository* 36 (1876): 401–7.

Webb, Alexander Russell Mohammed. "The Spirit of Islam." In *The World's Parliament of Religions,* vol. 2, edited by John Henry Barrows, 989–96. Chicago: Parliament Publishing, 1893.

Weber, Max. *The Sociology of Religion.* Boston: Beacon Press, 1963 [1922].

Wertheimer, Jack. "Surrendering to Intermarriage." *Commentary,* March (2001): 25–32.

West, Cornel. *Race Matters.* New York: Vintage, 1994.

Whitney, William D. "On the So-Called Science of Religion." *Princeton Review,* new series (1881): 429–51.

Wilder, R. G. *Mission Schools in India of the American Board of Commissioners for Foreign Missions.* New York: A.D.F. Randolph, 1861.

Williams, Raymond Brady. "Asian Indian and Pakistani Religions in the United States." *Annals of the American Academy of Political and Social Science* 558, July (1998): 178–95.

———. "Swaminarayan Hindu Temple of Glen Ellyn, Illinois." In *American Congregations,* vol. 1, *Portraits of Twelve Religious Communities,* edited by James P. Wind and James W. Lewis, 612–62. Chicago: University of Chicago Press, 1994.

Williams, Roger. *A Key into the Language of America.* Edited by John J. Teunissen and Evelyn J. Hinz. Detroit: Wayne State University Press, 1973 [1643].

Witten, Marsha G. *All Is Forgiven: The Secular Message in American Protestantism.* Princeton, N.J.: Princeton University Press, 1993.

Wolfe, Alan. *One Nation after All: What Americans Really Think about God, Country, Family, Racism, Welfare, Immigration, Homosexuality, Work, the Right, the Left and Each Other.* New York: Viking, 1998.

———. *Whose Keeper? Social Science and Moral Obligation.* Berkeley and Los Angeles: University of California Press, 1989.

Wood, Richard. *Faith in Action: Religion, Race, and Democratic Action in America*. Chicago: University of Chicago Press, 2002.

Woolever, Cynthia, and Deborah Bruce. *A Field Guide to U.S. Congregations: Who's Going Where and Why*. Louisville: Westminster / John Knox, 2002.

Wuthnow, Robert. *After Heaven: Spirituality in America since the 1950s*. Berkeley and Los Angeles: University of California Press, 1998.

———. "Anti-Semitism and Stereotyping." In *In the Eye of the Beholder: Prejudice and Stereotyping*, edited by Arthur G. Miller, 137–87. New York: Praeger, 1982.

———. *Creative Spirituality: The Way of the Artist*. Berkeley and Los Angeles: University of California Press, 2001.

———. *Experimentation in American Religion: The New Mysticisms and Their Implications for the Churches*. Berkeley and Los Angeles: University of California Press, 1978.

———. *Meaning and Moral Order: Explorations in Cultural Analysis*. Berkeley and Los Angeles: University of California Press, 1987.

———. *Producing the Sacred: An Essay on Public Religion*. Urbana: University of Illinois Press, 1994.

———. *Religion and Diversity Codebook*. Princeton University, Department of Sociology, 2003.

———. "Religion and Politics Survey." Princeton University, machine-readable data file, 2000.

Wuthnow, Robert, and Conrad Hackett. "The Social Integration of Practitioners of Non-Western Religions in the United States." *Journal for the Scientific Study of Religion* 42, December (2003): 651–67.

Wuthnow, Robert, and John H. Evans, eds. *The Quiet Hand of God: Faith-Based Activism and the Public Role of Mainline Protestantism*. Berkeley and Los Angeles: University of California Press, 2002.

Yandell, Keith. "Religious Pluralism." *Christians and Scholarship* 2, 3 (1999): 3–6.

Ziolkowski, Eric. "Heavenly Visions and Worldly Intentions: Chicago's Columbian Exposition and World's Parliament of Religions (1893)." *Journal of American Culture* 13 (1990): 9–15.